Straight Left

Straight Left
A Journey in Politics

Ruairi Quinn

HODDER
HEADLINE
IRELAND

The publisher would like to thank the following for allowing use
of photographs and cartoons: Tom Halliday, *Irish Independent*,
Mac Innes Photography, Graeme Keyes and Bill Hastings.
Despite best efforts, the publisher was unable to trace all copyright holders
prior to publication of *Straight Left*. However, the publisher will make the
ususal arrangements with any copyright holders who make contact after
publication.

First published in 2005 by Hodder Headline Ireland

1

A CIP catalogue record for this title is available from
the British Library.

ISBN 0 340 83296 7

Typeset in Sabon MT by Hodder Headline Ireland
Cover design by Anú Design, Tara
Printed and bound in Great Britain by Clays Ltd, St Ives plc

Hodder Headline's policy is to use papers that are natural, renewable and
recyclable products and made from wood grown in sustainable forests.
The logging and manufacturing processes are expected to conform to the
environmental regulations of the country of origin.

Hodder Headline Ireland
8 Castlecourt Centre, Castleknock, Dublin 15, Ireland

A division of Hodder Headline
338 Euston Road, London NW1 3BH, England

Contents

Foreword

I have enjoyed writing this book but it has taken longer than I expected. I also had, of necessity, to exclude and reduce sections and references that I had included in my original draft. I am indebted to the many people who encouraged me to write and who gave me great support. From the beginning it was Jonathan Williams who not only responded enthusiastically to my first approach but who helped me get the project off the ground. He is more than a literary agent because his knowledge of the subject matter, his own literary insights and his infectious enthusiasm conceal another invaluable contribution; his insights as a reader and skills as an editor.

Denise Rogers was central to this project, having travelled with me on this political journey and for the many helpful comments which she made as she typed the manuscript.

From the beginning, Breda Purdue of Hodder Headline Ireland was directly helpful and determined to assist me so as to produce the best book possible. This was because she recognised just how few books of this kind has emerged from modern Irish political life. In this task, she was ably assisted by her colleagues Ciara Considine and my attentive and committed editor, Claire Rourke.

I want to extend my appreciation to my extended family for the support and encouragement they have given to me over the years. Despite frequent differences of political opinion, my sister and four brothers have been wonderfully loyal over three decades and, for this, I thank them sincerely.

This is one person's account of a set of events in which many others have participated. In order to be as accurate as possible I sent various different chapters to a number of people requesting them to correct where possible any errors of fact. They were dutiful and helpful in the task and I thank them all, including Tony Brown, Una Claffey, Peter D'Arcy, Kevin Duffy, Brendan Halligan, Brian McLoughlin, Pat Magner, Coilín Murray, Ronan O'Brien, Seán Ó Laoire, Ciarán

O'Mara, Micheal O'Siadhail, Seamus Scally and Greg Sparks. Finally, Tom Butler, Tony Heffernan and Ita McAuliffe provided much needed assistance in the completion of this project.

For a long time I have intended to write a political memoir. While I have read many excellent modern histories and biographies of Irish politicians, I regretted the absence of their own version of events or explanations as to why certain things happened. Kevin Healy of RTÉ urged me to keep a journal when I became Minister for Labour in 1983 and Desmond O'Grady taught me the regularity of routine in keeping to one A4 page first thing in the morning when I got into my office. I managed to do that for about half of the time over the last twenty-three years. I have used the *IPA Yearbook and Diary*, since 1972 and these were an essential tool. Those volumes were invaluable in helping me remember events and check facts. Ted Nealon's *Dáil Guides*, since 1974, were another primary source of reference and information. I have tried to verify all dates and facts cited. Accordingly, any mistakes are mine, for which I apologise in advance.

I have taken the liberty of quoting people in conversation from my memory of the exchange and my journals rather than a recorded transcript. I have done this in the interest of telling the story as best as I can remember it. This book is not a comprehensive history of the last thirty years of Irish political life, it is one player's account of some of the events in which I was privileged to be involved. I have tried to tell my account from the inside, to give people added insight into some events of which they were, perhaps, already aware.

RUAIRI QUINN
July 2005

for Liz

Chapter 1

Going to the Country

Thousands of Dubliners pass the imposing structure on Merrion Street every day. Most know it as Government Buildings, the large classical set of buildings completed at the beginning of the last century. Some, but very few, know the inside but all, as citizens, are affected by the decisions that are made there. Government Buildings is an elaborate construction originally designed to house the Home Rule Administration, which had been approved by the imperial parliament in Westminster in 1914, only to be suspended with the outbreak of the First World War.

Access to the cabinet room, the centrepoint of Irish democracy, is through the entrance to the Attorney General's office on the buildings' northeastern corner, adjacent to the Natural History Museum. As a person climbs the stairs into the hall, a door on the left of a corridor directly in front of them opens into the communications room. Inside this small room, another door provides direct access to the cabinet room. There are, in fact, two doors back to back to provide sound insulation and protect cabinet confidentiality. This large, formal room has been used as the executive chamber since 1922 when the Irish Free State came into existence.

The government of the Irish Republic normally meets at 11.00 a.m. on Tuesday mornings when the Dáil is sitting and usually completes its business by 1.00 p.m. As the starting time approaches, this otherwise quiet area of Government Buildings becomes a hive of activity. Civil servants from the Taoiseach's Department move into the communications room, telephones are manned, messages received and documents delivered. Last-minute memos are printed and the photocopier hums, preparing the eighteen copies required for a full cabinet meeting. In addition to the fifteen cabinet ministers, limited to that number in Ireland's constitution, the Attorney General, the chief whip and the secretary to the government also attend.

Inside the cabinet room, a door at the far side from the communications room leads to a refreshments room, which has self-service tea and coffee. It is left deliberately empty when ministers arrive so that they can chat openly about the business of the coming meeting. Spontaneous bilateral discussions take place with cup and biscuit in hand, as two colleagues attempt to arrive at a compromise over some political issue which they can then present to the Taoiseach, or more importantly the Minister for Finance, as an agreed position. This informal canvassing distinguishes the effective and influential cabinet minister from the more innocent or less powerful cabinet colleague, whatever the portfolio.

Constituency problems are raised, where a minister can intervene to solve a particular problem. Impending announcements, bringing good news to constituencies, must, at all costs, be conveyed by the senior minister and not by a backbencher – this is particularly critical if the backbencher is in the same party.

Some ministers arrive deliberately early in order to make contact with others. It is, for many whose departments are located in other parts of the city, the only chance to meet informally and discuss matters of general interest. Not all come to Government Buildings by state car. As Minister for Enterprise and Employment in 1993–94, my office was located in the old government office built in 1941 on Kildare Street, which houses two departments and it is only a short walk through Leinster House into the back of Government Buildings.

Access to the cabinet room from the Department of Finance, which is part of the Government Buildings complex, is through an underground passage. However, on sunny days, both climatically and politically, the Minister for Finance walks along Upper Merrion Street to get to the cabinet meeting. If the political climate is challenging, reporters and photographers will cluster around the Attorney General's office entrance, waiting to doorstep ministers for impromptu interviews. This is the Government Press Office's bad-day scenario. The Minister for Finance is advised, in these circumstances, to use the underground passageway, and all other ministers are requested to drive through the wrought-iron entrance gate to the north road rather than run the risk of being intercepted.

Cabinet papers are circulated before the meeting by the Department of the Taoiseach accompanied by a *clár*, or agenda, setting out the twenty or thirty items to be decided. Some will be short and on the agenda for the first time. Others will be familiar and may not be disposed of, but will still be discussed. Legislative proposals start life on the *clár* with a formal request by the sponsoring minister to prepare legislation on a specific topic. The legislation may arise from a commitment in the programme for government, negotiated after a general election or from a directive emanating from the European Union which has to be transposed into national legislation.

The secretary to the government, sitting beside the Taoiseach, who chairs cabinet meetings, takes note of each decision as it is made on a pad of A5-sized pink slips. In many cases, if the decision being noted involves either money or personnel, the same pink slip is passed over the table to the Minister for Finance, who may, and usually does, qualify the text of the decision before handing it back. It is then held with other pink slips until the secretary presses a button beside him, linked to a signalling system in the communications room. Once an acknowledgement of his signal is received, by a light over the door, the secretary goes to the door and hands the pink slips to a civil servant from the communications room, from where their contents will be conveyed to the relevant government department for implementation.

When I first entered the cabinet in December 1983, one year after the election of the coalition Labour/Fine Gael government, the way this system worked intrigued me. Dick Spring, Tánaiste and leader of the Labour Party, had nominated me to fill the vacancy brought about by the resignation of Frank Cluskey. The Taoiseach, Garret FitzGerald, was the senior Fine Gael deputy in my constituency; I had known him when I was a student and he was a lecturer at

University College Dublin, but I had never attended a meeting at which he was the chair.

Coming into the cabinet a year after the government had been formed was a strange experience, not unlike going to a new school in the middle of term. Everyone else knew what to do and I was reluctant to draw attention to the fact that not only was I the new boy, but that I was also unclear about some basic procedures.

For that first meeting, I arrived early and, as with any first day, I was anxious and overly prepared. Dermot Nally, the secretary to the government, was the only person in the cabinet room. A senior and respected civil servant, Nally was a courteous man who came to public prominence when he played a critical role in finalising the 1985 Anglo-Irish Agreement. He wished me well, within the polite objective decorum that befits a non-partisan, non-political civil servant. I have since learned to admire the fine line that has been observed by so many civil servants, which does not confuse personal friendship or intellectual agreement with political neutrality and professional objectivity.

I was shown to my seat at the cabinet table, a large, oval table of polished mahogany. Each minister has his or her own place, which never changes. If absent, the minister's seat remains empty. The Taoiseach sat with his back to the centre window and immediately across from him sat the Tánaiste, Dick Spring, with Alan Dukes, the Minister for Finance, on his right. Directly across from Alan was Dermot Nally or sometimes his deputy, Frank Murray. That arrangement facilitated the constant flow of pink slips. I had a close view of this process because I was seated between Alan Dukes and Barry Desmond, the Minister for Health and for Social Welfare and also the deputy leader of the Labour Party.

My proximity to the Minister for Finance gave me an advantage over many of my colleagues. Without difficulty, because they were placed on the table right beside me, I could see Alan Dukes' cabinet papers as we moved from item to item, and was able to read the steering notes and other pieces of negotiating advice which Finance officials had written. Opening positions and bottom lines were clearly indicated. It was a facility that would be useful to me in the months ahead. I also learned from the way in which Alan scrutinised every significant draft decision on the pink slips that passed across the table. In my own time as Minister for Finance, I made sure to apply the same scrutiny, much to my own relief and sometimes to the bemusement of my colleagues. I am indebted to Alan for the example he set.

The evening before my first cabinet meeting, I took time to carefully study all thirty-one government memoranda that had come in the two large leather briefcases given to me by my private secretary, Freda Nolan, in the Department of Labour. I need not have bothered. By 11.10 a.m., a few other ministers had arrived and all had moved into the refreshment room until, ten minutes later, a knock on the door from Seán Barrett, the government chief whip, asked us to come in to start the meeting.

When we went into the cabinet room, the Taoiseach, the Tánaiste and the Minister for Posts and Telegraphs were in deep conversation. Jim Mitchell was in animated form and expressing great concern about some issue as we sat down at the cabinet table.

Dermot Nally read out the minutes of the previous meeting. The Taoiseach, after he had formally greeted me, proceeded to say that he wanted to discuss an item that was not on the agenda and he would need to have it disposed of before 12.30 p.m. He then proposed to deal with the *clár*, listing a number of different items before the non-agenda item he had mentioned earlier. Some ministers asked that other items on the agenda be considered priorities; others indicated that they did not want certain items to be discussed on that particular day. Bemused and a bit surprised, I made my first intervention by asking why we could not simply proceed through the agenda. This suggestion was greeted with some merriment around the table. Paddy Cooney, the Minister for Defence, smiled and Peter Barry, the Minister for Foreign Affairs said, 'Ah, listen to the new boy.'

I spent a lot of intense time in that room between 1983 and 1987, and again between 1993 and 1997, and I soon became very familiar with every detail of it, which did not change during that period. On the walls were charcoal drawings of Irish patriots, strong and robust, drawn by my former art teacher in secondary school, John Coyle. Robert Emmet, Henry Grattan and Constance Markievicz, among others, looked down on our proceedings. I also got to know every aspect of the view through the windows out onto the court-yard. Before the renovation of Government Buildings in the late 1980s, the UCD School of Engineering was located in part of the central complex under the dome at the western side of the court-yard. As a result, there was a constant flow of traffic, with students and staff coming and going from Upper Merrion Street.

Garret FitzGerald's great range of talents did not extend to chair-ing a meeting with direction or efficiency. Cabinet sessions were long and frequently draining. Contentious political issues, which should have been finalised, were reopened for discussion, despite having gone through the full interdepartmental consultative system. Yet there were other issues which were simply not easy to resolve because every proffered solution appeared too politically painful to grasp. Sometimes during the long discussions, I turned to drawing cartoons. I did so to ease my own stress. The drawings were then passed around and I watched with pleasure as a grin or smile would appear as a cartoon openly passed from minister to minister. Finally, Seán Barrett might or might not show it to the Taoiseach, allowing a bit of light relief for everyone.

Garret's eagerness on occasions could be the cause of great amusement. I remember him starting a cabinet meeting by telling us he wanted to clear the names of the Commission on Penal Reform, which the government was setting up. It was to be chaired by Ken Whitaker, a respected former secretary of the Department of Finance. Garret rattled off a list of eminent people as prospective members, including professor this, doctor so-and-so and sister somebody-or-other.

Jim Mitchell leaned forward, 'Taoiseach, can I make one observation on your list?'

'Certainly, Jim,' the Taoiseach replied. 'What is it?'

'There are no prisoners on it.'

'Very good,' came Garret's response. Then, turning to the rest of us, he asked aloud, 'Does anyone know a prisoner?'

'In or out of jail?' was the gruff response from John Boland.

'Oh, well, out of course,' replied Garret.

'What about Mannix Flynn?' I said.

'Who is Mannix Flynn?' asked Paddy Cooney, lighting his pipe.

'Will you tell him or will I?' Boland asked.

'You do,' I said, curious to hear how he would describe Mannix.

'He is the bollox who burnt Dockrells.'

A startled Paddy Cooney replied, 'We couldn't possibly do that on poor Maurice and Percy Dockrell', two former Fine Gael deputies.

At this point, Peter Barry, seated between Cooney and Boland, observed, 'I don't know about that. Didn't they get great compensation?'

The early 1980s were a difficult time to be in government. The three elections between June 1981 and November 1982 had not provided stability or helped the economy. The large financial deficits, generated before 1981 by the Fianna Fáil government, had become worse in the following period of uncertainty. By mid-1984, as we prepared for the January budget of 1985, the painful task of controlling public expenditure at a time of weak economic activity was far from easy. In addition, a significant part of the Labour parliamentary party and the trade unions were strenuously opposed to reductions in public expenditure, which would, in their opinion, harm the living standards of working people. We had few choices and all of them were difficult. The Labour ministers had three of the four big-spending departments and we were fighting a rearguard action against the proposed reductions.

The preparations for the budget began in July each year with the Estimates of public expenditure, which each department would put together and submit to the Minister for Finance. They were, supposedly, in accordance with the policy and expenditure guidelines issued earlier in the year by the Department of Finance. The first bids from each department were literally that. An elaborate process of bargaining, begun initially at departmental level but which, ultimately, became face-to-face encounters between the line minister and the Minister for Finance – encounters which always took place in the Department of Finance. It was, from a psychological and negotiating point of view, important for the Minister for Finance to be in control of the venue.

The place used was a small room, adjacent to the minister's private office. Referred to as the 'torture chamber', it was painted in a range of harsh green colours. Its walls carried black and white photographs of every Minister for Finance since the first, Michael Collins. The private secretary ushered the line minister, with three or four of his departmental officials, into this room. They were often kept waiting while the Minister for Finance received a briefing from his own budget team, though, sometimes, the line department minister and the officials were kept waiting deliberately. The Minister for Finance and his officials would then enter solemnly, like a jury returning to a court, to face the minister and his intimidated official civil-service team.

In time, a minister would get to learn the unspoken rules of this process. The use of bluff or the ridicule of particular policy measures considered important by the minister were commonplace. When a policy was defended, a well-informed Finance official would dismiss them out of hand. Submission would immediately involve loss of face with the minister's senior civil servants, and probably political humiliation when the full details of the cutbacks became known.

In 1984, Alan Dukes had a difficult job to do. I did not fully realise this at the time, but I would in another administration. His difficulties were compounded by his own political isolation in Finance with no Labour Minister of State. Labour's Joe Bermingham, a deputy for the then five-seat Kildare constituency, was the Minister of State for Finance but his job was confined to the Office of Public Works, located in a separate building away, from the main department. While Dukes and Bermingham shared the same constituency, they had little else in common.

In the 1980s, ministers did not have special advisers to act as political go-betweens within the system. The negotiations on the Estimates took place between civil servants from the line department and the Department of Finance. The line department civil servants would go only so far before a stalemate was reached and a ministerial bilateral meeting invoked. If that bilateral failed to reach the target set by Finance, the issue or issues were referred up to the final level – cabinet.

This was not the place to conduct detailed negotiations, department by department or vote by vote, as the various sections of the Estimates were called. A process of special pleading was now a part of cabinet meetings. Indeed, extra meetings were convened to deal specifically with the Estimates. Each minister, still resisting reductions, would argue his or her case over extended periods of time. In great detail, the defending minister would describe the impact of reductions, while the attention of other ministers would drift.

The best exponent of this method of defence was Barry Desmond, who once brought into the cabinet room an overhead projector and screen, to illustrate with tables of figures the impact upon the health services that would follow if the Finance proposals were accepted. While Garret and Alan would become engaged in a detailed discussion of the figures, the interest of other ministers waned. But Barry's technique was to refer, constituency by constituency, to the local impact – and of course all the constituencies he highlighted had a cabinet minister. Around the table the ministers were listening. At the far end of the table sat Austin Deasy, the Minister for Agriculture. For a lot of the time during these discussions, Austin would be avidly reading the *Racing Post*. However, if Waterford was mentioned, the paper would be lowered slightly and Austin would re-engage. Barry Desmond was not put off. He referred not only to the Ardkeen Hospital in general, which was located in Austin's Waterford constituency, but then took us on a tour of the hospital wards, identified the ones which might be closed and even went so far as placing labels of political loyalty on the patients who were occupying the threatened beds!

In preparing the 1985 budget, we had a couple of difficult meetings and made slow but painful progress. The final push was to take place at the next meeting. We arrived, aware of what was expected of us. Alan Dukes, as Minister for Finance, opened up with the necessity to deal with the deteriorating financial situation. He referred to what action had been taken to date and demonstrated how short of the mark the reduction in the level of public spending still was. Then Alan really got into his stride, his cigarette lit and nestling in the ashtray beside his three packets of John Player Blue. As he continued, he encountered new and even more determined resistance from his cabinet colleagues. His voice got stronger and the level rose as impatience changed to irritation and he exploded.

'Ah, fuck it. I have simply had it. I am fed up. I have had enough of the bloody obstruction and fucking prevarication.' When he stopped, he drew heavily on his cigarette before angrily stubbing it out in the ashtray.

The room went quiet. Dermot Nally lowered his head, looking down businesslike at his notes, so as not to make eye contact with any of us. I saw the Taoiseach gazing across at the Tánaiste. Quietly and hesitantly, Garret suggested in a low voice that perhaps a coffee break in the refreshment room with the Minister for Finance and the Tánaiste would now be in order. Greatly relieved, the rest of the ministers signalled assent to the Taoiseach's proposal.

As Alan rose, taking his files and cigarettes with him, Dick leaned over and indicated that I should come out with the three of them. I knew instinctively that he did not want to go into the refreshment room alone with two highly numerate economists. Last into the room, I closed the door. Garret and Dick had moved up to the coffee machine beside the window and were taking it in turn to pour a cup. Alan was lighting a cigarette, having banged the files on the small dining table in the centre of the room.

As I moved towards them, there was a sense of embarrassment rather than tension. Garret tried to smooth things over. We listened. Alan now had a cup of coffee and was pulling strongly on a cigarette. He responded to the Taoiseach. Very quickly, he was back up to speed, at the same pitch and on the same point he had reached in the cabinet room. He then took off, giving out about the line ministers in general and the Labour ones in particular. He was getting louder and, more importantly, closer to the real edge.

It was no longer a conflict between the Department of Finance and the other departments, but instead a point of deadly confrontation between the two government parties. Alan was in full flight, fluent and argumentative.

'I am fucking sick of it; it can't go on. Taoiseach, you have no choice: you simply have to go to the country.'

There was silence when he finished. I was looking at Dick, steely-eyed and showing no emotion but obviously under pressure. If anyone in the room knew how to take pressure, it was Dick Spring, who had played full-back for Ireland in rugby. Garret was flushed and, for a change, seemed lost for words. I do not know how or where the formulation came from, or what prompted me to speak before either the Taoiseach or the Tánaiste.

'Had you any particular country in mind, Alan?' I asked quietly.

The intense atmosphere was shattered by the spontaneous laughter of both Dick and Garret and, after a few seconds, by Alan himself. We were going to have to find another solution because going to the country was not an option.

Chapter 2

Growing Up in Dublin

The smell of petrol remains, to this day, a poignant evocation of one of my earliest memories. Uncle Kevin was dipping a cloth into the fuel tank of his Chevrolet to wipe off the tar that we'd got on our hands and legs from the sun-warmed surface of Moyne Road, Ranelagh, where we lived in 1950.

I was just four years old, the youngest child of Malachi and Julia Quinn. My sister, Moninne, had two other brothers, Lochlann and Conor. In time Declan and Colm would complete the family. Nineteen fifty was also the time when my father, with his father, sisters Una and Joan and brother Kevin went to Rome on a pilgrimage because Pope Pius XII had decreed it a Holy Year. On their return, after what seemed an age, I used an Italian coin, which looked deceptively like an old Irish shilling, to buy a slab of Cleeves toffee in the local sweet shop, opposite Morton's on Dunville Avenue. My swindle was quickly rumbled. Not many had been on a pilgrimage and few little boys could afford to buy an entire slab of that wonderful cream toffee. My parents scolded me, which was bad enough, but being obliged to go back down to the sweet shop and publicly apologise to the owner and hand over a real shilling was strong punishment.

One year later, we moved to a larger house in Sandymount: 23 Sydney Parade. My brother Declan had been born on 15 August 1950, the same day as Princess Anne. My mother used to taunt her strongly republican husband that, had they stayed in Newry where their married life had begun in 1936, she, like all the other mothers throughout the UK, would have received a present of a special pack of free nappies! He was not impressed. Fortunately, as a successful grocer, he could well afford the nappies and indeed another child.

We moved just before Christmas 1951. Uncle Kevin, who had come out of the Irish army in 1945 at the end of 'The Emergency' – neutral Ireland's euphemism for the Second World War – moved in with us. My mother used to say that Kevin came for a weekend and stayed for ten years. When he did leave to marry Ita Hynes, we missed him. My parents' last child, Colm, arrived in March 1953 and I remember still the Moses basket in the dining room, with aunts and uncles admiring him and asking his sister and brothers if they liked the new baby. Sydney Parade was a big family house and it turned out to be a happy home.

My mother was from Dundalk, south of the Border separating the northeastern six counties from the newly independent Irish state. I had a lot of cousins in County Louth. Two of my mother's three sisters had seven children each, and lived in Dundalk. Her other sister had two daughters.

Crossing the Border at Killeen in south Armagh was a tense experience because of the periodic searches of the car. We used to cross quite often with Uncle Kevin, who was en route to Warrenpoint, County Down, to visit his father, John Quinn, and his two sisters, Joan and Una, who remained single all their lives. In a way, we became their surrogate children and we saw them often. Kevin would take the trip north every fortnight or so, with Lochlann, Conor and me in tow, to give my mother a break and to amuse my grandfather and aunts. In later years, I stayed in Warrenpoint for a month every summer until I was nine, acquiring a tinge of a northern accent which soon disappeared when I returned to school, St Michael's, at the beginning of September.

I had started in that primary school after the Easter holidays of 1952. It was a small school in those days, with less than 130 pupils. Most went on to Blackrock College, which was also run by the Holy Ghost Fathers. On my first day, my father brought me in, after the classes had started, through the connecting corridor of rooms in the garden basement of that fine old house that still stands on the corner of Ailesbury Road and Merrion Road. The brushed timber floors had a smell of Jeyes fluid. We were greeted by Father Maguire, the school principal. After a few words, my father left. Father

Maguire tapped on the frosted window of the door into first class. The teacher welcomed me into a room with about six twin desks and I was asked to sit down on an empty bench seat beside Tim Crowe. All I can remember of that first day is the plasticine, or *mala* as we called it, and Tim Crowe's friendly greeting and sniffy nose. It was a good start.

Between playing at home, where we had a large hall and a separate playroom, and visiting Warrenpoint regularly, my early life was full. Times were good for our family. We had a housekeeper, Fran, like many other comfortable families at that time, who lived with us. A year after we moved to Sydney Parade, Moninne went to a boarding school in Roscrea, run by the Sacred Heart nuns. My mother felt that she was rather smothered by her brothers and needed the civilising influence of other young women. Lochlann and Conor were close in age and formed a natural pair. Too young to keep up with them, I had to find other ways to amuse myself as Declan and Colm were, in the early days, too young to keep up with me.

The first big Christmas I remember was 1953. Santa Claus was generous: I received a set of mini-bricks, the precursor to Lego, Conor got a mini billiard table and Lochlann got a German Marklin electric train set that my father bought second hand. The fact that it was Marklin and not Hornby was no accident. My father always encouraged us to look to other countries, indeed to any country other than Britain, for inspiration. The train set was an example and also a success; it soon had a permanent location in the playroom. In time, visits to the best toyshop in Dublin – Hely's of Dame Street – for birthdays or other occasions of celebration, resulted in more locomotives, rolling stock, level crossings, stations and related accessories. Everything about that German train set, with its overhead cables for the electric locomotives, was new to us. The only level crossing we knew, the one between Sydney Parade and Ailesbury Road, had cumbersome horizontal timber gates which opened and closed through the laborious turning of a cast-iron wheel in the tiny signal box that is there to this day, preserved but no longer in use.

Our model level crossing had strange and wonderful vertical lift-up poll barriers, which I thought were so daring and so different, but which are standard now in Ireland, including at the Sydney Parade crossing. The mini-bricks were converted into buildings and houses around the train set, with its mountain tunnel and viaduct. I know now that my father and brothers obviously got great fun out of making the set, and I am equally sure that the hours of enjoyment that I got probably steered me in the direction of architecture and town planning.

St Michael's was staffed mainly by Holy Ghost missionary priests returned from Africa, and seminarians who had completed a three-year Arts degree before commencing their theological studies. They wore black soutanes, and the seminarians were given the benighted prefix of 'Sir' to distinguish them from the ordained Fathers. I was to be taught by many Sirs and Fathers during my twelve years at St Michael's and Blackrock College and I felt secure throughout all that time. I had no sense of the undercurrents of abuse, physical or sexual, which clearly existed elsewhere. There were also a few lay teachers in St Michael's. Music and elocution were taught by Miss Muriel Morris. Drama was part of her curriculum and she produced her own operetta each year. I was the executioner in *The Royal Jester* and, in addition to the singing, enjoyed making my axe!

The original St Michael's house had a large glazed conservatory which was used as an art room and it was here that I was introduced to the wonders of drawing, painting and modelling. My natural talents were seriously enhanced by the encouragement and good teaching I received. Our art teacher, John Coyle, encouraged us to paint and sent the results into the Caltex Oil Company's nation-wide children's art competition, which had begun in 1954. In the late spring of 1956, I finished a painting that won first prize in the under-ten section of the competition. The prize was £10, a lot of money in those days, though the full value was not just the money but the encouragement and endorsement that the prize gave to my artistic ambitions and self-confidence.

However, my immediate priority was how to spend my prize money. After much deliberation, I bought a secondhand Rudge boy's bicycle for the princely sum of £6. I also decided to buy a seven-volume *Pictorial History of the War*, edited by Walter Hutchinson, for the substantial sum of £3.10s. The remaining 10 shillings were no doubt spent on sweets.

My interest in the Second World War was triggered, in part, by the Suez Crisis of 1956. In those days all our visual images of news came from the newspapers or from Pathé News clips in the cinema, which were spliced between the feature and the supporting film; its trade-mark opening was a crowing cock and patriotic music. The commentary of the mostly heroic stories contained an infectious mixture of excitement and exhortation. James McKenna, a neighbour and schoolfriend, had started to assemble a scrapbook, cutting out photographs from various newspapers of the military incidents from the Suez War. We were knowledgeable, with all the authority that only ten year olds can command, about the military equipment and the various aircraft deployed during that disastrous Anglo-French campaign.

James and I used to go into Dublin and he showed me how to make aeroplanes with balsawood and rubber-band-driven propellers. After some experimentation and development, we graduated to ether-fuelled motor engines with the same balsawood-framed aeroplanes. But while our unity of interest on the hardware of the war kept us engaged, we were seriously divided, and not for the first time, in our support for the two sides in the conflict.

Although we were now firm friends, our first encounter some four years before had not been amicable. I had accused James of being English when I had first heard him speak in St Michael's playground. He vigorously denied being English. I said that no Irish person could speak with an accent like that! One word led to another and fighting followed. One of the 'Sirs' separated us and we were confined to either end of the playground for the rest of the break.

James' father, C.B. McKenna, was an eminent senior counsel and professor of law at Trinity College. In those days, Trinity was a 'British' and a largely Protestant institution as far as I was concerned. Mr McKenna was completely different to my own father.

He was austere in manner, with not much interest in children. In retrospect, he was an old-fashioned man, who married a considerably younger woman named Rosalie after the death of his first wife left him with three children. Together they had three children and Rosalie, as a stepmother, seemed to me to be just like my own mother, but their house was quite different in nearly every respect, bar religion, to my own home around the corner.

The McKennas were what one might now describe as Castle Catholics and were reluctant nationalists. So reluctant indeed that when they took their olive green Ford Consul on a continental holiday, it carried a GB rather than an EIR sticker. I had a heated argument with James about this which lasted for at least two days. These things mattered immensely in the 1950s, but I was forever in the McKenna household and James in mine and our friendship endured. At the end of sixth class at St Michael's, he went to boarding school in Clongowes and that in itself was a breakthrough within the McKenna household. James' older brother David had been sent to Stonyhurst, the renowned Jesuit public school in Britain, and his sister Lisa to a similar British Catholic public school. It was the time of the last stages of a form of conscious Anglicisation of middle-class Irish children by parents who believed that, by sending them to such schools, they were doing the best for their children.

The other main event of 1956 was my father's visit to the Holy Land. A small group, including my Uncle Kevin and Aunts Joan and Una, flew in a Douglas DC3, hopping across Western Europe, from northern France to northern Italy, across to Cyprus and on to Israel. The journey took approximately three days, incredibly slow by today's standards. My mother, who had an intense fear of flying, became devoutly religious for the few weeks they were away and we recited the rosary each evening, more with a sense of insurance than worship.

They returned with exotic gifts and great photographs. At weekends, as my father went to take his after-lunch snooze, he would adjust the dial on the Bush radio, and the strains of Arab music would waft around the room. As he dozed, he was drifting in his mind. As a young man in the 1920s, he had travelled to the Weimar

Republic and had got as far south as Budapest because the collapse
of the German deutschmark had enhanced the value of his sterling.
In 1936, he took his young bride to Germany for their honeymoon.
He remained an admirer of Hitler's Germany, at least in the initial
stages of the Second Word War, because of his antipathy to Britain.
When I confronted him about this later, he said that his eyes had
been opened only when he had heard Lord Haw-Haw, aka William
Joyce, the Irish mouthpiece for Nazi Germany, on the radio. Lord
Haw-Haw was justifying why the coalmining village of Lidice in
Czechoslovakia had been razed in June 1942, why all its menfolk and
many of its women had been executed and why the rest of the population had been incarcerated in concentration camps as a reprisal for
the assassination of Reinhard Heydrich, the local Nazi governor, by
Czech partisans.

I played rugby and soccer in St Michael's, but these sports did not
attract me as much as they did my older brothers. Looking back
now other events have a stronger presence in my mind than sports.
In autumn 1953, my mother told me to repeat to my father something I had said to her earlier that day. I told him that I was going
to have my own gang when I went back to school, a declaration that
I think amused them both. When school started, I became the
leader of Quinner's gang and, in second form, our big enemy was
Sully's gang, led by Donal O'Sullivan.

One of our main activities in those halcyon days was the building
of forts across and along the stream that provided the boundary
between the edge of the grounds of St Michael's and the fields
beyond. They had become a building site, with a plentiful supply of
fort-making material. Across the road, work had started on what
had been half of Elm Park golf course to make way for St Vincent's
Hospital. To replace the lost nine holes, new ground was found
between Woodbine Avenue and Stillorgan Road. When it was time
to go home from play in Derek Scally's home on Woodbine Avenue,
we climbed over the back garden wall and headed across the new
Elm Park golf course until we were out on Nutley Lane, dodging

and weaving between the trees. The two building sites, St Vincent's Hospital and the houses under construction, came to a halt in the deep economic recession of the mid-1950s, but we youngsters were not perturbed by the consequences of such a social setback. On the contrary, it ensured that we had one of the most exciting and happiest playgrounds that any group of young kids could wish for. The only very minor downside was that I could never remember to clean the builders' muck off my shoes, and my mother's anguished cries in response to the trail of mud I brought into the house are something I can still hear. When she had calmed down and I had cleaned up, she would console herself with the observation that it was at least clean dirt!

By the age of eleven, I knew every building site within walking distance of our house. The RTÉ complex at Montrose was another large construction of curiosity. Security was light and we frequently went on explorative hunts, scavenging bits of timber for construction or model-making at home.

During the week the family normally ate in the kitchen; it had an Aga cooker, which was our main source of heat. We also had an Agamatic boiler, which supplied the entire house with hot water – provided the fire was kept lit. Sometimes the roster of three stokers – Lochlann, Conor and myself – accidentally allowed the fire to go out. The task of relighting the appliance was not pleasant and the lack of either hot water or warm food was the only strong reminder we needed not to let it go out again.

Our house had two reception rooms. During the winter, the folding doors were kept closed, the fire lit and the wireless turned on. Before television arrived, we used to retreat to the dining room in the evening. The only other places of warmth were the kitchen or the bed. There was a hierarchy of seating places in the dining room, from my father down, along the armchair and couch in front of the fire. On Sundays, after mass, we ate dinner in this room and not in the kitchen. The meal was formal in the sense that it took about twenty-five minutes to eat the food and another hour to finish the discussion of the day. There were six, sometimes ten, people for dinner: Uncle Kevin was usually there, sometimes we had a visiting cousin from Dundalk or other female cousins working in Dublin and living in flats; they were my mother's nieces and she felt she should feed them properly and keep an eye on them in a maternal way, which they obviously liked. Sometimes my mother's bachelor brother, James Hoey, who was sure to spark controversy, would be there. The issues of the day – the Hungarian Uprising, the Suez Crisis or the ongoing injustice of partition – would get an airing. The serialisation in the *Sunday Press* of nationalist and republican books such as John McCann's *War by the Irish* or Dorothy MacArdle's *Irish Republic* would prompt a debate about the Civil War. The politics of religion, and the call by Archbishop Dr John Charles McQuaid for Dubliners not to attend the 1955 Ireland vs Yugoslavia football match because of the imprisonment of Archbishop Stepanic, was another big topic, along with many others, both mundane and profound.

My father presided over these proceedings, careful that each of us got our say, and careful also not to impose his own strongly held opinions. Every so often, someone would be interrupted in the middle of a contribution. Father would then intervene, insisting that the speaker should be allowed to conclude. 'Let him finish and then – and only then – you can argue back.' It was an effective way of learning how to hold your audience and make your point quickly. To this very day, the cry, 'Let me finish' is a catchphrase within our extended family when we gather around the table.

My grandfather had been in poor health for some time, though I was not conscious of it. I did realise, however, that we were not visiting Warrenpoint as often as we had been. His condition probably explains why we had a special Christmas dinner in 1954. The dining room table was extended with its drop-in leaf and extra chairs were brought in to seat the fourteen people there in honour of our Mór Dada, as we called him.

John Quinn had started his family in Liverpool in the nineteenth century where five of his ten children, including my father, were born. Returning to Newry in 1910, he bought a small grocery business known as the Milestone. The five younger children were born in Newry and their father prospered, becoming a leading businessman in the county and a major figure in the emerging self-confident Catholic nationalist community of south Down and south Armagh. My grandfather was a Sinn Féin judge during the period before independence.

Unlike most of his nationalist business colleagues, my grandfather had taken the Sinn Féin side in the 1918 general election and was one of the signatories to the nomination of Éamon de Valera, as a candidate in that election for both Clare and South Armagh. Three of my grandfather's sons, including my father, fought in the War of Independence and went on to fight on the republican side in the subsequent Civil War. His eldest son, Seán, died in that war and another, Pádraig, was wounded and lost a leg.

The new unionist government in Northern Ireland had brought in a law enabling it to confine persons deemed to be a security risk to live in certain locations. My father was ordered to the Banbridge area, a unionist stronghold. After hanging around the Border on the Free State side for a number of months, he, along with others, returned to their homes. Back in Newry, he was arrested and jailed for six months in Crumlin Road Prison, Belfast. He was just twenty.

Mór Dada lived on to see his family settled between Warrenpoint and Dublin and to enjoy the company of his grandchildren. That last Christmas he was at the head of the table surrounded by two generations celebrating a long life. Imagine then my surprise when my father called on me, his third son, to propose a toast to the health and happiness of all present. Flushed and embarrassed with the honour he had bestowed on me, I did it. Was it a portent of things to come? I don't know why he asked me and not Lochlann, the eldest of his beloved sons, or indeed Moninne, his only daughter.

Two lay Irish teachers in St Michael's, John O'Donoghue and Ivor Kenny, had a great influence on me. Both also worked as news announcers with Radio Éireann. It was four years before the television service, Telefís Éireann, would come into existence with its first broadcast on New Year's Eve 1960. When it did, John O'Donoghue went on to become a senior presenter in various current-affairs programmes. Ivor Kenny, who taught us Irish, would eventually move to the Irish Management Institute and then to Trinity College Dublin.

The new principal of the school, Father Seamus Galvin, was a progressive teacher, full of American ideas about education. Micheal O'Siadhail, who lived in Nutley Park, had a deep interest in the Irish language and culture. We were close friends and our young minds were tentatively beginning to explore the world of language. Happily, we were well encouraged. Ivor Kenny was from Galway and, through him, Micheal got the name of a family on Inisheer, the most southerly of the Aran Islands, and the address of a bed-and-breakfast in Galway, near the harbour, where the island ferry, the *Naomh Éanna*, docked.

In the early summer of 1960, aged fourteen and thirteen, Micheal and I hitchhiked to Galway. We got a lift from Lucan to Loughrea in the cab of a large cattle truck and eventually reached Galway. The *Naomh Éanna* sailed the following morning; it was a slow three-hour journey. I can still hear the excitement in the raised voices that ran around the ship when the three islands came into view. Then the commotion, below decks, when calves were thrust into net-rope sacks, their legs bound together, ready to be winched onto a currach bound for Inisheer, the ferry's first stop. Both of us were keen to learn Irish. However, Micheal was deeply committed and stayed on after I had left and is now one of our outstanding poets.

It was during that visit that, influenced by my new-found interest, I decided to change the spelling of my name from the English form of Rory to Ruairi. I had been reading one of my father's books about Roger Casement, who had translated his name Roger to the Gaelic form Ruari. For a year or so I spelt it like that until the correct spelling in modern Irish, the way I spell it now, was brought to my attention and I have kept that ever since.

Micheal and I arrived on Inisheer in time to see the end of a period romanticised by many and captured on canvas by the artist Seán Keating, one of Ireland's social realist painters. There was no electricity on Inisheer and no outboard motors on the currachs. Red petticoats and coarse homespun tweed jackets and trousers were still everyday wear, along with woven woollen belts known as *crios* and raw cowhide shoes which the islanders called pampooties. This was a completely different world for us and we both knew we were seeing its final days.

Inisheer raises its back to the roaring waves of the Atlantic, and the sparse settlement of houses take shelter behind the rocky ridge on the east looking back inland towards Galway. A wide, sandy beach runs across the centre linking the villages on the eastern side. Our house was to the north, beyond the harbour pier, but it could barely be called a harbour. In the middle of the beach, a single house with a slate roof stood, half-buried by the surrounding sand. In the coming days, as we explored the island, we met the occupant of the isolated beach house, Knut the Dane. He was a refugee from the modern world. We listened with intense interest to what he had to say about the devastation of the Second World War and his disillusionment with continental Europe. We were both in our early teens and anxious to explore the very world from which he was retreating. Outside, the shoal of porpoises that frequently cruised along the eastern coast seemed to symbolise that desire for exploration. Their soaring leaps signalled to me that the world would be both exciting and fun.

Chapter 3

Coming of Age in Blackrock College

Going to Blackrock College in September 1960 was a big step. St Michael's only went as far as second year and then, of the twelve students who had completed the final year, ten of us went on to Blackrock, where my two older brothers had gone and where my two younger brothers would follow. By now, Lochlann was studying Commerce at University College Dublin and Conor was in sixth year, accommodated in the Castle. This last year was seen as providing a transition between secondary school and the adult world. The Castle was a separate three-storey, self-contained building with its own classrooms, refectory, library and bedrooms. It had its own chapel on the top floor over the hallway with some fine stained-glass windows by Evie Hone. The Castle was the first building that a visitor met as they came up the driveway from the Rock Road. On the left of the Castle, across the upper playing field, you could see the main complex of buildings with its square tower. The Jubilee Hall at the end of the driveway was on the other side of the main entrance.

I was now in third year with 120 students, most of whom I did not know. The garden basement room of the Jubilee Hall was our informal gathering place. I had just finished playing a game of table tennis, which I had lost, and my opponent asked if I was related to Lochlann or Conor. When I said that I was, he announced loudly to the group that he had just defeated one of the Quinns at table tennis. I quietly decided to myself that I would not be playing table tennis again. Following in the footsteps of two brothers created an unsustainable expectation. So I determined that whatever sport I pursued, it would be of my own choosing. Large families have, as I know, many strengths but they can also create expectations from others that all the members of the family have the same abilities and similar interests.

There were five classes in third year and each pupil was streamed, subject by subject, on the basis of academic ability. I had been placed in the top two streams. The first days enabled those of us who had come from St Michael's or Willow Park, the other feeder school, to get to know the students who had started in first year. Most of these were boarders and they made up nearly half the student body.

Seamus Grace, my English teacher in third year, had natural authority as a schoolmaster. On our first day he instructed us to take out our intermediate poetry books and to turn to a particular page. When we did, some of us informed him that the poem in question was not on that year's course for the Intermediate Certificate examination.

'I know,' he said, and asked Kevin Connolly to stand up and to read it aloud. 'It is an excellent poem and I want you to listen to it.'

When Kevin had finished reading, Mr Grace asked us to take ten minutes to write down what the poem meant to us. I was astounded, as were others. We had come from St Michael's or Willow, prepared to sit the Intermediate Certificate in third year because we were in the top streams – so we had concentrated only on those poems that were on that year's course. Mr Grace then asked three pupils to read out their written thoughts. He proceeded to ask us, at random, what we thought about the remarks. This method of education by question and discourse was new, but very welcome. In Seamus Grace's classroom, I soon lost any academic inhibitions. My memory more than forty years later is obviously selective but I still retain the sense of liberation that this way of teaching engendered, not just by Seamus Grace but by other teachers in Blackrock. At a time when Ireland was still an insular country, such invitations to think aloud and to have an opinion respected was not the norm – even if was for me at home.

I looked forward most to the art classes, held in the library under the direction of John Coyle. He was very different in personality from Seamus Grace, but carried similar authority. Students committed to art and design were identified early on and were given additional encouragement. Over the next couple of years, I did extra classes with John Coyle and worked at the top table with four or five students from different years; all of us went on to pursue art or architecture. John Coyle encouraged me to transfer from watercolours to oils and ensured that I persevered despite my initial difficulties. It was around this table that I first met Coilín Murray, who was a year ahead of me and who would become a respected artist.

'I suppose you have read Camus?' he asked one day.

'I have, but not *The Outsider*.'

I told him that while on the island of Inisheer, I had been enthralled as I read *The Plague*'s tale of siege and philosophical confrontation. It was the beginning of major conversations about writers and ideas, through which we became close friends. I introduced him to William Faulkner, as he enthused about John Steinbeck and we eagerly swapped other books.

I decided to play rugby because my friends were keen on it. I was barely a competent player and just made the squad of the Under-15 Junior Cup Team. As a prop, I was too light and not sufficiently aggressive. Undeterred, I persevered, even though it was a long time before I made it to the first team. My first full match – the result of an injury to another player – was in the first round of the championship.

Competitive team sports generate their own group dynamics and bonds of friendship. Tim Crowe and David Browne were on the team. Tony Amoroso, David Cantrell, Seán Kelly, Brian McLoughlin and others who had come through from Willow Park were also part of a group whose friendship became central to my time in Blackrock. David Browne, a natural athlete, was team captain. We made our way through to the Junior Cup final but were beaten by a strong Belvedere side.

The Holy Ghost Fathers developed an approach to team motivation years before the advent of modern sports psychology. Group bonding and team spirit were things they instinctively understood and reinforced. After each cup match, the winning team, junior or senior, was fed in the refectory. Meanwhile the boarders sang Blackrock songs as the team ate their meal of bacon, sausages and eggs, with bread, jam and cream cakes. The singing boarders had to be satisfied with tea, bread and jam. A victory resulted in a generous rendition of songs culminating with the school anthem 'Rock Boys Are We', for which we all stood.

As a losing Junior Cup Team, we were treated with the same food and songs but then had to address the assembled boarders. David Browne stood on a dining table to thank everyone for the great support and to apologise for having lost. As he stepped down from the table, he was replaced by another and then another as each player was called to stand 'up, up' on the table and address a demanding group of disappointed Blackrock men. I can remember it still and, as I spoke, I steeled myself with the private resolution that I would never again lose a match.

It was powerful stuff and certainly made Blackrock a formidable force on the rugby pitch, irrespective of the quality of the team. Three years later, I was delighted to be a wing-forward on a Senior Cup Team, led to championship victory by Brian McLoughlin. David Cantrell, my roommate in the Castle when I was a boarder for the last year, was the other wing-forward. During the final, after a touchline throw-in confrontation, we kept a mildly concussed captain and lock-forward on the pitch for at least eight or nine minutes, and managed to hold on to our 3–0 lead over Terenure. Brian was so injured that he could not accept the cup from his mother, the tradition then as now, but his departure from the pitch, without a substitute, was too big a risk for us to take. Today he shows no signs of any residual damage!

My brother Conor, whom I saw infrequently in school, displayed great athletic skill on sports day in the half-mile. He was a smoker and so I figured that I could at least be as good as he was and, towards the end of third year, the idea of athletics took shape in my mind.

Early in the autumn at the start of fourth year, Father Jerome Godfrey, known affectionately as Goddo, asked me if I would be interested in cross-country running because I was now too old for the Junior Cup Team. The memory of Conor's sprint in the finish of the half-mile was still strong when I went across to the sports fields after school ended.

A man with tightly cut hair and angular features, wearing a light brown overcoat and smoking a cheroot, was speaking to some boys. Tony Farrell lived in Blackrock and ran O'Leary's Bakery. He was very keen on athletics and had been given permission to use the school sports fields to train a squad of middle-distance runners from the Donore Harriers Athletic Club. Tony was a serious and knowledgeable coach. In gratitude to Blackrock's generosity, he offered to train any students interested in the sport. It was a demanding afternoon. We ran, in a single file, around the boundary of two football pitches between Blackrock and Willow Park. Each runner at the end of a 30-metre line had to sprint up along past the file of other runners and take over the lead position, gratefully slowing down to the median speed and pace of the group.

I had never done interval running before. Between a growing stomach stitch and weary thigh and leg muscles, I got a glimpse, and a sense of the exhilaration, of the rhythm of running.

'You're all going to be sore and very stiff this evening and first thing tomorrow,' Tony told us when we had finished. 'The only cure for that stiffness is more running, so I'll see you here at the same time tomorrow.' I changed and, stiff and sore, limped back up to the House. There along with a number of other day students, I did supervised study for two hours, finishing at seven o'clock.

By the middle of fourth year, I was beginning to enjoy school in Blackrock. I had a good group of friends, most of whom lived around Booterstown. The second time sitting the Intermediate Certificate examination involved us doing a whole new course in English and History. I was more self-confident in the classroom and enjoyed the method and style of teaching. There were more lay teachers and the priests who did teach, like Father Roche, were getting older and fewer even at that time.

We were aware of the African Missions, to which the order of the Holy Ghost Fathers had been dedicated since its original establishment in France. One priest, Father Joe Fullen, referred to the missions in a different way to others; while other European countries may have had large territorial empires, we, the Irish, had an enormous spiritual empire! However, the reality of the missions was often present in our classroom. Father John Roche, affectionately known as 'Da' because he called everybody 'son', was the rugby coach of the Junior Cup Team and had spent more than twenty years in West Africa; the ravages of that hot, humid climate left their mark and he would often be missing from the classroom, suffering from a recurrence of malaria. When he did not appear in the classroom, the Dean of Day Boys, Father 'Spud' Murphy, or the Dean of Studies, Father 'Bing' Corless, would put his head around the door to tell us that Father Roche was indisposed. We were instructed to use the period for study and asked to remain quiet, but I do remember wondering how I would have coped with a parish the size of Leinster with only a motorbike for transport.

Harold Macmillan's 'winds of change' had started to blow across Africa and the process of independence and decolonisation would be a major issue not just for Britain but also for France, Belgium and Portugal. The Holy Ghost Fathers were proud of the fact that they had educated some of the emerging leaders of the newly independent states. Tom Mboya, one of Jomo Kenyatta's bright young deputies in Kenya, was a past pupil of the Holy Ghost secondary school in Nairobi. When he subsequently came on an official visit to Ireland, he visited Blackrock and publicly gave thanks to the retired priests who had been his teachers in secondary school. Long before the jargon of overseas aid became commonplace, we acquired a sense of solidarity with the Third World. I have no doubt that this influenced Bob Geldof, a Blackrock past pupil, to work so effectively to organise Live Aid in 1985 and his subsequent Live8 campaign for debt relief.

By Easter 1962, I was approaching my sixteenth birthday. Athletic training had moved on to the athletic field in front of the main college building which had a quarter-mile running track with six lanes. Interval training had also changed and now consisted of a series of sprints interspersed with a slow jogging recovery period. Cross-country running was not then formally organised in Irish schools as it is now; most of the focus was training for the athletics season in the short summer term.

I had set my sights on the half-mile (800 metres). Through Tony Farrell I joined Donore Harriers and took part as a junior in road races in and around the Phoenix Park. There were a number of young adults in the Donore Harriers. Every weekday evening, they would arrive from work and change in the Blackrock Rugby Clubhouse on the college grounds, before heading out for one of Tony Farrell's training sessions on the athletic field. Since we trained together these young men in their twenties were a good influence on us. Their commitment to training and work, which they combined with evening courses related to their jobs, displayed real dedication.

There was little athletic competition in the Republic because the sport had been split by the 'national question'. The National Athletic and Cycling Association, like the Gaelic Athletic Association, did not accept the existence of partition and the confinement, for the purposes of international competition, of athletes coming only from the Irish state. On the other hand, the Amateur Athletic Union had six clubs in Ireland, including Donore Harriers. We got to travel to Belfast for competitive road races against the Northern Ireland section of the British Amateur Athletic Association. The competitive season was short and tight. The Leinster provincial athletic competition took place in the Iveagh Gardens, Crumlin, and the All-Ireland finals were held a fortnight later in Ballinasloe, County Galway. In the four half-mile races that were held for that title, I came a close second to Seán Fallon on three occasions and succeeded in beating him just once – in Ballinasloe. In Dublin on the same day, the awards in the national Caltex children's art competition were being presented, so I was not able to collect the first prize I had won in the intermediate category. The combination of running and painting that early summer was intoxicating, and I finished my fourth year in great form.

The money I won in the art competition funded an exchange trip to France. I was excited about going there to improve my knowledge of the language. My mother heard about an exchange programme between Irish and French families being organised by a French priest, Père de Rocquois, and signed me on. I would stay with two different families for one month each and, in turn, two French boys, not necessarily from the same families, would stay with my family in Dublin. The journey to Lyons was by a chartered Air France Caravelle jet, then the state-of-the-art technology. I sat beside Shane de Blacam, a fellow student in Blackrock, who would become a colleague in the School of Architecture in University College Dublin.

Lyons sits at the junction of the rivers Rhône and Saône in south-eastern France. The suburb in which my first family was living was to the west, on an elevated ridge above the city, a typical middle-class district. The father was a schools inspector for an independent Catholic federation of schools and the mother was warm and maternal, a *pied noir* who had left her native Morocco many years before but who, emotionally, still remained there. The Algerian independence struggle was at its zenith and the sentiments of my French hosts in support of the French settlers were not in any doubt. Their eldest child, a young adult in her twenties, was a nurse in the city. Her arrival home to the suburban house, with its high-walled garden and solid timber gates, was proclaimed by the familiar honking – three short and two long – on the horn of her car 'Algerie Française'.

I had great expectations of meeting young French people, but the reality came as a bit of a shock. Irish society was more relaxed and Dublin social life more open than the narrow lifestyle of Jean Pierre, my sixteen-year-old counterpart, who was polite but not friendly. When I was bored or lonely, I consoled myself that at the end of the month I would be in a different place, possibly on the Mediterranean coast with a family who were exciting and who would be enjoying the traditional four-week French holiday. Imagine my disappointment when my new family turned out to be living in the same neighbourhood. There, however, the similarities ended. The father of the house was a lovely man who took to me instantly. They had two sons: the eldest was in his mid-twenties and not around that much, but Bruno, the younger at nineteen, was my first introduction to male adolescent rudeness and selfishness.

However, my real new friend was the father of the house. We spent a number of evenings, in the warm August heat, talking on the terrace of their modest house. He was an active trade unionist and supporter of the socialists in France – then known as SFIO. The crisis in Algeria was frequently in the news and I related to him my experience with the mother of the previous host family. He explained the difficulties of the *pied noirs*, French white settlers returning to metropolitan France, with few resources, having lived for three or four generations in Algeria. I was familiar with the issues because I had read *The Plague* and *The Outsider* by Camus, who had been born in Algeria. The tension of the settlers and the revolt of the OAS, the secret army organisation, and the reaction of de Gaulle were the major topics we discussed. I also told him that I noticed on my arrival in Lyons airport, a plaque on the wall indicating that the new arrivals building had been opened recently by Jacques Soustelle, the former Gaullist minister who was now on the run as one of the leaders of the French settlers' rebellion, cam-paigning against de Gaulle's U-turn decision to recognise Algeria as an independent country. My friend was surprised that I would have noticed this, a young foreigner entering France for the first time, but I had then, and still retain, a great interest in French politics.

Coming back to Dublin after nine weeks and little contact with my parents, except for a few letters, was more emotional than I expected. I knew I had changed. I was a wiser young man than the one who had left at the end of June. When we came into the small arrivals building at Dublin Airport, a large group of parents and siblings were waiting for the planeload of young students. I could make out my father in the crowd – small, baldheaded, smoking a cigar – and I rushed over and hugged him warmly. Sixteen-year-old boys did not usually hug their parents but, as I did, I realised that he really welcomed my big embrace and homecoming.

By that autumn of 1962, I had known for some time that my father's grocery business was failing. An illness some six years earlier had pushed him into premature old age and he did not have the drive to modernise the shops and convert them into self-service supermarkets. My parents decided to wind down the family business. I didn't know the details of what was happening but I did know that, while we were comfortable, times were tight. Money was scarce and so my mother started to take in Spanish students throughout the year as paying guests, something she did for the next ten years.

During my fifth year, my running and painting proved to be particularly successful. I won the coveted title 'Victor Ludorum' – Winner of the Games – at the school sports in the summer term. I was now concentrating on the mile and 3 mile distances (1,500 metres and 3,000 metres today). The success meant that I got a place on the Irish team to participate in the Catholic Student Games in Lisbon. Our group consisted of twenty athletes and three supervisors, including Declan Grehan, a neighbour and architect who gave me great encouragement. We flew to Paris in July, took the night train southwest to Hendaye, where we transferred very early in the morning to an awaiting Spanish train. By 7.30 a.m. we were high in the Basque country, overlooking verdant hills and the orange-coloured roof tiles of the whitewashed rural houses and farm buildings of that part of Spain.

By midday we were in the flat dry plains of northwestern Spain. The dining car, with its high-collared, uniformed waiters and dark-varnished timber panelling, evoked images of the American Wild West. The long horizontal landscape had a palette of burnt brown colours which I had only seen before on a cinema screen. It was as if I was back in the Stella Cinema in Mount Merrion looking at a classic western, except this was the real thing. The summer landscape and the smell of heat was visually exciting and wonderfully new.

Later on, in the dull heat of the afternoon, the steam train stopped in a dusty, isolated station to take on water. I stepped down from the carriage, curious to explore the quiet station with its few people and eerie silence. In the bar I succeeded, with some linguistic difficulty, to buy a bottle of red wine. The high-ceilinged room, with a slow-turning ventilator fan, was empty except for the barman and me. I returned to my friends on the train to share the wine, unaware at that time that I had just had my first experience of the Spanish siesta.

After ten days in Lisbon, where we competed with eight other countries, we set off on the return rail journey. The games were enjoyable, but I was out of my league in the 1,500 and 3,000 metres. I left the group to take a train to Zaragoza where my mother's summer Spanish lodger, César Alierta, lived. I arrived at their city-centre apartment block in the middle of the siesta and was quietly admitted into a spare bedroom with shuttered windows. All was still in the early afternoon, but a few hours later the place was transformed with the noise of traffic and people rising from the streets.

I had never been in a large family apartment before. The Aliertas home took up half the third floor of their building, and had a long central corridor with some rooms overlooking an indoor courtyard and others looking out onto the street. Showered and changed, César led me on a tour of the streets of the town, visiting bars where he would call out 'Dos blancos', and we would nibble tapas set out on small plates along the counter. As César ate, he scanned the room for male friends and female talent. As soon as the white wine was consumed and the place adequately surveyed, it was off to another bar and more blancos. After four or five such visits, and plenty of excitement, chatting to the local young women, we headed home for dinner and my formal introduction to the Alierta family.

I returned from Spain at the end of August to begin my sixth and last year in school and, for this year, I was a boarder. While I had been away from my family many times before, I had never lived in an institution or shared a bedroom with anyone for any length of time. In September 1963, I arrived in the Castle. My roommate, chosen by mutual agreement, was David Cantrell. I had played with him on the Junior Cup Team in third year, he had gone on to concentrate on playing rugby while I had focused on athletics.

I was elected president of the Students' Representative Council, an

institution designed to help prepare students for the responsibilities of adult life. Soon I was leading a group of students to the
Dean, Father 'Pop' McCarthy, to try and improve conditions for the
students. One of our first requests was to have the daily newspaper
– four pages pinned up in a glass display case on the corridor –
changed. The *Irish Press* was what we had to read in Blackrock,
perhaps in deference to the paper's founder, Éamon de Valera, who
had attended Blackrock College at the turn of the century. Many of
us, though, wanted to have *The Irish Times* displayed instead as it
contained more news and it did not have the *Irish Press*' Fianna Fáil
bias. Father McCarthy listened to us politely and said, 'How could
we have boys, particularly those from the country, reading *The Irish
Times*? What would their parents think if the college authorities
were encouraging students to read a Protestant paper?'

By the time I was sixteen, my personal interest in religion, spiritu-
ality and belief began to intensify. Influenced initially by Camus but
now provoked by writers including Robert Graves, James Joyce,
Evelyn Waugh, J.D. Salinger and Ernest Hemingway, I began to
question my received set of religious beliefs. At home, my father, a
devout Catholic, attended mass every day during Lent and we – my
brothers – went with him. His commitment had an influence on me
despite my growing reservations and in Blackrock I joined the
Legion of Mary in 1963.

While streaming took place for subjects on the basis of ability, for
Christian Doctrine or Religious Instruction, it was simply a case of
students staying in the same room after the previous class ended,
waiting for the religion teacher. Towards the end of fifth year, I
learned that Dr Michael O'Carroll, known affectionately as the
Doc, was the Christian Doctrine teacher in 6C. I had been in his
History class in fifth year and wanted to be in his sixth-year
Christian Doctrine class because he was such a great teacher. I made
my transfer request which was considered unusual but it was
granted. The students of 6C were the hard men of the year, not
studious but definitely not stupid! A lack of intellectual curiosity
among some of them was compensated for by a streetwise self-
confidence which was seldom displayed in the higher streamed

classes. Indeed, 6C Christian Doctrine class was a lively and stimulating place and Doc Carroll responded firmly to the frank and provocative questions from the slightly cynical pupils.

During that sixth year, I was busy painting and had decided to study architecture, which appealed to me because it was both artistically and socially engaged. I came to this decision slowly over two years. While I loved painting, I did not want to become an art teacher, which at that time was the only route open to me to continue with art. Alongside my intention to be an architect, I developed my interest and belief in politics. I continued to follow current affairs, but felt that the type of political debate taking place at national level did not tackle the concerns I considered important. The poverty of distant Africa was brought into our classrooms by our returned missionary teachers. The inequalities at home were to be seen in the row of cottages across from St Vincent's Hospital where a home for six or more people was the size of a single room in my own home. Among the books I had read, such as Steinbeck's *Of Mice and Men*, was a clear direction towards the construction of a different political reality.

Closer to home, the British Sunday newspapers lambasted the failing Conservative government now led by Sir Alec Douglas-Home, the hapless successor to Harold Macmillan. A momentum was gathering behind the British Labour Party. Politics of both a national and international dimension became a frequent subject of school conversation. A classmate, Pat O'Connell, introduced me to the *New Statesman* and I became a regular reader. In 1962, an essay I wrote on the political developments in Africa won the fourth year gold medal and was published in the 1963 Blackrock College annual. Sadly it now reads prophetically:

> But the Africa of 1980... What of that? Will it be a development of Europe today? Will delegates from Accra, Lagos and Nairobi and other capitals sit around the conference table and seek a united Africa? An African Common Market? Or will the African states wage pitiless wars upon themselves? Is there a future Hitler or Mussolini lurking in the background?

Looking back, this was clearly the opening up of a developing political mind. For me there could be no other set of political beliefs but a socialism of the head and the heart. As my attachment to orthodox religious belief began to wane, my need for an alternative value system saw me turn increasingly to the politics of the left.

One of my friends in school was Stephen Coughlan. His father Stevie, a past pupil, was the Labour TD for Limerick East and a controversial figure. Stephen and I were part of a regular group who took our meals at the same table in the refectory where we frequently talked about politics and the Irish Labour Party. Stevie Coughlan had been in Clann na Poblachta, the leftist republican party founded in 1946 by Seán MacBride. In 1963, the Labour Party was growing. Seán Dunne, an Independent TD, had formally joined the party and Dr Noël Browne and Jack McQuillan, the two radical Independent TDs who made up the National Progressive Democrats, had also joined. Brendan Corish from Wexford had been the new, young and handsome leader since 1960, when William Norton finally retired after more than twenty years at the helm. I was following this mostly by reading *The Irish Times*, which I still had to buy outside the school.

Towards the end of the first term of sixth year, Stephen Coughlan showed me a newspaper report of how the Cambridge Union in Britain had restructured its normal debating configuration to replicate the United Nations. Students proceeded to have a series of debates on topical issues while reflecting the format and structure of the General Assembly. In response to Stephen's suggestion that we copy the Cambridge Union's initiative, I proposed the idea to the sixth-year Debating Society Committee, of which I was a member, and they agreed. Our UN General Assembly, in a rearranged refectory, would be all participants and no audience. Stephen and I were asked by the committee to bring it about and so twenty countries were selected with a controversial agenda in mind.

In order to retain control of the meeting, we decided that Stephen should become the Secretary General of the General Assembly. We also needed an authoritative president, because some people did not think that the set-up would work, and could degenerate into chaos.

Father Walter Finn, ex-padre to the British Eighth Army during the Second World War and an outstanding rugby player in his time, accepted the position.

We now had to match the individuals and the states as best we could. The hard men and the tough guys, many from 6C, were to be representatives from Khrushchev's USSR and Castro's Cuba. Pat O'Connell, whose father was English, volunteered to represent the United Kingdom. Some of our ten Hong Kong Chinese students agreed to represent Taiwan, which in 1963 was occupying the permanent seat on the Security Council retained for China. Stephen and I worked out the main issues to be debated: the admission of the People's Republic of China to the Security Council, the apartheid regime in South Africa and that country's abuse of its UN mandate in Southwest Africa (now Namibia).

Decolonisation in the rest of Africa was why I had volunteered to represent Portugal, the last belligerent colonial power on that continent. I got Stephen to take on one additional motion which we placed in the middle of the agenda. When all was agreed, I proceeded to hand print the notice, announcing our first UN General Assembly meeting, which was pinned up proudly on the noticeboard on the Castle corridor.

I was surprised later that day to come across Father McCarthy, Doc O'Carroll and Father Flood berating a bewildered Stephen Coughlan, his back against the wall beside the noticeboard. 'How could the college authorities explain to the parents of the boys, whose care, education, faith and morals had been entrusted to the Holy Ghost Fathers, that their son would advocate that the receipt of United Nations aid to Third World countries was conditional on the recipient state having a national programme of family planning and population control?'

I had drafted this motion in the name of Sweden, but it failed to get past the clerical heavyweights. However, our UN experiment did and the General Assembly meetings were very popular.

After Christmas I was asked to play as wing-forward with the rugby Senior Cup Team. I was surprised to be asked because I had been concentrating exclusively on athletics at this stage and did not consider myself a good rugby player. I was nervous of injury, which might hamper my US athletic scholarship prospects. I also had a yellow streak as I looked at the size of second-row forwards like Neil 'Barney' Mullen and Mick 'Porky' Whelan. The task of tackling men that size terrified me. Father Godfrey felt that the team was short of talent in the pack and knew I was fit; besides, I was flattered to be asked. I had many friends on the team, with whom I had been on the Junior Cup team.

In our first championship encounter, against the superior High School team, I managed, in a late tackle on their talented out-half, to break the arm of our wing-forward, my own roommate, David Cantrell! With only four minutes to go, Brian McLoughlin levelled the score with a converted try taken with nerves of steel. In the closing minutes, Tim Crowe scored our winning try. Progress through the next rounds was difficult but successful. The final was set, as usual, for Lansdowne Road on St Patrick's Day. David was still injured. Here I was, a game away from a coveted Senior Cup medal, sharing a room with someone who wanted little else. Fate intervened in the form of an influenza epidemic, which closed college and the final was cancelled. The Easter holiday came and went and a few weeks later David Cantrell, fully recovered, naturally regained his place on the team. In the meantime, his replacement, Hugo Hynes, had performed well and had replaced me. But in another twist, Hugo became ill, compounded by an injury, on the eve of the final and failed a fitness test that morning. I was back on the team, filled with righteous indignation and a determination to prove my worth.

To run out onto the pitch at Lansdowne Road as an eighteen year old is a daunting experience. Fired up with the tension in the changing room, with its smell of fear and nervousness, combined with the deep odour of wintergreen, we charged out on to the field. Earlier that year I had submitted a scene inspired by rugby as my painting for the Caltex art competition. The main assessor, John Fitzmaurice Mills, was complimentary and told me privately that he thought I had caught perfectly the angst of the prisoners, enclosed in their cramped cell. I explained to him that it was a rugby team, togged out in a crowded dressing room! The pale blue and white horizontal stripes of the Senior Cup Team jersey could easily be mistaken for a prisoner's uniform.

In the second half of the match, our scrum-half, Liam Hall, slid over the line from a scrum close to the Terenure College line. It was the only try of the match and ensured victory. I don't think I'll ever forget the emotion that these intensely contested games evoked.

We were now weeks away from the end of secondary school and I concentrated on studying and my athletics training. Father McCarthy allowed me to take an hour off in the evening to do intensive interval work on the top sports field with Tony and his troop of athletes. My target for the Leaving Certificate examination was to get a basic honours result: 60 per cent or more in at least three subjects. Although the athletic season that year went well, I didn't win the senior All-Ireland gold medal for which I had hoped. However, I did qualify, once again, for the Catholic student games that year in Gerona, Spain, and spent two weeks there in June running in the half-mile. I was also delighted to be able to visit the Alierta family in Zaragoza again.

Back in Dublin in July 1964, I spent the rest of the summer months crossing that difficult but invisible threshold between youth and adulthood. I had many nights of chat and earnest teenage conversation with my family and friends which were more than matched by going to dances, falling in and out of love, and anxiously wondering about my next date and the next dance as we left the pub after a few pints.

Chapter 4

UCD and the Gentle Revolution

A lthough I had the experience of going to a big secondary school, I found my entry into University College Dublin intimidating. The imposing neoclassical building at Earlsfort Terrace, just off St Stephen's Green, housed around 3,000 students and was the major centre of UCD; today it is the home of the National Concert Hall. I remember well how its central hall became immensely congested on the hour, every hour, as lectures ended and others began.

Thomas Aiken Austin and Neil Downes, the two part-time studio masters in first year, were good teachers. First year was an intense period of study in which I learned the basics of the five-year course: how to measure, how to draw and how to organise spaces so as to begin to accommodate and successfully house different kinds of human activities. In first and second year, we spent two afternoons a week in the National College of Art (NCA), which in those days was located beside Leinster House. Because of my friendship with Coilín Murray, a second-year student at NCA, I got to meet and became friends with a wide circle of people, including Ciarán MacGonigal and Charlie Harpur.

By second year, after working for the summer in a pea-canning factory in Essex, I had become close friends with an extraordinary group of people in the School of Architecture. Friendships naturally develop among a mixed group who are thrown together for six or seven hours a day, five-and-a-half days a week in a relatively confined space, but they only occasionally develop a great dynamic. Years later when I taught architecture as a studio master, I saw the phenomenon of a dynamic group emerging within an arbitrarily selected class of twenty-five students but I don't think I would have recognised it so readily if I had not benefited greatly from a similar formation.

The village of Enniskerry in County Wicklow was chosen by our studio masters as the location for our second-year work. We got to know every part of that attractive village and learned a lot about architecture. Educational projects developed into social functions, get-togethers in someone's home or flat, usually after the Saturday deadline for the study project hand-in.

Although the camaraderie at college was good, the education curriculum in the School of Architecture was bad. Professor Desmond FitzGerald, the oldest brother of Garret, was an arrogant man who, despite his considerable intelligence, had lost touch with developments in architectural education and could not relate to the new generation of students. Our group was bright, keen, confident and pushy. We knew that our architectural education was substandard and we groused about it. I decided, with the support of the group, to stand for the post of auditor of the Architectural Society, a position normally reserved for a senior student. My candidacy against Kevin Brady, of third year, was seen as cheeky, but we had an agenda for change and, at the end of a tightly fought campaign, I was successful. One of my pledges was to connect the school with the outside world and, as part of that, I wrote to Father McDyer, a priest from Donegal. He wanted help for his radical co-operative company, designed to sustain his declining rural community. He replied saying he would be in Dublin and would like to meet us – the 'us' in question were Larry Fewer, Edward O'Cleary, Seán Ó Laoire and myself. Father McDyer wanted to build a folk house that would reflect traditional life in Donegal. The building would be a tourist attraction to supplement the community's meagre agricultural income.

The Donegal priest told us to contact Kevin McDermott, a UCD lecturer who had done research into rural Irish housing. He knew about the design and the construction of the roof structure and the timber truss, or 'couple' as he called it. Early dwellings used timber from the branches of trees, which retained their original rounded shape; they were pinned together with timber pegs, or dowels. On the west coast of Ireland, the paucity of forests and the prevalence of bogs meant that the only reliable source of suitably sized timber was bog oak or pine.

Two months later, in June 1966, I arrived on my Lambretta scooter to collect Seán Ó Laoire from his Finglas home. Travelling to the northwest, Seán and I went through Donegal town and out along the coast road. After Killybegs, and before we reached Kilcar, we began to come across a few derelict single-storey cottages. We could see the profile of their roof structure and soon were recognising the iconic couples. We began shouting excitedly to one another as we neared our destination and could understand the tangible context in which we were to work. About half an hour before we arrived at the crossroads of the little village of Glencolumcille, a strong summer mist descended on the upland bog road along which we were travelling. We dropped out of it and rode along the curving road into the glen.

We were accommodated in the local pub, which doubled as a bed and breakfast. The following day Larry Fewer and Edward O'Cleary arrived in Edward's Mini Minor with our drawing equipment. Father McDyer told us that we had a very open brief and no specific site. Our first task was to explore the valley. It was mid-June, with glorious weather, long evenings and beautiful landscapes. The pattern of housing was of small clusters of three or four dwellings with accompanying outhouses and farm buildings. These clochans formed the centre of a series of townlands or loosely structured villages. The church, pub, shops and community hall in the centre were close to where we were staying, as were some holy wells and derelict structures. There were also some closed-up houses, complete with furniture and household effects, left by people who had moved into newly built houses nearby, gone to Letterkenny or emigrated farther afield.

In those two wonderful weeks, we established as our design objective not one house but a clochan. We began to survey the existing dwellings, locating furniture and artefacts. We drew up our plans and presented them to Father McDyer, who made one constructive suggestion: the three residences that made up the clochan should be built and furnished to represent traditional life as it was at different times – 350 years before, 150 years and a more modern house from fifty years earlier, about the time of the Easter Rising. The outhouses would reflect the farming methods and other activities related to life in Glencolumcille. We left Donegal exhilarated and full of theories about vernacular architecture, aestheticism, the cult of monumentalism, and how the human scale was reflected so differently in these folk buildings, compared to the official buildings of church and state. It was a theme to which I would return.

After our trip to Donegal, I went to London, which in the summer of 1966 was at the heart of the cultural revolution that was the swinging sixties. The globalisation of pop culture was in its infancy and the city was one of its capitals. I had travelled from Liverpool with Coilín Murray, on my Lambretta scooter initially to work again in the Goldhanger Pea Factory near Maldon in Essex. However, there was no work for Coilín and one look at the place convinced me that I did not want another seven weeks on the night shift there. We headed for London, armed with addresses and telephone numbers. I contacted Michael Burke, a third-year architectural student who was already in London and, in a pattern that is so familiar to Irish people in Britain, I soon got a job. We shared a flat in Notting Hill Gate and I buzzed around on my Lambretta. Together we explored the city and thoroughly enjoyed the cosmopolitan atmosphere, so different to Dublin. The bonus was the good money that could be earned as a contract draughtsman.

Back at UCD in 1966 for third year, I was the auditor of the Architectural Society and an active member of the universities branch of the Labour Party, which combined both UCD and Trinity College. Freshers' Week, at the beginning of October, enabled the student clubs and societies to set up stalls and promote their activities in the hope of attracting new members. The Great Hall, now the auditorium of the National Concert Hall, was where this intellectual, social and sporting fair took place – I was there to attract people to the Labour Party.

My involvement with Labour began back in November 1964 when I saw a notice outside the gates of Earlsfort Terrace for a meeting of the universities branch of the Labour Party to be held in Moran's Hotel on Talbot Street. The UCD authorities would not allow political parties, of any hue, to organise in college, hold meetings or even put up posters. All posters had to have the stamp of sanction, usually administered by Brian Farrell of later RTÉ fame, or they were quickly taken down by the college porters. There were fewer than twenty people at the meeting, including members of the Trinity Fabian Society, who were then part of the branch. I joined immediately. Michael Ryan, a neighbour and ex-St Michael's pupil, was now in Trinity and we became friendly again through this organisation. He invited me to a meeting of the Philosophical Society to hear Brendan Corish address the students.

I was impressed by Corish's oratory and sincerity, but I was also excited by a young man with distinctive black hair who spoke passionately and eloquently. Michael O'Leary had recently left University College Cork and was an education officer with the Irish Congress of Trade Unions (ICTU). This recently reunited All-Ireland body was growing in influence under its secretary, Ruaidhrí Roberts, and research director, Donal Nevin. Michael O'Leary and Barry Desmond were part of a new generation working for the ICTU, and together represented the new face of the Irish Labour Party. In 1964, Harold Wilson had ended 'thirteen wasted years' of Conservative rule in Britain. Publicly challenged about Labour welcoming the victory in Britain, Corish stated that as a Christian socialist he was happy for the change and hoped that it would be good for Ireland.

In March 1965, Eileen Desmond had won a by-election in Mid-Cork, caused by the death of her husband Dan, but before she could take her seat, Seán Lemass called a general election. Dr John O'Donovan, a UCD economics lecturer, had been nominated by the universities branch to contest Dublin South-Central and I intended to campaign for him. He was a respected figure, a one-time Minister of State and an ex-member of Fine Gael. He had fallen out with Gerard Sweetman's right-wing orthodox policies and was among many who had made the political journey to Labour.

But then, a few days after the election was called, Michael Ryan phoned to say that Michael O'Leary had been nominated to stand in Dublin North-Central and asked if I would help with the campaign. The Easter college holidays were due to start and I plunged in, wholeheartedly. O'Leary's headquarters were on the top floor of a union office in Parnell Square. He had few workers because he had only just arrived in Dublin and did not live in the constituency. The two other Labour candidates were Cllr Susan Bowler-Geraghty, a solicitor who had joined the Labour Party on the day the election was called in April 1965, and Tom Hammond, a trade unionist from East Wall in the heart of the four-seat constituency.

It was a typical political apprenticeship: handwriting the names and addresses of registered voters on envelopes, putting up posters, canvassing in parts of the city that were new to me and meeting old and young people, all with the common bond of socialism. My driver's licence meant that I soon got the job of driving the blue van, which we had hired as the major piece of equipment of our campaign. Typically, we would go out with Michael O'Leary and a couple of canvassers, stopping on his instruction at street junctions where he would alight onto the pavement and address passers-by using the loudspeaker mounted on the van's roof.

O'Leary was a good street orator and made quite an impact on the voters, something his running mates also noticed. Some days later, when we got back to Parnell Square, O'Leary took a phone call from Susan, who was not at all pleased with his progress; angry words were exchanged. It was decided that the two candidates should have a peace meeting and I drove Michael to the venue off the North Circular Road. He returned after the pow-wow fuming at what he called Susan's patronising attitude. She had accused him of using the word 'socialism' and said that he was not suitable to be a TD. As far as Susan was concerned, she was a city councillor, publicly known, with a successful legal practice and a big purse.

Leaving the comfort of Sydney Parade, getting the bus across town to Parnell Square and canvassing through the tenements of Mountjoy Square, Gardiner Street and other streets in that derelict part of Dublin was a daily journey between two worlds within one city. I had never seen such overcrowding – large families all in one room, where frayed curtains acted as dividers between the sleeping space and the living area. There was no kitchen as such. Food was prepared with water obtained from a tap downstairs and cooked, if lucky, on a gas cooker or else in a frying pan over an open fire. The old Quinn farmhouse in Tullyframe, County Down, had such a fire, but that was the countryside. The tall elegant Georgian rooms were impossible to heat and the one toilet, located down the stairs in the backyard, was used by as many as ten families. The smell of poverty was everywhere, making me want to throw up. This was particularly true when I called on two old bedridden ladies in a high tenement room. I'll never forget the crumpled clothes on the bed, the rickety table with half a batch loaf on it, and the overwhelming stench of stale urine.

These housing conditions were the other side of the tragedy that had become public when a tenement building on the corner of Holles Street and Fenian Street, just off fashionable Merrion Square, collapsed in June 1963. Two little girls on their way to a sweet shop were killed instantly. The Dublin Corporation officials panicked. Within weeks, hundreds of families were homeless, forced out of condemned tenements; women and children were temporarily housed for months in a reopened debtors' prison, Marshalsea Barracks, and the men told to seek shelter where they could.

Radical social change was needed. Campaigning every day for two-and-a-half weeks generated an intoxicating energy and enthusiasm. The evening conversations in Mooney's of Parnell Street fuelled my heart with passion and informed my mind. Theory and practice could and would combine. Socialist solutions would have to be implemented. Young canvassers like Bernard McDonagh, Paul Gillespie, Michael Ryan and myself were made wise in the ways of the real world by activists such as Jim Quinn from Dublin Port and Sheila Conroy from the Irish Transport and General Workers' Union (ITGWU).

Sheila had been the first woman elected to the executive of the ITGWU. An active trade unionist, she married John Conroy, a widower who was a major figure in the Labour movement. He, along with young Jim Larkin, had been responsible for the reunification of Congress in 1959 and had played an active role in getting Michael O'Leary on to the ticket for the Dublin North-Central constituency. I canvassed East Wall with Sheila and, between houses and across streets, got an education from her on the realities of the Labour movement.

At home in Sydney Parade on the evening of the election, Lochlann, Conor, my father and I watched the Telefís Éireann coverage of the count. It was a first for the five-year-old station and John O'Donoghue, my old school teacher, was one of the anchormen on the programme. It appeared that while Fianna Fáil would get a majority, which pleased my father, Labour would do remarkably well, which upset him. By ten o'clock, Michael O'Leary looked as if he might win a seat because Alderman Frank Sherwin was clearly going to lose his. Sherwin was a councillor and one of the four Independent TDs who had supported Lemass' minority government with the introduction of the unpopular turnover tax, a forerunner to VAT, in November 1965. Finally, I asked my father for the car so I could go to the count centre on Bolton Street. Upset with the result, I suspect, he refused until Conor persuaded him to let me go. Conor had worked tirelessly in Fianna Fáil's expensive campaign in Dublin South-East where they had managed the vote so as to win two seats out of the three, defeating Dr Noël Browne in the process.

As I arrived at the count centre, there was tension and excitement in the air. The final count had to come and O'Leary could make it. So unsure were we of success, and he of victory, that he was not there; exhausted, he had gone home to sleep. Searchers were dispatched to find him and he arrived in time to thank his election workers and the staff of the returning officer. We had won. I had been part of it. I felt elated by it all and knew immediately that this was definitely something I wanted to do, some day.

Back at UCD, third-year architecture marked a shift in my life. I was approaching my twenty-first birthday and was the oldest living at home. Moninne was married with two very young children and living in Rathmines. Lochlann was in London with the big accountancy firm Arthur Andersen, and Conor was in Canada working with General

Foods. Declan and Colm were still at Blackrock. I had the use of the large attic bedroom where I had installed my drawing board in the dormer window. There were two divan beds in the room – one was used for sleeping, the other as a couch – which were also ideal for laying out A1-sized drawings of work in progress. I could pretty well come and go as I pleased so long as my parents, my mother in particular, knew vaguely where I was.

One evening, before I was going out, I asked my mother to come down into the kitchen because I wanted to talk to her. This was unusual for me and she seemed apprehensive.

'Is anything the matter?' she asked immediately, obviously worried, as she closed the door behind her.

'No, I just want to tell you that I will not be going to mass any more and I thought you should know. I do not intend to make an issue of it in the house and I will be out every Sunday midday in the Merrion Inn, reading the papers and having coffee with James McKenna and Tom Power. I don't want to influence either Declan or Colm and do not want to upset Da.'

She paused, looked for her handbag and lit a cigarette. 'When did this all come about?'

I told her that since fifth year in school I had had my doubts and that I had gone into the whole question in detail. Through the Legion of Mary, I had got involved in a Christian theology group run by Opus Dei, which ran evening meetings, more like discussions really, in one of their houses at the corner of Ely Place and Hume Street. I explained to her that these discussions, combined with my reading, had led me to reject the Christian concept of a personal god.

The more I had investigated the Catholic content of my religious education, the less convincing I found its tenets. As its attractions began to recede, the array of ideas and concepts surrounding socialist thinking assumed a greater importance and a stronger resonance for me. The physical poverty of the society around me and in the world was compounded by the intellectual restrictions on me. I felt the lack of freedom to think, to reach my own conclusions, denied the potential of my mind and so was bad for the soul. Where, between those two, did one begin and the other end? The Christian message of love, so powerfully conveyed by Jesus, was not unique to his followers or to his Church. It was a long way from the Sermon on the Mount to the grandeur of the Vatican. I found that very sermon, on intense reading, to be defeatist and even self-serving. It was hard to equate it with the emerging profile of what I understood to be the theology of liberation. The body of orthodox Catholic doctrine, as it was self-described, appeared to me to be impenetrable to reasoned critique or analysis, even that of a curious teenager. The fact that it could not be understood was what made it a mystery and that very mystery, I was informed by my Christian doctrine teachers, made it a gift in itself. But the acceptance of such a gift seemed to require the suspension of my own naïve attempts at analysis. From a position of faith, I was moving hesitantly to a platform of reason.

The world in which all this was taking place for me was changing rapidly, and I wanted so much to be a part of that process, to help it to change and more importantly to steer it in the direction I felt it required. The values of the gospel, with which I agreed, could now be recast in another context, given a new foundation and a new rationale, but it would be one I could understand and accept. Its succinct expression was contained in Albert Camus' *The Rebel*, his philosophical work whose French title, *L'Homme révolté*, is a more accurate description of the theme of the book. Rejecting the certainties of absolutism, either religious or historical, Camus places man in the centre, struggling to define values from his experience of the world around him.

I was by now an atheist, but that alone was not enough for me. I knew that I had to consciously construct a set of values and a system of behaviour within which I felt comfortable and secure. The values of socialism were an obvious foundation on which to start.

It was then, and only then, that I made the formal break and decided to tell my mother. My father, now retired and not in the best of health, was ageing. He was a devout Catholic and my love for him was such that I would not willingly confront him. I knew my mother was less committed and would be easier to talk to about my decision.

'Why are you telling me this?' she asked, after she had smoked a second cigarette and shed a tear.

'Because I don't want you asking me what mass I had gone to or what I thought of the priest's sermon.'

I was offering a diplomatic deal: my external compliance on a Sunday for her silence and acquiescence at home. She accepted it.

Retrospective journeys can be misleading. The point of arrival is never finite, and the original route taken is more tangled than one might remember. But whether talking to Coilín Murray, or listening to John Coyle, the process of reaching out had begun in school, beyond the very familiar set of ideas with which I had grown up. The Cuchulainn saga which my father recounted to us repeatedly as we travelled from Dundalk to Newry, I now read in Standish O'Grady's heroic version. I had found it discarded in the school library. Tom Barry's *Guerrilla Days in Ireland*, and Dorothy MacArdle's *The Irish Republic* added to my detailed knowledge of an intense and political struggle, all of which seemed disconnected from the rest of history. The Versailles Treaty negotiators had dismissed the Irish delegation contemptuously, I had been told. Ireland's history of oppression had links to other countries – Catholic Spain, Republican France and the liberated Irish in the United States – but the focus of the story was, always, on Irish freedom.

When, at last, it came in 1921, it was betrayed by compromise and civil war. 'How did Uncle Seán die?' Declan asked, as we were seated at the table. My father was home for lunch as usual. I was beside Colm.

'He was shot by the British,' came the direct reply.

I paused, but only slightly, and said to my father and Declan, 'That's not true. He was shot by an Irishman and died in an Irish hospital, probably through lack of proper care,' I added hurriedly.

Declan and my father looked at me, as I went on to explain to my brothers, that it was during the Civil War. 'It's all the same,' my father asserted; 'they caused it.' But civil wars were not always about national freedom.

When I travelled across Spain towards Lisbon for the Catholic Student Games, the place names in Hemingway's novel of Spain's

Civil War, *For Whom the Bell Tolls*, which I was reading on that rail journey, appeared on the sign boards of the stations. Later, on my first visit to Madrid, César Alierta insisted that I see Franco's monument, The Valley of the Fallen, a cavernous cathedral carved within a mountain out in the countryside beyond the capital city. A giant cross visible for miles bestrode the top of the mountain.

'It was built by republican prisoners,' César quietly told me, 'a form of forced labour.'

He described, in part, the way Franco, who was then still alive, had dealt with his opponents. Reading Hugh Thomas' history of that war put George Orwell's *Homage to Catalonia* in context for me. The savagery on both sides was matched by the intensity of political debate. This was not a civil war about territory or borders or oaths of allegiance, but about poverty and class, freedom of expression and social equality. This was central to Spain's history, and to César's understanding of it, but it did not connect to my thorough knowledge of Irish history, as I had received it.

'Read that,' Coilín said one day in fourth year, as he came down the corridor alongside the study and the refectory. 'The brother Seán says its brilliant.'

Arthur Koestler's *Darkness at Noon* introduced me to the horrors of Stalinism, but these were not the horrors, of which I had been told so many times, which forced Cardinal Mindszenty to seek refuge at the US legation in Budapest in 1956, or had Archbishop Stepanic imprisoned by Marshal Tito. Communism was a very bad thing and socialism, was really, a milder version, according to the textbook we had in secondary school on the principles of Catholic social thinking.

The problem with the Mother and Child Scheme, I was told, in response to my youthful enquiries at home and in the classroom, was that it was not means-tested. This meant that everyone could avail of it. That resulted in the state undermining the family and interfering with parents and their responsibilities to look after their children.

In first-year architecture in UCD, Shane de Blacam gave me a file of papers about Noël Browne's clash with the bishops and politicians. Amongst the papers was an article in support of the bishops' line, written by a curate in Westland Row, Father James Kavanagh. The scheme interfered with people's liberties, he argued, because it was financed out of general taxation. Since everyone was compelled to pay tax, it followed that they were compelled to avail of this service. My inward response was that we were therefore equally compelled to burn turf briquettes because of the state support for Bord na Mona. By now, the same James Kavanagh was a bishop in the Dublin diocese.

Albert Camus had been briefly a member of the Communist Party. Pablo Picasso was openly associated with the French Communist Party, and Franco had forced him into exile to France. The world of my teenage years had been clearly divided between goodies and baddies, but not everyone agreed on who qualified where. To James McKenna's father, Gemal Abdul Nasser was clearly a baddie when he nationalised the Suez Canal in 1956. But, to my father he was a hero because of his defiance of former imperial powers.

In fifth year in school, we had earnest political discussions. In October 1962, our intense conversations were overshadowed by world events. Would the Cuban crisis end the world? Would we come of age or would we even be alive by Christmas? My diary entries are studded with references to Kennedy and Khrushchev, the balance of terror and the necessity to defend the free world. In our school debating society, the rhetoric flowed into argument as Pat O'Connell rebutted my aggressive assertion.

'You cannot defeat communism with force,' he said. 'It is an idea, which must be confronted with a better idea, not bigger guns.'

Getting our hands on better ideas, in those days, was not easy. The Sunday Press regularly ran extracts from War by the Irish by John McCann, Four Glorious Years by David Hogan and other accounts of the Irish war of independence. But other papers came into the house after Sunday mass. The Observer or The Sunday Times for my father and the Sunday Express for my mother. Kim Philby had gone over to the Soviet Union. Harold Wilson had begun to look like a prime minister, especially beside Harold Macmillan's successor, Sir Alec Douglas Home. Somehow the new prime minister's riposte to the Labour leader, that he was the fourteenth Harold Wilson, did not diminish the aristocratic gap between the two of them.

Then, one birthday, my eldest brother handed me a brand-new paperback. 'If you're going to be a socialist,' he said, 'you'd better read this.'

I had never heard of *The Ragged Trousered Philanthropists* or its author, Robert Tressell. But its message, relentlessly repeated, was in tune with my heart and head. It was the story of a group of house painters working in desperate conditions in Victorian Britain, and was located in the typical town of Mugsborough, based on the real town of Hastings. In their midst is a dedicated socialist who continuously promotes an alternative social and economic system. But the duped workers, who continue to vote for the politicians who exploit them, are reluctant to change. When I had read it, I reflected on how very English it was, not unlike aspects of the novels of George Orwell, and far from the Irish political, popular literary tradition. Years later, in May 1991, in Wexford Street I listened to Paddy Coughlan, president of the Dublin Trades Council and general secretary of the Painters' Union when he was unveiling a plaque to commemorate the birthplace of Robert Tressell. His famous book, it was claimed, had been handed around the British armed forces during the Second World War much like Samizdat underground publications that were privately circulated in Poland or Czechoslovakia in the 1970s and 1980s. Some commentators argued that it had been a key factor in helping Clement Attlee replace Winston Churchill as prime minister in 1945, when he won that famous post-war Labour landslide.

We were gathered in front of the president of the Dublin Trades Council on that crowded street because Robert Tressell's real name was Robert Noonan and he had been born above the shop at 37 Wexford Street. The illegitimate son of a Royal Irish Constabulary inspector, he had left the country after his father's death when his mother had married a man with whom he could not get on. But he had never been part of Ireland's literary family and there was, in my growing up, no connection between the island of his birth and the evangelism of his politics.

The universities branch of the Labour Party got involved in the protests organised by the Dublin Housing Action Committee, which had grown in strength in the wake of the housing crisis. Local elections were due to be held in June 1967 and the party was making preparations to consolidate the successes, particularly in Dublin, of the 1965 general election. I decided to stay in Dublin to work in those elections and to postpone my return to London and my contract draughtsman's job with J.E. Lessor in Hounslow.

Dublin city was divided into twelve electoral areas and I lived in the No. 12 ward, which had three seats. I was involved with the Dublin South-East constituency organisation, though to call it an organisation is an exaggeration. It had two branches: one was in Ringsend, established by John Kennedy, Michael Gregg, Jim Kenny and others; and the Connolly branch, based in Gaj's restaurant at the corner of Lower Baggot Street and Lower Pembroke Street. Margaret Gaj, a Scotswoman, radical socialist and feminist, ran a very successful eating house which was a veritable home from home for many people living in the area. Niall Greene, a young Labour Party activist, a member of the administrative council of the party and the executive of the Workers' Union of Ireland (WUI), worked in Aer Lingus and lived in digs on Mespil Road. He was nominated, along with John Kennedy and Jim Kenny, as a local-election candidate. Although I had not worked politically in the ward, I was considered a campaign veteran and, most importantly, I had transport in the form of my Lambretta. However, the critical factor that saw me become the local director of elections was that I was not working and had plenty of time to devote to the campaign.

Labour ran a successful campaign across Dublin generally, going from three seats to thirteen on the fifty-two-seat city council. However, ours was the only ward not to elect a Labour councillor. John Kennedy was narrowly defeated and the surprise victor was an Independent, Jack Torpay, who campaigned to save Sandymount Strand from a grandiose expansion plan put forward by the Dublin Port and Docks Board. The three weeks of managing a campaign – helping to write and design the literature, collecting it from the printers in time to go canvassing with our volunteers each summer's

evening – added to my knowledge of electioneering and deepened
my commitment to politics.

Because I had not gone to London at the end of May, I was able to
enter the McCarthy Memorial Travelling Scholarship, with a
substantial prize of £160, which was open to students who had
completed third-year architecture. The terms of the scholarship
required the submission of a project for architectural study; if
successful the winner would get £100, with an extra £60 being paid
when study-trip report was submitted.

Around this time I came across a provocative book, *Architecture
without Architects*, based on an exhibition organised by Bernard
Rudofsky in New York's Museum of Modern Art in 1962.
Primarily a global photographic survey of vernacular housing, but
with particular emphasis on North Africa, the Mediterranean and
the rest of Europe, it was striking in its range. It also was unusual
in that most of the illustrated building types had never been in our
recommended textbooks. I immediately connected the multiple
images with my experience in Glencolumcille and our efforts to
derive some theoretical architectural framework from the work we
had done there. There was a similarity in scale and decoration that
seemed to relate more to the geographical region in which the
dwellings were located than to the national boundaries within
which they were constructed. In preparation for the scholarship
submission, I did some research on Italian hill towns and the
fortified enclosed villages of the Mediterranean, including the
Cycladic Islands. Some academics had suggested that the complex
and maze-like pattern of streets had been designed as a form of protection from intruders. Konrad Lorenz, in his book *On Aggression*,
also developed a set of spatial territorial theories which reinforced
this initial analysis.

I was very happy with my proposal when it was finished and was
pleased with the range of topics I had covered, but in truth I also
wanted to visit Greece after seeing the film *Zorba the Greek*. I had
no previous image of Greece, other than the typical historical

classical references. The theme of Nikos Kazantzakis' novel, so dramatically transposed onto the screen, greatly appealed to me. I had seen the film by chance, one dank winter evening in the Ormonde cinema in Stillorgan. The black and white images, combined with the music of Mikos Theodorakis, bowled me over. When it ended, the auditorium burst into spontaneous applause, something I had never heard before in an Irish cinema.

My interview with the external examiners for the scholarship was difficult, but I was successful. However, I decided to postpone the study trip until the following year and, instead, return to London to make some money. At the end of the summer of 1967, I travelled to France on my Lambretta to visit some of the work of the famous Swiss-French architect Le Corbusier. The quality of Le Corbusier's work, particularly his church at Ronchamp in eastern France, with its play of light, form, space and texture, was fantastic. Back at the youth hostel in Belfort, I figured that since I was close to Switzerland and northern Italy, I could travel through those countries on my way to Marseilles, the location of another Le Corbusier classic, the complex apartment building known as L'Unité d'Habitation. Images of *The Sound of Music* and Steve McQueen in *The Great Escape* filled my head as I cruised along the roads of Switzerland, blithely unaware, as I looked up and admired the snow-capped Alps on either side, that I would ultimately have to go over them on my Lambretta, via the St Gotthard Pass. It was a really testing experience, particularly coming down the zigzag road past a line of cars and trucks. The fading daylight, with the sun on the other side of the mountain, was an additional hazard, so much so that when I finally got to the flat terrain, a few espresso coffees, a large brandy and half a dozen Gauloise cigarettes were needed to soothe my nerves.

I looked at the map in Milan and determined to travel even farther south. After all, a good Catholic Irish boy – even if now an atheist – could simply not be in Italy for the first time and not go to Rome! For budgetary reasons I had to make a choice between petrol or food. Travel won the day and so I made do on a strict diet of black coffee, Gauloises and white bread. The rest of the trip, along

the Mediterranean coast, was truly memorable. I completed my
tour of Le Corbusier's buildings with a visit to his dramatic mona-
stery at La Tourette, outside Lyons.

At the end of September 1967, I was back in Ireland and ready for my
fourth year. In America, students at the University of California in
Berkeley had begun to make demands for social change, which were
compounded by protests against the Vietnam War. Harold Wilson's
Labour government in Britain could not bring itself to openly oppose
the US efforts to prop up the corrupt South Vietnamese puppet regime
because of divisions in his own party. I suspect now that the weakness
of sterling at the time, the role of the dollar in supporting it and the
bitter lessons of the Suez debacle ensured Wilson's compliance. But it
was a compliance that did not extend to many of his MPs or most of
the left in Britain and elsewhere in Europe. It has some striking
parallels with the situation in which Tony Blair found himself with
the Labour Party and the British public over the invasion of Iraq in
March 2003. In 1967, the mood for radical change had deepened, and
students in many parts of the world, but particularly in Germany,
France and Britain, were at the forefront of its articulation.

Closer to home, the Civil Rights Movement in Northern Ireland
had been established to confront major discrimination in the
allocation of houses and jobs in favour of Protestants. The fundamental equality of one person, one vote, did not exist across
Northern Ireland's distorted political landscape. Even in those towns
where unionists were not in the majority, the Stormont government
ensured that the gerrymandered wards would deliver a unionist
dominance. All this was happening in Labour's United Kingdom
where 'the mother of parliaments' could not, by convention, inquire
into the internal administration of its subservient regional government in Northern Ireland.

The universities branch had brought together supporters of
Labour and socialism from other universities, particularly Queen's
in Belfast. The British general elections of 1964 and 1966 saw Gerry
Fitt win West Belfast for Labour. Among his young supporters were

Michael Farrell and Rory McShane, who, along with Paul Gillespie in Trinity College, played a major role in establishing the Irish Association of Labour Student Organisations (IALSO). The IALSO organised a number of meetings and conferences in Belfast and in the Graduates Memorial Building in Trinity, where visiting speakers made a considerable impact on the relatively few but highly committed students. It was in this context that I first met Gery Lawless. A veteran of the 1956 IRA campaign, and a member of the left-leaning Saor Éire, Lawless famously was the first person in 1960 to take a case about civil liberties against a signatory government, Ireland, to the Strasbourg-based European Convention on Human Rights. A committed Trotskyist, he ran an organisation called the Irish Workers' Group whose aim was to radicalise the left by infiltrating the mainstream Labour Party with supporters and/or secret members. Years later Joe Higgins and the Militant Tendency were to successfully pursue the same strategy. Notwithstanding the Byzantine intricacies of Trotskyist ideology, Gery was a wonderful communicator. One of his eyes was badly turned, the result of an industrial injury, and so when he engaged in powerful speeches, you never knew just which eye was making the connection. We were transfixed with his combination of theory, experience and his knowledge of history.

It was Lawless who first introduced me to the full story of the 1913 Lockout. 'It was always a lockout and never a strike,' he insisted, reinforcing our comprehension of the fundamental difference between the two. 'Never forget,' he said, '1913 happened three years before 1916. Those conservative nationalists Griffith and Pearse knew exactly what they were doing when they co-opted the power of the working class into their nationalist crusade. They had seen the strength and courage that had run from August into the harsh winter and Christmas. They had witnessed the solidarity of workers across the water, sending food and support in one direction and offering to provide secure lodgings for the hungry children in the other.' Later, James Plunkett's *Strumpet City* would tell the full story. Included in that novel was how the Church authorities feared that hungry children, being fed in English workers' homes, might be exposed to spiritual contamination.

James Connolly had written the first Marxist history of Ireland. Lenin had spoken positively, we were told, of this radical Irish socialist. It was claimed that, in the evolution of socialist thought, Marx himself had borrowed heavily from a radical Irish landowner, William Thompson, for his theory of surplus value, a core element in *Das Kapital*. Thompson inherited the estate of Roscarbery, County Cork, in 1814, but, ashamed to be living off 'the produce of the efforts of others', he gave his tenants very favourable terms and ran the estate as a co-operative. In his will he left Roscarbery to the co-operative, but his relatives argued that these radical and irresponsible actions could only be the act of a deranged mind. The courts agreed and the rightful relationship of landlord and tenant was rescued from such a dangerous precedent!

The years of the mid-1960s were a time of political and aesthetic discovery for me. I knew where I was going and why I wanted to do the things that I did. I felt then, and even more so now, that I belonged to a large extended political family with shared values, different traditions and common objectives. Years later, when reading Donald Sassoon's *One Hundred Years of Socialism*, I was enthralled by the diversity of our socialist family. First published in 1996, it describes the development of radical politics in Europe. Starting with the establishment of socialism in Europe before 1914, it sets out in chronological order the progress of the political movement right through the century. It concludes with the fall of the Berlin Wall and what it terms the new revisionism. My deep regret on reading it was that it had not been available thirty years earlier.

In all this activity through the year, the universities branch, of which I was now the chair, began to make contact with other groups within UCD to build a broad, radical political front. Basil Miller, auditor of the Politics Society, was an intelligent and intense activist. The late John Feeney had moved left along a political journey from the Student Christian Movement. Active in supporting the Anti-Apartheid Movement, he famously disrupted a cricket match against South Africa by damaging the pitch at the Leinster Cricket Club in Rathmines. The political temperature was rising. In recognition of the branch's strength, Labour Party head office divided it between UCD and Trinity. The Fabian Society, which qualified for funding by Trinity College, was effectively the Labour Party branch in that university.

In January 1968, the UCD branch organised a public meeting in the Kevin Barry Room in Earlsfort Terrace, entitled 'Student Power'. The invited speakers were Howard Kinlay, president of the Union of Students in Ireland (USI); Denis Reen, president of the UCD Student Representative Council; Sister Benvenuta, otherwise known as Margaret MacCurtain, a lecturer in the college; and Kadar Asmal, the leader of the Irish Anti-Apartheid Movement, an active leftist who was a law lecturer in Trinity. The meeting attracted a crowd and I subsequently learned it was the subject of discussion in the college's governing body, the Academic Council. On the night, Kadar could not attend and instead Justin Keating, a television journalist and veterinary lecturer, took his place. I knew nothing about Justin but, for me, his contribution was the highlight of the evening.

After the successful meeting, some of us went to Kirwan House at the bottom of Leeson Street for a few pints and further discussion. 'You have to get into their pockets as well as their heads if you want to reach the wider audience of the general student body,' Justin said in reply to our question on how to radicalise the largely apolitical students. 'Talk to them about things that affect them directly, like the quality of their accommodation, or the poor levels of lecturing, or the standard of education in different departments.'

All this struck a chord because of our struggles in the School of Architecture. It also resonated with Basil Miller, Una Claffey, Dave Grafton and others who were frustrated at the narrow intellectual dimension of both the politics courses and the teaching of economics. But it did not stop there. The same complaints were being made about the teaching of sociology and other related subjects. The truth was that UCD was more like a Catholic academy than a modern university. By the end of the 1960s, it was a tight shoe that no longer fitted the aspirations of its overcrowded and increasingly challenging students.

I realised, along with others in the universities branch of Labour, that we had to broaden our approach. At the small regular meetings we held in a room on the top floor of 22 Earlsfort Terrace, the

Labour Party headquarters, we came to the conclusion that we should radicalise students first and presume that they would subsequently vote for Labour. To achieve this, we had to include activists who were not party members, such as Kevin Myers and John Feeney, and so we formed an organisation called Students for Democratic Action (SDA). Our monthly publication *Confrontation*, run off on the Labour Party Gestetner printing machine, lived up to its name. We demanded information on how the college was being run, looked for openness in decision-making, and student representation on the governing body, the faculties and departments. We denounced the narrow Roman Catholic scholasticism of the intellectual base of the college.

Our radicalisation matched the tempo of student action which was rising across Europe. The Labour Party had joined the Socialist International in 1967, which gave IALSO access to the youth section and its programme of meetings across Europe. Una Claffey, the international secretary of IALSO, attended a Young Socialist meeting in Strasbourg in the early spring. Weeks later some of the French participants were involved in the initial demonstrations, which culminated in the events of May in Paris 1968. The branch sent a telegram of solidarity to our comrades in Strasbourg. Around the same time the King of the Belgians attended a garden party in Trinity College. It was one of the highlights of College Week, a series of snobby social events culminating in the Trinity Ball. As an alternative to the Trinity Ball, the Internationalists, a group of radical Trinity students, who supported Mao Tse Tung, organised 'An Anti-Imperialist Céile in the Bricklayers' Hall in Cuffe Street!

The Internationalists placed a protest picket on the garden party in opposition to the Belgian government's interference in the newly liberated Congo and its neo-colonial support for the breakaway copper-rich province of Katanga. There were only a few protesters, but scuffles ensued, provoking a heavy reaction from the gardaí. The following day, the *Evening Herald* denounced the students in strongly reactionary language; an insult to distinguished visitors to Ireland had been made by pampered and unrepresentative students. Reading the piece in O'Neill's bar in Suffolk Street, a group of us became infuriated. It was either Basil or Una who suggested that we should organise a march from Earlsfort Terrace to Trinity College in solidarity with the students. After lunch the following day, as students began to return to Earlsfort Terrace, we gave out leaflets and made speeches calling for solidarity, even though we were heckled by some commerce and medical students, who tended as a group to be very conservative.

The march began and wound its way around the Green, down Grafton Street, causing congestion and annoying shopkeepers. We swung around College Green, through the front gate of Trinity and up to the steps of the dining hall. Assembled there were our comrades, the victims of the *Herald*'s insult. More speeches were made in front of a couple of hundred students. Calls were made to march to the offices of the *Herald* on Middle Abbey Street, but we couldn't reach an agreement on what to do. After the meeting had fizzled out, a small group went down to Middle Abbey Street nonetheless.

John Hume once said that the trick about street politics is knowing when to come in off the street, but we had yet to learn how to manage or control street politics. When we did our analysis, some lessons were clear; have a plan, have an exit strategy, have a limited but achievable objective and ensure that there is control of the agenda. This meant selecting who was going to speak. The disarray on the steps of the dining hall and earlier at Earlsfort Terrace had been caused, in part, because we had no microphone or loudspeaker. We would not make this mistake again.

Our group plotted further moves as the summer term was coming to an end and also agreed that, in order to make an impact at the autumn Freshers' Week exhibition, we would pool the allocated stall space for the branch, with the Politics Society, *Campus* newspaper and the Republican Club, which was not even recognised by the college authorities.

Our last act of protest was to disrupt the graduation ceremony in the Great Hall. As the assembled deans and professors took their places alongside the president and registrar in gowned magnificence, the graduating students and their proud parents sat patiently in their carefully allocated sections. We had written radical slogans and demands for change on our placards and concealed them near the Great Hall. I led about fifteen students with raised placards past the startled porters and down in front of the assembled gathering and the authorities of the college. Our protest, dignified and with little noise, did not last long. But we were not to know just what impact it would have until later.

One of SDA's objectives was to ensure that every student, whatever they were studying, would be confronted with a socialist alternative to how Irish society could be organised and governed. Whether it was medicine or engineering, economics or sociology, there was a better way to what Ireland was enduring under Fianna Fáil with Éamon de Valera as president and Jack Lynch as Taoiseach. We wanted to bring the college to a halt to achieve this objective.

Student power was now real, or so it seemed. France had been convulsed by the events of May, leading to a national political crisis. Other countries in Europe experienced protests and demonstrations. There were a number of short-lived but disruptive occupations on campuses throughout Britain.

When UCD reopened in the autumn, we were surprised and then highly dismissive of the college authority's proposal to establish student–staff committees in every faculty. Our reasons were simple. The composition of ten students and five staff meant that such committees would exercise no effective power. Conservative college authorities did not readily convert to change, certainly not on this scale! Their offer was a sop made purely in response to our agitation of the previous term, rather than representing a fundamental shift in their thinking.

At a crowded meeting in the first-year studio of the School of Architecture, Professor Desmond FitzGerald struggled to explain the college's proposals. As a member of the Academic Council, he should have known better, but fumbling and contradictory statements provoked sneers, followed by anger. After an hour or so of inconclusive discussion, an annoyed and frustrated Hugh Murray announced aloud that he had heard enough of this nonsense and was leaving. By the time he reached the door, he was leading a walkout.

In 1967 the School of Architecture had received an unscheduled visit from the Royal Institute of British Architects (RIBA), whose regular five-year visitations monitored the standard and quality of the course. The holders of a UCD degree were accepted for membership of the British institute and this in turn was recognised in the Commonwealth and the United States. Professor FitzGerald and the college authorities had been put on notice by the RIBA that, without an improvement in educational standards, the UCD degree might not be recognised. This was a serious prospect because more than half the graduates usually went abroad and many never returned. The Architectural Society attempted to plug some of the perceived gaps in our education. Every Friday we met in 86 St Stephen's Green, where up to three-quarters of the school's 120 students would listen to a variety of guest lecturers, most of whom spoke on topics related to the general course content of the school. This indicated the concern and hunger of the students. It gave us, certainly me, a great sense of the necessity for change and was an integral part of the movement for student power.

The word now from the Royal Institute of British Architects was not good since no changes had been made or even planned for the curriculum in the School of Architecture. We had to take further action. The internal crisis within the School of Architecture coincided with the upturn in the political temperature of discontent. Now was our opportunity.

The occupation of the School of Architecture was meticulously organised. Our demands were for decent academic standards and an effective student participation in the running of the school. I was, with others, central to the planning and had learned some lessons from my political activities. I asked Owen Lewis to prepare a report establishing how long we could last in the school if the college cut off the water supply to the toilets. We surveyed the entrances to ensure a speedy occupation and the subsequent erection of firm barricades. A Friday morning in November 1968 was our D-Day and, when we did occupy the buildings, we announced that the occupation would end at midnight the following day. Owen's report, carefully calculated and including an assessment on the impact of the regular bowel movements of a hundred plus students had concluded that forty hours was our limit. The weekend would give us plenty of publicity and we would be out on Sunday to tell our story.

In the event, the occupation was a success. Pressure mounted relentlessly on the college authorities. Mass meetings, attended by up to 2,000 students and staff, took place in the Great Hall. Young college lecturers actively supported the students. Some senior figures, particularly Garret FitzGerald, then a Fine Gael senator, journalist and college lecturer, spoke in support of us. Ireland, not yet in the European Economic Community (EEC) and still running a protected and closed economy, was very isolated, but at least we students were part of the modern world and we had many supporters, both open and secret, who admired us for that.

The activity continued through Christmas 1968, but my role had to be limited because I was in the final year of my studies and I had to complete the report for the McCarthy Memorial Travelling Scholarship to collect the outstanding £60. Through the early months of 1969, SDA maintained the pressure. This resulted in the authorities agreeing that the final two days of the winter term, for every class, would be devoted to a discussion about the role of the university and its contribution to Irish society. It was a mixed success.

However, the steam was beginning to escape from the cauldron. An occupation of the administration offices, led by Dave Grafton and others, had a minimal impact, but change was clearly coming – concessions were made or were at least promised. In advance of any formal legislative change, the government, through the Minister for Education, appointed the president of the Student Representative Council to the university's governing body. For me, the act of completion was the publication of a book of essays which took as its title the commentators' description of what had happened in UCD – *The Gentle Revolution*. Kevin Myers wrote a chapter in his inimitable style: 'Only victorious generals write memoirs and the staff are writing this.'

In retrospect, I do believe that UCD was greatly changed by that Gentle Revolution. Other factors played a role in transforming that conservative academy to the vibrant university it is today. But one thing is certain: there was no generation of students before, and none since, who made such a mark. The university authorities did take action in restructuring the School of Architecture in the following year. A new sinecure post was created for Desmond FitzGerald. Ivor Smith, a British architect, was appointed director and given the job of running the School of Architecture, ensuring that it retained its recognition by the RIBA. I had wanted to complete my thesis on a public housing project but was told that it was not a suitable subject. Instead, I did a design for a new College of Art located on the Trinity College campus.

Brendan Halligan, the general secretary of the Labour Party, understood the college work I had to do and did not expect me to take an active part in the preparations for the general election in June 1969. Once again Noël Browne had been nominated to stand in Dublin South-East and John Kennedy was selected as his running mate. I was no longer living in the constituency because my family had moved to Booterstown in Christmas 1968. The family was now smaller and my parents decided to sell their house. As a result, I completed my thesis in a much smaller space than that to which I had been accustomed in Sydney Parade.

I promised, however, that I would work with the campaign after I had submitted my college work. Hence I borrowed an old Renault 4L and for the duration of the election drove regularly to printers in Bray and back to Earlsfort Terrace ferrying election posters and literature. The election results were mixed for Labour: a triumph in Dublin but a setback in the rest of the country. However, I was more interested in my academic results, which were due at the end of June. When the results went up on the noticeboards in Earlsfort Terrace, most of us had merely passed. All those who had been active in the student disruptions obtained results significantly below our normal academic levels. I was disappointed because I had

hoped to go on to post-graduate studies. To obtain a scholarship in
any US college would require, we presumed, an honours degree. I
suspected that we had been marked down from the results we had
obtained from the external examiners at the instigation of the
college authorities.

Over the previous two years, my mother had repeatedly told me
that if I did not behave myself and stop confronting the authorities
in UCD, I would emerge without any degree! I laughed, aware that
I had already concealed from my parents a lot of the student and
political agitation in which I was involved. On graduation day I was
reminded of my protest in the Great Hall. My parents were proud
to see their fourth child graduate from UCD. It was an achievement,
considering the cost of fees and maintenance. Like so many of their
generation, they had devoted all their energies and denied themselves many pleasures to finance an education which they valued for
their children because they had not received it for themselves. 'No
bank or economic depression can ever deprive you of, or take away,
your qualifications,' my father had said to me on a number of
occasions when I had found my studies hard going.

As the names of the graduating architects were being called to
receive their parchment, I had begun to reflect on how my parents
must feel. It was only after Smith, Troy and Unger had gone to the
rostrum that I realised that I had been passed by. All my mother's
warnings rushed through my head. I had been denied my degree,
my architectural future! Yet everyone else had been called. Why just
me? There must be some mistake. There was, and I was the one who
had made it! I had not completed the forms for the graduation ceremony properly. So, later that morning, in the sanctuary of the
Academic Council Room, outside of which I had organised sit-in
protests in the past, I was conferred in Latin with my formal quali-
fication, a Bachelor of Architecture.

Chapter 5

Exploring Europe

In July 1968, we had stood on the platform at Victoria Station in London. The train tickets with student concessions, our passports, student cards and the £100 first instalment from the McCarthy Memorial Travelling Scholarship had got us this far. I had completed my fourth year at UCD and had decided not to work that summer but instead to travel and return to my final year. My girlfriend, Nicola Underwood, was coming with me for the six-week trip. We liked the idea of the train journey across France and Switzerland and down through Italy to the port of Brindisi.

The journey took nearly three full days. The original six passengers who got into the train compartment became five, when one, happily for the rest of us, left at Calais. That night, two of us, myself included, slept on the luggage racks; two on the bench seats and the other on the floor. Like Chaucer's travellers, we became good companions and spent an eight-hour waitover together in Milan. A completely different landscape steadily unfolded as we travelled through the country south of Rome. During the previous winter, I had had time to do more research on my original study proposal of Greece and I also looked at modern architecture in that country. There was very little in the reference books except repeated mentions of a C.A. Doxiadis, a new name to me.

On 27 April 1967, the Greek colonels had staged a coup in Greece, deposing the Centre Union government of George Papandreou. They subsequently also got rid of King Constantine II, who had acquiesced in the military seizure of power. This was the third southern European country I had visited which had a fascist dictatorship. In contrast to Spain and Portugal, however, the signs of the recent takeover could be seen everywhere. Banners and posters were erected on buildings when we came off the ferry in the western port of Patras. It was assumed at the time, and later confirmed, that the CIA and the White House had allowed the military to snuff out democracy in its very birthplace.

In July Athens is a hot city. Although we had become partially acclimatised to the weather because of our long, slow journey, the blast of heat in Syntagma Square as we got off the bus was intense. Two days later we boarded a ship for Mykonos where we stayed for a few days before carrying on to Santorini, the other island on our itinerary. We planned to spend most of our time on the islands, and later make a tour of classical sites on the mainland before returning home.

Disembarking from the ship and getting into a motorboat for the final leg into the pretty harbour of Mykonos was an experience I shall never forget. I had never associated the Mediterranean with storms, but the wind had made the sea choppy. Old women dressed in black and looking like extras from Zorba the Greek were at the pier to meet the tourists with offers of rooms to let. Furious bidding and counter-bidding ensued, and all those who had disembarked were quickly led away to their accommodation. Later that evening, Nicola and I had our first meal in a taverna on the edge of the harbour. I thought the ouzo and retsina had gone to my head when a large pelican started wandering between the tables snatching food or being fed. We were told later that the bird was a beloved mascot of the island.

Our onward voyage to Santorini took us past many islands, including Paros. We spent a few days on the dramatic Santorini where an earthquake in 1954 had wreaked great damage and changed the shape of the island to a horseshoe. A new housing development had been built as part of the reconstruction and I made an extensive study of it and also of the traditional buildings.

By the time we returned to Paros, my head was full of theories about vernacular architecture. Paros provided me with many more examples, both of isolated dwellings in the countryside and the complex street pattern of its port, Parikia. The Cycladic Islands were like the Aran Islands or even Glencolumcille, but with blue sky and strong sun. The way the buildings naturally rose out of the landscape, the relationship of doors and other openings to shelter from the wind, were similar to what I had seen in Ireland. The homes were simply plastered and whitewashed. In contrast, the buildings used to house the animals or for storage stayed as they had been built, in rough uncut stone. This delineation between human and non-human habitation was striking, both in visual appearance and cultural similarity to the west coast of Ireland.

The aesthetics of architecture, which we had been taught in UCD, did not include this vernacular language of architectural statement or urban design. I began to formulate theories, or at least explanations, about why modern architectural solutions for public housing needs were so unsuccessful for their inhabitants. The high-rise flats in Britain and the towers in Dublin's Ballymun may have solved the problems of inadequate and overcrowded shelter but they did not facilitate the transformation of dwellings into homes. The high-rise flats did not work, and the architects and engineers who designed them did not know what it was really like to live in them.

I knew from my involvement in the protest marches of the Dublin Housing Action Committee, and from frontline activists like Paddy Behan, that people wanted houses, not flats. Young children living on the tenth or eleventh floor of a block of flats would, when drawing a picture of home, invariably produce an image of a two-storey dwelling complete with pitched roof, chimney and front garden. In Greece I certainly felt that I had come across an alternative, if parallel, tradition of architecture which was quite different to what was expounded in the School of Architecture.

Although architectural aesthetics are derived from the examination and study of existing buildings, I now began to realise that the source material for that body of orthodox architectural aesthetics was the buildings of the powerful. Castles, palaces, temples and cathedrals, while very different in so many ways, were similar in one overriding respect: they were designed to intimidate, protect, or create a sense of wonderment and awe. The large, high entrances, at the end of a series of rising stairs, interrupted by paved level surfaces, signalled to approaching visitors that they were about to enter a place of power or importance, or both. The use of this vocabulary of space and design was inappropriate for the construction of everyday buildings.

A new vocabulary was required, and a systematic analysis of what ordinary people had designed and built for themselves, whether in Greece or Ireland, was a good place to start. I became excited with this conclusion because, as a socialist, I felt that it underlined the power and intelligence of ordinary people to develop and implement appropriate solutions for themselves. Victorian paternalism in our public housing design seemed to clash with workers' control! I knew that this was not the full story, but it did reinforce my emerging thesis. I was anxious to get home and write about what I had observed, develop the photographs, complete my drawings and submit the report.

I also had another reason for wanting to get home. I had received news by post when we were in Santorini that I had failed the structures component of my fourth-year exam and would have to repeat in September. I was shocked by the news and took myself off for a walk to think about what had happened. This was the first exam I had failed and, in retrospect, it was a necessary lesson in intellectual humility – but it did not feel like it at the time!

After our return to Athens, we visited Corinth and Mycenae in the Peloponnese. The ancient site of Olympia revived memories of athletics and the impressive stone-built stadium in Lisbon, six years before. I had not pursued athletics when I went to UCD for the very simple reason that I was not prepared to give it the time it required. I knew that even if I did a bit of training, I was going to be psychologically on the defensive if the athlete in front had been training harder than me. However, in the historic Olympia stadium, I ran a lap of the track in homage to all the heroes of the games, ancient and modern.

There are two prominent hills in the centre of the sprawling modern city of Athens. The Parthenon, the definitive symbol of classical Greece and a building whose sheer majesty never ceases to thrill me, stands on the Acropolis. The other cone-like hill, Lycabettus, with a small white Greek Orthodox church perched on its top, is covered with dark-green pine trees. The buildings climb up the side of Lycabettus to be met by a road that runs around the perimeter of the hill. That road defines the limit of the building line and many elegant apartment blocks are located close to it. In between are some hotels and offices. Close to where the Doxiadis office complex was located on that perimeter road is the fashionable Kolonaki Square.

When we had first arrived in Athens, I had made my way up the steep streets to the offices of C.A. Doxiadis and the Athens Center of Ekistics. Through the entrance, I could see a courtyard with a pool and fountain. These features were more than decorative; they acted like modern air conditioners, refreshing and cooling the surrounding air. Across the courtyard were the main doors of the seven-storey building.

I could see through the floor-to-ceiling windows a large group of people sitting and listening attentively to a speaker at a rostrum. Posters in the foyer announced that the Athens Ekistics Month was in session. I made enquiries at the desk and introduced myself as an architectural student from Ireland. Soon the director of the centre welcomed me. Panayis Psomopoulos, a jovial man in his late thirties, ushered me into the meeting room. The speaker at the rostrum was C.A. Doxiadis. Speaking in fluent, if slightly accented, English, he was addressing his attentive audience about shelter in rapidly growing cities. I listened for a while with interest and then asked Mr Psomopoulos about the centre.

The conference over, the director explained that at the heart of the enterprise was a very successful international consultancy firm – Doxiadis & Associates – founded by Constantinos Doxiadis, an architect and town planner. The firm provided planning, engineering, architectural and related services to clients in Europe, the Middle East, Africa, Pakistan and North America. Funded by the consultancy firm, and a grant from the Ford Foundation, there was also a research centre with a school for graduate students from around the world.

Ekistics, a word coined by Doxiadis and derived from ancient Greek, means 'the science of human settlements'. The centre had a number of ongoing research projects, and graduate students, who came on a year's scholarship funded by the centre, took part in the research programme whilst also studying related subjects. To qualify for a scholarship, student graduates needed at least two years' experience. I sat in the simple office, listening to this amiable Greek, as the whirring electric desk fan did its best to dissipate some of the summer heat. Afterwards I lingered, drinking a Greek coffee in the small cafeteria on the mezzanine floor. Across the courtyard, I could see the specially constructed air-conditioned computer section. At the corner of Syndesmou Street was a publishing company, also part of the group.

As I walked down towards the city centre, my mind was racing. The conversation with Panayis Psomopoulos had excited me. I wanted to study at the centre. The list of luminaries who were participating in the conference and seminars would have endowed any third-level institution with immense prestige, and that was exactly the point.

One year later, in October 1969, Nicola and I were married. Two months before that, I had started working with Patrick Campbell & Associates, whose offices in Upper Hatch Street were just across from the back entrance to the School of Architecture. Brian Conroy, one of the associates, had offered me the job. Pat Campbell met me at his home and asked me why I was not going to start my professional working experience within my own family. Paul Burke-Kennedy, Moninne's husband, had started with his uncle Joe Kidney, and was rapidly developing a reputation as an up-and-coming architect with a thriving practice. I told Pat that I believed that serving an apprenticeship is best done outside one's family. He welcomed my answer. His was a small practice and that meant a lot of hands-on experience for someone coming straight from college. Brian Conroy was a good teacher and I learned a lot from him in the twelve months I worked there.

For me, politics had taken a back seat after the 1969 general election and my trip to Greece. By August the domestic political agenda, which had dominated our concerns about housing and other social conditions in the Republic for the previous decade, was shattered by the political eruption in Northern Ireland. The dramatic manifestation of this was captured on television and transmitted around the world. The stark, black and white images of Royal Ulster Constabulary policemen rampaging through the unarmed civil rights marchers in Derry swinging truncheons revealed in an instant the horror of sectarianism and state oppression within Britain's Northern Ireland. The rest of the world was now seeing what we had long since known and, as a result, the direction of Irish politics changed.

My direction, however, was focused on being accepted for study abroad. I applied to a number of colleges in the United States, to do a postgraduate degree either in architecture or urban design. Five years of endeavour, captured on 35 mm photographic colour slides, combined with a CV and letters of recommendation, including one from Dr Garret FitzGerald, whom I had got to know well during the Gentle Revolution, obviously made an impact. Despite my disappointing degree result, my portfolio studio work stood me in good stead. I received an offer of an attractive scholarship from Rice University in Texas and, for a couple of weeks, considered accepting it.

In 1970, the Architectural Society in UCD had invited C.A. Doxiadis to address them. When his visit was confirmed, An Foras Forbartha (the Irish Institute for Planning and Development) invited him to give a public lecture in their offices on Waterloo Road. Eventually, the Architectural Society and An Foras Forbartha sensibly decided to combine their meetings into one. Because I had met Doxiadis, however briefly, Robin Mandal, the auditor of the Architectural Society, kept in contact with me. As the details were confirmed and Doxiadis' arrival imminent, I asked who was to meet him at the airport and how he was to be brought into the city. When I discovered that the architectural students had no plans to collect this eminent scholar at the airport, I volunteered my services and the use of a Volkswagen Beetle.

This was no mere generosity on my part. I wanted to make an impression on Doxiadis because, attractive and all as the offer from Rice University was, I was haunted by Greece and excited by my conversations in the centre. While two years' professional experience was a prerequisite for the course, I was prepared to argue my case. When Robin and I arrived at the airport, some people from An Foras were already there. When Doxiadis was offered an option of how to get into the city, he announced that, since he was the guest of the students, he would travel with them. I was silently delighted as Robin got into the back of the car and Doxiadis took his seat beside me.

As soon as the journey began, his questions started. Why was there no urban tradition within ancient Ireland? What was it about the Celts, a developed civilisation, that they had not created an urbanised culture like so many other civilisations? What was the pattern of settlement in Ireland and what was its history? Had there been any studies undertaken and what were the conclusions?

I replied enthusiastically, describing how the Celts, who had settled in Ireland and elsewhere on the western fringe of Europe, had been driven there repeatedly by other civilisations, including the Romans. The earliest urban settlements in Ireland had indeed owed their origins to the monastic needs of their occupants. In effect, the Celts were the last nomadic civilisation in Europe. Even to this day, great cultural festivals, such as the Eisteddfod in Wales, do not have a fixed annual venue but instead move to a different place each year, in contrast to classical Greece with, for example, the fixed location of the Olympic Games.

This was Doxiadis' first, and only, visit to Ireland. I delivered my passengers to their destination in the city centre and then turned round and drove to Hodges Figgis on Dawson Street. There I bought a number of impressive books on Celtic civilisation and the Irish dimension. I delivered them, appropriately inscribed with my name, to Doxiadis as the small group was having a meal before his lecture. Afterwards there was about an hour before he had to return to the airport for his late evening flight. Once again he turned to his student hosts. A pint in Doheny & Nesbitt's was suggested. There, in the back snug, concealed from the Foras officials who had promised to follow us, five of us continued to talk about planning. By the time we had come to the top of Gardiner Street, he turned in his seat and invited me to come to Athens to study with him.

'Write to Psomopoulos and tell him that you and I have met. I will organise it for you,' he said authoritatively.

I think that I must have glided the rest of the way until I got home to the flat in Grosvenor Road, Rathmines. Some weeks later, after I had responded to the invitation with a formal letter of application, I received confirmation of my correspondence from Athens. This was followed by a formal offer of a place and details of what was to be a generous scholarship. I now had to choose between Rice University, and its master's degree in Urban Design, and Athens, with a Higher Certificate in Ekistics from a centre with a strange name that no one could understand. In my heart I knew what I wanted, but I was not sure what was the right thing to do. I put my dilemma to Lochlann. He was now back in Dublin with Brenda, his wife, and their first son, Oisín. Lochlann's reply was characteristic. 'If you do not wish to pursue an academic career, then the master's degree is not really that relevant. What is relevant is the quality of the education you obtain in relation to what you want to do. Which would help you most in the future? Only you can decide that.'

In the end it was a simple choice. I wanted to explore the urbanisation of Ireland, to understand the dynamics of the physical change that was occurring in my own country so that I had a picture literally of where the people, if not the country, were going. I knew I wanted to become actively involved in politics and that this knowledge would be of considerable help in this goal. Greece had many attractions and Doxiadis had impressed me greatly. The decision was made and the necessary preparations had to be put in place. The course in Athens was due to start at the beginning of September and I negotiated that I would finish work in the architectural practice at the end of July. The intention was to take a leisurely, four-week tour across Europe, arriving in Athens just before the course began. Whilst making preparations, I learned with delight that I was to become a father.

Making the travel arrangements required a lot of research and detailed planning. The plan was to fly to Paris, buy a car there, and drive down through France to visit César Alierta in Zaragoza and then follow the Mediterranean coast through southern France and on to Milan. We would meet up with Seán Ó Laoire and Liam O'Herlihy, who had recently started working there, before travelling south. From Brindisi we would once again take the ferry to Patras and then travel on to Athens.

In April 1970, the Irish banks had locked out their staff in a bitter industrial dispute that lasted for nearly seven months. It seems hard to imagine now, but the economy apparently continued without too much disruption. I was a beneficiary since I gave myself an overdraft which enabled me to buy a Renault Dauphine car in Paris. Equipped with an international driving licence and provisional insurance, I assumed that buying a car in France would be the same as in Ireland. When we arrived, we went straight from Orly airport to a reputable motor dealer. However, we did not leave that wonderful city for four days because French law required us first to have a certificate of residence, which we got that evening from a small hotel off the Boulevard Saint Michel. The following day, when I had handed over US$300 for the car, I was informed that the registration plates had to be changed, the police notified, a new number issued and new plates fitted.

The journey to Athens was varied and exciting and the return to Greece was like a homecoming. After checking in with the centre, where Panayis Psomopoulos warmly greeted me, enquiries were made about suitable and affordable accommodation. The flat was in Sarantapichou Street and was the garden basement of an old four-storey building. The landlord and his family lived on the ground floor, and in two of the three flats above were other graduate students and their families. John Reid, a geographer and town planner, was from Belfast and Don Stastny, an architect, had come all the way from Portland, Oregon.

Our landlord had been with the French army in the First World War and I soon became the unofficial spokesperson for the three families because our negotiations were conducted in French. In time, however, the necessities of daily life meant that we picked up street Greek.

Even though I had been a the centre before, it was not until I started working there that I realised how extensive the Doxiadis organisation was. There was a special computer facility, a steam engine by today's standards, that required a separate air-conditioned room. It was used, in a pioneering way, to generate multiple town-planning options, which could then in turn be evaluated against a set of numerically scored physical and social criteria. This was used by the main organisation, Doxiadis & Associates, who had a wide range of international contracts. The Ekistics Center was a small part of the entire operation but it did share the substantial library. In there first few weeks there, I spent a lot of time reading about the different ongoing research projects and marvelling at the scale of resources that were now available to me, a far cry from those at UCD. I was even more convinced that I had made the right choice.

At the centre, everything was done in English. There was an international group of ten students from China, Canada, New Zealand, Uganda, India and elsewhere. Dusan Botka, a Slovak, had left Czechoslovakia with the arrival of Soviet tanks in August 1968 and Milos Perovic from Belgrade had Greek relations living in Athens and a wife still back in Yugoslavia.

Two of our lecturers remain strong in my memory for their intellectual rigour and their humanity: John Papaioannou and Jacqueline Tyrwhitt. John had worked with Doxiadis for decades and was a man of many parts. Formally trained as an architect, he was a highly skilled generalist. I still have my notes of the course he gave on ecology, which to this day are a tribute to the depth of his knowledge. He was a talented musicologist, as well as being one of the main forces on the large research project of the centre, entitled 'City of the Future'.

Jacqueline was a lively woman in her sixties. She had met Doxiadis many years before and was not only lecturing in the centre but also acting as editor-in-chief of many of its publications and research projects. An architect of Welsh origin, she had been involved in the modern architectural movement of the 1930s. Later she was a senior figure in the Harvard School of Architecture and Urban Design. She had moved to Athens, building a magnificent house outside the city, because she suffered from chronic asthma and the New England climate did not suit her. I learned a lot from her about planning and development, and worked with her the following August as she compiled and edited the comprehensive report on the Athens Ekistics Month.

Soon my main research project took shape. I wanted to work on the coming urbanisation of Ireland. As it happened, so did John Reid. We decided to work together and treat the island as one entity, using census and other data from both jurisdictions. John was a member of the Royal Town Planning Institute and his skills in geography were particularly helpful as we set out to construct our matrix of the map of Ireland, divided into 10-kilometre squares. We proceeded to map in all the statistical details, building layer on layer of information and developing a profile of the emerging shape of urban Ireland. We then began to make assumptions about growth and development, based on the available research and forecasts and the data in our study. It is rewarding that today, more than thirty years later, its conclusions remain substantially valid.

Life in Greece was itself a great adventure because everything then was so different. With the car we got to travel quite a bit and saw a lot of the countryside. Our son, Malachi Dimitri César Quinn, was born on 15 February. Shortly after his birth, I left Nicola and himself in the care of the staff of Maeteron Athinon Hospital, and returned to Sarantapichou Street, where in the Stastny's flat we all celebrated the new arrival.

I booked a telephone call to Dublin and had to wait just over two hours for the various connections to be made across Europe. When the call finally went through, my father answered and I proudly announced the arrival of his seventh grandchild, named after him. A Greek name, we felt, had to be given and Dimitri served two purposes. It was the name of my favourite composer, Shostakovich, and Dimitri translates into Irish as Séamus, my father's second name. César was for the Aliertas and for a European future for us all.

Some weeks later, my father came to visit us. He stayed in a hotel but visited us every day and I took time off to show him around. Until then I had never had a drink in a pub with my father. Now, seated outside a taverna, as I confidently called in my street Greek for food and drink, our relationship became totally different – something I relished. We spoke and talked of many things, but as adults. The three of us, father, son and grandson driving in a French-registered car on the right-hand side of the street, with me acting as guide and interpreter in a foreign city was something I particularly cherish now because within a year my father had died. When we were going back to Ireland, at the end of September 1971, we got news that he was not well. I thought then how fortunate I was that he had come out to Athens.

Arrangements were made for the organisation of the Ekistics Month, which would take place in July. The centrepoint of this was a week-long conference known as the Delos Symposium on board a Greek cruise ship. There were no more than thirty participants but the observers, invited guests, partners of participants, graduate students and the staff of the centre made up 150 people, including young children. As the ship sailed from Piraeus to visit different islands with their historical monuments, the participants had a seminar on board each morning. Doxiadis led off the discussion or introduced a theme and awaited the response of different person-alities who were present. After lunch the passengers would a visit a historic place, to be followed by a traditional Greek meal and return in the evening to the ship. It would cruise, through the night, to our next port of call as passengers continued to discuss the themes of the morning's debate. The amount of open, unstructured time and the confinement of passengers, either on board or on tour, meant that there was ample opportunity to listen and learn, question and discuss. An informal rule of the week was that the passengers moved around the different tables for breakfast and lunch, which ensured that I ended up sitting beside and talking to among others Arnold Toynbee, Margaret Mead, Jonas Salk, C.H. Waddington, Barbara Ward Jackson and Buckminster Fuller. The seven-day symposium spent its last evening on the small island of Delos which, in classical times, had a venerated status amongst the competing city-states of Greece and was seen as a place of pilgrimage and inspiration.

The primary focus and content of the Ekistics Month, including the week-long Delos Symposium, was on the problems of human settlements and how no single discipline or set of skills could provide the necessary solutions. The return to the port of Piraeus, a dirty and shabby harbour – as it is to this day – was a depressing contrast to the beauty and cleanliness of the islands.

The last weeks in Athens combined work in the centre and entertaining visitors from Ireland. Hugh Murray and his brother Eugene were among the many we fed and entertained over the summer. We enjoyed a long and discursive night on our garden terrace arguing and proclaiming our own solutions. We were conscious of the police state in which we lived and the prevailing absence of democracy. During one of the seminars in the Ekistics Month, two uniformed and armed policemen had walked in to a seminar and had stayed for more than half an hour. Their presence reminded everyone that they and the state were in control and that the deliberations of the seminar were taking place, in effect, on their terms. There were political prisoners in Greece and many Greeks in exile who, had they not fled their country, would have been flung into jail.

There was also much political discussion among the students in the centre. My own views were known, but I was anxious to learn what others thought and about their own political experiences. Since fleeing Czechoslovakia, Dusan Botka had seen his parents only twice, in Switzerland. His view of the situation was one of slightly cynical resignation:

During any war, the generals do not allow the troops on the frontline to have wavering doubts about the validity of the struggle. Their lack of commitment would undermine the strength of their defence or their ability to attack. The Cold War had placed certain countries, by arbitrary chance, on the frontline of the ideological divide that ran across Europe. Just as the occupants of the Kremlin could not tolerate any equivocation in Czechoslovakia, the White House had a similar view of Greece, and both sides had found willing local nationals to replace Papandreou in 1967 and Dubček in 1968.

One of my acquaintances, a young Greek engineer, had married an American woman, much to the concern of his father and brothers because she had come to Greece with no dowry. One evening, I met him for a drink. As we were sitting on the terrace of the taverna near Kolonaki Square, he casually informed me that he had never revealed his political beliefs to his wife. 'If she does not know them, the authorities could never extract them from her' was his simple explanation and another reminder of the different approaches needed in a police state.

Throughout the year I was in regular correspondence with Niall Greene and others at home and was aware of what was happening politically. The 1971 Labour conference in Cork City Hall saw a walkout, led by Noël Browne, before a vote was taken which authorised Brendan Corish to participate in a future coalition government. Niall and Nuala Greene were still members in Dublin South-East, but were not active because the organisation had fallen into disarray following Browne's withdrawal, who had, in fact, not been well and was taken ill soon after his successful return to the Dáil in 1969. Never a good constituency worker, Browne had not been seen in the constituency for quite a while, mainly because he lived in Bray. I was concerned at the breakdown of political activity in the constituency, but there was little I could do.

As the year progressed, I began to concentrate, more and more, on the topic of public housing. I read extensively on the subject in the Ekistics Center's library. The ekistics framework was a good one within which to research the topic of housing. In addition, some senior and excellent British public housing architects had participated in the Athens Ekistics Month and the Delos Symposium.

So many things had begun to make sense and come together for me. Public housing in Ireland appealed to me despite all its problems. It was where I could combine, and put to productive use, what I believed and what I had learned. Besides, Dublin Corporation's Housing Architects Department was advertising for architects. We also had another reason for wanting to return to Ireland. Malachi was less than four months old when we learned that a sibling was now on its way to join him and us. It was time to go home.

I wrote to the Personnel Department of Dublin Corporation. Over the summer, I experienced the slow correspondence that flows to an anxious applicant from a lethargic bureaucracy. The message I received was that no, they would not pay my fare back to Dublin for an interview, but yes they would see me on my return, and yes there were vacancies and, in addition, I could probably start to work right away. I now know, and soon learned on my return, that things do not always work that way. Every written word from a bureaucratic public body like Dublin Corporation, which was housed in different offices scattered across the city, should be carefully parsed and analysed before a definitive conclusion is drawn. In my enthusiasm, I had failed to do that necessary bit of scrutiny.

By the end of August my work in the centre had come to an end. I now knew that I wanted to do some architectural teaching, if possible at UCD. With that in mind, I gathered a lot of material from the center and sent it home. I was returning to Ireland, which had now become well known across Europe because of the violence and counter-violence in the North. 'Belfast boom-boom' was the frequent reply that I would get when I told Greek people where I came from.

At a farewell gathering with colleagues and friends on the terrace of his Athenian apartment, my host, having answered my political questions, turned to the Irish problem and asked me to explain it to him. I was anxious to present a balanced view and was clearly taking some time to do so when he interrupted and asked, 'How many people are on the island?'

'Altogether?' I responded.

'Yes, altogether.'

'About 5 million.'

'How many are Catholics?'

'Four million.'

'What's the problem then?'

I looked at him, beginning to understand what he meant as he slowly drew his outstretched index finger across his neck. I reacted strongly. Such action was impossible to even contemplate.

'Why not?' was his laconic response. 'In Crete, it worked for us in 1912.'

Chapter 6

Public Architecture and Party Politics

'What's it like outside?' was the question put to me on the top corridor of the interconnected Georgian houses on Mountjoy Square that formed the offices of the Housing Architects Department of Dublin Corporation. I replied to the senior architect that it was a pleasant spring day, but he had been enquiring about the economic climate within the Irish building industry. In 1972 there was quite a bit of construction activity, so my decision to seek employment in the public sector puzzled a number of people.

I was the first young architect to join Dublin Corporation in quite some time. Despite my expectations and the fact that vacancies had been advertised, for reasons that I never fully understood I was back in Dublin six months before I finally got full-time employment with the public service. I succeeded in getting permission, set against my annual leave, to teach in the School of Architecture at UCD on Fridays during term time.

Our daughter, Síne Lisa Quinn, had arrived safely in the Coombe on 17 February, a year and a day after her brother had been born.

In Dublin Corporation I worked with Jack McDaid, from whom I learned a lot. Our team – Brenda Gaffney, Philip Thompson, Jack and myself – were responsible for the design of a new, low-rise, high-density housing scheme on a greenfield site close to Ballymun. I found the experience stimulating but frustrating because of the slow response of other sectors to my quickly designed proposals. Teaching as a studio master provided a balance that made up for this frustration.

Because I had left UCD only three years earlier, I knew many of the final-year students personally. In fact, I found engaging with them stimulating. Education is a two-way street, and I feel I learned as much as I taught.

I was anxious to see how the School of Architecture had changed after the recent struggles. The director, Ivor Smith, was doing a good job. Philip Geoghegan had come from Britain and shone a new light on the matter of housing and urban renewal, a taboo subject under the old regime. Shane de Blacam, after an apprenticeship with Louis Kahn in the US, taught first year. He and Pat Hickey, the artist/ architect, provided inspirational teaching. Slowly, but surely, the school was rebuilding itself. A symbolic part of that was the construction, in the large first-floor studio, of a multi-levelled timber mezzanine to provide much-needed additional floor space. But the radicalism of the students had dissipated and this was a disappointment to me.

I suspect that the new tolerant and liberal approach in the school and university was the cause. Tom Murphy, the university registrar during the Gentle Revolution, was now president of UCD. The Arts Block and Administration had moved out to Belfield and the extra space and modern facilities there had taken away the irritation of overcrowding, which had been a hallmark of Earlsfort Terrace. But Andrzej Wejchert's design of the Arts Building had no obvious central gathering place, which, like the crossroads of the main hall in the terrace, could easily become the focus of a mass meeting. Some radical students thought this to be deliberate, but the UCD authorities were frankly not that cunning. Besides, the campus layout and the main building design had been the subject of an international design competition which the young Polish architect had won.

I was surprised at the architectural students' lack of interest in becoming involved in the management of the school. The staff–student committee had soon run out of steam; it appeared that the students simply wanted to be taught and expected the teachers to do the teaching. In retrospect, this was not unreasonable. When things are going well, and there is a good management in place, most people want to get on with their lives. Demands for change surface only when things are clearly not going well.

Seán Ó Laoire was now teaching in Bolton Street College of

Technology. Eugene Murray was involved with the Union of Students in Ireland and, through him, Seán and I got a contract to prepare a report on the provision of student accommodation. 'Students Housing Students' was the result, but sadly the leadership of the union changed and the new regime did not pursue the report's recommendations. To this day, dedicated affordable student accommodation remains a real problem for third-level students in Ireland. At the same time, I was also trying to start a debate on urbanisation and the future shape of urban Ireland. To this end, I wrote a number of newspaper and magazine articles, spoke to different groups around the country and participated in radio and television programmes.

Throughout this period I was actively involved in the Labour Party in Dublin South-East. Even though I would not live in the constituency until a year later, I made contact with Niall Greene on my return to Dublin in September 1971. To put it mildly, nothing was happening, much to the concern of Niall and the disgust of John Kennedy. Ringsend was the emotional heart of the constituency, as far as Labour was concerned, and John its undisputed leader. He was a central figure in the community; a founder member of the local credit union, he had been involved in establishing a youth club, and had worked closely with Cathal Fleming, the principal of the boys' national school. When he formed the Labour branch, he was joined by Dickie and Michael Gregg, Jim Kenny, Ben Moran and others. Mattie Merrigan, the Irish secretary of the Amalgamated Transport and General Workers' Union (ATGWU), had urged John to develop his trade-union activities into local political work.

Despite John's near success in the 1967 local elections, he was enthusiastic for Noël Browne to stand in the 1969 general election. He was selected as Browne's running mate, with an eye to the next local elections, but campaigned selflessly for Noël, even to the point of persuading his family and friends to give 'the great man' their number one vote. He still managed to get votes himself and helped secure Browne's election. Imagine his frustration when, soon after the election, Noël Browne was not to be seen within the constituency.

Individual representations on behalf of constituents are a central part of a politician's job. This was particularly so at that time, in working-class communities, where low levels of education and the lack of understanding of how bureaucracies worked, deepened the poverty that existed there. John had campaigned vigorously for Noël; now his neighbours were coming to John, seeking help from the TD he had urged them to elect.

One day, in anger and disgust, John advised a person who had called to his house that they really would be better off going to see Seán Moore, the local Fianna Fáil deputy. John was no longer in contact with Noël, even though the Labour deputy drove past his house in Irishtown every day on his way from the Dáil to his Bray home. I was taken by John's anger as we sat in the Yacht pub in Ringsend. He was a loyal Labour man and would become involved again if we got things moving. Others expressed interest. John Byrne, who worked for the Corporation and who had joined Labour when Noël Browne did, was anxious to be active, as was Paddy Perry, a train driver and a militant socialist. We decided to call a meeting of all Labour activists with the objective of doing political work in the constituency. Brendan Halligan, the party's general secretary, encouraged me in the task.

I became the secretary of what we called the Central branch of the constituency. Even though there were four branches in Dublin South-East, it was felt desirable to combine all the activists into one branch until we had the strength and the numbers to recreate local branches that had ties to their own community.

The work of rebuilding the organisation in Dublin South-East was a priority for me, together with looking after my family, teaching in UCD and working in the Housing Architects Department. As long as I completed all my work and continued to meet deadlines, I was free to do anything else. This consisted of making phone calls, drafting leaflets and doing the correspondence work of a constituency secretary. As part of our campaign to promote the party and our deputy, I secured Noël Browne's reluctant agreement to run a clinic in City Quay, a part of the constituency where we were weak. Premises were found in Dowlings Lane and leaflets distributed, inviting people to 'Help Labour to help you' by availing of the services of the Labour deputy. Noël did not attend the clinics and constituents were not impressed with the presence of an unelected activist. The clinic was quietly closed down after four months.

The campaign to have Merrion Square opened to the public as an amenity did come from that clinic experience. A frequent complaint from constituents was of the lack of safe play areas for local children. The square had originally been the shared, semi-public open space of the houses on Merrion Square. All householders had a key to the locked gates, a system that prevails to this day with Fitzwilliam Square. But the Catholic archdiocese acquired the square in the 1930s and intended to build a cathedral on it. From my school days, I had heard priests complain that the Protestants had not one but two cathedrals in Dublin – St Patrick's and Christ Church – while the Catholics had none. To add insult to injury, they further claimed that the two cathedrals had been taken from the Catholic Church after the Reformation. In the 1920s, there was talk of building a new Catholic cathedral and Merrion Square was acquired as the site. However, the Second World War intervened and the grand design to build the new cathedral facing Leinster House did not proceed. When the war was over, the rapid expansion of Dublin meant that the energies of the archdiocese were redirected towards constructing churches in the burgeoning suburbs.

I designed a leaflet with an aerial photograph of Merrion Square which was distributed in the area, and a public meeting about opening up the square was held. *The Irish Times* carried a piece on its front page in 1972 in which I was described as a Labour party activist and Dublin Corporation architect.

The next day Mr Ó Loinsigh, the head of personnel in Dublin Corporation, summoned me to his office. While my job was permanent, I was still on probation and was nervous as I came across the city to his tall, imposing office in City Hall. The assistant city manager with responsibility for my department was also present. Mr Ó Loinsigh read the riot act. How dare I suggest that the Corporation was running a campaign to have the square opened. Who did I think I was? I explained that I was not trying to involve the Corporation and regretted any embarrassment I may have caused. Towards the end of the meeting, the assistant city manager offered me the kind advice that I should choose between public service and public life because I could not combine both. I thanked Frank Feely for his helpful opinion and left City Hall to return to my office in Mountjoy Square. Following a prolonged campaign, Merrion Square was finally opened to the public in May 1974 by the new archbishop, Dr Dermot Ryan, who handed it over to Dublin Corporation. I was present at the opening and felt that I had helped to bring it about.

I was the first architect to join the Local Government and Public Service Union (LGPSU), at that time made up of the clerical and administrative staff of local authorities and health boards. Evelyn Owens, an official in the Corporation, was a former president of the LGPSU and a Labour Party member. I knew Harold O'Sullivan, the LGPSU general secretary, and through him met Phil Flynn, the assistant general secretary. Phil and I got on well and he gave me a job to extend the union's offices on Gardiner Place.

The 1972 annual Labour conference was held in the Ard Mhuire Hall in Wexford town. I went as a delegate and a candidate for the administrative council, the party's ruling body. I did badly in that election and it was some years before I learned the intricacies of campaigning for positions within the party – battles that can be more complex than public elections.

Since my days as a student, I had helped Brendan Halligan to organise the annual conference and design the backdrop to the platform and speakers' rostrum. We had not had a conference in Wexford in living memory, although it was a Labour stronghold and the hometown of Brendan Corish. I knew the place quite well, having done architectural work there. I went down early to Wexford to help with the preparations and it was only when the timber was cut, the pieces assembled and the nails driven home to complete the platform and speakers' rostrum that Tommy Carr conceded, with affection, that I was more than just a radical student! A Labour stalwart, he had known me from previous conferences and was one of the senior local people in charge of running the conference. Drawings of James Larkin and James Connolly were hung on either side of the stage, reflecting equally the respect in which the founders of the Labour Party were held.

This was more than a historical courtesy. When Larkin returned to Ireland, having gone to the US after the end of the 1913 Lockout, the 1916 Rising was over and the general election of 1918 had given Sinn Féin its landslide victory. Labour, having stood down in favour of what was akin to a broad national front represented by Sinn Féin, lost political influence as a result. It is easy to say now that a strong Labour leadership at that time would have demanded a number of those seats reserved for Labour-nominated candidates in some form of united electoral pact, given the Westminster election system, but by 1918 Connolly was dead, executed by firing squad, propped in a chair in the yard of Kilmainham Gaol, and Larkin was in Sing Sing prison in New York for his trade-union activism there. In Ireland, the leadership of the ITGWU had concentrated on building the union across the country rather than bargaining for seats in the Dáil.

On his return, Larkin was confronted with a very different organisation, compared to the one he had left. Within a short while, differences arose between Larkin and the leaders of the trade-union movement, and Larkin and his followers split to form the Workers' Union of Ireland (WUI). As a student, I had encountered some of the strength of feeling of this legacy.

In 1967, at Brendan Halligan's request, I was erecting a large photograph of Brendan Corish as part of the backdrop to the stage in Liberty Hall at that year's conference. My task was to frame and mount it. As I continued working, the porter in charge of the auditorium stopped me and said that I could not put up a photograph of anyone who was a member of the ITGWU, even Brendan Corish, unless Connolly's picture was also displayed. Given his strength of feeling, I had no doubt about the seriousness of the situation. I made a quick phone call to Halligan and soon a framed portrait of James Connolly was also displayed.

In Wexford, the big issue of the annual conference was the party's response to the crisis in the North. Conor Cruise O'Brien – otherwise known as 'the Cruiser' – was Labour spokesperson on Northern Ireland. He was and remains a formidable character who articulates a controversial point of view and defends it vigorously. Conor was the great revisionist of nationalist politics in the Republic. As the sectarian conflict continued in the North, he challenged the sacred cows of a united Ireland and the four green fields of a unitary state for a united people of Catholic, Protestant and dissenter.

Labour recognised that an accommodation with the million Protestant and predominantly unionist population was essential. The Social Democratic and Labour Party (SDLP) had been formed in 1970 with the direct help of the Irish Labour Party. Labour had an organisation in parts of the North and there were Labour members and local councillors in centres like Newry and Warrenpoint. When the SDLP was being established, all Labour members and organisational units in the North were directed to join the new sister party.

Gerry Fitt was a frequent visitor to Labour conferences and was close to the leadership. Paddy Devlin, who had moved from republican Labour to the Northern Ireland Labour Party, was also familiar to Labour delegates. Both he and Fitt had come from the nationalist/Catholic side of the community; they were socialists and internationalists in their politics and values and had little time for the narrow nationalism that fuelled the sectarian tensions that were now so real.

From the unionist tradition, Erskine Holmes represented a young generation of Labour people from the Northern Ireland Labour Party, and he remained in close contact with the Labour Party after the SDLP was formed. That party's creation brought together the nationalist civil rights campaigners and mostly Catholic trade unionists, some of whom were elected members of Stormont. Gerry Fitt, MP for West Belfast, became leader of the SDLP. In addition, the energy and political vision of people like John Hume, Ivan Cooper and Paddy O'Hanlon provided its driving force. Fitt seldom travelled west of the Bann and, no doubt because of his membership of the House of Commons, seemed to be more focused on London than Northern Ireland. The constitution of the SDLP was based on that of the Irish Labour Party. Frank Cluskey, a protégé of young Jim Larkin and a former official with the WUI, had become very close to John Hume. Cluskey's wife, Eileen, was from Donegal and while there on holidays in the late summer, after the June 1969 election, Frank saw with John Hume the reality of the conflict in Derry.

Frank Cluskey, who had been elected for Dublin South-Central to the Dáil in 1965 on the first count, alongside Seán Lemass, was close to Brendan Corish and shared the revisionist analysis espoused by the Cruiser. Indeed, the Larkin–Connolly faultline between the two unions was about more than personalities. The WUI contained, within its senior ranks, members who had fought in the British army. It was the WUI, and not the ITGWU, that succeeded in unionising the enormous workforce of the Guinness brewery. Jack Harte, an ex-British army man, played a major role in the union organisation within the brewery. On the other side, in Liberty Hall, Michael Mullen, the only Labour deputy in Dublin city in the early 1960s, had been interned in the Curragh during the 'Emergency' because of his IRA membership. Mullen's successful organisation of the hotel and restaurant workers, as their branch secretary within the ITGWU, saw him rise through the ranks to become its general secretary. He retained strong republican sentiments.

The tension between Mullen and Paddy Cardiff, the general secretary of the WUI who succeeded young Jim Larkin, was legendary. In a row that nearly came to blows, Cardiff accused Mullen of supporting fascism during the war, while he, as a sapper in the British army, was bent on its destruction. Mickey Mullen retired from the Dáil in 1969 because of his increased union duties. Dr David Thornley retained Mullen's seat in Dublin North-West in 1969; he was a brilliant Trinity College academic, who had worked for many years with Noël Browne and was a noted political commentator on RTÉ. He readily agreed to stand for Labour at Brendan Halligan's invitation, but like many people with a British family background and schooling, he felt obliged to demonstrate his adopted Irishness by espousing the traditional nationalist republican project, which was now the target of revisionism.

The fiftieth anniversary of the 1916 Rising was celebrated across the country. Illuminated copies of the Proclamation were framed and hung in every national school. The major railway stations in Dublin, Cork and Galway were renamed in memory of some of the signatories of the Proclamation. In 1966, the Department of External Affairs (as it was then called) produced a new, modern-designed booklet entitled Facts about Ireland, which caused an outcry, because it was written from an exclusively Fianna Fáil point of view. Its near Stalinist exclusion of Free State heroes, such as Collins and Griffith, as well as Labour's role in ensuring democracy through the provision of a constructive opposition in the Dáil, caused uproar. Fine Gael and Labour leaders did not take their places on the review stand in front of the GPO on Easter Monday 1966 because they were not officially invited.

That year, combined with the subsequent outbreak of the communal conflict in the North and the arrival of the British army on the streets of Belfast and Derry three or four years later, had another silent effect. The sacrifice, and its public memory, of the thousands of Irish men and women who had fought in the two world wars was driven underground and could not readily be referred to or commemorated. For many Labour families and supporters, joining the British army had been an economic necessity more than a conscious political decision. Many had died, particularly in the Great War, and their sons and daughters honoured their memory in private, because any public display could be seen as not being fully Irish. In the Second World War, the fact that these brave people had fought against fascism and Nazism was more than enough of a vindication for their decision to join the British army.

I vividly remember a radio interview with Kevin Myers on Gay Byrne's popular morning programme. It was November 1972.

Myers, an authority on Irish participation in the First World War, was speaking about the background to Armistice Day. Young soldiers, mere teenagers, who took fright in the trenches and refused to obey orders to go over the top, had been summarily shot by their officers. Class division across Europe ensured that the officers were upper class, the troops working class. If there were courts martial, they were short and execution immediately followed. Myers put the behaviour of the British authorities into historical context. The serial execution of the leaders of the 1916 Rising was normal and quite mild in the context of the way the British army maintained order and discipline amongst its own, and its reaction to the people whom it perceived had stabbed the Empire in the back. Gay Byrne had uncles in the British army in that war, as indeed had many of his neighbours along Dublin's South Circular Road. His questions reflected the angst of many of his listeners.

What Myers described appeared new to Gay Byrne and to most of those who phoned in. They were surprised to learn that their relative had possibly died from the revolver of his own officer and not from a German Mauser. This was in stark contrast to the Christian Brothers' version of Irish history with the savage martyr-dom of Connolly and Pearse on the one hand and, on the other, the casual killing of seventeen- and eighteen-year-old uneducated and shell-shocked boys who, rigid with fear, were shot by their own officers. At the 1972 Wexford conference some of the delegates let this private family history inform their public politics. For others, the certainty of the republican cause and the imperative of achieving Wolfe Tone's Republic, with or without the consent of dissenting unionists, were fundamental to their understanding of history. These two conflicting positions and the political necessity to find a way between them characterised that great debate. It was typified by the personalities of Conor Cruise O'Brien and Seán Treacy. A Labour deputy for Tipperary South since 1961, Treacy had great presence and spoke with that elegance which seems to flow with the River Suir, and gives to some of the inhabitants of such towns as Clonmel and Carrick a distinctively polished accent. Both points of view were ardently argued by speaker after speaker.

In the end, compromise was reached and symbolised by a display of unity between the two men on the platform.

The Wexford conference was the first I attended as a constituency delegate. I had missed the coalition conference in Cork and was chairman of the UCD student branch when I last attended conference. There were few delegates from Dublin South-East. I observed with admiration the size of delegations from constitu-encies like Limerick East, Kerry North and Carlow–Kilkenny, as well as from Wexford. I realised that to develop the party in Dublin South-East, and the rest of Dublin, a lot of effort would have to be put into the recruitment of members. But I also knew that that in itself would not be enough. Local campaigns would be necessary, both to attract support and to energise members. All these things required the active encouragement and participation of the local deputy. But Noël Browne had little or no interest in this kind of activity. He would give half-hearted support to proposals and then would not follow through with the promise of engagement. His attendance at constituency functions was periodic and I could never be sure when he would show up.

By now, I had definitely decided that I wanted to be a candidate at the next general election. The City Council had been suspen-ded since 1969 and it appeared probable that a general election would take place before the local elections were due to be held in 1973. Some senior party people believed that Noël Browne would not stand again, but he had not made his intentions known. Through the early part of 1972, political work in the constituency took up lots of time. As soon as I had the job with Dublin Corpora-tion, I was able to look to buy a home, because we could now get a mortgage.

Seafort Avenue runs east from Sandymount Green to the sea at Strand Road. It broadens out between these two points and part of it forks off to link up with Marine Drive, creating a triangular space at the junction. Seafort Terrace faced south onto this urban space of two-storey terraced houses. We bought No. 6.

When we finally got possession, the detailed surveyor's ins-pection revealed some defects and dampness in the kitchen. While of no great significance in themselves, in my eagerness I had not seen them. I learned one lesson which I subsequently put into effect. Architects, when looking for a house of their own, have a tendency to see the home and not the building.

We now had our new home, located strategically in the heart of the constituency and back where I had come from. I was now ready, at last, to get stuck into politics.

Chapter 7

Dublin South-East
and the 1973 General Election

The door of my office in Mountjoy Square was open as I sat working at my drawing board. It was after lunch on 5 February 1973. I had taken a quick soup and sandwich in a pub on Hendrick Street, behind Ellis Quay, where I was doing a survey of the licensed premises for a friend of mine.

'Did you hear the one o'clock news?' Jack McDaid asked me.

'No,' I said, explaining that I had been busy.

'I thought you'd missed it,' he said. 'Jack Lynch has called an election for the 28th.'

I thanked him as I closed the door, my mind racing. Lynch had seized the opportunity, created by the volatile and violent political situation. The government had introduced amending legislation to strengthen the powers contained in the Offences Against the State Act in the Dáil in November 1972. Fine Gael had been split on the contents of the bill and its leader, Liam Cosgrave, faced a vote of no confidence within his own parliamentary party. As the Dáil was debating the committee stage of the controversial legislation on 1 December, two car bombs exploded in Dublin before the Fine Gael vote was taken. In politics, timing is critical. It so happened that Richard Burke, the Fine Gael chief whip, was asked on television in Leinster House what his party leader would be recommending following the explosions in Dublin. Burke said that he would go and get Liam Cosgrave himself into the studio to answer the question. Cosgrave announced, live on television, that, in view of the crisis facing the country, Fine Gael would be abstaining on the government's legislative proposals, thereby ensuring its passage. The motion of no confidence was abandoned and Cosgrave survived.

From that point on, as Christmas approached, talk of an election grew, even though Jack Lynch had a clear mandate and eighteen months before his term expired. But a lot had happened since June 1969. The eruption of the sectarian conflict in the North had major repercussions south of the Border, particularly within the government. Jack Lynch had forced his Minister for Justice, Mícheál Ó Moráin, to retire, allegedly on grounds of ill health. Some people believed that Lynch suspected that Ó Moráin was involved in arms importation. Lynch's dismissal of C.J. Haughey and Neil Blaney from the cabinet, and the resignation of Kevin Boland and Paudge Brennan, a parliamentary secretary, after the Arms Trial, had convulsed that party. The Arms Trial and the conflict of evidence between Jim Gibbons, Minister for Agriculture, and Haughey had spilled over into the Dáil. It was a period of political turmoil and intrigue within Fianna Fáil. Election talk was more than just speculative.

I re-read the letter I had written earlier that day to Noël Browne. It informed him of the next meeting of the constituency council and asked if he could be certain to attend because a number of people who had joined the party since the previous June had yet to meet their deputy. Following the 1972 Wexford conference, new branches had been established in Dublin South-East. Bill Lloyd, who worked in RTÉ, helped to establish the Donnybrook branch with Nancy and Michael McInerney. Nancy was a radical Dutch feminist with strong political views. Michael, the political correspondent of *The Irish Times*, was well known for his left-wing outlook, but he was essentially a backroom party member offering invaluable advice, particularly in the field of publicity. The widow and son of Tom Johnston, who now lived in Clontarf, were asked to join the branch, named after him. (Johnston had been a Dáil deputy for the Rathmines area and was the first parliamentary leader of the Labour Party in the Free State Dáil.)

Ringsend had gone from strength to strength, with John Kennedy enlarging the branch and running a very successful quarterly draw that brought in a lot of money. A new branch was also set up in Sandymount. Rory and Fionnuala Brennan, returned from working abroad, had bought a house on Tritonville Road and became enthusiastic activists. At that time, the constituency of Dublin South-East was a three-seater whose boundaries extended from Sandymount Strand, through Ranelagh, to the Dodder at Milltown, and from City Quay on the Liffey out to the edge of the city at Merrion Gates and as far as the Tara Towers Hotel.

The EEC referendum campaign in June 1972 helped our small organisation to grow. People opposed to Ireland's membership gravitated towards Labour in the constituency, because we were the only party providing opposition. I campaigned vigorously within Dublin South-East, seeing it as an opportunity to develop the party organisation after it had declined rapidly following the 1969 general election, the pro-coalition decision of the Cork conference and Noël Browne's walkout. But, I was not comfortable with the party's position because I believed in European integration. My experiences in Spain, France and Greece strengthened my profound sense of being a European of Irish nationality.

Labour did not oppose the concept of European integration. Along with the Irish Congress of Trade Unions (ICTU), we rejected the terms of Ireland's entry. It was clear that Irish agriculture would benefit enormously and immediately from the Common Agricultural Policy (CAP). The national finances would no longer have to support Irish farmers in the way that they had in the past. But the jobs of industrial workers, who were the mainstay of union and labour support, in a number of protected sectors would be at risk – for example, car assembly would come to an end. The reality of tangible job losses concentrated the minds of those in danger. Promises of new employment were a poor and vague substitute for those whose actual jobs would disappear. Justin Keating was Labour's principal spokesperson during the campaign, while Fine Gael's Garret FitzGerald personified the pro-EEC lobby. Both were articulate and knowledgeable about the subject and encountered each other in many halls and hotels around the country.

The internal political difficulties within Fianna Fáil and the continued problems of the North distracted the government during the referendum campaign. However, Labour was not united in its opposition to Ireland's membership, even on the terms negotiated by

Paddy Hillery, the Minister for Foreign Affairs, and didn't take advantage of Fianna Fáil's disarray. Barry Desmond, the Labour deputy for the then Dún Laoghaire–Rathdown constituency and a former official of Congress, supported Ireland's entry. Barry was the first person I heard describe himself as a European social democrat. Along with many others who shared his view, he remained silent during the referendum campaign out of loyalty to the party.

When the result was announced, a foregone conclusion even in the days without political opinion polls, the figures were 83 per cent in favour and 17 per cent against. That evening Brendan Corish stated that the Irish people had spoken in a clear and decisive manner. Labour, he said, would respect that decision and seek to work within the EEC to promote Ireland's interests and in particular to defend the rights and working conditions of Irish workers. I welcomed the clarity of his announcement as did many other party members. As far as we were concerned, the issue had been decided and Labour subsequently never attempted to reverse or obstruct Ireland's membership.

This was in contrast to the Labour Party in Britain where EEC membership took effect on the same day as Ireland's and Denmark's, 1 January 1973. It was not until Harold Wilson held a referendum in 1974 that the issue was partially resolved. However, as late as 1983 the anti-European faction proposed British withdrawal from the European Community in the election manifesto under Michael Foot's leadership. The triumphant return of Margaret Thatcher's beleaguered government led to that infamous manifesto being described as 'the longest suicide note in history'. By contrast, Corish's clarity and leadership ensured that no such ambiguity remained within Labour in Ireland.

I never posted my letter to Noël Browne on 5 February 1973. Instead, I phoned his home and spoke to his wife Phyllis. Noël was not available. The selection convention was set for the coming Thursday, 8 February. I seriously began to think that Noël might not stand. I made a number of phone calls to him over the next two days, but without success. Eventually I told Phyllis that I wanted to speak to Noël before Thursday evening's meeting because I wanted him to know that I was putting my name forward as his running mate. It was with some sadness that I said this to her, and I was disappointed that I had not been able to speak directly to Noël because I felt that our relationship would not be the same again after the Thursday meeting.

On the night in question, we gathered in Earlsfort Terrace and decided to contest the election with two candidates. I was proposed by Dermot Scott, son of a Donegal Presbyterian minister, who had joined the Labour Party because he was a supporter of the party's line on the North as articulated by Conor Cruise O'Brien. At that stage Noël rose to speak. His quiet voice filled the room as he began to express his concerns about the fourteen-point election programme that had been agreed between Labour and Fine Gael. He had reservations about the policy content and had refused to endorse the programme the previous day. He said quietly that he could not let his name go forward as a Labour candidate. The meeting erupted with many people speaking loudly at the same time across the room to each other. John Byrne, Paddy Perry and others wanted him to reconsider. Pat Carroll got agreement that the meeting be adjourned for fifteen minutes.

David Neligan, Brendan Scott, John Byrne and Pat Carroll surrounded Noël. I was standing at the window of the first-floor room where I could see the group through the door huddled together on the first landing. Noël was shaking his head, and his supporters could not persuade him to change his mind. My heart was leaping. I would, at last, realise my ambition and become a Labour candidate with a real prospect of victory.

When the meeting resumed, Noël, having formally declined a nomination, thanked his supporters. But we had already decided to run two candidates, and so Francis Kenny, a recent recruit who lived in Portobello, put his name forward. I could now see myself with an unknown running mate and the added complexity of two candidates, instead of one. David Neligan said that it was bad enough not having Dr Browne on the ticket but that it would be madness, in a three-seater, to run two unknown candidates. The meeting shared his view. Francis Kenny withdrew his name, leaving me as the sole candidate.

It was all a frantic rush to put a campaign in place. I received great encouragement and help from many quarters, including my immediate family. Des Windle became a daily activist in our election headquarters on Serpentine Avenue. Nearby, Allied Irish Banks had purchased a set of buildings, including a vacant shop adjacent to their present Bank Centre. We were able to rent this for the campaign. Aonghus McDonnell, prominent in the UCD branch, lived on Serpentine Avenue and was a student with time on his hands and plenty of ability. He became director of elections – Labour's youngest in the country. However, Des provided a bit of maturity and became the parliamentary agent, a title that no longer exists in today's electoral law. A lot of young people from UCD and Trinity came to help and what we lacked in experience was more than matched by their energy and enthusiasm. After sixteen years of Fianna Fáil in government and the internal divisions within its ranks over the North, the public mood for change was palpable.

The concise nature of the fourteen-point election programme, including a commitment to declare a housing emergency, had a lot of appeal. Michael McInerney wrote a sympathetic profile of me in *The Irish Times*, as one of the new generation of young candidates. In it, I said that I hoped to achieve as much for housing as Noël Browne had done for health. The day the profile was published, I arrived at the election headquarters to find Aonghus shocked and angry. He had just had a phone call from Phyllis Browne who had given him an earful, telling him that I should not compare myself to her husband. We knew then that we had no hope of getting the public endorsement of support which we had requested from the former deputy. Given his reputation, it would have been of enormous value. No reason was given for Browne's refusal.

Bob Dylan's classic song 'The Mighty Quinn' had always struck me as an obvious theme tune for a campaign if I ever became a candidate. Now that I was, Charlie McDonald, my brother Conor's future partner in Quinn McDonnell Pattison, suggested that I use the Manfred Mann version because it was more melodic than

Dylan's original. Conor's normal Fianna Fáil allegiance was swamped by the tide of filial blood – much thicker than political water.

Name recognition in such a short campaign, he and Charlie argued, was my biggest problem. So with their help, a van with a wooden box on its roof proudly displaying my name was continuously driven around the constituency while Paul Jones' voice announced the Mighty Quinn, and then my recorded voiceover articulated policy on an amplified cassette tape. While the idea was not new, it made an impact. But was it enough? Given the size of Noël Browne's 1969 vote, I would have to shed more than half of it in order to lose the seat. Brendan Thorne and Tom Gaffney claimed that this was just not possible, having scrutinised some canvassing returns.

On the day of the count, the mood in the Bolton Street College of Technology was electric because many people present sensed a change of government. My initial vote was a disappointing 2,927, compared to Noël Browne's 5,724 first preferences in 1969. But as the candidates were eliminated, the transfers started to come my way. Garret FitzGerald was comfortably elected on the first count, followed by Seán Moore from Fianna Fáil, on the fifth count. Sitting in the Four Seasons pub, across from the count centre, I was caught up in that incredibly intense and unreal world of suspended animation in which candidates find themselves. The long intervals of time between each count are filled with every possible rumour, coming allegedly from the most experienced tallyman, or complicated analysis and speculation as to where the transfers of the recently eliminated candidate would ultimately land.

I had not realised how different electioneering is for the candidate, as distinct from party activists and personal supporters. Sport and drama enable performers to shine or sparkle. Spectators and audiences may be disappointed by the result or lukewarm in their applause at curtain call. But politics and elections are about the pursuit of power, not the provision of entertainment. While many citizens and commentators relish elections as a spectator sport, the experience for candidates is very different. Most candidates believe that it is just possible they might win. Some – but very few – believe they are secure. I have never met a politician who personally felt that they had got too many votes. To stand for election, to seek a maddate, to aspire to office and the exercise of power, is a very public act. It requires a particular form of self-belief and a strong ego – but every ego, no matter how robust, has its Achilles heel, irrespective of public displays of stoicism.

Word came from the count centre in Bolton Street to the Four Seasons pub that the last count had started. I was 121 votes ahead of Garret FitzGerald's running mate, Fergus O'Brien. The last Fianna Fáil candidate, Pat Cummins, was being eliminated with 4,042 votes and, given the Fianna Fáil tradition of a plumping vote – that is to say one, two, three and stop – it was impossible, I was told, that I could be caught. I urged caution to some excited supporters who congratulated me in the hall of Bolton Street as I made my way, half-dazed, up the stairs to the room where the count was being held. I passed Fergus O'Brien in the corridor, his back slumped against the wall, his ashen-faced head shaking in disagreement as two of his supporters told him that he could still just about make it.

A slow swell of excitement began to form within me. Scrutineers from all parties were crouched over the barriers. Andy Smith, the Official Sinn Féin candidate, had transferred 748 votes to me, a significant and critical number, at an earlier stage. Now the eliminated Cummins' preferences were being adjudicated on and allocated to either O'Brien or myself. The gap was steadily closing. Fergus, an ESB worker, had stood with Garret in 1969 and had subsequently worked hard, particularly in the City Quay area where Cummins had his council seat and much support. It was, I believe, that factor which gave O'Brien a thirty-nine-vote lead and victory at the end of that seventh count. Significantly, 3,210 votes of Pat Cummins' total did not transfer, nearly the same as his first preference figure of 3,329. This was in the days when Fianna Fáil did not believe in working the proportional representation system.

It was a cliffhanger of a result, one of the few in that election, and the only one in Dublin which got much publicity. I was devastated, as were Labour's South-East activists. After a quick consultation with Des Windle and Aonghus McDonnell, we agreed to ask for a recount of the last round of votes and their distribution. When the recount was over, the margin of defeat was reduced only by one vote. I had lost by 38 votes.

Defeat was partially numbed by the victory of the Fine Gael/Labour coalition and the sense of expectation and change. The physical and emotional aftermath of an election campaign, particularly for candidates and those close to them, is not unlike the aftereffects of a funeral. The sheer excitement of intense activity and the exuberance of electioneering is followed by exhaustion. Victory brings with it the balm of success, but defeat, particularly a narrow defeat, compounds the tiredness and depresses the spirit. I mustered enough energy and courage, when thanking the returning officer and his staff, to inform Fine Gael to mind well the Labour seat in Dublin South-East because we would be taking it back at the next election.

Back in the Four Seasons, despite the result in South-East, our supporters were jubilant about the defeat of Fianna Fáil and the prospect of Labour participation in the new government. I had not fully absorbed the impact of my defeat as I shared the excitement of political change that would at last happen after sixteen years. There was much talk of Seanad seats and of me being one of the Taoiseach's eleven nominations, since I had been the most successful of the defeated Labour candidates. But, as is common in politics, it is very easy to speculate authoritatively on the outcome of decisions that you have no power to shape.

The next day, on Sandymount Green, I met Larry Flood. He commiserated with me and said that if he had known that I was going to go that close, he would have given me a number one. It was, for me, a telling introduction to the truism that everyone wants to be on the winning side. Larry subsequently did support me and, when he retired from the Revenue Commissioners, became my unofficial tax consultant, to whom I referred many constituency taxation queries.

It has often been said that the next election campaign begins the day after the count is completed. That was my own view and the opinion of the people around me. The narrow defeat gave me one victory, which was beyond dispute: I was the heir apparent in Dublin South-East. Noël Browne had retired. What had to be done now was to consolidate the organisation.

I was encouraged to run for the Seanad and easily achieved a nomination from the Royal Institute of Architects of Ireland. I had been the first architect in modern times to stand for the Dáil and the profession had given me a lot of support. But I could not get a Labour Party nomination for the Seanad because of the intense competition and so I decided, with the advice of people around me, not to contest the Seanad election.

Within weeks of the general election, to the surprise of many and the anger of John Kennedy among others, Noël Browne announced his intention to stand for the Seanad on the University of Dublin panel. He declared that he would not be taking the whip or joining the parliamentary party. While Browne's supporters were delighted, many Labour Party members in Dublin South-East were annoyed.

The formation of the cabinet gave Labour five of the fifteen ministerial posts, with Brendan Corish as Tánaiste and Minister for Health and Minister for Social Welfare. Already there was tension between Corish and Browne over the politics of medicine. Natural resources and the future of the enormous zinc ore deposits in Navan were also a controversial issues. A student-led organisation, the Resources Protection Campaign, argued that the wealth of the ore body, combined with a state-controlled smelter, would give the Irish economy vast revenues which the government could use to redress poverty, and provide for health and housing. Labour Conference resolutions reflected this position and the matter was now a hot potato on the desk of the new Minister for Industry and Commerce, Justin Keating.

Browne was easily elected to the Seanad, and his name was put forward to be the constituency delegate at the October annual conference in Cork. For me, this was a trial of political strength and for the party leadership a potential problem. The meeting to select the Dublin South-East conference delegate took place in Newman House on St Stephen's Green. Rather than run myself, in case I might lose, I proposed that the constituency secretary, Seán Mistéal, should be our delegate. This meant that there would be no clash, ostensibly, between the new senator and myself. Characteristically, Noël Browne did not attend the meeting, but his supporters did, led by Neligan, Carroll, Byrne and Perry. When the result of the secret vote was announced, it was a tie. I then exercised my casting vote, as chair of the constituency council, and announced that the constituency secretary would be our delegate to conference. This was greeted by angry protests, but I held my ground. Neligan, Carroll, Byrne and Perry walked out in protest, leaving the meeting and, in the case of Pat Carroll and Dave Neligan, the constituency organisation. It was a tough decision for me but it sent a signal about my intentions in Dublin South-East and my future ambitions. The news travelled quickly – at a funeral some days later Conor Cruise O'Brien congratulated me as we stood in the graveyard overlooking Dublin Bay.

Liam Cosgrave, as Taoiseach, and Brendan Corish, as Tánaiste, got on well together, having, among other things, a common interest in horse racing. They had been in government before as cabinet ministers in the Inter-Party Government of the early 1950s. Corish had a talented team in cabinet. Michael O'Leary, the young dauphin as he seemed then, was Minister for Labour. Jimmy Tully, the tough deputy party leader from Meath, was appointed to the Custom House where he relished being Minister for Local Government. Conor Cruise O'Brien was in Posts and Telegraphs and also retained his spokesperson's role on Northern Ireland. He worked closely with Garret FitzGerald, the surprise appointment to Foreign Affairs. Cosgrave, it is claimed, displayed some canny skill in reversing the opposition roles of Richie Ryan and Garret but, four years later, FitzGerald's outstanding performance in Foreign Affairs made him the undisputed successor to Cosgrave.

There was rivalry, although I was hardly aware of it, among the Labour ministers. The transformed parliamentary party after the 1969 election was legendary for its clash of personalities, ideological divisions and the tensions between the liberal/urban versus rural/conservative viewpoints. Many long-established provincial deputies, such as Dan Spring, Tom Kyne, Stevie Coughlan and Jimmy Tully, ran their constituencies more like personal fiefdoms than open democratic organisations, and some urban Labour deputies were not much different. Frank Cluskey was not unique when it came to his control of Dublin Central; similarly Dr John O'Connell's control of Dublin South-West.

Soon after the 1969 election, following some fractious parliamentary party gatherings, Corish had had enough. In the middle of a very disputatious meeting, he stormed out of the room. In the stony silence that followed, Cluskey's deep flat voice was heard to say, 'Here we are now, fifteen contenders and not one of us with a seconder.' Frank's characteristic humour diffused the situation. However, the tensions, while abated, still remained.

There were seven parliamentary secretary posts, the equivalent of ministers of state, to be filled. Corish could nominate two. Michael Pat Murphy from Cork South-West went to the Department of Agriculture and, to some people's surprise, Frank Cluskey went to the Department of Social Welfare. Barry Desmond was widely expected to get office, but was overlooked. Seán Treacy became Ceann Comhairle, opening the way for Michael Ferris to start his long campaign to win a Labour seat in Tipperary South. David Thornley and Liam Kavanagh were nominated as members of the European Parliament. Corish, in both Health and Social Welfare, had two parliamentary secretaries: Cluskey and Dick Barry, the Fine Gael Cork East deputy, who took an office in the Custom House. Cluskey moved into the office of the secretary of the department because Corish wanted him to be beside his ministerial office in Busáras. It was here that the Department of Social Welfare was housed in Michael Scott's modern architectural office block, combined with a bus terminal, and its own small theatre, the Eblana.

Frank, as many people knew, had a serious drink problem and had only gone on the 'dry' when the general election was called. He was still not drinking when the government was formed and his appointment announced, but many colleagues predicted that it would not be long before he was back on the sauce. The Dáil then sat late because many members were part-time legislators with other jobs. Question Time began at 3.00 p.m. and the Order of Business at 4.00 p.m.; this meant that the barristers, solicitors, teachers, businessmen and trade-union officials could get in most of a day's work before being required to attend to their Dáil duties. The sitting went on until 10.30 p.m. and often to 11.00 p.m. if matters were raised on the adjournment. Facilities were very meagre, with deputies sharing rooms and having restricted access to telephones and no secretarial support. All correspondence was written in long hand. It was usual to see many deputies in the Dáil chamber listening to the debate while addressing envelopes and doing their correspondence because it was one place where they could find a bit of space. The other place of refuge was, of course, the members' bar.

Here the speculation about Cluskey remaining 'on the dry' mounted; soon a book was opened and bets were placed. When Frank heard about this, as inevitably he did, his response was typical. He pondered a while and told his informant to go back and enquire as to what the odds were.

'But why?'

'Well,' said Frank, 'if they are good, we should put some money on. After all, I may not stay on the wagon and if I do fall, we'll need the drinking money.'

Happily, Frank applied himself vigorously to the job and was, in effect, the Minister for Social Welfare, since Corish concentrated his energies on being Tánaiste and Minister for Health.

In December 1973, the British and Irish governments, with the participation of the SDLP and the Ulster Unionist Party, made a major breakthrough on Northern Ireland. Ian Paisley and Sinn Féin would have nothing to do with the negotiations, which took place at a country club retreat, Sunningdale, in England. Corish, having the confidence of Gerry Fitt and Paddy Devlin, played a considerable role. This meant that it fell to Frank to bring forward a series of radical reforms to the spartan and puritanical social-welfare system.

Prisoners' wives, unmarried mothers and deserted wives would all now qualify for welfare payments. The Combat Poverty Agency was established in 1979. It was a political initiative taken by Frank Cluskey and was informed by a Labour Party policy document. He subsequently persuaded his fellow ministers in the Social Affairs Council to adopt a European-wide anti-poverty programme based on this Irish model.

Labour's participation in government brought about an innovation which initially created considerable difficulties. Influenced by other socialist and social democratic parties in government within Europe, the leadership, under Halligan's initiative, proposed the appointment of special advisers to the Labour ministers. This was agreed, and soon Tony Brown, Willie Scally, Niall Greene, Flor O'Mahony and Nicholas Simms were working with Labour ministers. Jimmy Tully refused to have one and Garret was the only Fine Gael minister who took on an adviser – the economist Brendan Dowling. Problems arose for the Labour advisers when they were told that they would have to resign as members of the party, in order to be temporary civil servants. Willie Scally and Tony Brown worked in the Sugar Company, where Halligan had worked as an economist before becoming party general secretary. Flor O'Mahony was a lecturer in the College of Technology in Kevin Street and a councillor in Dún Laoghaire. Niall Greene was in Aer Lingus. All were active and influential Labour Party members; they were also highly committed and refused to resign from the party. The matter was referred to the Attorney General, Declan Costello, for legal advice. A meeting of the Taoiseach, Tánaiste and Richie Ryan, the Minister for Finance, was held in which an exasperated Brendan Corish, reaching into his wallet, exclaimed that you could not expect a party member to give up his card. He produced his membership card, to the intense curiosity of his Fine Gael colleagues. They had never seen such a thing, because they did not have that sort of political organisation.

Labour's advisers remained as party members and provided essential help to their ministers and departments. Initially many civil servants were suspicious. They feared that, on departure from office, a minister might appoint an adviser to a permanent post,

which would obviously have promotion implications for the professional civil service. In the end, their fears were groundless and
did not materialise when Labour left office. Nonetheless, in the
following government Frank Dunlop, the Fianna Fáil press officer
and subsequent government press secretary, persuaded Jack Lynch
to appoint him, in the public interest, as a permanent civil servant,
with the rank of assistant secretary when he became press secretary
to the government in 1977. When C.J. Haughey was defeated in
1981, Dunlop was transferred to the Department of Education. But
the need for political advisers did not go away and the issue would
surface again.

As Labour prepared for its annual conference, one issue – the future
of the zinc ore mine in Navan and the role of the state in maximising
its value and distributing its wealth – dominated the agenda. Justin
Keating was under great pressure to acquire the mineral body and
build a smelter to ensure that the added value of the ore would
remain in Ireland. Noël Browne arrived at the Cork conference as a
delegate and ordinary party member. Although he was now a
senator, he was true to his word and did not take a seat on the
platform as we was not a member of the parliamentary party. The
main debate on the Saturday afternoon was about the future of Tara
Mines.

   Browne led the case for the nationalisation of this priceless
resource which, he said, should belong to the people. He spoke in
his quiet, almost whispering, voice to a packed hall. As he lowered
his voice slightly, the delegates, straining to hear his every word,
created a concentrated silence that was tense. Browne ranged back
in time, reflecting on how we had all been told that Ireland was a
poor country, that we had no natural or mineral resources of value,
unlike the coal and iron ore of many other European countries. That
was why our development had lagged far behind other countries;
particularly our neighbouring island. But this was no longer true.
Buried beneath the ground, in the fields of Meath, lay untold riches
that could be ours, that *should* be ours. All we needed was the

political vision and courage to take what was there and spend what was so clearly needed on our hospitals and our schools. But did we have that will and did Labour have that courage? It was a magnificent speech, wonderfully delivered and heart-rending in its message to every delegate. When Browne finished, there was a spontaneous standing ovation and sustained applause.

The platform had a serious problem. The strength of feeling that Browne had unleashed could result in the leadership being directed by Conference to take a course of action which it could not deliver in government. This was exactly what the left wanted to achieve. Still opposed to coalition, even though they had been defeated two years previously in the same hall, they wanted to show that coalitions did not work, that a socialist project could not be obtained within a coalition with a right-wing party. They knew that Fine Gael would not agree to nationalise Tara Mines, but wanted Conference to resoundingly pass the motion. Failure to implement it would then be an indictment of the leadership. Under the constitution of the Labour Party, Conference was the supreme decision-making body.

Corish and Halligan knew what was going on. Corish had changed his principled opposition to coalition after the 1969 general election and the crisis in Irish politics, which developments in the North had brought about. He was convinced, based on his private dealings with Jack Lynch, that Irish democracy was at risk and that the prospect of an alternative government was essential. Corish was not forgiven for this change. Yet, it was Justin Keating who was the man in the hot seat. He was the minister who had the actual responsibility to implement the decision of Conference. Naturally, he did not want a position hung around him which he regarded as impossible to deliver. Furthermore, he had his own ambitions, or at least many people in the party, myself included, had leadership ambitions for him. He had a radical past, was the son of Ireland's first socialist realist artist, Seán Keating, and was a talented television presenter.

I watched the platform from the body of the hall, surrounded by people who, like myself, had given Noël Browne a standing ovation. He had taken us up to the top of the mountain. No one could resist the strength of his emotional appeal and yet many of those same people were the ones the leadership was relying on for support. The stakes were very high. Since this was the start of a new government, the outcome in Cork would have a major impact for the following years. A number of speakers came to the rostrum, one after another, supporting either Browne's line or the compromise with reality which coalition entailed. Slowly, the charged atmosphere of the hall changed. Some speakers were boring and others antagonistic, but all insisted on their three-minute contribution.

By the time Keating came to reply to the debate a great space of emotion and time had opened up between Browne's contribution and the opportunity to respond. He began with generosity and praise for all the previous speakers, recognising the essential validity of the case. Yes, there was new wealth discovered in Ireland, wealth that we had never known was under the ground near Navan. It was essential that we get it, that we put it to good use. If Fianna Fáil was back in power, it would be squandered or wasted. 'Was that what Conference really wanted?' he asked

'No,' was the clear response from the audience.

Justin continued, 'Yes we are in government, but not the majority in government because Conference has not persuaded the electorate to make us the majority.'

He, the minister, did not have the votes. They, the delegates, had not delivered the votes, but did they want the party to leave government so that the alternative would then control the future of this priceless resource?

'No' again was the even stronger response of the audience, going quiet as they listened to Justin, patiently and earnestly, lead them back down from the mountain top. To each reasoned step that he presented, with his relentless logic, they gave their consent. He would not betray them. The best possible deal, which he would negotiate, would be obtained. No other party, or even minister, would or could do better and Labour would deliver in government. The same delegates, in the same hall and on the same day, who one hour earlier had cheered Noël Browne, now gave Justin Keating a standing ovation and voted for the decision which he and the leadership wanted.

Even as he was speaking, I was aware that I was listening to an extraordinary historic debate. To this day, I can remember the whispered words of powerful, emotional rhetoric, the compelling logic and the generous praise, combined with reasoned conclusions. It was the essence of political discourse. It combined everything between what had to be and what could be obtained. I was not alone; many in the hall felt the same. Conference adjourned after that vote. Later, I spoke to Ted Nealon and Brian Farrell, television journalists who were covering the conference for RTÉ. They could not, in their experience, recall such a political performance, and a performance it undoubtedly was.

Corish's speech, as party leader and Tánaiste, made later that evening, was well received. He was in good mood, understandably, and always spoke well. His speech was greeted as ever with affection and applause from the delegates. By midday on Sunday, the conference was over and I returned to Dublin.

Meanwhile, Jim Tully had reinstated all the elected Dublin city councillors who had lost their seats when the City Council was abolished. In their place, Kevin Boland, had appointed John Garvin, a former secretary of the Department of Local Government, to be the sole commissioner. This, in effect, gave to Matt Macken, the city manager, full control of the decision-making process. Now, Garvin was gone and the city councillors were back for one year. The next local elections would take place the following year, in June 1974.

I had to make some decisions about my own political future. According to the regulations, I could not be employed by Dublin Corporation in the Housing Architects Department if I was elected to the City Council. I wanted to stand in the local elections for the Pembroke ward, which included Ringsend and Sandymount where I had grown up. John Kennedy was keen for me to stand. He had no ambitions for himself but plenty for me. So I began to look to a change of job and positioning myself to run in the forthcoming local elections.

Chapter 8

Combining Private Practice
and Public Service

When I arrived at the Harcourt Hotel, Des Doyle was not there but when he did arrive, full of apologies for being late, he was his usual self: enthusiastic and deeply committed to architecture. He had worked for Bord Fáilte, specialising in hotels, before he became a partner in Kidney Burke-Kennedy & Partners. The company was changing. Joe Kidney, the firm's founder, was still involved but was soon to retire. When I told Paul, my brother-in-law, that I intended to leave Dublin Corporation, he said there might be room for me in the practice. It was with Des that the terms and conditions of my employment were to be negotiated, so as to remove any taint of family bias. Des suggested that I come in as an associate and, after a year, partnership would be discussed. He considered my experience in public housing to be a particular asset. In addition, I could continue my teaching in UCD and make up for any time lost by additional work.

In anticipation of leaving the Corporation, I had been looking out for projects that I could bring to the practice. I was introduced to Jonah Jones, a Welshman who was director of the National College of Art and Design (NCAD). There had been a crisis in the college similar to that in the UCD School of Architecture, and a new regime was installed. The word 'design' had been added to the college's title, to become the NCAD, and additional staff were employed, mostly from the Britain. In the meantime, space was a major problem in the confined complex of old buildings and prefabs that were formerly the outbuildings of Leinster House. While the proposal for a new college on a greenfield site at Morehampton Road in Donnybrook had been announced in 1969, nothing had been done on the project. Jonah

Jones needed a short-term solution and my name had been suggested
to him as a suitable architect. We got on well together and soon I was
working closely with David Sherlock, Jonah's deputy.

The expanding NCAD rapidly occupied my redesigned extra in
fill rooms. But more space was required and a disused garment
factory in South William Street was rented on a temporary basis,
because the new college building was still on the 'promised' list in
the Department of Education. While the temporary accommodation was basic, it was within walking distance of the rest of the
college. It was also in the city centre, an important factor for staff
and students. At one meeting, I asked, 'If a part of the NCAD could
be housed in a recycled industrial warehouse, couldn't the whole
college be so accommodated?'

'Of course,' said Campbell Bruce, whose Fine Art students were
happy with their new space.

'But this is your city,' Jonah Jones said, 'and you know it better
than us, so see what you can find.'

Some weeks later at a party I was talking to John Tierney, an
accountant with the Irish Distillers Group, who had recently consolidated their production in one location, Midleton, County Cork.
The Powers Distillery on Thomas Street in the Liberties of Dublin
was in its last year of production before being closed down.

'What are you going to do with the building?'

'Sell it,' he said.

Tierney was not sure who would buy such a large site because the
property market was flat and the distillery was outside Dublin's
central business district. I asked if I could visit it with a client. A few
days later, David Sherlock and I went to the premises and were shown
around. We started on the street and entered through the large
archway, under which the grain lorries passed when they were
delivering the basic raw material for the making of Irish whiskey.
There were two drying areas, with pyramid-shaped roofs at either
end of the seven-floor warehouse, with its solid timber beams, cast-
iron columns and low ceilings. The mixture of space, the play of light
and the sounds of the city were now flavoured with the pervasive
aroma of whiskey.

David and I exchanged glances; we knew this place could work. When the tour was finished, we made our way back to Kildare Street hardly able to contain our excitement. It was simply perfect, but we had to persuade Jonah and the college and then the department. Our first task was to define in spatial and service terms what the NCAD needed. This was now a substantial project in the practice and Noel Kidney was working with me. The building's potential to match the needs of the NCAD was presented in 1976 to Jonah Jones, David Sherlock and Oscar Richardson, a senior architect in the Department of Education, and we were given the go ahead. Our proposals were then lodged with the Department of Education and the Office of Public Works (OPW) in 1978 – little did we know then that we would hear nothing for three years.

In June 1981, as a result in the increase of the country's population, the total number of Dáil deputies was increased from 148 to 166. This put enormous pressure on the limited space within Leinster House and its adjoining accommodation. The NCAD project was quickly, dusted down with instructions to get it moving at full speed. Those parts of the empty distillery building which could be used were to be ready by the following September and the rest would be phased in as a matter of priority. There was the minor matter of obtaining planning permission, which normally would take a minimum of two months.

I made an appointment to see the senior planning officer responsible for that part of the city, Liam Tobin. It was, I informed him, more of a courtesy call because I did not really think that a formal 'change of use' was necessary. His quizzical expression conveyed great doubts about how a distillery and an art college were the same thing. I listed many of the activities of the NCAD: metalwork, woodworking, painting, drawing, meetings and administration. I then identified the various activities in the existing buildings, which included administration, meetings, design work, metalwork and woodwork. Liam smiled benignly, asking what all this had got to do with a distillery becoming an art college.

'Would you not agree,' I asked him, tongue in cheek, 'that the distilling of Irish whiskey was more of an art than a science?'

His response was correct, constructive and supportive. 'Put in a formal application for a change of use and its passage will be given speedy attention,' he assured me.

He was true to his word and the rest of the project proceeded in 1981 and was finished two years later.

Outside of my architectural work I was very involved with the local politics of the Pembroke ward, Ward 9, as it was now known. This was the ward where I intended standing as a candidate in the forth-coming local elections. Back in 1967, Jack Torpay had been success-fully elected as an independent environmental and community candidate. 'Save Sandymount Strand' was his slogan. There had been a proposal to expand Dublin Port and to construct a motorway across the strand. I knew from my urban studies that, once constructed, such a major transport artery would forever create a major barrier between the city and the bay. The special relationship between sea, sand and city, which characterises Sandymount Strand, would disappear. The character and quality of Irishtown and Ringsend would also be des-troyed. This was a major local issue and of citywide importance. Now restored to the City Council by Jimmy Tully, Jack Torpay personally told me that he would not be a candidate in the 1974 local elections.

The Labour Party began its preparations in earnest for the local elections after the October 1973 conference in Cork. Our initial local team had been consolidated by the addition of people who had cam-paigned in the general election and who had stayed active. Caroline Hussey and Anna Doyle took on increasingly important roles. Caroline, a senior lecturer at UCD and subsequently the registrar, would become the director of elections for the 1974 local and the 1977 general elections. John Kennedy strengthened his influence in Ringsend and I finally got my clinic up and running that autumn. There was no community facility in Ringsend from which a clinic could be run. In desperation, John suggested that I might approach the local general practitioner, Dr Rutledge, who had suitable premises in the heart of Ringsend. 'All he can do is say no, but if it is a yes, then you'll be made up.'

Tony Rutledge had been in school with Brendan Corish and liked what he was trying to do as Minister for Health and Minister for Social Welfare. Yes, I could use his rooms in Thorncastle Street and no he would not take payment for the two hours every Sunday when I would use the rooms. It was a major breakthrough, and we had the use of that generous facility for many years.

Since I was no longer in the public sector, my membership of the Local Government and Public Services Union had come to an end. For political reasons I wanted to maintain a union connection, particularly with a union affiliated to the Labour Party. Through my part-time teaching in UCD, I joined the No. 15 branch of the WUI, a section that catered for white-collar workers in UCD and which also included RTÉ and the Industrial Development Authority (IDA) amongst its members. I was not that active but, through the union, I met Eoghan Harris, a prominent RTÉ television producer and then a covert political activist in Official Sinn Féin.

Because of its large size, we decided to run three candidates in the four-seater No. 9 ward, in order to appeal to as wide a cross-section of the community as possible and so maximise our vote. Paddy Perry was keen to stand and, since he had been active in the constituency for many years, he was nominated. Mary Freehill, originally from Cavan but who had lived all her adult life in Dublin, was a prominent young member of the Rathmines branch. Living in Terenure, she was a professional welfare officer with the National Rehabilitation Board, and had joined the party because of the lack of housing in the city.

One event occurred around this time that was to have a major influence on my political career: I happened to meet Denise Rogers. One of our political tasks was to call door-to-door collecting money for the Labour Party. A door in Durham Road was answered by Denise, a young woman of slight figure and short red hair, and she put one shilling into my box. She told me that she had, that day, got a copy of Labour's equality document from Labour Party head office because she was interested in what the various political parties had to say about the role of women.

I invited her to a Sandymount branch meeting, but she did not want to get involved with the Labour Party because 'they were communists and reds'. Denise was from Sligo, her mother voted Fianna Fáil and her father Fine Gael. Even so, I persuaded her to come to the meeting and listen. During the course of the meeting, the branch wanted to send a letter to Noël Browne. In those pre-computer days, typing was a skill I did not have and Denise, who worked in UCD, offered to type the letter. In O'Reilly's pub after the meeting, I told Denise that I intended to be the next Labour TD for Dublin South-East and asked her if she would type for me, on a voluntary basis. This she did and we have worked together ever since. Between 1974 and 1977, I dictated clinic queries and dropped them off to her on a Sunday evening.

On polling day, 17 June 1974, Alderman Carmencita Hederman, a dynamic conservation and community activist, topped the poll. Fine Gael's Peter Kelly, the young brother of the government whip, John Kelly, was elected. The veteran Seán Moore was comfortably returned for Fianna Fáil and I became the first Labour councillor elected for Ward 9 in over thirty years.

In all, forty-five councillors were elected, ten of them for Labour. I knew early on in the count that I would be elected, so I set about seeking the post of secretary of the Labour group on Dublin Corporation. The position involved extra work, which I knew I could handle, and my early declaration of interest meant that I had no competition when the group met. Paddy Dunne was elected as our chair.

As chair of the Dublin Regional Council of the Labour Party, I was by now well aware of the special influence vested in the hands of the person in any group who wrote the minutes of the meetings and correspondence. Frank Butler, secretary of the Dublin Regional Council for years, gave me many examples, though I am not sure if he knew it.

Fine Gael and Labour now had an overall majority, without re-course to independent councillors or the newly formed Community group. Business had to be done before the newly elected council met. Positions such as the Lord Mayor and the chairs of the various committees appealed to everyone. An interest in position and power is common to all politicians. I have long grown suspicious of elected politicians who solemnly declare that they have no interest in power. The motivation to achieve and exercise power does vary, but the desire with which it is sought remains constant and common amongst all those with whom I have been elected.

Our own group decided that we should enter into exclusive talks with Fine Gael to agree a division of posts and responsibilities. Our final meeting took place after 11.00 p.m. upstairs in the room of a pub on Store Street, either owned or controlled by Paddy Belton. He was a big man in every sense. A successful publican and business-man, he was a Fine Gael TD who had not been made a minister by Liam Cosgrave in the 1973 coalition cabinet. Fergus O'Brien TD, now newly elected to the City Council, was a strong voice within the Fine Gael group. Both men represented the conservative wing of Fine Gael. Belton was tough but, as I was to see later, loyal to any deal to which he had given his word. By the end of the evening, the details were resolved and the deal was agreed, but with one excep-tion. We could not agree on the post of Lord Mayor because both parties wanted to have the first term. Such pride was costly because on the night, as Fine Gael and Labour nominated their candidates, the gap was adroitly filled by the nominally independent councillor, Tom Stafford, who seized the prize with the votes of the Fianna Fáil group. His election to the Mansion House ensured subsequent unity on every other position. I became the vice-chair of the housing committee, with Fergus O'Brien as the chair. So it was that, within less than twelve months, the department in which I had been a junior technical official now had me as their number two political head. I like to think that my previous experience in work-ing with Dublin Corporation enabled me to make a more informed political contribution on different policy issues.

We were blessed with a senior official, Jimmy Molloy, promoted from assistant city manager, by Jimmy Tully, Minister for Local Government, to the newly created post of housing co-ordinator for Dublin City and County. Tully's response to the housing crisis was direct and decisive. He put an end to the disastrous policy of low-cost housing, brought in by the previous inexperienced Minister for Local

Government, Bobby Molloy. Local authority houses under construction, but for which no provision for a solid fuel fireplace had been made, were now to have such facilities as part of a revised contract. The escalation in energy prices, following the Yom Kippur War, had made nonsense of the cheaply built, poorly insulated houses, which substituted the traditional chimney with a simple electricity or gas-fired, warm-air heating system. Tully's instinctive understanding of how low-income families could better manage a 'pay as you go' solid fuel heating system, rather than run up expensive monthly bills, contradicted the middle-class management decision which had concluded that the elimination of the fireplace was a substantial capital saving. Solid fuel could be acquired, for cash, with no recurring monthly liability. There had been tragically sad cases of people whose houses were burned because they had tried to light a fire to keep their families warm in low-cost units that did not have fireplaces.

Jimmy Molloy, under Tully's direction, was on a mission to find land, anywhere and anyhow, which could be brought quickly to the point of development and allocation. Good-quality construction and well-designed buildings were the new priority. High-density, low-rise housing would meet the social and accommodation needs of people on the housing list. Soon the newly completed scheme in the Coombe set the standard in public housing, which the market-driven private sector followed.

Paddy Logue, Jimmy Molloy's principal officer, used some of his weekends to scour the alleys and back lanes of Dublin, looking at under-utilised land. He found many small plots that we developed for housing. Molloy used Fergus O'Brien and myself to reinforce his own personal contacts in the Custom House to speed up housing decisions, such as the development of a large tract of land adjacent to the Irish Glass Bottle Company and Ringsend Park.

Jimmy Molloy was a man of quiet strength, considerable intelligence and great integrity. I learned a lot from him during my three years on the City Council. Because of the tight voting arrangements in the Dáil, Fergus O'Brien would sometimes ask me to chair the housing committee meeting until he could get away from Leinster House after the order of business. This was at a time when the dual mandate, whereby deputies could also be councillors, was still allowed. I noticed at our meetings that the clerk of the committee, seated beside the chairman, would write into the large ledger the decisions that had been reached. Sometimes this might be qualified with an additional clause, such as 'as soon as possible' or 'subject to the agreement of the manager'. After seeing these constraints appearing in the minutes of the previous meeting, I resolved to prevent this from happening whenever I was in the chair.

When I next found myself at the head of the long broad table in the members' room, I opened the proceedings in the normal way. The clerk, who was on one side of me, with Jimmy Molloy on the other, proceeded to start to hand write in the decisions. I gently requested the large ledger, which he let me take, and the meeting proceeded. Now the boot was on the other foot and I would, within reason, emphasise the urgency of the committee's decisions for inclusion in the minutes.

In July 1975 a housing committee meeting was about to start, with me in the chair, when I noticed that four Fianna Fáil TDs had come into the members' room together. As we began, Cllr Frank Sherwin raised an objection. Seated at the end of the table, directly facing me, he challenged the proceedings, declaring that since this was a quarterly meeting of the housing committee, the first item on the agenda, according to the standing orders, should be the election of a chair and vice-chair. I looked at the two officials on either side of me and then back down the table. Now the punctual presence of the Fianna Fáil deputies and the involuntary absence of Fine Gael and Labour TDs, confined to Leinster House until after the order of business, began to make sense. This was a raid and I was one of the targets, but so too was the entire deal we had negotiated with Fine Gael for the other committees. I began to inwardly panic, but did nothing, letting the voluble Frank Sherwin argue his case with all the ferocity and intelligence of a barrack-room lawyer. 'It is not on the agenda, so there is no election,' I said, continuing to respond to his repeated demands for an election.

'But it should be on the agenda. It is in standing orders,' he argued.

A chorus of strong support now came from Fianna Fáil's Ben Briscoe and Jim Tunney. The Fine Gael and Labour councillors present expressed counterviews but not with the same conviction, because the standing orders, printed in the members' yearbook and diary, were not to be doubted, even if the practice of quarterly elections had long since been ignored. The law agent was called for and confirmed the validity of the standing orders. He also accepted the need to have a written notice of a motion for any election, particularly for the positions of the chair and vice-chair. As the heated argument intensified, I turned to the two officials beside me, telling them, under my breath, that if I got up to leave the meeting, they were to come with me and not remain behind. To make sure that there could be no mistake, I began to close the large ledger. With inner nervousness but outward calm, I declared aloud that the meeting was adjourned and quickly headed for the door, amid much protest.

Walking up Castle Street to the car park, Jimmy Molloy was supportive and reassuring. He quietly advised that it is usually better to adjourn a meeting to another day, rather than *sine die* as I had done. I agreed but said that I had been a bit flustered. He expressed surprise at that and then went on to say how I reminded him of Denis Larkin, former councillor and the younger son of Big Jim. At Molloy's first housing committee meeting, many years earlier, Denis was in the chair. An unruly debate was taking place. In the middle of this, Molloy observed Denis Larkin beginning to write in the large ledger.

'What is the chair now doing?' Molloy asked a senior colleague.

'He is writing the decision of the committee' was the reply.

'But they haven't finished the debate.'

'Correct, but when they do, he will read out what he has written and the majority will agree to it.'

I was soon to find myself at a meeting chaired by the same Denis Larkin, now a senior figure in the WUI, in its headquarters on Parnell Square. Five of the Labour councillors were members of the

WUI. In the run-up to the mayoral elections, which this time was to be Labour's turn, a caucus was called to agree the WUI candidate. Initially, Denis had not invited me. I had to phone and remind him, firmly but politely, of my membership of the No. 15 branch of the WUI. We discussed the post of Lord Mayor and the competing claims of the different councillors present. Under Denis' guidance, it was agreed that Paddy Dunne would have the support of the WUI councillors. This, of course, was to the great irritation of the rest of the Labour group. Indeed, Brendan Halligan had asked me if the group might nominate Dr John O'Connell. Brendan Corish, Minister for Health, was getting grief from his Labour back-bencher, who was knowledgeable about the politics of medicine; the feeling was that the reward of the Mansion House would soften his cough. But then, as now, the party leadership had no say over the determination of such a prized position, no matter how compelling their political arguments.

In order to run for the local elections, I had had to move from the public to the private sector. The stimulus of the practice was one thing, but the understanding of how the private sector worked was another. When my first year with Kidney Burke-Kennedy Doyle & Partners was coming to an end, I was gearing myself to talk to Paul and Des about the question of partnership. A lot had happened in those twelve months. By the autumn of 1974 the country was carrying the brunt of an economic downturn. The oil crisis, precipitated by the latest Arab–Israeli war, had created a worldwide economic slump. The construction industry is a good barometer of the health of any economy. Architects are at the start of the supply chain and when demand slows or stops, it is the architect's office that gets the first phone call. Our assessment of projected income for the forthcoming year showed a drop of more than 30 per cent at a time when inflation was already running high.

Paul and Des took a critical decision which consolidated the practice and led to greater architectural and financial success in years to come. Instead of letting staff go, as was the norm in other

practices, a 20 per cent across-the-board reduction in salaries for all
was implemented, combined with a four-day week for those who
wished to avail of it. Few did, and we put considerable focus into
trying to generate extra work. Against this background, I went
formally to see Paul about the partnership commitment. As he
closed the door and sat down behind his desk, he looked bemused.

'But you know the figures; you've seen the projections. This is the
worst possible time to be talking about new partners.'

'On the contrary,' I replied, 'it could not be better. First, you will
be giving me a percentage of fuck all because of its present value.'

'And?' he asked.

'And secondly, instead of just Des and yourself worrying about
the future, you will have me and whoever else you decide to include
to share the burden and build up the practice.'

Soon afterwards, following Joe Kidney's formal retirement, Paul
and Des announced the creation of three new junior partners – Jim
Crowley, Damien Dillon and myself. The office, now known as
Burke-Kennedy Doyle & Partners (BKD), consolidated itself and
weathered the tough years of 1975 and 1976. A comprehensive
bonus scheme, open to all in the practice who had been there for at
least one year, also helped to strengthen the spirit of the team.

Not long after my election to the City Council, I began to realise
that my narrow defeat in the general election had been a blessing in
disguise. There are skills involved in every job, and serving an
apprenticeship to learn the trade is essential. Some things, like
riding a bicycle or swimming, cannot be learned from a book; they
just have to be worked at and that involves getting very wet or
hurting oneself with the falls of failure.

Membership of a local authority places politicians in direct
contact with public officials, from clerical assistants and maintenance staff to the manager. Because there is no elected executive
group on a council, councillors are required to interact directly with
the responsible officials in the planning, housing and other sections
of the local authority.

This is different from what happens in the Houses of the Oireachtas
where an elected member in opposition can at least try to hold

ministers to account. A government backbencher is denied such opportunities and has no practical experience of the operations of the civil service, except through the narrow line of contact of the minister's private secretary. Depending on the personality of the minister, irrespective of party, and the tenacity of the deputy, the opportunities for interaction with the public service for new backbenchers are very scarce. For a local councillor, with bright ideas, the situation is quite different, but converting such ideas into council proposals, capable of being implemented, is another task and one that requires its own set of skills.

I remember bringing to a committee meeting a proposal that Dublin Corporation should buy the Martello Tower at Merrion Strand, which had come on the open market, and use it as an interpretative centre for Dublin Bay. The initial response from various councillors, including Seán Dublin Bay Loftus, was enthusiastic. I slowly began to get excited at what looked like a local political coup. There was no apparent opposition. The officials did not raise any principled objection. Then Seán Moore, my fellow councillor who had not opposed the project in public, but was also not inclined to let his young opponent have a successful home run, asked the senior official present at the committee what he thought of the idea. Did the Corporation have the expertise, the resources and staff to carry out this imaginative proposal? The response was as Seán expected.

Confronted with an innovative idea, not of their making, and for which no budgetary provision has been made, most public bodies simply say no. That has since been my experience, but back then I was at the early stage of my apprenticeship. Seán Moore solemnly regretted that the idea could not be undertaken. He looked at me across the large members' room table, his eyes inviting me to figure out how best to deal in public with my dashed hopes and premature press statements. Similar setbacks occurred from time to time, but with each came the lesson of understanding how the system worked so that a young and enthusiastic councillor could start to steer it in the direction required.

David Nowlan, a journalist with *The Irish Times*, rang me early one morning in November 1974. The proscenium arch of the Olympia Theatre had collapsed. The tenants were responsible for the maintenance of the structure, otherwise the lease would be forfeited back to the owners. Unless action was taken quickly, the old theatre would disappear. Along with the Gaiety Theatre, the Olympia was now the only one of its kind left in the city.

As I stood listening to David's pleadings for help, I knew that I had to move very quickly. I met Brendan Smith, the director of Olympia Theatre Productions, the tenants of the theatre, and he gave me all the details I needed. The building could be saved but the cost was beyond the range of the 'production company'. I had discussions with senior officials from Dublin Corporation. They could make money available under the new 1974 Arts Council legislation, and the rates could be increased to cover the cost. Gathering the technical and administrative support from the officials was one thing, getting all the councillors, or at least a majority, on board was another. Brendan Smith was a good friend of Jack Lynch, leader of Fianna Fáil. I told him that the Fianna Fáil councillors, in opposition in the City Council, would have to be onside or at least neutralised. The Labour group was in full support and others, such as Community councillor Kevin Byrne, were enthusiastic. Slow, but steady progress was made as I patiently gathered cross-party support against the relentless clock of time. The Olympia Theatre remains open today, strengthened and consolidated by that critical intervention that was made nearly thirty years ago by Dublin City Council, with the assistance of taxpayers' money. From that exercise I learned that, in order to achieve success, it is sometimes necessary to share the political reward.

Those were difficult financial times and I found the necessity of earning a living, while nursing serious political ambitions, time-consuming. My experience in public housing enabled the architectural practice to register for future work with the National

Building Agency (NBA), the semi-state body charged with helping local authorities meet their social housing obligations. Meantime, the land-hunting energies of Jimmy Molloy and Paddy Logue bore fruit, and a number of sites awaited the appointment of design teams to take them to the contract construction stage. One big site was in Irishtown, opposite the Irish Glass Bottle Company, located in my ward. At Jimmy Molloy's suggestion, I had met the owner some months earlier and tried to persuade him to sell voluntarily, and so avoid the delays which a compulsory purchase order would entail.

Stephen O'Flaherty subsequently sold the site to Dublin Corporation. Imagine then, my excitement and concern when I learned that the Corporation had asked the NBA for help in advancing this project. Burke-Kennedy Doyle & Partners was identified as the firm for this job, our first public sector housing contract. When the item formally appeared on the housing committee agenda, I was in the chair. I brought to the attention of the members and officials that I was involved, as a partner, in the relevant architectural practice and accordingly sought leave to absent myself from the chair and the proceedings of the committee, while the decision was being made. In my absence, the committee accepted the officials' recommendation. Burke-Kennedy Doyle & Partners got the job, the first of a number of public housing projects.

I had some concerns about the public perception of this decision, even though I had been open about my declaration of interest. I was anxious that Jimmy Tully was fully aware of what had been agreed. I met him, by designed accident, outside the dining room in Leinster House and began to tell him that I thought I might have a possible conflict between public office and private practice. He cut me short, clearly already briefed about what had been decided. 'I would never publicly apologise for obtaining a public project, particularly a housing project, in my own backyard,' he said.

The office was excited about this new design challenge. A team led by Paul Burke-Kennedy, Peter Duffy, Peter D'Arcy, Noel Kidney and myself started preliminary design work. Initially, some very exciting sketches were circulated within the office, with proposals for pedestrian passageways and courtyards. I intervened in the discussion and suggested that we get into a car and drive around the neighbourhood. When we did, I showed them the sort of houses that the people, currently accommodated in the flats in Ringsend and Irishtown, would like to live in. I pointed out to my passengers the long terrace of two- and three-storey red-bricked houses with their small front gardens on Ringsend Road, opposite the large CIÉ bus station. We travelled through South Lotts Road, comprising a network of terraced on-street houses with no front gardens, over the humped bridge at Ringsend and then on to Irishtown.

As I drove, I told my colleagues that the houses they were looking at, traditional as they were, were what people aspired to. It was our task to design and build the kind of houses that people could easily turn into homes. My theoretical work on vernacular architecture and study of public housing had strongly consolidated these views. The site conditions, on reclaimed land, required piling, making three-storey terraced houses the most cost-effective to design and build. It also ensured that we achieved relatively high densities – a requirement of our brief. Cost considerations came down in favour of sand and cement, plastered walls that subsequently would be painted, instead of redbrick walls which would be maintenance-free. In retrospect, the multicoloured carefully selected shades for each house have stood the test of time. The local children dubbed the new estate 'Legoland'!

There had been five by-elections during the Twentieth Dáil and unusually the government won three of them, even though times were not easy. The one by-election that directly affected me was in Dublin South-West. It took place in June 1976 and was caused by the death of Fianna Fáil's Noel Lemass. He was the son of a famous father and former Taoiseach and, like so many who follow in the footsteps of an illustrious parent, did not live up to the expectations of those around him, who measured him against his father. His wife, Eileen Lemass, a more able politician than her husband, was already a city councillor and clearly would be the obvious candidate for Fianna Fáil. Jim Mitchell, a city councillor from Ballyfermot ran for Fine Gael. A by-election candidate in 1970, Mitchell had un-selfishly encouraged Declan Costello's return to politics and stood aside in the 1973 general election to allow Costello to become elected to the Dáil and subsequently become Attorney General. Labour's candidate was not so obvious. The Dublin South-West constituency was controlled by Labour's Dr John O'Connell, who was semi-detached from the party leadership. It was clear that a candidate would have to be found quickly, since the convention was that the party which had suffered the loss had the right to move the writ for the by-election.

At this stage, the talented and politically active general secretary of the Labour Party, Senator Brendan Halligan, had clear ambitions to stand for the Dáil. A vacancy seemed likely in the new consti-tuency of Dublin Finglas and Brendan had already made prepara-tions to stand in that constituency at the next general election. He was, therefore, as surprised as everyone else when Dr John O'Connell announced to the media that the only Labour candidate who could win the seat from Fianna Fáil was the same Brendan Halligan. Many people saw a Machiavellian hand being played by the sitting Labour deputy, who not only controlled the votes at the selection convention but who had a formidable personal election machine at his disposal. For Halligan to spurn both was to court disaster. On the other hand, to abandon Finglas was not the best way to present oneself as a by-election candidate to another consti-tuency when he intended returning to Finglas at the next general election. With a heavy heart and an external display of enthusiasm, Halligan accepted the nomination. The vigorous campaign saw Fianna Fáil lose and Labour win, with the critical support of Jim Mitchell's transfers.

Two political opportunities now presented themselves. Deputy Brendan Halligan's success meant that his nominated seat in the Senate was available and the position of Lord Mayor would soon become vacant when Labour's Paddy Dunne left the Mansion

House. Its new occupant was the Fine Gael nominee, Jim Mitchell. Some days later, I received a phone call from Brendan Corish's private secretary. Would I go to the Custom House to meet the minister? I waited in the long, dark, mahogany-panelled corridor on the first floor outside the minister's office. Brendan greeted me warmly and, after a few preliminaries, told me that he intended to nominate me to the Senate. Would I accept?

Would I what? was my inward impulsive reaction, but I managed to control my reaction and said that I would be honoured.

'No,' he said, 'it is not about honour. You have a good chance of winning an extra Labour seat in the general election. In fact, our best chance, and that is why I am nominating you.'

Many other people were also looking for the Senate nomination, and it was essential to keep the matter confidential for a couple of days. Moreover, it was a vote of confidence in my ability to win back the Labour seat in Dublin South-East.

Meanwhile, Fergus O'Brien had already indicated his intention to move to the newly created Dublin South-Central constituency, one of thirteen new three-seat constituencies in Dublin. Jimmy Tully had redrawn the boundaries to favour Labour and Fine Gael. This political attempt to give additional advantage to the coalition parties was denounced by Fianna Fáil as a 'tullymander' – which was rich, given the gerrymandering that had been done by Fianna Fáil's Kevin Boland.

The extra resources that the Seanad gave me were significant, along with an enhanced political profile. The Seanad timetable meant that I was not able to make my maiden speech in the Seanad before it adjourned in July 1976. Denise Rogers, who had worked extremely hard since 1974 as my unpaid secretarial assistant, now had an addition to her workload, since senators had an allocation of Oireachtas freepost envelopes that I used fully in the lead-in to the general election.

The Dáil and Seanad were convened at the beginning of September 1976, before the normal autumn return, in order to deal with some items of constitutional importance. A declaration of emergency, made by the Oireachtas at the outbreak of the Second

World War, enabled successful governments to suspend, in the interests of the security of the state, certain provisions of the Constitution. The IRA murder in July of Sir Christopher Ewart-Biggs, the new British Ambassador as he left his official residence in Sandyford was a major challenge to the authority of the government. In the light of this murder, developments in Northern Ireland and a perceived threat to the state which these constituted, the government introduced a new declaration of emergency under the Emergency Powers Bill. This was considered legally necessary before the Oireachtas could pass new security legislation. Many of my constituents and my political activists were aghast.

A great political argument arose for and against the need for the legislation. I was uneasy but initially kept my opinion to myself, even though I was doubtful that the set of measures proposed or the procedure outlined was necessary. However, many around me were more unhappy and unconstrained. I had no choice, they argued passionately. I could not, as a Labour senator, vote for this set of measures. They had worked long and hard with me in Dublin South-East. We could not deny that journey its political success, but neither could we betray it.

What was I to do? Abstain was the proffered advice. Do not take a position by taking a non-position. It sounded easy and looked straightforward. What did it matter? Who would really care? A majority was assured anyway and the government would carry the day. Yes, but not with my vote, or indeed without my vote, because I would not be casting it either way. I told my constituency council that I could not abstain. Whatever I did, I could not abstain. That would be a denial, a betrayal of a different kind. Why go to all the lengths of political struggle, as we had done together since 1973 and indeed before, to make it into Leinster House, where my very first political act would be not to act at all. 'No,' I replied, I would vote with the government, albeit with a heavy heart. My only other choice was to go back to Brendan Corish and return the Senate seat which he had entrusted to me on behalf of the Labour Party. If I could not use it decisively, then I should not use it at all.

They were hard times. At the end of that evening in Newman House, a number of people, keen and loyal party activists and personal friends, took their leave. While some probably voted for me in subsequent elections, they never again were active within our local party organisation. I deeply regretted their departure, but remained convinced that my difficult decision had been correct. The subsequent action of President Cearbhall Ó Dálaigh to resign because of the failure of Paddy Donegan, the Minister for Defence, to step down after he publicly insulted the office of president for referring the emergency legislation to the Supreme Court, compounded the real sense of political disquiet and menace that the special September session had engendered.

I was now a member of the Parliamentary Labour Party as well as a novice senator, late in a parliamentary session that would soon end. While I had heard about the tensions within the Parliamentary Labour Party, I could not have imagined the level of disunity and lack of cohesion that I experienced at my first meeting.

Room 114 in Leinster House is a long narrow space, set at right angles to the landing at the top of the processional flight of stairs, which leads from the ground floor up to the main ceremonial entrance into the Dáil chamber. Its very narrowness thrusts people on either side of the table close to each other. If the humour of the meeting is sour or sullen, there is no place to conceal it. I sat there, in anticipation, observing at first hand people who were now colleagues but who previously had been somewhat remote and senior figures in the party. I experienced that sense of slight disappointment which proximity and familiarity with famous names and personalities can sometimes bring. Stevie Coughlan, the father of my good friend from school and the man who first opened the doors of Leinster House to me in 1964 as I made my way to the visitors' gallery to witness the turnover tax debate, was now directly opposite me. As Justin Keating moved down the three steps to the level of the meeting room floor, Stevie Coughlan began to exclaim. 'There he is, here he comes,' in his raspy Limerick accent. 'The minister for prices, the minister for prices. Sure isn't it good of you to visit us at all at all.'

I was horrified, but I made no show of it. Justin's disdain and Stevie's angry rant cancelled each other out. The business of the meeting was dealt with and, when it was over, everyone concentrated on what was ahead, the general election.

Chapter 9

Victory and Defeat
1977–1981

As I came out of the Carlton cinema, the sunlight of the June afternoon contrasted strongly with the dark and almost empty auditorium. My eyes took time to adjust, but soon jumped into focus when I saw the *Evening Press* headline: 'Ministers gone, others to follow.' I stopped at the top of O'Connell Street, looking in amazement at the newspaper's front page. Justin Keating and Conor Cruise O'Brien had lost their seats. It was 17 June 1977 and the general election count was well underway.

The campaign duration was twenty-two days. My team and I had, in anticipation of a summer election, prepared material in advance. From the previous Christmas, we had been planning the campaign. While I took an intense interest in these matters, I was blessed in having Caroline Hussey as director of elections, leading a strong team of activists. Caroline had become involved with the Dublin South-East Labour Party during the 1974 local election campaign and was no stranger to the world of politics. In fact, she was tough, particularly with her candidate. In addition, she was ably complemented by Denise Rogers, who was still working in UCD, when not working voluntarily for myself.

On the evening of 25 May, we were knocking on the doors in the compact streets of South Lotts. Many who opened them were taken aback because they were not aware that an election had been called. In the run-up to the general election, we had canvassed and leafleted the constituency intensively – but received a mixed reaction. The recession, caused by the 1973 oil crisis, had created considerable un-employment. The fallout for the Labour Party following the enforced resignation of Cearbhall Ó Dálaigh and the stubbornness of Paddy

Donegan and Liam Cosgrave had been destructive. On top of that, the anti-coalition forces within the party had not gone away. Urged on by supporters such as David Neligan and Mattie Merrigan, Noël Browne was encouraged to look for a nomination to run as a Labour candidate in Dublin Artane, a new three-seater with no incumbent Labour deputy. Head Office had intended that Labour's candidate would be Cllr Paddy Dunne, the former Lord Mayor. The organisation in the new constituency was divided, however, and Browne won the nomination. Nonetheless, the party leadership refused to ratify his candidacy. The administrative council ruled that members of the Houses of the Oireachtas, who were not members of the parliamentary party, could not be accepted as party candidates. Browne could have easily moved to avert this situation, but chose not to. Instead, he stood as an Independent in Dublin Artane and, after his election, was helped by others to establish the Socialist Labour Party.

The early months of 1977 had not been easy. Richie Ryan's final budget was a good one, providing a positive fiscal stimulus to an economy that was slowly recovering from the oil shock recession of the previous few years. But the lag in public perception of the improving economic circumstances was made worse by media commentators and a wickedly funny television satirical programme, *Hall's Pictorial Weekly*.

While a member of the Senate, I had concentrated on winning the Dáil seat for which I had been nominated by Brendan Corish. Shortly before the general election campaign began, I managed to secure a commitment in the government manifesto for the establishment of a Dublin Transportation Authority. That experience gave me an insight into the way the government leadership was approaching the campaign. It did not inspire confidence in me: little strategic preparation had been done. There were also hotspots of trouble. The keen hand of Brendan Halligan was now focused on the constituency of Dublin Finglas, to which he had returned, as he said he would. There were bitter words within the party about his role in the administrative council's thwarting the ratification of Noël Browne for Artane, and this led to Mattie Merrigan standing against him in Dublin Finglas.

Fianna Fáil, in opposition for over four years, had had plenty of time to prepare. Despite the tensions between Charles Haughey and Jack Lynch, which ultimately saw Haughey invited back onto the frontbench by a politically enfeebled Lynch, their head-office team had prepared well. Soon after 1973, Lynch appointed Seamus Brennan as the new, young general secretary. Frank Dunlop became the energetic press officer and Esmonde Smyth was given the responsibility for policy formation to run the campaign. Martin O'Donoghue, an economist and adviser to Jack Lynch between 1970 and 1973 in the Department of the Taoiseach, also played a key role. Now back in Trinity as Dean of the Economic and Social Science faculty, O'Donoghue was a major figure in devising the economic section of the Fianna Fáil manifesto. Partially published in the autumn of 1976, when many people felt that the economy needed a major stimulus, it was repackaged and its priorities reversed when it was launched in late May 1977.

In essence, O'Donoghue proposed that if the government could persuade workers to accept wage moderation, then the resulting savings, combined with an increase in the level of borrowing, would enable a new government to cut taxes dramatically. However feasible such a course of action might have been, the strategic planners within Fianna Fáil – including George Colley, Des O'Malley, Seamus Brennan and Martin O'Donoghue – effectively put the cart before the horse when they wrote the manifesto. All the 'goodies' – the abolition of domestic rates, the removal of car tax and an enormous hike in the first-time house buyers' grant to the colossal sum of £1,000 – and no requirement to adhere to the wage restraint on which it was predicated was the incredible offer made by Fianna Fáil, desperately hungry to return to office. The voters, at first publicly sceptical when I met them whilst canvassing, quietly did their sums. This Fianna Fáil offer was one they could not refuse and wasn't it being made by two honest men – Jack Lynch and George Colley? It seems incredible that two former ministers for Finance actually went along with the economics of the manifesto. The country subsequently took more than ten years of painful adjustment to try to recover from the negative impact which it caused.

Since late 1975, the bi-monthly Irish Marketing Survey's opinion polls indicated that Fianna Fáil would get an overall majority in the next election anyway. It is hard to believe now but the coalition government, in deciding to call an election for June 1977, only commissioned a poll after the announcement. The results were discouraging.

Standing outside the Ringsend polling station on Cambridge Road on the evening of 16 June 1977, Garret FitzGerald spoke briefly to me as we canvassed the voters. He mentioned that the polling data was very bad. I did not fully realise the implications of this. Opinion polls and market research were not then part of the basic equipment of electioneering in Ireland. Many learned and most well-informed commentators had dismissed the few polls that were published. Besides, this was the first time that such data were available and the media did not trust the results.

Caroline Hussey, Denise Rogers and the Dublin South-East crew, including Ciarán O'Mara, an undergraduate law student, ran a good campaign. Our headquarters was the old national school on Beaver Row, Donnybrook, which was a great location with plenty of space. The secondary school year was over, the exams were on and we had many young people in and out looking for things to do and anxious to be involved. The Lacey family lived close by and Dermot Lacey, a Leaving Certificate student, cut his teeth in that election. Dermot, who has held a number of positions in the Labour Party, is now an elected councillor for the Pembroke ward and served as an excellent Lord Mayor of Dublin in 2002.

The bright sunshine that Friday afternoon seemed incongruous with the dark news of electoral defeat. I walked distractedly across O'Connell Street to Cathal Brugha Street, where I had parked. The car radio made it plain that things were black. Many reporters in the count centres were predicting a major victory for Fianna Fáil. My mind was racing. If the big names on our side had fallen, what about the rest of us? I headed towards the count centre on Bolton Street.

In those days, before mobile phones and the absence of instant hard information, there were long periods of time during which the imaginative political mind could torture itself. At the door of the room where our count was taking place, I was greeted by smiling faces and a happy director of elections. Caroline Hussey, clipboard in hand, gave me a great hug. It was looking good! She had checked tallies and analysed previous results. The electoral field in Dublin South-East, with eight candidates for three seats, was tight. Ciarán O'Mara, a small transistor radio held to his ear, told me excitedly that John Horgan was going to be elected in the then Dublin South County constituency. Nuala Fennell, an Independent, was being eliminated and a huge transfer was underway to Horgan. Surrounded by exuberant people, I did a short television interview alongside Frank Cluskey. In response to a number of questions about the implications of the results that were now flooding in, I replied that I did not know since I had just come from the pictures and all I could say was that the good guys had lost there as well.

But I had won a Dáil seat and the implications of the bigger picture could not suppress my delight and the joy of the Labour South-East team.

Finally, when the dust had settled, Fianna Fáil had an unprecedented overall majority of twenty-two seats. The 'Real Taoiseach', as Jack Lynch had been referred to by many of his admirers, murmured, in response to Brian Farrell on television, that maybe a majority of twenty-two was too big.

The Fianna Fáil Dáil majority was larger than Labour's parliamentary party. Seventeen deputies had been elected, including Seán Treacy, who, as the outgoing Ceann Comhairle, was returned automatically. He remained outside the parliamentary party between the completion of the count and 5 July when the newly elected Twenty-First Dáil met, which was also the last few weeks of the outgoing coalition government. Brendan Corish announced his resignation as party leader and a meeting of the sixteen members of the parliamentary party was called to elect his successor.

Two candidates declared for the leadership: Frank Cluskey and

Michael O'Leary. I was close to both, but for different reasons. I had cut my political teeth in O'Leary's successful campaign during the 1965 election. Cluskey I had got to know and respect from his work as Junior Minister for Social Welfare. The years between 1973 and 1977 saw tension, probably based on political competition, between Cluskey and O'Leary, which was intensified because of the requirement to work at European level – a new experience for the Irish political system. Both departments, quite separate at national level, worked through the one Social Affairs Council and the one European Commissioner, Paddy Hillery. O'Leary, as Minister for Labour, was clearly the senior and was immensely influential in transposing progressive EEC measures into Irish law. However, Cluskey, representing the Tánaiste and leader of the Labour Party, had overseen a substantial improvement and expansion in the social-welfare system.

Late one evening after the 1977 election, Tony Brown, who was in Luxembourg attending a Social Affairs Council meeting, phoned me to see if I would take a call from Frank Cluskey. I said I would. Some minutes later the phone rang and Frank's gruff voice was at the other end, asking for my support in the leadership contest, I told him he had my support. It was not an easy choice. I had decided not only to vote for Frank but to openly support him. In my opinion he was the steadier of the two, although not as politically charismatic as O'Leary. When I told Michael O'Leary of my decision, he was naturally disappointed. His response, not bitter, was prophetic: he said that I depended on a lot of middle-class support in Dublin South-East and that Garret FitzGerald, the newly elected leader of Fine Gael, was going to seriously affect that support base if Frank became the new leader of the Labour Party.

The parliamentary party meeting was opened, and the business tersely conducted. The result of the secret ballot was 8:8. What to do now? Corish's resignation, before the convening of the Twenty-First Dáil, had effectively excluded Seán Treacy from our ranks. Was that a deliberate choice on his part? Would Treacy have voted for Michael? On balance I thought he would, but that was just a hunch. After a few moments of general discussion, I suggested to the chairman, Joe Bermingham, that we should vote again. He asked what the point was because we would get the same result. 'Not necessarily,' I replied. 'Just try it – it may resolve our problem and we've nothing to lose.' A new ballot was called and the result announced. This time it was 9:7 in favour of Cluskey. O'Leary was unanimously elected deputy leader and the meeting ended. I never found out who changed their vote.

When the Dáil resumed business in October after the summer recess, the full parliamentary party contained Seán Treacy and Mick Lipper, who as an Independent Labour candidate, had defeated Stevie Coughlan in Limerick East. His subsequent application to join the parliamentary party had been accepted without difficulty. Seven senators – Jack Harte, Justin Keating, Mary Robinson, Fintan Kennedy, Conor Cruise O'Brien, Tim McAuliffe and Michael Moynihan – brought our ranks to twenty-five. Within a short time the Cruiser left the parliamentary party, but not the Seanad, because he had clashed with Frank Cluskey over policy on the North. Frank's assertion that he, and he alone, would speak on that controversial issue was not acceptable to Conor. It soon emerged that Justin had recurring health problems and sadly, from my point of view, he slowly disengaged from active involvement, choosing not to stand in the next general election.

Jack Lynch's new administration began with a great flurry of activity. George Colley immediately proceeded to implement the financial provisions of the Fianna Fáil manifesto and Martin O'Donoghue, now Minister for Economic Planning and Development, worked closely with him. O'Donoghue was amongst that rare breed, one of three in fifty-three years, of newly elected deputies to be made a cabinet minister on his first day in the Dáil – Noël Browne and Kevin Boland being the others. However, O'Donoghue never fully made the transition from economic adviser to party politician. This was particularly evident during Question Time, when his replies were open and discursive, giving many hostages to fortune, rather than the tight, guarded replies that a seasoned politician would have offered.

Brendan Corish, much more relaxed having relinquished the

leadership after seventeen years, was now an elder statesman within the party. Early in the autumn, I asked him what advice he had for a new deputy like me trying to acquire the skills of a parliamentarian. He told me to attend the hour-long sessions of parliamentary questions, when ministers give oral responses to questions and the follow-up supplementaries. Furthermore, Corish advised me to attend the opening of each session, the order of business, which would set out the work to be done by the Dáil that day. It was good advice, and I followed it rigorously.

My electoral success meant that I had to change the way I did my architectural work. After the August holidays, I sat down with Paul and Des to work out a new relationship with the practice, because as a deputy I would be busier than a senator or a councillor. I had already decided to resign my seat on the City Council because I did not believe in the dual mandate. This I did in the autumn of 1977 and Mary Freehill, who had polled well as my running mate in the general election, was co-opted. I became, in effect, the office manager at BKD, with responsibility for finance, personnel matters and servicing the monthly partners' meetings. It relieved the two senior partners of much administrative work and fee-gathering, and I continued to generate some work. These new arrangements enabled me to stay involved in the architectural practice in Hatch Street and continue my teaching engagements with the School of Architecture in UCD.

As regards Denise Rogers, I asked her to give up her permanent and pensionable job in UCD and to work full-time with me at Leinster House. Room 120 in the 1932 extension of Leinster House was located to the side of the main complex, adjacent to the National History Museum and what is known as the Fisheries Yard. I shared this room with John Horgan, who agreed to allow Denise to work in the room with us. The usual provision of secretarial assistance to deputies was based on a pool system – one clerical typist to every ten deputies – and there was always a substantial amount of work waiting to be typed. Denise's arrival in Leinster House led to some minor problems, inconceivable in the context of the level of support that deputies now have. For example, where would you find a plug for an IBM electric 'golfball' typewriter in a building that had manual-only typewriters?

Former Minister for Local Government, Jimmy Tully, decided that he did not want the responsibilities of a frontbench job and I was appointed spokesperson for the Environment (the Department of Local Government had been renamed the Department of Environment). I threw myself into the work. I was a new deputy, the fifth youngest of that election's intake and the youngest, by some years, of the Labour deputies.

Learning to operate effectively in a national parliament is daunting. There are rules, procedures and formal meetings. There are also groups, allegiances, friends and opponents. However, not all the rules are written down, the procedures are often evolving and the set encounters are frequently disappointing when compared to the chance flashes that spill over into real argument and sharp political conflict. While the formal party allegiances are a fair guide, learning to distinguish between your opponents and your enemies, and keeping sight of your friends, requires both a measure of time and attention which at least in the initial stages is all-absorbing.

After many years of yearning, this was where I now found myself. The sheer exhilaration of being a part of the place, of being able to enter the Dáil chamber, take a seat, listen to or even ask a minister a question, remains to this very day part of the pull of politics. But in the initial stages, it was more than tempered by a lack of certainty about the procedures and a sense of intellectual intimidation when confronted with the printed text of a piece of draft legislation. My experience of moving from primary school into secondary school or from there to university was such that, even though I was standing on the bottom ladder in the lowest year, the final-year students were only a few steps ahead of me. I knew, instinctively, notwithstanding my inner terror, that fairly soon I would have the swagger of the middle years and in a relatively short time the gravitas of the sixth-year students. This helped me face the immediate tasks that lay ahead.

But Leinster House contained politicians nearly twice my age;

men – nearly all men – many of whom had been there for decades. Some had ministerial experience during times with which my only connection was through the pages of history books. How could these gaps of experience be closed? When would I have the ability, never mind the confidence, to make a casual but authoritative intervention in the middle of a complex legislative debate? Such inner doubts could never be publicly disclosed. In time, I made the passage to journeyman status, but looking back now, thirty years after having first sat in the chamber of an elected assembly, the sense of intimidation remains stronger in my memory than the process of learning, which self-evidently I must have gone through.

The first eighteen months of that government appeared to me to be going well for Fianna Fáil and the public. Jack Lynch was a hard man to confront or argue with. Not unlike one of his successors, Bertie Ahern, he would reluctantly dispute with you and give out a kind of muffled sigh, suggesting that we should not even bother to disagree. But we all knew from his previous period in government that he was a man of steely nerve when he had to be. He was also a man of great courtesy and kindness, particularly to new deputies, and, some days after he had been elected Taoiseach in 1977, I had direct experience of this.

He was coming along the corridor in Leinster House which runs from the main ceremonial steps to the Dáil chamber, which he had just left. On either side of him walked two or three officials, one of them talking earnestly to him, as they headed towards the main hall. As the group approached, taking up most of the width of the corridor, I stood into a side passage to let them pass. Jack caught my eye, smiled, stopped the group and came over to me. He shook my hand, congratulated me on my election and wished me well, before resuming his journey, entourage back in tow. I was naturally delighted, pleased to be so publicly acknowledged, but also conscious of how very political his action had been.

The considerable coverage of the proceedings of the Dáil in the printed media depended on commentators like John Healy in *The Irish Times*, Michael Mills in *The Irish Press* and Chris Glennon in the *Irish Independent* to give the colour and record the tone of the political debate. The arrival of radio and television, which would not be for at least another ten years, totally changed the way Dáil business was reported. Garret FitzGerald's new dynamic leadership of Fine Gael was seldom seen in Leinster House since he was frequently absent for normal Dáil sessions. In contrast, Frank Cluskey was hardly anywhere else and he developed a sharp incisive parliamentary style that was initially to ruffle Jack Lynch and ultimately to get under the skin of Charles Haughey.

I applied myself diligently to the work of the Dáil chamber. I was not alone. Barry Desmond, our party whip, had an immense knowledge of a wide range of political issues. He was assiduous, to the point of obsessiveness, about taking cuttings, filing documents, storing papers and keeping notes on nearly every political topic of the day. He would frequently come and ask either John Horgan or myself if we would go down to the chamber and make a contribution. Since I had been a member of the Seanad for the previous year and had spoken on a number of occasions, I was familiar with the way Leinster House worked. In the beginning, the part I found hardest in the Dáil was asking supplementary oral questions to senior ministers during Question Time.

Soon I learned a lot about the making of law. The most comprehensive way in which to do this as an opposition spokesperson was to debate a bill with the sponsoring minister from the beginning of the second stage right through to the committee and report stages and to its conclusion or fifth stage. When I was learning my trade, I made an effort to get in touch with individuals or groups whom I thought would have an interest or expertise in the subject covered by the bill. Sometimes they would contact me. Without the help of researchers, I developed a brief and formulated a view in keeping with what I understood to be party policy and apply it as my critique of the bill at second-stage debate. Most pieces of legislation have an explanatory memorandum published with them. This sets out the purpose of the bill and explains, section by section, how the proposed law will work. The second stage is a debate in principle on the subject matter of the bill. The committee and fourth, or report, stages go through the text, line by line, making amendments, if accepted or if considered necessary.

Back in 1977, both from personal interest and at the insistence of the aforementioned Barry Desmond, John Horgan and I spent a good deal of time in the Dáil chamber on legislation. Some of our older and wiser colleagues observed cynically that they had seen many deputies who had talked themselves out of Leinster House.

There are other aspects to the range of parliamentary and political skills a young deputy has to acquire. Early in 1978, I found myself in the lobby of a hotel on Rue Charlemagne, close to the Berlaymont Building, headquarters of the European Commission in Brussels. This was my first time there as part of a group from the Oireachtas European Community (EC) legislation scrutiny committee, whose task was to review and scrutinise EC draft legislation. Seated opposite me, that early morning in the hotel foyer, was Oliver J. Flanagan, a legendary figure, first elected to the Dáil in 1943, three years before I was born! He had been Minister for Defence in the last year of the Cosgrave–Corish government and was an old-style conservative Fine Gael politician. We were waiting for the rest of our delegation. I looked at Oliver J. as he lit his pipe.

'Would you mind if I asked you a question?' I enquired.

'Ask away,' was his response.

'You have been in politics a long time, in opposition and as a minister in two governments.' He nodded to me, drawing on his pipe. 'How do you manage the transition from power to opposition, from being a minister to becoming the deputy again, out of government? Does it not reduce your appeal within the constituency and undermine your political support.'

'It can,' he replied, 'but, then again, you can put that to advantage as well.'

'Well,' I said, 'I am a new deputy, serving my apprenticeship.'

He paused and then began to speak. 'A woman came into my clinic in Mountmellick some months ago, seeking help for her son, the youngest of six. I knew her and the family well. The young fellow was not that bright and she wanted not only to get him into the Garda Síochána, but to have him made a sergeant after a couple of years. I said to her that it was a terrible pity that she had not come to see me when I was a minister. Then I might have been able to do something for her, but now that many of her family had voted for the "other crowd", there was nothing I could do. She claimed that she had always voted for me. I said that I knew, but many of her family had voted for Fianna Fáil the last time and she would have to go and see Paddy Lalor, the senior Fianna Fáil man in the constituency, and the government chief whip. "But I don't even know him," she said, "and he is away down in Abbeyleix." "But he will certainly know your family. Well sure, go down to him and tell him what you want; after all, your side put him in." "What will he say if I ask him?" she said. "Well," I replied, "he will probably tell you that what you are looking for is impossible." "And is it, Oliver?" she asked. "You know, Mary, before I was a minister, I used to think that it was. But go down and ask him yourself. Come back then and let me know how you get on."'

Oliver smoked his pipe and smiled at me. 'She was back to me the following week. "Oliver, you were dead right. He said that he couldn't do it, but I knew that he was not even going to try, after all the votes he got. Well that's that. I've told them all at home: from now on, we'll stick with you."'

'Did you really know what way they had voted?'

'No,' he said, 'but I had a suspicion and her response confirmed it. As far as she was concerned, Fianna Fáil had seriously let them down.'

The first direct elections to the European Parliament were due to take place in June 1979. The government decided to hold the local elections on the same day. I was not a candidate and so became director of elections for the European and local elections for Dublin city and county. We had three candidates for the four-seater Dublin European constituency: Jane Dillon-Byrne, a prominent councillor in Dún Laoghaire, Dr John O'Connell and Michael O'Leary. O'Leary had not taken his defeat in the leadership election well. As deputy leader, he had played little or no role in the party, largely because Cluskey had excluded him from the leadership circle. He was the Labour Party spokesperson on Finance but became increasingly disengaged from the politics of Leinster House. John O'Connell was also semi-

My parents' wedding, 14 April 1936.
Uncle Kevin is seated beside my mother. Uncle Eamon, father of Senator Feargal Quinn, is in the top-right corner and my grandfather, John Quinn, is standing to the left of my father.

l-r: Declan, Father, Lochlann, Mother, Colm, myself, Moninne and Conor at 23 Sydney Parade, 1955.

The 1964 SCT final, Rock v. Terenure, played in Lansdowne Road.
I am at the end of the line with David Cantrell and Brian McLoughlin in front of me.
Liam Hall, our scrum-half, scored the only try of the match.

Combining sport and art in
Blackrock College.

My landscape won first prize in the Caltex
(now Texaco) Art Competition and I won
the Victor Ludorum trophy in the school
sports, 1963.

Waiting for the start of a mass meeting held in the Great Hall, UCD.
It was organised by Students for Democratic Action. I am in the centre with
Una Claffey to my left, 1968.

Addressing the meeting.

Detailing Labour Party policy at a press conference during the 1981 general election.

With Dick Spring

left: at Áras an Uachtaráin when I became Minister for Labour, December 1983.

below: discussing policy in the Merrion Street Lawns, 1996.

CLÁR GNÓTHA

Dáta an Chruinnithe	Am	Áit	
Dé Máirt, 13 Nollaig, 1983.	9.30a.m.	Seomra Comhairle	

ON AIRE SAOTHAIR

Ábhar	Aire	Scríbhinní Ábhartha
MINUTES OF LAST MEETING.		
1. BUDGET TRENDS: Seventh Report.	Airgeadais	Memorandum dated 8/12/83.

The *clár*, or agenda, of my first cabinet meeting, 13 December 1983.

As can be seen from the *clár* above, the budget difficulties were top of the agenda.
My cartoons caught the mood of my colleagues.

The New York Times

NEW YORK, WEDNESDAY, JANUARY 21, 1987

Dick Spring, right foreground, in Dublin yesterday after resigning as Deputy Prime Minister of Ireland.

I was surprised that we made the front page of *The New York Times* after we resigned in protest at the massive public-spending cuts. The photograph was taken on the steps of Government Buildings.
l-r: Liam Kavanagh, myself, Dick Spring, Barry Desmond.

OIFIG AIRE NA SEIRBHÍSE POIBLÍ
(Office of the Minister for the Public Service)
BAILE ÁTHA CLIATH 2
(Dublin 2)

20 January '87

Dear Taoiseach

I wish formally to tender my resignation as Minister for Labour and Minister for the Public Service with effect from today.

I wish to thank you for your courtesy during my period of service in Government.

yours sincerely

Ruairi Quinn TD

GARRET FITZGERALD

TO WHOM IT MAY CONCERN.

I have known RUAIRI QUINN for several years and have a high regard for his abilities. In University College, Dublin, a difficult period in the College he showed considerable leadership and a strong sense of social commitment. He has an exceptionally alert and lively mind. In U.C.D. he combined an outstanding academic record with extensive involvement student activities and also travelled very widely during holiday periods.

I would expect him to play an important role in this country in the decades ahead and I know he is committed to making contribution to the future of this country.

Garret FitzGerald, T.D.

Little did either of us think when Garret wrote a reference for me back in 1969 that, eighteen years later, I would be resigning from his government detached and became more and more alienated from Cluskey. To make matters worse, it was anticipated that both Cluskey and O'Connell would be sharing the same constituency when the new Electoral Boundary Commission made its report.

So two powerful personalities within the parliamentary party, both disaffected with the leadership, had decided to run for Europe. Head office was not disappointed because this was a strong team for Dublin. Elsewhere, Eileen Desmond in Munster, Liam Kavanagh in Leinster and Michael D. Higgins in Connacht–Ulster completed Labour's team of candidates. A striking black and white poster of the six of them was produced for the campaign with the slogan 'Labour is giving its best for Europe'. The response was magnificent. We won four seats, two in Dublin and one each in Munster and Leinster. I was congratulated on my role in Dublin, but I knew it was the strength of O'Connell and O'Leary which had triumphed.

What did worry me, however, was the attitude of Frank Cluskey towards the relatively poor results for Labour in the local elections, both in Dublin and throughout the country. While voting for both elections had taken place on 7 June 1979, the count for the European elections had to be deferred until the following Sunday, so results across the whole of the European Community could be announced at the same time. Frank's response to my concern about a relatively poor showing in the local elections was that when the good results, which he anticipated from the European Parliament, were announced on the Sunday, the setback would be forgotten.

While he was right in the short term, he failed to realise the full significance of the major gains made by Fine Gael at local level. In an election post-mortem radio programme, Peter Prendergast, the Fine Gael general secretary, congratulated me on our European performance. As he did, he remarked how Fine Gael had succeeded in bringing forward a new generation of bright young candidates. Two years later many of them would sweep into Dáil Éireann, giving Garret FitzGerald the second largest representation the Fine Gael Parliamentary Party had ever had.

In 1979, the big losers were Fianna Fáil and Jack Lynch. The majority of twenty-two backbenchers now looked nervously at their security of tenure. A tired Taoiseach did not appear like the leader who could return them safely to the Dáil. Charlie Haughey did; and so the plotting began. The emotionalism of Irish national- ism, forever the political mortar that binds together the uneven components that make up Fianna Fáil, was the faultline which was used to weaken Jack Lynch's leadership. Síle de Valera and Tom McEllistrim allowed themselves to be the vehicles of dissent, ex- pressing righteous nationalist concern about overflights of the national airspace along the Border by British army helicopters. By implication, Lynch's government was conniving at this heavy- handed military security by way of explicit acquiescence, or alter- natively was failing to assert Ireland's sovereignty pending the reintegration of the national territory!

The autumn skies darkened politically. Two by-elections, in ad- joining constituencies, caused by the death of Labour's Pat Kerrigan in Cork City and Fianna Fáil's Seán Brosnan in Cork North-East, were held on 7 November. Fianna Fáil lost both seats, a disaster for Jack Lynch. His home city had let him down and the final heave against him was now mounted. By December 1979, weeks before Ireland completed its second presidency of the EC, Lynch resigned and was no longer Taoiseach.

The ascent of Haughey to the leadership of Fianna Fáil and the office of Taoiseach was watched with fear and awe by many within Leinster House. The entire nation followed the public drama. Some events stand out to this day, particularly the eleventh hour political desertion by Michael O'Kennedy of the Fianna Fáil/ Lynch loyalist ranks, within which he had been such a beneficiary. O'Kennedy's public reward, a year later, of nomination as Ireland's European Commissioner to succeed Dick Burke, was to end ignominiously in a retreat to the constituency of Tipperary North. Liam Lawlor, who had been at Haughey's side during the years of political exile, supported Lynch's candidate, George Colley, who lost the leadership by twenty-two votes. From the sidelines, the spectacle of the pursuit of power between the Haughey and the Colley camps affected everyone in Leinster House. The intensity of the contest spilled out into the corridors and touched us all – visitors, staff and even non-combatants in the opposition parties.

The new Haughey cabinet contained some surprises: Albert Reynolds became Minister for Posts and Telegraphs and Minister for Transport. More surprising, as much for its brutality as for its decisiveness, was the sacking of Bobby Molloy from Defence. Martin O'Donoghue not only lost his cabinet job, but his new Department of Economic Planning and Development was abolished. George Colley remained as Tánaiste, but was shunted to Energy to make room for Michael O'Kennedy in Finance, before his departure to Brussels when he was succeeded by Gene Fitzgerald. Seán Doherty became Minister of State at Justice, though Gerry Collins remained as Minister for Justice until 1982 when Doherty took over. Fianna Fáil was now badly split. George Colley made a public declaration of conditional support to Charles Haughey as the new Taoiseach. It was seen by all as a sign of weakness that Haughey did not have the strength or courage to sack Colley for such a display of disloyalty.

On the evening of Haughey's election as Taoiseach in December 1979, I was in the chamber to hear Garret FitzGerald's famous speech, denouncing Haughey and referring to his 'flawed pedigree'. Many people, including myself, thought he had gone too far and that there was an element of class snobbishness about his words. But later revelations have undoubtedly endorsed the judgement, if not the rhetoric, of Garret's words. Cluskey was equally condemnatory. When I expressed some reservations about the personal nature of both his and Garret's contributions, he said vigorously. 'It would be a bad day for this country if we in the Dáil had to be easy on C.J. Haughey.'

Later that evening, I listened to the contribution of Noël Browne, who as an Independent had been called to speak long after the debate had started. Sitting in the chamber, I looked across at the impassive face of Haughey, who had sat in the chamber, Taoiseach-designate, throughout the entire debate. Some seventeen years previously, Alsatian dogs under the control of the Garda Síochána, answerable to Haughey as Minister for Justice, had attacked Noël

Browne and other demonstrators outside the American embassy during a protest march against the United States treatment of Cuba. Browne spoke quietly, but with some vehemence, in his opposition to Haughey's election as Taoiseach. There were only three people in Irish public life who ever really scared him, he said, and Haughey was one. When asked openly by me in the chamber, to name the other two, he mentioned Gerard Sweetman, the late Fine Gael Minister for Finance in the Inter-Party Government of 1954–57. He could not remember the third person. Later, in the corridor, he told me that Seán MacBride was the third person. Six years after the 1973 general election, Noël and I were again on civil talking terms, but only just.

One of the indications of Haughey's determined rise to challenge Lynch had taken place in the Dáil the previous October soon after the House resumed after its summer recess. The British satirical magazine *Private Eye* – commenting on the growing political storm in Ireland – made reference to Haughey's affair with the journalist Terry Keane, a subject that received no media coverage in Ireland while being widely known at the same time. In a memorable phrase, *Private Eye* referred to the activity of 'horizontal jogging', much to the amusement of people in the know.

In October 1977 during the first days back in the Dáil, Jack Lynch was asked by Labour's John Ryan during Taoiseach's Question Time if he proposed to appoint a Minister of State to the departments of Health and Social Welfare. Lynch replied that he did not. Ryan responded by pointing out that every other department had a junior minister and surely the workload in these two large departments required at least another pair of political hands. On Brendan Corish's advice, I was in the chamber, sitting beside Frank Cluskey. Across from us, on the government side, Jack Lynch was alone on the ministerial frontbench, except for the presence of C.J. Haughey, who was both Minister for Health and Minster for Social Welfare. There were quite a few Fianna Fáil backbenchers present and they all sniggered loudly when, in response to a third question from John Ryan, a reclining C.J. pre-empted the Taoiseach and replied, 'The reason why we are not appointing a minister of state is because the last one was such a disaster.'

I watched Cluskey's face respond to this calculated insult, which was accompanied by the echo of laughter around the chamber. He showed no reaction.

Haughey now rose, closing over his suit jacket and buttoning it deliberately in a characteristic mannerism, and moved slowly along the frontbench. He was halfway up the middle stairway on the government side of the chamber when John O'Connell pressed Lynch on Ryan's parliamentary question.

'Was the Taoiseach not aware,' he hurriedly asked, 'that there was now so much pressure upon the minister's office that letters were coming out of it and they were not even signed?'

'Very hard to sign letters when you're jogging,' said Frank Cluskey loudly to a chamber that suddenly stopped sniggering and instead awaited a response from Haughey, who had paused on the stairs. His steely eyes closed slightly as he looked down towards Frank, who had barely moved, but whose face was now returning Haughey's glare. Both Dubliners, they knew each other well and disliked each other even more.

'You don't half pull punches,' Haughey hissed.

'And aren't you lucky I don't ask supplementaries?' Cluskey retorted.

The relief of laughter was felt everywhere as Haughey smiled weakly and continued his measured exit from the chamber. Frank allowed himself a perceptible grin and Question Time continued.

The following day, still chuckling to myself about the exchange, I sought out the official draft record of the previous day's debates to see how the stenographers had officially recorded the event. Sadly, but not surprisingly, the printed text carried the Taoiseach's replies and reference to various interruptions, but no more. Today's live television record would be different.

In the early months of 1980, after the new Taoiseach, Charles J. Haughey had famously addressed the nation on television about how we were all 'living beyond our means', the mood and atmosphere of the Dáil had changed dramatically. The reduction in business confidence, caused by Fianna Fáil's crazy 1977 economic policies and exacerbated by the second oil shock in 1979, affected the economy. Cluskey turned the order of business session into an ordeal, which Haughey hated because he was forced to answer questions, clearly and audibly, in front of deputies and before the journalists in the press gallery. Haughey, whose natural demeanour was imperious, bristled every so often with tangible anger. Whereas Jack Lynch had remained gracious with a steely stoicism, Haughey's cruder personality and lust for unchallenged power displayed itself regularly. However he may have dealt with his ministers and public servants in private, he clearly hated being held to public account, particularly by people whom he felt to be personally inferior.

Nevertheless, it was Garret FitzGerald who was to reap the harvest of the parliamentary advantage that Cluskey had done so much to sow. The disquiet with Haughey within Fianna Fáil and its many marginal supporters, who had been attracted by Jack Lynch's perceived honesty and strength, was to flow to Garret and his reinvented Fine Gael. Fianna Fáil soon floundered in the face of public resistance because of the proposed harsh austerity measures promised in Haughey's national television address.

In Britain by 1981, the poor relationship that had already existed between Haughey and Margaret Thatcher was slowly inflamed by the increased tension in Northern Ireland. When the hunger strikes started in the Maze Prison, the Taoiseach was politically cornered and the British prime minister's intransigence compounded his problems. To add human tragedy to political insult, his stage-managed pre-general election Ard Fheis in Dublin's RDS had to be abandoned after its first evening because of the Stardust Ballroom fire disaster in Artane, Haughey's own constituency. Haughey's leader's address, due to be televised that Saturday evening, was cancelled out of respect for the dead and injured. The carefully planned curtain raiser to the 1981 general election had now to be cast aside. A period of political drift created a vacuum, but it would soon be filled. The increasingly critical position of the hunger strikers brought a new dimension to the election that was finally called for 11 June 1981. Two of the strikers, Paddy Agnew and Kieran Doherty, in jail in Northern Ireland, were elected to the Dáil for Louth and Cavan–Monaghan respectively, depriving Fianna Fáil of two critically important seats.

The new boundaries, established in 1980, extended the Dublin South-East constituency into the city centre, and included Labour strongholds around the Iveagh Buildings and Mercer Street. Rathmines, Terenure and Harold's Cross were now part of the enlarged four-seater constituency. I felt that the work of the Labour Party nationally, my own profile locally and an excellent organisation would all help to hold the Labour seat. We had local councillors in all three wards, along with myself as a TD, and a permanent headquarters in a converted shop on Charlemont Street.

The rain on polling day was dismal but soft and all day I had a bad feeling about how things were going. Some days earlier, just before the big televised debate between Garret FitzGerald and C.J. Haughey, Frank Cluskey was interviewed by Brian Farrell on RTÉ. We all gathered in the upstairs room in Charlemont Street to watch the programme on Caroline Hussey's black and white portable television. Frank was hesitant on the issue of coalition. When Brian Farrell asked why someone should vote Labour and not Fine Gael, he stalled and staggered. We all groaned and felt that we had taken a hit. We certainly had. Not only did I lose my seat but so too did John Horgan and Frank Cluskey, and along with that loss went his party leadership on election night.

There were five outgoing deputies contesting four seats in Dublin South-East, and I was the most junior, so I was worried. On the last count of the 1981 general election, I was 767 votes behind Richie Ryan, who was elected to the fourth and final seat. He had started off with 1,722 first preference votes as against my 3,559. Some weeks later, nursing my wounds over a pint in Doheny & Nesbitt's, I asked an old friend, economist Colm McCarthy, to explain how Richie could get over 80,000 votes to be elected to the European Parliament but only manage just over 1,700 first preference votes in a Dáil election.

'Simple,' was his sardonic reply. 'Eighty thousand people wanted Richie to leave domestic politics but only 1,700 wanted him to stay!'

Our collective pain was eased, somewhat, by the success of Michael D. Higgins in Galway West and Mervyn Taylor in Dublin South-West, along with Michael Moynihan in Kerry South, who had been contesting that seat for many elections. Dick Spring succeeded his father Dan in Kerry North and Toddy O'Sullivan consolidated his impressive by-election performance with a solid victory in Cork North-Central. In all, we had won fifteen seats, a net loss of two.

The real victor of the elections, though, was Garret FitzGerald and his revitalised Fine Gael party. He now had sixty-five deputies, an increase of twenty-three; just over one-third of them were newly elected, reflecting the gains made two years earlier at the local elections. Garret was impatient to start negotiations with Labour to put a government together, but Labour had some preliminary business to do, like electing a new leader.

In the end, the decision was fairly straightforward. Michael O'Leary was elected as the new leader days after the election with Jimmy Tully, surprisingly, becoming his deputy. It emerged some days later that he was positioning himself for inclusion in the cabinet.

After five years of being around Leinster House and a member of the parliamentary party, I was now excluded. As an ex-deputy, I had rights of access to the building, but not to the inner circle of parliamentary power. This exclusion was a daily reminder of my defeat, made worse by the commiserations of people who, on meeting me in Leinster House, would shower me with questions like 'How could you have lost?'

I had no coherent reply. Toddy O'Sullivan greeted me warmly on his first day in Leinster House. Throwing his arms around me, he was affectionate, supportive and speechless. 'What can I say?' he offered a few times before moving on to the first meeting of the new parliamentary party.

Many activists took the loss of the Labour seat in Dublin South-East hard. At a constituency council meeting, chaired by Ciarán O'Mara, many delegates expressed a strong anti-coalition mood. They were suspicious of the new leadership of the party.

A programme for government was negotiated between Labour and Fine Gael. On its completion, the Gaiety Theatre was booked for a one-day special Labour delegate conference to take place for a couple of hours on a bright, warm Sunday, 28 June 1981. The Gaiety conference concluded its deliberations late that afternoon, endorsing the leadership's recommendations to enter into government with Fine Gael.

The delegates spilled out onto South King Street. I had not spoken because I was now a candidate for a nomination to run in the Senate elections, which would start immediately after the Dáil met on 30 June, with the count in early August. Given the divided nature of the conference, I did not need to let my views be known until such time as I had secured a clear run for the Senate, thus ensuring my political survival, but I did not feel particularly brave standing outside Sinnott's pub, opposite the Gaiety, with a pint in my hand speaking to some of the delegates. A man, whose face I knew very well but whose name escaped me, came bursting into our company. He was one of Frank Cluskey's loyalists and an active member of the Federated Workers' Union of Ireland (FWUI). 'There you are, Ruairi,' he said. 'How are you?'

'Fine,' I offered in response.

'Ah Jaysus,' he said, 'the party is bolloxed in Dublin, what with Frank, you and John losing your seats.'

'Ah, it's not so bad,' I tried to reassure him.

'What do you mean?'

'Well, Mervyn Taylor has won a new seat in Dublin South-West and both Michael O'Leary and Barry Desmond were re-elected.'

'Will you get out of it, for fuck's sake! Two Cork men and a Jew! Get away,' he said as he moved along the street downcast at the defeat of his hero.

Meanwhile, across in the Mansion House, the Fine Gael Parliamentary Party also approved the programme for government with, it was reported, one dissenting voice, John Kelly's. But government was not necessarily in the bag. The arithmetic was uncertain, since Labour and Fine Gael had eighty seats between them to the seventy-eight seats won by Fianna Fáil. There were eight other elected deputies: six Independents plus Noël Browne, one for the Socialist Labour Party, and Joe Sherlock, newly elected as the first deputy for Sinn Féin The Workers' Party (SFWP).

The uncertainty of the outcome ran up to midday on 30 June. Then it emerged along the Labour corridors that John O'Connell had accepted a proposal from Jimmy Tully and Peter Barry to have his name put forward as Ceann Comhairle. This undoubtedly tilted the balance in the coalition's favour. Haughey was defeated, receiving only one Independent vote, that of Neil Blaney. By contrast, FitzGerald had the support of Fine Gael and Labour, along with that of Jim Kemmy, an Independent socialist, who had been elected for the traditional Labour seat in Limerick East, displacing Mick Lipper in the process. The other Independent deputies, Noël Browne, Seán Dublin Bay Loftus and Joe Sherlock abstained. The two H-Block deputies were on hunger strike in the Maze Prison.

Garret FitzGerald was elected Taoiseach and went to Áras an Uachtaráin. When he returned to the Dáil as Taoiseach, he listed the departments and announced the names of the new cabinet, the new ministers sitting beside him on the government frontbench. There was a debate on the formation of the new government, followed by a vote. That evening, there were great celebrations, even though the visitors' bar was closed because of a fire. Leinster House was packed with jubilant supporters of the new administration and present in their misery were friends and former employees of the defeated office-holders. In the following days, junior ministers were appointed.

Once again Labour was in a coalition government.

The race for nominations for the five Senate panels now commenced. Fortunately, I got a clear run as the sole Labour Party candidate on the Industrial and Commercial panel. I was anxious to get on the road and call individually on every Labour county and borough councillor from Dungarvan to Donegal and from Louth to Listowel; about ninety in all. Notwithstanding their party loyalty, councillors expected, if not demanded, that Seanad candidates should make that visit and ask, face to face, each of the Labour Party councillors for their number one vote. However, I could not get going for a couple of weeks, until the entire nomination process had been completed and the identity of all the candidates was known.

Because of this delay, I found myself betwixt and between my architectural responsibilities in Burke-Kennedy Doyle & Partners and my political aspirations. I had no option but to let Denise Rogers go because I was no longer a deputy. Since there was no facility for her to claim a redundancy payment from 69,149 constituents, who had not given me my job back, she signed on for £45 a week unemployment benefit in Townsend Street! It was not my proudest moment, considering that I had persuaded her to leave the security of UCD.

I was sitting, after lunch in early July 1981, in the small temporary members' bar, having coffee with Frank Cluskey. He was waiting for Michael O'Leary to resign his seat in the European Parliament so that he could get the co-option. This was the procedure whereby a vacancy in the parliament could be simply filled by the affected political party without the necessity of holding a by-election. John Horgan was waiting for John O'Connell to do the same. I sat talking with Frank about the issues of the day, my mind focused on the future but my head still locked into the recent past. 'Why did we lose?' I asked again, though to no one in particular because, at 3.00 p.m. on a Friday, this small uncomfortable bar was empty except for us.

'Ah, son, is it not obvious?' I heard him pronounce. Cigarette lit, Frank sat back and continued, 'All this canvassing is a load of bollox!'

'What did you say?' I asked, not sure that I had heard him correctly.

'I said that all this canvassing is a load of bollox.'

'But sure what else would you do in an election campaign but knock on every door and canvass?'

'Exactly,' he replied, 'and is it any wonder that we lost our seats. Ringing on bells, knocking on doors, interrupting people in the private moments of their personal intimacy.'

'But what else could we do?'

'The counter-canvass,' he replied.

'The what?' I said, asking Frank to explain.

'The counter-canvass would be different. For a start you wouldn't make a meal of it; you would only call on every tenth house or so.'

'And then what?'

'Well, you'd knock on the door and when they opened it, you would stare them straight in the face and say, "Fuck ye!"'

'You can't be serious!'

'Well,' he said, 'I won't guarantee that you'd get a lot of votes but, I can tell you this, son, they'd remember you called!'

Chapter 10

Recovery and a New Life

The summer of 1981 was a disturbing time. I travelled the Seanad trail with no great enthusiasm, but with a determination to survive politically by staying in Leinster House, until the next general election. Then we would all work hard to regain the Dáil seat.

There was some substance to this hope. Garret FitzGerald's first cabinet contained surprises. While there were new anticipated faces, such as Jim Mitchell and John Bruton, Alan Dukes' appointment as Minister for Agriculture on his first day in the Dáil was not expected. Yet it was the omission of some of the Fine Gael heavyweights of the previous Cosgrave–Corish coalition that caused so much comment. Richard Burke, who had just completed a term as Ireland's European Commissioner in Brussels, had been invited to stand with Jim Mitchell and Brian Fleming in the large Dublin West five-seat constituency. He had previously represented Dublin South County and his move to Dublin West was seen as a major risk, but he succeeded in taking the third seat. On the morning of 30 June, I heard him on the radio speculating with the interviewer about which cabinet post he might be offered.

No offer was made to him, or to Tom O'Donnell from Limerick East or to Richie Ryan, the former Minister for Finance, whose exclusion from the cabinet seemed to signal his exit from Dublin South-East and domestic politics, and he concentrated on his membership of the European Parliament.

The toughness of the manner in which Garret had appointed his cabinet members was a subject of discussion between John Long and myself. John was active in the Dublin South-East Labour Party. He had worked as a volunteer for the Simon Community before going to Britain where he qualified and worked as a social worker in London, before his return to Dublin. A big, strong and compassionate man, he had been a major figure in our election team. Now between jobs, he offered to accompany me on the Seanad trail.

I would collect him from his home off the South Circular Road, drive to Werburgh Street employment exchange, where he would sign on and then we were off for a long day. Every Labour councillor, along with friendly Labour-leaning independent councillors, had to be met personally.

The Seanad trail takes the supplicant candidate to places in the country that he would otherwise never see. Seanad votes, or at least the people who possess them – county councillors and members of the Houses of the Oireachtas – about 900 in all, are located across the country. The preparations for a Seanad election campaign are quite different from Dáil elections. Letters are sent to all electors at the outset of the campaign, when nominations have closed and the precise field of candidates is known. A map is prepared locating every voter, and a campaign route devised.

The Seanad has traditionally three categories of politicians: those who are on their way to the Dáil, those who, like myself, are temporarily out of the Dáil, and a residue of dedicated senators who have no Dáil ambitions. These dedicated senators have to make sure of their own electoral support between elections, so as not to be vulnerable to a sympathy vote, within their party, drifting from them to a high-profile Dáil casualty in the recent general election.

Within the parliamentary party, Senator Tim McAuliffe had the best inside knowledge and understanding of the intricacies of the Seanad trail. He had been successfully re-elected for the Cultural and Education panel in five Seanad elections. He was relentless in identifying potential votes in between elections and making sure to consolidate them. There was a story told of how outside Maynooth, on his way home to Milltownpass, County Westmeath, Tim gave a lift to two young female students who were going home for the weekend. He discovered that one of the students, who lived outside Sligo, was the daughter of a county councillor. Imagine her surprise, and the delight of her parents, when Senator Tim McAuliffe delivered her safely to her hall door! His act was not forgotten. Tim was a generous man and shared some, but not all, of his knowledge with myself and others who had the sense to request it.

The summer days of July were fine times to be on the road. John Long acted as navigator as we set off on a circular loop that would take us out of Dublin in the morning and across one part of the country, designed to enable us to make contact with the maximum number of electors that day. Late in the evening, we would begin the return journey to Dublin, where the long day's work was compensated for with the pleasure of a good meal and a few pints. Paul Brady had just released his album *Hard Station* and his music sustained us for many a mile when our conversations had run their course.

The political situation at national level was disastrous. Haughey's delay in calling the election, abandoned because of the Stardust fire tragedy, had, among other effects, a major impact on the public finances. John Bruton arrived into the Department of Finance to discover an enormous gap between projected spending and the Book of Estimates. The rhetoric of Haughey's fiscal rectitude, from the year before, had been replaced by a manic drive to spend and appease every lobby group in order to win the election and stay in power.

It should be remembered that Haughey, an ex-Finance Minister, had total control of the Department of Finance as Taoiseach. Gene Fitzgerald had replaced Michael O'Kennedy in that portfolio but he was beholden to 'The Boss'. A less than impressive Minister for Labour and Minister for Public Services in the previous administration, Gene was not fully up to the difficult task of Finance. Senior Finance officials, after completing their discussions with their minister, were subsequently called to the Taoiseach's office in Government Buildings and there given final instructions by the Taoiseach, their former boss.

Many years later, in the Department of Finance, I experienced something similar. After we had completed our first Estimates negotiations within the department, the senior officials, including the secretary general, asked me if it was OK for them to go over to John Bruton's office to brief him. I enquired why they should, only to be told that it was normal practice and had happened with my predecessor, Bertie Ahern, and his Taoiseach, Albert Reynolds, also a former Finance Minister. Politely, I told them that I would personally inform the Taoiseach of our progress, by telephone, after I had spoken to the Tánaiste. The revelations of the tribunals in the 1990s have now explained in part why C.J. Haughey exercised this control.

Back in the summer of 1981, the prospects for the economy were bleak. With cabinet agreement, Bruton brought forward a mini-budget in July and prepared the country for a comprehensive spending review and a full budget in January 1982.

At the beginning of August, I had left for holidays, before the start of the three-day Seanad election count. Denise Rogers and Caroline Hussey were to phone me in a hotel on the island of Paros with the election result. On the day, I waited in reception for hours but there was no phone call. The next day, however, I got the good news.

The autumn of that year was politically difficult. I was back in the Seanad but not wanting to be there. Internal tensions were worsening within the Labour Party. Michael O'Leary, Tánaiste and Minister for Industry and Energy, had gone missing for a number of weeks in the middle of the summer. It was then revealed that he was staying in a suite in the Royal Hibernian Hotel on Dawson Street. His house was being renovated and he was completing his legal studies so that he could qualify as a lawyer and have the option of practising as a barrister! Meanwhile, Jimmy Tully was in his element as Minister for Defence; frequently in the past he had referred to his service as a corporal in the local defence forces, the FCA. Liam Kavanagh was one of Labour's stars in that cabinet and brought a steady and knowing hand to the departments of Labour and Public Services. Labour's only woman deputy, Eileen Desmond, started off very well in the departments of Health and Social Welfare. She secured probably the largest ever increase in social-welfare payments in that July mini-budget, but the 25 per cent was more a reflection of the enormous levels of inflation than a major shift in redistribution. Later that year, Eileen was hit with a serious illness that knocked her back and she did not contest the 1987 general election.

On the evening of the January 1982 budget, there was considerable tension and excitement after John Bruton had concluded. Fianna Fáil responded and a short adjournment was called before the debate resumed on the budget measures that had to be voted on that evening. Fergus O'Brien had replaced Gerry L'Estrange as government chief whip on 11 November in a small reshuffle. He was now charged with making sure that enough of those Independent deputies who had supported the government in June would keep them in office that January evening.

While tough measures had been announced, I did not have any sense of crisis or the possibility of the budget being defeated. Evelyn Owens, a former senator and member of the parliamentary party, had come into Leinster House that evening. Evelyn and I were seated in the temporary members' bar. There the black and white television monitor indicated that the Taoiseach was speaking to financial resolution number one. It is the normal practice for the Taoiseach to take these resolutions after the main budget speeches have been made. This provides the Minister for Finance with a break and enables him to give television and radio interviews. There were a number of members in the bar, including Lorcan Allen, Ray Burke and Brian Lenihan. After a while, the division bells began to ring and the television monitor showed up the card with the word *vótáil* printed on it. It was time to vote. Even so, the three Fianna Fáil deputies continued to stand with their drinks, chatting earnestly, knowing that they had some minutes before the division bells would go silent and that, anyway, the members' bar was close to the Dáil chamber. As Lorcan Allen, the last deputy left in the bar, lingered over his drink, Evelyn Owens jokingly said to him not to bother voting and to stay where he was. But he left and I was soon back chatting with Evelyn when she looked at the silent monitor and said, 'They're gone, it's over. The Taoiseach is on his feet. Look at the monitor: they must have lost the vote.'

The monitor now showed Garret replying without reference to the second resolution. I dashed out of the bar, turned left into the corridor heading towards the office of Labour Minister of State Joe Bermingham, situated on the ground floor of the 1932 Annex. Joe's private secretary was seated, legs outstretched, looking at the monitor and listening to the cackling noise of the wall-mounted voice box, which relayed the debate in the chamber throughout Leinster House. I did not have to ask and he did not turn around. 'We're gone,' he was saying; 'we're gone.'

I turned on my heels and was now beginning to speed along the corridor, meeting other people hurrying in different directions. I ran to my desk and phoned home. Malachi, my eleven-year-old son, answered. I spoke slowly to him, trying to contain my excitement. 'Malachi,' I said, 'listen carefully to me. There has been a vote in the Dáil, and the government was defeated. That means there is going to be a general election.'

'Great, Dad,' he said.

'What do you mean?'

'Well, you'll get your seat back.'

Delighted at his response and flattered by his political judgement, I told him to be ready to answer the phone and door.

'A lot of people from the South-East Labour Party are going to start phoning. Tell them, when they do, that there is a meeting being held tonight at eleven o'clock in our home to discuss the campaign.

I then rang a number of people, including Ciarán O'Mara, in case they had not heard the news.

As I left Leinster House, there was a sense of disbelief, mixed with panic, around the building. It was later that I heard the story of how Garret was seen, in the chamber, apparently pleading with Jim Kemmy for his vote.

Seán Dublin Bay Rockall Loftus, who had finally won a seat in the Dáil after decades of effort, blew himself out of it forever by bringing down the Fine Gael/Labour coalition. The government had been defeated by a single vote. That evening we had our own objective, which was to win back the seat in Dublin South-East. We had expected an early election, but no one anticipated that it would be caused by a defeat of the budget.

Denise and I, along with a few close associates, had attempted to analyse the reasons for my defeat the previous June. I had spent a lot of time working on legislation and had expended great energy researching and drafting an Urban Land Bill, designed to control the price of building land and so reduce the cost of housing. Even though I had also done an enormous amount of clinic work, spending a lot of time pursuing the concerns of voters, they did not reciprocate with a vote for me on polling day. We came to the conclusion that to ensure that the clinic and representational work was made electorally efficient, it would have to become more personalised. Constituents had come to see me in a clinic office, but the canvassing call was not necessarily done directly by me. Instead, they got the same attention as everyone else when their area was canvassed by our team of workers. I did hold clinics because I wanted to serve my constituents, but I felt that my main contribution was as a legislator. Caroline and Denise came to the conclusion that, if I got the chance again, I would have to do more clinic and canvassing work and spend less time on legislation.

We decided that when the election was announced, I should personally call to the house of every constituent who had come to one of my clinics and ask directly for their number one vote. In order to do this, up to 3,000 individual clinic files were transferred from our records and put onto a card index system. In addition to the name and address, the card had details of the case – whether it was housing, social welfare, telephone or whatever – and the date of last written contact. All this work was done by hand; there were no computers. This meant that Denise spent hours that autumn after my election to the Seanad, typing, writing and organising our 'blue-card' system.

When I got home, Malachi told me that Dermot Lacey, John Kennedy, Ray Kavanagh and Anna Doyle had already phoned. By eleven o'clock, we had a full meeting of the election committee around the dining-room table. Caroline Hussey, who had agreed to take on the job of director of elections again, assigned various tasks. The Dublin South-East office in Charlemont Street had been kept open as a constituency and clinic office, but now it became an election headquarters.

From ten in the morning I was going to start calling on every clinic constituent. Using the card index packs, I would renew contact with those who had come to see me. It was hoped that the sole presence of the candidate at the door of a clinic constituent would re-ignite the original contact and so reinforce my claim for their number one vote. A personalised letter would also be sent out that week. In the evening time I would go out with supporters and do a general canvass in a particular area.

The mood on the doorstep was difficult to gauge. The tactic of personal calls seemed to be working well. Most people met me warmly. With a few odd exceptions, I was guaranteed a number one vote, with an additional expression of regret at my loss of the seat in June. A small number were antagonistic and I was very direct with them. People do respond to clear, blunt and honest replies, if candidates have the courage to give them. But for all candidates, and certainly for me at that time, there is a fine line between being courageous and being reckless.

Polling day was Thursday, 18 February 1982. Labour in South-East had run a very good election campaign. During it, my brother Conor arranged for Lochlann, Moninne and myself to have lunch on the day of the count in Caspar and Gambini's, a restaurant on Wicklow Street, where Conor and I used to meet monthly for lunch. My two other brothers were abroad: Declan, a psychiatrist, was in Canada and Colm was working as a doctor in the refugee camps in Sudan. At lunch, the four of us talked about everything except the count. A phone call from Denise earlier that morning had been positive and during the meal she phoned the restaurant with even better news. Our mood changed considerably. I was grateful for my family's support. Indeed, it became a feature of all subsequent elections that my brothers and sister made a point of being with me, for lunch, on the day of the count. It was a great manifestation of solidarity, which meant a lot to me then and still does. After lunch I went to the pictures while the others returned to work. By the time I got to the count centre, the results were clear. I was a Dáil deputy again. I sought out Frank Cluskey, whose count centre was close by, and congratulated him on his regaining his seat.

But the coalition government did not fare well and so it was another hung Dáil. Fine Gael had marginally increased its support but had lost two seats. Labour won fifteen seats, the same as in June 1981. The composition of the new Dáil was such that I could not see a new Fine Gael/Labour coalition achieving the support of the Independents. Moreover, there was now a new dimension to the composition of the Dáil. Joe Sherlock, the lone Sinn Féin Workers' Party deputy, had been joined by Paddy Gallagher from Waterford and Proinsias De Rossa for Dublin North-West. The 'Stickies', as they had been nicknamed, had now arrived as a serious political force. In Dublin, their strength was in direct proportion to our weakness. Noël Browne and Tony Gregory also represented a left-wing vote in the capital and within the Labour Party there was a feeling of real concern, if not fear, that some of our clothes were being stolen.

If we were to be in government, with Michael O'Leary again as Tánaiste, I felt that the party would continue to lose support, because the leadership's attention would be on the responsibilities of government and not on the party. Our countrywide organisation was weak, because we were divided and unclear of our future political direction.

In Britain, the defeat of Jim Callaghan by Margaret Thatcher's Conservative Party had forced the Labour Party to the left. Michael Foot's leadership was weak and vacillating, allowing Tony Benn to drive the party even farther from the centre of political gravity. The rise of the Militant Tendency, a Trotskyist organisation, led to a major campaign of 'entryism' within Labour. But Militant was not confined to the United Kingdom. In Ireland, it had a small but growing membership. John Throne from Derry was at first its senior member in the Dublin area, but he was soon to be outshone by Joe Higgins, who happened also to be a Labour Party member in Dublin South-East. Joe had joined the UCD branch and remained a very active member, until he, along with many other Militants, was expelled years later, but that's another story.

For the previous eight months, I had had time to reflect on the party's internal problems and divisions. I was deeply concerned for its future because I felt that the left across Europe had lost the intellectual, if not the moral, high ground. The sense of clarity with which social democratic and socialist parties in other parts of Europe, with the exception of the Nordic countries, had dealt with the economic and social problems that confronted the continent at that time seemed to have disappeared. However, this political confusion, as manifested in Britain, further affected the confidence and sense of direction of a structurally much weaker party, like the Irish Labour Party.

The combined meeting of the administrative council and the parliamentary party to decide Labour's future parliamentary strategy was held on 3 March. Back then the divisions between the parliamentary party, whose members largely supported coalition, and the members of the administrative council, who didn't, were very deep. The annual conference elected the members of the administrative council as well as the chair and vice-chair of the party. Michael D. Higgins had been elected as chair in 1978, defeating Dan Browne, the leadership's preferred candidate. For his part, Michael D. was opposed to coalition and to the direction the party had taken under Cluskey and most certainly under O'Leary.

In the days before this meeting took place, there had been a lot of speculation about the possibility of Fine Gael leading a new coalition. The influence of Thatcherism was already beginning to dominate the political agenda and many commentators regarded the swingeing cuts in public expenditure to redress the macro-economic problems of the country as the only option open to any Irish government. But the burden of such cuts would fall disproportionately on working people. The trade unions were vehemently opposed to such action. There was, sadly, a lack of clarity about an alternative strategy. But what I did know for certain was that within government, dominated by such an economic point of view, Labour would continue to lose electoral support. When the vote was taken, very late that evening, I voted against our participation in coalition, much to the dismay of the leadership. It was really of academic interest, because it was clear to many in the meeting that Haughey would be elected Taoiseach, probably with the support of Tony Gregory. In Dublin South-East, many Fine Gael activists, who had given me a high preference vote, were very disappointed. When the Twenty-Third Dáil did assemble, Haughey was elected Taoiseach, leading a minority Fianna Fáil government.

Within days, Haughey moved boldly to obtain an effective working majority. Michael O'Kennedy, who had sought the glittering prize of European Commissioner, received that reward from Haughey towards the end of 1980. However, in the division of tasks and responsibilities among the new commissioners, made by Commission President Gaston Thorn, O'Kennedy lost out badly. He misread, it is claimed, what was on offer. In the cruel commentary of Frank Cluskey, Kennedy thought that he was being made Tánaiste but instead ended up as Parliamentary Secretary. O'Kennedy soon became disenchanted with Brussels and when the general election of February 1982 was called, he announced his decision to re-enter Irish national politics. He fought for his old seat in Tipperary North, displacing his colleague Michael Smith and resigned from the European Commission. In the event, Haughey did not appoint him to his new cabinet.

However, Haughey did offer the now vacant Irish commissioner's post to Richard Burke of Fine Gael, who had been successfully re-elected to the Dáil for the constituency of Dublin West. Excluded from office by FitzGerald the previous June, Burke did not take long to decide to return as commissioner in Brussels and so complete O'Kennedy's term of office.

Haughey's move was seen as a great stroke, even by his own Fianna Fáilers, who normally would have baulked at the sight of such a plum job going outside the family fold. However, it was widely expected that Fianna Fáil would win the Dublin West by-election since they had a ready-made candidate. Former deputy Eileen Lemass had just lost her seat in the same constituency from which Burke would have to resign his seat in order to return to Brussels. Many in Fine Gael were incensed at what they saw as Burke's lack of loyalty. Others recognised that his talents and experience had been conspicuously passed over by Garret FitzGerald the previous June.

The prospect of a by-election in Dublin West, where we were

weak and Sinn Féin The Workers' Party strong, was another difficult challenge for Labour. President of SFWP, Tomás Mac Giolla had taken early retirement from the ESB, moved house from Stillorgan to Inchicore and had been, since 1979, a Dublin city councillor for Ballyfermot, then at the centre of Dublin West. He had been gathering strength and now, with the prospect of a by-election, was poised, like Joe Sherlock in 1979, to make a decisive impact. Once the prospect of a by-election became known, Michael O'Leary, now back as full-time leader, took action.

A tentative feeler was put out to Noël Browne to ask if he would rejoin the Labour Party and stand for us in the by-election. Apparently, Fine Gael had conducted a private opinion poll in the constituency with Browne's name on the ballot paper. It showed that he would defeat Fianna Fáil in a by-election. Browne had decided not to contest the previous general election and his seat had gone to Fine Gael's Richard Bruton in Dublin North-Central.

Despite Browne's earlier antagonism towards Labour, it appeared that he was now prepared to stand once again for the party, provided that he was the unanimous choice of the local organi- sation. This proved impossible. The Dublin West organisation, suspicious of O'Leary and contemptuous of his authority, was already under the influence, if not the effective control, of Militant. Having vetoed Browne by denying him a unanimous nomination, the constituency council selected a political novice, Brendan O'Sullivan, who was so humiliated by the by-election result that he subsequently disappeared, politically, not even contesting the gen- eral election of the same year. Meanwhile, Mac Giolla did very well, as we feared, and placed himself in pole position.

However, the real story, as far as the public was concerned, was the surprise victory of Fine Gael's Liam Skelly over the Fianna Fáil racing certainty Eileen Lemass. Jim Mitchell, already an electoral legend within Fine Gael, had recruited Liam Skelly when Labour failed to nominate Browne. A political novice but a successful businessman, Skelly was a local boy made good, and had been living in Canada for a number of years before returning to Dublin. His candidacy was unveiled with some panache. The entire Fine

Gael organisation, galvanised by Burke's departure, rallied to the campaign and carried the day. Haughey's stroke had backfired.

Another by-election was held on the same day, 11 May 1982. Kevin Dwyer, a teacher from Tuam, was selected to stand for Labour in Galway East, following the death of Fianna Fáil's John Callanan. This was truly barren country for Labour. Yet Michael O'Leary decided that he would give it his wholehearted attention. He pledged himself to the campaign, effectively taking himself out of Leinster House for three weeks and thereby losing the opportunity to hold the government to account, because the Dáil was still sitting, notwithstanding the by-elections in both constituencies. His absence attracted widespread negative comment within the parliamentary party because the results of the two by-elections seemed to be a foregone conclusion.

On my return to the Dáil, after the February 1982 general election, I resumed occupation of my old room. My new roommate was Dick Spring, who, the previous July, had become Minister of State in the Department of Justice on his first day in the Dáil. He had succeeded his father Dan Spring to Dáil Éireann. Some have claimed that the large delegation that Kerry North brought to the Gaiety Theatre in support of Michael O'Leary's coalition proposal was the instrument of Dick's instant promotion. This was an unfair comment, whether it was true or not, because he was undoubtedly the most able and brightest of the new intake to the parliamentary party. In the late autumn of that year he survived, but only just, a dreadful car accident outside Nenagh on his way to Dublin in his ministerial Mercedes. German engineering, the wearing of a seatbelt and the skill of his garda driver all contributed to his miraculous survival. But Dick was badly injured and was out sick for a long time. Even then, in those early weeks in April leading up to the Dublin West and Galway East by-elections, he was still periodically in considerable pain.

Dick's constituency secretary, Sally Clarke joined Denise and myself in Room 120. I was now back on good terms with O'Leary. Spring was particularly close to O'Leary, but Michael himself was increasingly disconnected. Dick and I played an active part in the Galway East campaign, but it was a fruitless exercise.

The by-elections were disastrous for Labour. The sense of drift and hopelessness carried through to June and on to the summer recess. I was back in the Dáil, but the party was going nowhere. On top of everything, my personal life was now at a critical stage. My marriage was coming to an end. For the previous three years, there had been increasing difficulties, and Nicola and I were effectively living separate lives. We subsequently separated in May 1983 and I moved to a small house in another part of Sandymount.

The party's annual conference was scheduled to take place in the Leisureland complex in Salthill, Galway, a bleak, windswept build-ing, designed in the 1960s. We had been reassured that its modern-isation made it a suitable venue, but it was with some dread that I went to Galway that October weekend. The main item on the agenda was coalition and how the party was to decide the matter. It had been clear from the joint meetings of the administrative council and the parliamentary party in the previous March that the party leadership regarded the present arrangements as very unsatis-factory. Many activists felt that the parliamentary party could not be trusted to decide by itself this critical issue. Frank Cluskey had been instrumental in changing the party's decision-making proced-ures before the 1981 general election. This led to the Gaiety con-ference and the presentation of a draft programme for government. O'Leary was unhappy with this and his experience of the various meetings that took place immediately after the snap February election did not enamour him to the process. He was not alone.

Running parallel to this debate in Ireland was the experience of the Labour Party in Britain and a sense, fostered by Tony Benn and Militant, that parliamentarians could not be trusted to care for the future of the party. Rank and file members must have the final say, it was claimed. Yet other people argued that you could not, or indeed should not, have a democracy within a democracy. This would leave the final decision about the shape of future coalition governments in the hands of a relatively small group of party activists, rather than the electorate.

It is important to set the context in which this debate was taking place. Ireland had a limited experience of coalition or inter-party government. Fianna Fáil had made single-party government a core value, denouncing the very principle of coalition governments as being inherently unsound and internally divisive. There was also the sense that political clarity of purpose was required during an election campaign and immediately afterwards. A new prospective government had to be in place when the Dáil met for the first time, usually about two weeks after polling day.

Some thought the Dutch or Italian political culture of caretaker governments, operating for a number of weeks while coalition negotiations took place, to be unstable. How could a country function if there was not clarity about the shape and mandate of the government? It is against this background that the Labour Party was considering holding a special delegate conference, after an election result, to decide on a programme for government. Notwithstanding the experience of the Gaiety conference, many people thought this procedure was unwieldy and would delay the formation of a new administration. Others felt that the decision about the shape of the next government should be made exclusively in the ballot box on polling day and nowhere else. In all this there was the clash of two political cultures. The two-party, first-past-the-post, Anglo-Saxon model was one; the multi-party proportional representation model, used in continental Europe, as well as Ireland, was the other.

Going into the Galway conference, Michael O'Leary wanted the delegates to give the leadership and to the parliamentary party a dominant say in how the question of coalition was to be decided. This was rolling back the decision that had already been put in place. Frank Cluskey, Barry Desmond and the unions, particularly Billy Attley of the FWUI, wanted the existing system maintained and the role of a special delegate post-election conference left in place. They were arguing from a pro-coalition point of view, believing that the anti-coalition element would not only lose in such a conference, provided a reasonable programme for government was represented, but that the party would take greater and bigger ownership of Labour's participation in government if its position was agreed in this manner. They also argued that this would give a much stronger hand to Labour's negotiators with any prospective coalition party, if they could play up the difficulty of getting the draft programme through a delegate conference.

While there were many other issues of concern to the delegates, the conference had really only one item of political importance. In the key debate that took place on the Saturday, O'Leary went for broke and did not accept Cluskey's amendment, which would have retained a post-election delegate conference. O'Leary lost the vote and, notwithstanding his leader's speech later that evening, the conference was in disarray.

A very unwilling party leader turned up on the Sunday morning for the last session of conference, but by midday he had gone missing and was not in contact, it seems, with his office or advisers. By late Monday afternoon, rumours started to circulate. Chris Glennon, political correspondent of the *Irish Independent*, contacted Seamus Scally, the party's general secretary, who had served out his three-month notice of resignation in the job to coincide with the Galway conference. The question Glennon put to Seamus was: 'Has O'Leary resigned as leader and from the party and is it true that he's going to join Fine Gael?'

Late on Monday night, back in Dublin, the phone rang at home. I got out of bed to take the call – it was from Michael D. Higgins – and I sat at the end of the stairs listening to him. As chairman of the party, he had adopted his grave, deep tone of voice, and informed me that Michael O'Leary had resigned as leader and from the Labour Party. Michael D. went on to say that he was putting himself forward as a candidate for the leadership and wanted to know if I would support him. I told Michael D. that I would have to consider the situation and that I needed time to think the matter through, because O'Leary's resignation had come as a major surprise. O'Leary's pre-emptory departure created its own drama and there were more telephone calls that night.

After I had spoken to Michael D. and a couple of others, I reflected on the situation. I had long since decided that Dick Spring should be our next leader. I had said this to him, outside Hayden's Hotel in Ballinasloe the previous May, during the Galway East by-election. Since then, my view had strengthened. Dick had a safe seat, a good organisation and a great political legacy. He presented a new image for the party. Having shared an office with him for six or seven months, I did not need to reconsider my opinion.

An emergency meeting of the parliamentary party was called for Friday morning. When we were assembled, Joe Bermingham was in the chair. Senator Timmy Conway, the party's financial secretary, described the cryptic messages both Joe and he had received the previous Monday from Michael O'Leary. There was a lot of coverage in the media about his defection to Fine Gael. I privately felt some compassion for him. He could not live a lie; he was completely at odds with the party and had been for some time. And I think that, on balance, he did the honest thing in going. What I could not accept was that he would join any other political party, especially Fine Gael. But thinking about his dilemma, and indeed some of my own mixed feelings on the party's political direction, I concluded that if I ever reached such a position, I would resign from political life rather than cross the floor.

When the issue of O'Leary's resignation had been fully discussed, the parliamentary party went on to deal with the leadership vacancy. By consensus, it was agreed that no decision should be taken at that morning's meeting. Instead, we should meet again on the Monday afternoon. We would all have had the weekend to take soundings in our own constituencies and to reflect on the situation. Before that Friday was over, I spoke to Dick, reminding him of our conversation in Ballinasloe and confirming, once again, my support for him if he would stand. I also spoke to Liam Kavanagh, asking him to encourage Dick to put his name forward.

Meanwhile, the situation of the minority Haughey government was precarious. Ray MacSharry, Minister for Finance since March 1982, had forced Haughey to begin to face the crisis. The public finances had to be put on a sound footing whatever the short-term political cost. In August, a suspected murderer, Malcolm MacArthur, was arrested in the apartment of Haughey's Attorney General, Paddy Connolly. This scandal severely damaged the government. Conor Cruise O'Brien coined the phrase 'the GUBU factor', picking up on Haughey's reaction to the Macarthur–Connolly incident as 'grotesque, unbelievable, bizarre and unprecedented'. Fianna Fáil's maintenance in office by the three SFWP deputies could not last long. Following his successful performance in the Dublin West by-election, some five months earlier, Tomás Mac Giolla, the party president, was anxious to have a general election as soon as possible so that he could consolidate his position and be elected to the Dáil. As a further sign of the party's democratic, political evolution away from its abstentionist, nationalist origins to a Marxist socialist position, the prefix Sinn Féin had been officially dropped in October and it was now known as The Workers' Party (WP).

A meeting of our constituency executive was called for the following morning, after the Friday parliamentary party meeting. All fourteen members were there. I wanted to hear what people had to say about the leadership, while telling them that the Labour Dáil deputies would make the final decision. All were aware of the looming general election, and so the discussion of the prospects of various candidates took place in that context. Michael D. Higgins and Barry Desmond were mentioned, as speaker after speaker offered their point of view. My own name was also mentioned, but the general opinion, which I shared, was that the lack of certainty of my holding Dublin South-East was a major factor and that any move on my part would be premature. It was a constructive and positive meeting.

I spoke at length about Dick Spring and the potential which he possessed for the party. It was agreed that no vote would be taken and I was asked to use my judgement, informed by what I had heard that morning. When the meeting was over, we went into the Barge pub on Ranelagh Bridge. We were in the middle of a round of drinks and some food when a newspaper boy came into the back lounge with the early edition of the *Evening Press*. Tuthill's, the bookies, was quoting Dick Spring at 10–1 in the leadership contest.

Quickly, I asked Ciarán O'Mara, our treasurer, what was the constituency debt.

'A thousand pounds,' came the reply.

I then turned to the barman and asked him to cash a cheque for a £100. I told the others that I thought it was a very good bet and it would be an easy way of clearing our debts before the forthcoming general election. Runners were dispatched to place the bet, but they soon returned empty-handed. The book was closed, if it was ever truly opened.

Over the weekend, Barry Desmond phoned to seek my support. I told him that I was backing Dick. I think he was hurt because he had presumed on the support of the Dublin deputies. Meanwhile, I heard that Cluskey had been told by his constituency organisation not to even consider contesting the leadership, since his seat was still far from secure.

On the Monday, Dick Spring was nominated by Liam Kavanagh and seconded by his colleague from County Kerry. Michael D. nominated himself and was seconded by Mervyn Taylor. It was only to put Michael D.'s name on the ballot and not necessarily, as Mervyn explained, an indication of his support. Subsequently, Cluskey nominated Barry Desmond. This time Michael D. withdrew his name and when the votes were counted there were two for Barry and thirteen for Dick. We then made our way over to Kildare House for a press conference. There was a sense of excitement because we were aware of the courage and risk in electing our youngest TD, aged thirty-two, as the new leader.

On Wednesday, The Workers' Party rejected the recently published Fianna Fáil austerity programme entitled 'The Way Forward' and announced that they would be supporting the opposition motion of no confidence. This was the death knell for Haughey's minority government. The Dáil was dissolved on 4 November 1982. Another general election was on us and, even though it had been well signalled, I was terrified at the prospect of a third contest within eighteen months. Denise had moved with great speed and immense preparation: within days, all the essentials were in place. Meanwhile Leinster House was like the lower deck of the *Titanic*. Every deputy was stockpiling envelopes, while senators wearily eyed their upcoming campaign.

Now leader, Dick Spring moved, with Sally Clarke, from our office to the next room. He began his leadership cautiously and with some apprehension. I had suggested that we use the services of Quinn McDonnell Pattison (QMP), the advertising company in which my brother Conor was a partner. They had recently been joined by Dave Holden, a former army officer, who had brought his own public relations company into the QMP fold. Dick agreed and they were asked to prepare election material as quickly as possible for our consideration.

Before calling the general election, C.J. Haughey had published the wording to the eighth amendment to the Constitution, the so-called 'pro-life amendment', proposing to protect the life of the unborn in the Constitution. Immediately Garret FitzGerald endorsed it, promising a referendum the following April. The media now turned to Dick, who refused a blanket endorsement, looking for time over the weekend, keeping the media and the country waiting. It was a good political move and a lesson for me. I watched in admiration as he proceeded to work on an alternative amendment and produced a clear opposing position on the Monday. It became headline news, and was dramatically praised as a courageous stand for Labour under its new leader.

QMP and Dave Holden met the party leadership – Dick Spring, Barry Desmond, Michael D. Higgins and party vice-chair Michael Ferris, along with myself – and presented their proposals. 'A voice that will be heard' was to be our central slogan. They also produced a range of captions aimed at a variety of policy issues. Given our very limited budget, they came up with the stark but extremely effective set design for a television party political broadcast. I was particularly pleased on two counts. Conor and his colleagues had done an excellent job, and, at last, we were becoming seriously professional about the presentation of Labour's message. It became clear on the canvass that we were picking up votes.

The funeral of Michael Mullen, the former Labour deputy for Dublin North-West and general secretary of the ITGWU, took place at the Pro-Cathedral on the Thursday the Dáil was dissolved. At the funeral I spoke to Michael Bell, a group national secretary of the union and Labour's candidate in Louth. He told me that his selection convention was being held that Sunday, but he had no chairman for the meeting. My offer to preside was quickly accepted. I was anxious to give Michael support and to get a feel for the political mood of the country outside Dublin. The meeting took place in Castlebellingham. The question of actively seeking second preferences from Provisional Sinn Féin supporters was put to me after Michael had been formally selected. My reply was simple. Labour had fought on two successful occasions to retain the proportional representation system and we should encourage every voter, even Provisional Sinn Féin supporters, to use it effectively.

The only other visit I made out of Dublin during that short, tight campaign was to Meath where Frank McLoughlin was standing. Despite having being a candidate on a number of previous occasions, he did not run in February 1982 and the seat had gone to Fianna Fáil. I knew Frank well and had spoken to him on the phone after Dick Spring had phoned him and encouraged him to stand for Labour. He was hot and cold on the matter because he had had a big falling out with Jimmy Tully. In essence, he was not sure of the sort of vote he would get from Tully's supporters. When Anwar Sadat was murdered in Cairo in October 1981, Tully, as Minister for Defence, had been on the review stand, a few seats away from the Egyptian president and was wounded in the cheek by a stray bullet. The story, jokingly told in Labour Party circles, was that Frank had sent a hit party to take out his rival Tully, but that the bullets had ricocheted off the minister's neck and killed Sadat!

I met Frank and his team on a Saturday afternoon and my four hours in Meath with the ebullient candidate convinced me that not only would he win, but that a change of government was definitely going to happen.

Back in Dublin South-East, the campaign was going well, despite an effort by Fine Gael to defeat me since I was perceived to be anti-coalition following the vote of the combined parliamentary parties meeting the previous March. They had targeted a number of

Labour Party candidates whom they felt were not sound on this issue. In my case, they did not succeed, but Michael D. Higgins, another target, was a victim of their action and he did not serve in the Twenty-Fourth Dáil, but ended up in the Seanad on the National University of Ireland panel.

On the day of the count, I met Conor for our now traditional lunch. Hugh Byrne, a Fine Gael TD, came through the gates of Leinster House and gave me the thumbs up. He told me the early word from the count was that I was going to be elected. I was understandably in good form when we met Moninne and Lochlann. A phone call from Denise during our meal confirmed the good news. For the first time in my memory, the count was not to be held in Bolton Street but in different centres around the city. Ours was in Marian College, beside Lansdowne Road stadium. I was greatly relieved because I would no longer have to visit the Four Seasons pub across from the old technical college, long associated with electoral defeats. After lunch, I hid in the Academy cinema for a couple of hours, before heading to the count centre for a pre-arranged interview with RTÉ. There was a great mood, and the expectation of a change of government.

As the results were coming in from around the country, the focus was all on Garret FitzGerald, who was clearly the Taoiseach-in-waiting. He asked me for Dick Spring's phone number, as we stood waiting for the final Dublin South-East results to be declared, but I did not have it, nor could I remember it then or the following January when I desperately needed it. When the results were finally declared, I had increased the Labour vote, and combined with The Workers' Party vote, there was now effectively a left quota in the constituency. In the end, Labour and Fine Gael had sixteen and seventy seats respectively, a clear overall majority against the combined opposition of eighty-one.

When the new parliamentary party met, Dick got a mandate to open negotiations with both Fianna Fáil and Fine Gael and to report back to a special delegate conference. The inclusion of Fianna Fáil was a formality, since few believed, given Fianna Fáil's attitude to coalition, that anything would come of it. Yet it was considered necessary to maintain a balance. He asked each of us to prepare a shopping list of policy items for inclusion in a programme for government. As Environment spokesperson, I took to this task enthusiastically. I sought the help of my friend Dick Hargaden to make contact with representatives of the Irish pension fund industry with a view to exploring their potential role in underwriting our infrastructural needs. Then there was a round of meetings and interviews with economists, planners, trade unionists, banks and the construction industry. John Long accompanied me and we compiled a substantial and radical report that I presented to Dick in a matter of days. It was, I subsequently learned, the only one he received.

I was not directly involved in the formation of a new government and, though I felt excluded, I was in public very supportive of Dick. He was engaged in difficult talks with Garret and he hadn't much experience of such negotiations. A group had formed around him, including Joe Revington and John Rogers, two of his old friends from Trinity College. Pat Magner, a major figure in the Labour Party organisation, had come up from Cork and provided solid advice to the new party leader. Finally, agreement in principle was reached and a report was prepared for a special delegate conference in the Savoy cinema, Limerick. The joint programme was given to delegates when they entered the hall.

Dick's speech, proposing the adoption of the joint programme between Labour and Fine Gael, was particularly good. This was the first of many documents that were written by Fergus Finlay, who was unknown to me and most party members at that time. Pat Magner had asked him to do the job for the party leader, at short notice, and he clearly rose to the occasion. When Frank Cluskey was called to second the motion, I knew instantly that he would be in the cabinet and that probably I would not. The choice of Frank was inspired, as it was a clear reaching out to those who had been suspicious of the O'Leary leadership, with which Dick was still associated in the minds of many.

Frank spoke in favour of coalition. It was, he said, a tactic and not a principle, as far as the Labour Party was concerned, and the joint programme presented the party with a great opportunity to make progress. The rest of the speeches were intense, the mood expectant and the contributions predictable. But three elections in eighteen months had persuaded doubtful delegates of the merits of a stable coalition government above the electoral uncertainty of another minority government. In the end, the motion was carried by 846 to 522 votes.

The following Monday afternoon, I finally got to speak to Dick in the privacy of his office in Leinster House. 'I have good news and bad news,' he said, clearly uncomfortable as I entered the room.

I was not to be in cabinet, but was to be Minister of State at the Department of Education, responsible for school buildings and with a special role attached to the Department of Industry and Commerce to introduce the National Development Corporation, a policy flagship of the Labour Party. Whatever about my external response, I was inwardly dismayed, because I knew I could do little about the National Development Corporation from the lowly position that was being offered.

'Who is getting Environment?' was my first question.

'I am,' he replied and I immediately relaxed a little.

It was the job I really wanted and the thought of it going to someone else after all my work was unbearable, but the party leader taking on the portfolio was quite different. Dick then informed me that Fergus O'Brien was to be his Minister of State in the Custom House. We began to talk, and I slowly suggested that instead of what he was proposing, I should be appointed Minister of State at the Department of the Environment. Fergus O'Brien could take up the original post offered to me and there would be no net loss to anybody. I argued strenuously that, as party leader and Tánaiste, he would be extremely busy outside the department and would need someone there in whom he could place trust and confidence. This line of argument seemed to make some progress but our conversation was interrupted by a phone call from Garret.

As I got up to move, Dick waved for me to stay in my place, and so I listened to one half of the conversation. The other half I could only guess at, even though Garret's voice could be heard from time to time. Names were mentioned, posts were suggested and numbers counted and in the end Dick informed Garret that he now had sixteen ministers of state, instead of the limit of fifteen. Some rethinking was necessary, and the receiver was put back into its place. Dick grinned at me. He had accepted my suggestion, but I was not to talk to anyone until it was all agreed. I did, of course, tell Denise because she was not included in the 'anyone'.

Chapter 11

In Government
1982–1983

The new government was sworn in on 14 December. Tom Fitzpatrick of Fine Gael replaced John O'Connell as Ceann Comhairle and Garret FitzGerald was comfortably elected Taoiseach with eighty-five deputies in favour and seventy-nine against. Neil Blaney and the two Workers' Party deputies voted against him, while Tony Gregory and John O'Connell abstained. I had to learn the virtues of silence and political stoicism, required by all involved in public office, as many people around Leinster House expressed their surprise that I was not in the cabinet.

'There were many responsibilities on Dick's shoulders,' I replied, indicating, in a general but non-specific way, that he had to accommodate the party and include Frank Cluskey. I was happy that Dick would deliver what he had promised the previous day, but I had to wait until 16 December before the Taoiseach announced the names and responsibilities of the ministers of state.

My mother, Moninne and Conor were in the public gallery when the announcement was made and joined me in the visitors' bar for a celebration. I was excited about my responsibilities for Urban Affairs and Housing in the Department of the Environment. As soon as my family had left Leinster House, I returned to my office and phoned Margaret Cullen, private secretary to the Ceann Comhairle. 'What do I do next?' I asked her when I was in her office.

In the absence of the four Labour ministers, who had gone to their own departmental offices, there was no obvious person to whom I could talk. However, by the time I left Margaret Cullen, I had a guide detailing how to make contact with the Secretary of the Department, Gerry Meagher, whom I vaguely knew. I made an arrangement to go to the Custom House the following morning.

The other matter that I had to deal with there and then was the appointment of two ministerial drivers, recruited from the Garda Síochána Transport Section. Dr John O'Connell had suggested that I take on Joe Coggins who had worked with him. Michael Smith and Ber Cowen of Fianna Fáil recommended Nashie Grady. When I said that I did not want a black Mercedes, the Barrack Master told me that a Peugeot was available. I was conscious that the 'Mercs and Perks' tag had damaged the perception of the Labour Party in the minds of both our detractors and supporters.

That evening Joe Coggins arrived at Leinster House and drove me to the Barge pub where a large number of Dublin South-East activists had gathered to celebrate our success. A number of us went to the Kingsland restaurant on Dame Street but could not get a table, and so went on to the Calcutta, a favourite curry house of mine on Camden Street. The following month *Magill* magazine published a fictitious story of how I had arrived into the Kingsland restaurant, throwing my weight around, trying to jump the queue while all the time the state car was double-parked outside. It was a salutary lesson in how some elements of an event can be woven together with a set of political prejudices to create an erroneous account.

The next morning, John Long joined Denise and me in Leinster House I had asked him to come and work with us in the Department of the Environment. John was the only one of us to have worked in a government department and, despite my outward expression of confidence, we were all apprehensive.

For a symmetrical, four-sided classical building, perhaps the finest in the city, the public entrance of the Custom House was located in an out-of-the-way corner. Gerry Meagher, Secretary of the Department, ushered us through the door and up the stairs to the first floor of the ministerial corridor. I was struck by the dirt and dowdiness of the areas through which we passed. The dark-varnished mahogany panels of the corridor seemed even gloomier than the last time I had been there, eight years before, when Brendan Corish told me I was to become a senator.

The secretary opened a door to a room that overlooked one of the two internal courtyards. 'Now, Minister,' he started, as I tried to adjust to the title. 'What about a private secretary? Do you have a preference or indeed a particular person you wish to propose?' I asked him whom he recommended. The existing private secretary, who had worked with the previous minister of state, Gerry Brady, was declared to be excellent. He then introduced me to Frank Kelly, a nervous, young civil servant. After a chat, I told Frank that we would have a month together, at the end of which either of us could decide if we no longer wished to continue working with the other. I did stress, when we were alone, that he would have to get on well with Denise. I said she would be with me when I left the Custom House, so he had no doubts as to the importance of our working relationship.

Next I was introduced to the four clerical staff in an adjacent room, accessed by a connecting door as well as its own door, directly onto the ministerial corridor. Denise and John Long were taken off to the constituency office, cut off from the ministerial corridor. I was not happy with this arrangement and made immediate changes. Before long Denise was installed alongside Frank, because I wanted her to be working next door in the ministerial staff office, but there was no space for John.

The suite of the Minister of State's offices in O'Connell Bridge House were immediately offered, but I rejected it out of hand. I did not want to be physically isolated from Dick Spring and the rest of the department's senior public servants, all of whom were on the same floor in the Custom House. A few days later, I took a walk around the building, partly out of architectural curiosity, but mainly to look for an alternative office. I had little success. In one room two buckets were strategically placed to catch the rainwater from a leak in the roof. In the elegant circular space beneath the architecturally impressive dome, facing the Liffey, four very old wooden drawing cabinets were surrounded by metal filing cabinets, broken pieces of furniture and discarded materials. I was appalled at the disarray and the condition of the building. In part, this was because it was occupied by three government departments, including Environment, so no one was in charge.

Back in my office I reflected on what I had to do. There were a number of immediate priorities for our programme for government. I knew some, but not all, of the senior officials. Accordingly, I asked for a meeting with each of the six assistant secretaries, to enable them to outline their section's priorities and to enable me have a sense of their work and policy priorities. I asked Denise and John to sit in on these meetings so that they would get to know the officials. Some weeks afterwards, as confidences were built and relationships developed, Gavin Freeman, the press officer, told me that some of the assistant secretaries did not take kindly to being interviewed in the presence of two juniors, not to mention a female member of staff. On hearing this, I was taken aback and saddened. I admired John McGrath and Des Malin and, though I was a bit annoyed at their old-fashioned attitude, I had not intended to upset them.

By early January 1983 it was obvious that our office accommodation was a problem. My room was too big for one person but too small for Frank Kelly, Denise and the four others next door. Meanwhile, John Long was on another floor. I knew that I could not work like this for the next four or five years and that now was the time to act. Immediately, I asked Frank to get me a set of floor plans of the building, but he told me that, for reasons of security, he had been told that they were not available. Jocosely I told him that any book on classical Irish public buildings would give me all the plans I needed and he soon was back in my office with a broad grin on his face and a roll of plans under his arm! A large rectangular corner room, with three western windows and one northern one, cried out for detailed inspection. Airy, spacious and well lit, it was occupied by a number of civil servants who were startled by the unprecedented and unannounced ministerial visit. Some six weeks later, that generous space was subdivided into an integrated and efficient ministerial suite of offices which brought us all together.

Since I had shown such an interest in the building, Gerry Meagher gave me a file for advice and action. Gandon's Custom House masterpiece had been burned down in a costly open attack by the IRA at Éamon de Valera's insistence during the War of Independence. It was one of the last major conflicts before the 1921 truce. The heat of the fire had melted the lead cladding that was wrapped around a cast-iron necklace of metal bars which tied the large building together structurally just below parapet level. The subsequent repair work and reconstruction in the early days of the Free State did not replace this waterproof seal and over time the rusting metal expanded, dislodging parts of the stone and opening crevices for more rainwater to enter, lodge, freeze and expand. A major job was urgently needed because sections of stone were falling from the parapet onto the pavement. Gerry wondered if I – as an architect and minister of state – could run the file by the Office of Public Works and the Department of Finance to have the fabric of the building sealed so that restoration and modernisation could begin. I duly obliged. It was an illustration of how the permanent staff could harness the enthusiasm of a temporary office-holder to achieve success with projects that had been stalled.

I was fortunate with my two garda drivers. The civil service is supportive of ministers when you are behind your desk, in the Dáil or attending an official function. What is less clear is how to handle informal occasions, such as Christmas social functions. I was invited to many of these by organisations related to the work of the department, but whereas before I had arrived as an Oireachtas member, I was now the guest of honour. I realised how helpful both Joe and Nashie could be when a minister was expected at three or four functions on the same evening. During that time, I became a close friend to both of them. When Joe Coggins retired many years later, Gay Bradley maintained his high standards.

The new government had to come to terms with two political priorities that first Christmas: the forthcoming budget and the Northern Ireland question. I had no role in the former but accidentally got to centre stage on the latter. Months earlier, John Hume and the SDLP had been calling for the establishment of a body, which they named a Council for a New Ireland. Its task was to summon the democratic nationalist parties in the North and South to meet and attempt to set out an agreed description of what a democratic Ireland might be. Presented with this non-threatening proposal, unionists could then be invited to explore a negotiated political settlement on the basis of trust and respect for diversity. The SDLP could not readily advance this plan as long as Fianna Fáil, Fine Gael and Labour had different positions on the same question.

Some years previously, relations between Labour and the SDLP had grown cold, despite our shared membership of the Confederation of European Socialist and Social Democratic Parties, and indeed within the socialist group of the European Parliament. Cluskey, having fired Cruise O'Brien as Northern Ireland spokesperson, retained his disdain for nationalism in general, and for 'green' nationalism in particular. The departure of Gerry Fitt from the leadership of the SDLP and Séamus Mallon's prominence exacerbated Cluskey's disregard for the SDLP, which the Irish Labour Party had done so much to help bring into existence. O'Leary's leadership tenure had been too short and Dick Spring's leadership precipitated both the general election and the change of government that had made him Tánaiste. There was much on Dick's mind in those weeks before Christmas 1982, so when I indicated that I would like to attend the SDLP January conference in Belfast, he agreed. In our political discussions I told Dick that I hoped we would get closer to the SDLP and reconstruct Labour's previous positive relationship. I knew this was something John Hume desired too. No senior Labour parliamentary member had attended four or five of the previous SDLP conferences and it had been left to a defensive Seamus Scally to represent the Labour Party to less than enthusiastic SDLP delegates.

A few days before I left for Belfast in January 1983, I asked Dick if there was any particular line that I should take. I would be speaking to the conference after the leader's speech as the delegate from the Confederation of European Socialist and Social Democratic Parties. Dick gave me a free hand. As I travelled north, my mind was full of old memories. We drove through Dundalk and then on to Newry, past the church where my sister and eldest brother had been christened and near where my parents had begun their married life.

The conference hall in Belfast's Imperial Hotel was full for John Hume's address. Twenty years later the cadences in his speech retain their poetry, even if the charge of 'the single transferable speech' is harsh but true. I know of no other politician who has stayed on message for so long on such a single theme. His call for unity with diversity, spilling our sweat and not our blood, was the basis on which the work of a Council for a New Ireland could bring forward an agreed blueprint around which nationalist Ireland could agree. This would open the door to a constructive dialogue with unionists. It was a powerful speech, superbly delivered and cogently argued. I agreed with John Hume's analysis and was formulating my reply, while listening to the fraternal delegate of the British Labour Party, Alex Kitson. A senior trade unionist, he was a member of the party's national executive and a Glaswegian. He congratulated the leadership, pledged solidarity with the party, wished the SDLP well in the future and sought the forgiveness of the delegates because, owing to pressing business, he had to leave for 'the mainland' immediately after his speech.

There was polite applause as I then made my way to the rostrum and greeted the delegates. I conveyed greetings from the Labour Party and saluted their efforts in difficult times. Having outlined my Newry and Warrenpoint connections, I observed that had events not taken a particular course back in 1939, I would have been a member of their parliamentary party and not a visitor. I expressed my regrets that the previous speaker had had to leave for 'the mainland' and then said that I thought we were already on the mainland. There was a spontaneous outburst of applause and I knew the audience was with me. I then told the conference that Dick Spring and the new government warmly endorsed the establishment of a Council for a New Ireland and sat down to loud and sustained applause.

As I settled in my seat, having spoken for about ten minutes, John Hume thanked me warmly, and Bríd Rogers, Séamus Mallon and Denis Haughey expressed their delight at the government's position and their pleasure at my announcement. Seán Farren asked me if there had been much of a difficulty in getting the government's agreement.

To all this I remained open, but silent, as I nervously realised that I had gone much further than the government might wish.

Later in the bar among the well-wishers who greeted me was Daithí Ó Ceallaigh, a senior diplomat in the Department of Foreign Affairs with responsibility for Northern Ireland. 'Minister, that was a fine speech, if I may say so,' he said as he introduced himself.

I immediately manoeuvred him into a corner where we could speak. In response to my questions, he confirmed that yes there had been discussions about this matter, but the Taoiseach and the government had not agreed to Hume's proposal.

'What should I do?' I asked, my stomach tightening, thinking of how my brave words might be perceived when televised. 'Well,' Daithí said, 'I think you should phone the Tánaiste, before the six o'clock news, so that he will at least know what you have said and does not learn about it for the first time on the television.'

I did not have Dick's number. It was a Saturday afternoon and people were not at home. Twenty years later we have all forgotten what life was like before mobile phones. After many frantic calls, when I finally got to speak to Dick, his relaxed tone and obvious amusement at my discomfort were reassuring. He confirmed that there had been discussions and that Garret was a bit concerned about the Council for a New Ireland. Apparently, the new government did not want to be seen to be led by John Hume. Within weeks the government agreed to the establishment of the New Ireland Forum, based on Hume's proposal.

On Sunday morning, as Joe Coggins drove through the empty Belfast streets, I started to dictate the first draft of a memorandum to the Minister for the Environment. It was a proposal for a Roads Finance Agency, something that had emerged during the course of discussions I'd had with Dick Hargaden and pension fund managers before the formation of the government. The need to invest rapidly but coherently in Ireland's deficient primary road system was self-evident. Pension funds had substantial resources and they clearly wanted new outlets for investment. The Housing Finance Agency, established by the 1981–82 Labour/Fine Gael government to provide soft loans for housing, was my model. I also suggested that a system of tolls on new motorways would help service the cost of the roads capital programme.

Dick was not averse to the idea, but was concerned about the public's reaction to road tolls. To my delight, he allowed me to go to the Department of Finance to present the proposal. Senior Finance officials, including John Loughrey, met myself and civil servants from the Department of the Environment. When I had finished presenting my case, every point was knocked down; the proposal was not acceptable to Finance. They were not prepared to have any other government body borrowing money in the financial markets. Moreover, it would not be helpful for line departments to have independent sources of finance. My last chance was to get a local authority to agree to a toll. If this could be done, then I might be able to change the collective mind of the Department of Finance. The Naas bypass was about to open and, with Dick's agreement, I made a proposal to Kildare County Council and the Urban District Council; in return for agreeing to the establishment of a toll, they would get a percentage of the toll revenue for the first five years. The monies would be additional to their annual road grant.

I argued that, in fifteen years' time, the nation would have a national motorway system that would transform the country. The birthplace of the system would be Kildare and the County Council's decision would go down in history. My enthusiasm was matched only by my political naïveté. Fianna Fáil voted against the scheme, while congratulating me in private on its creativity. The Fine Gael councillors were supportive, but the Labour councillors were split and their division was enough for me to lose. With my tail between my legs, I had to let the proposal die. Twenty-five years later, we still have one of the worst road systems in Western Europe considering our levels of wealth.

One morning I received a call from Jim Mitchell, now the Minister for Transport. He wanted to bring a deputation to see me about a major roadway that was affecting residents in his constituency at Lower Ballyfermot and Inchicore. It was not usual for a minister to ask for a meeting with a minister of state, and I readily agreed. The problem for Jim's constituents, who lived in a complex of redbrick terraced houses known as the Ranch, was that they would be cut off from the rest of Inchicore and Lower Ballyfermot if the proposed route for the alignment of the dual carriageway, which would link the city to the M50 and on to the Galway and Sligo roads, was confirmed. As Minister of State, I had the final say.

The deputation arrived on 28 September 1983, and Jim asked them to wait outside so that he could see me alone. I asked the attending officials to give us five minutes. Quickly, Jim explained the issue and brought me up-to-date on what had been proposed, none of which was acceptable to the locals or himself. Immediately north of the Ranch, open ground sloped down to the banks of the Liffey. It had been used as a refuse dump but was now to be included in a linear park. It seemed an obvious location to him, the residents and me. Its position also meant that the new road could be built independently of the existing one.

At the formal meeting the residents expressed their concerns. The departmental officials responded with the recommendations of the technical staff. This included offers to lower the level of the dual carriageway and provide connecting bridges to the Ranch from Inchicore. In response, Jim Mitchell said the residents wanted a quick solution. He asked if the route could be moved. I then proposed shifting the alignment north of the Ranch. This would cost more was the official response.

'More than the additional costs of sinking the road?' I asked. There was no answer to that question because no cost analysis had been done. So we agreed, there and then, to make the change. After the happy deputation had left, the officials remained. I had made a firm decision and they were content to proceed. My satisfaction at being decisive was matched with an understanding that I had made a clear and sensible choice. Back in time, someone had proposed the original alignment and it had simply got stuck to the point where it could not be questioned. I did not realise it at the time but the unfolding view of the Wellington Monument and the spires and steeples of the city, with the Liffey between them, is a particularly attractive vista as you come into the city from the west. The stretch of the road from Chapelizod into Kilmainham, with its extensive planting of trees, is now the most elegant entrance of any of the roadways into the city of Dublin.

I first met Pádraig Ó hUiginn in Brussels in the early 1970s. At that time he was working with the secretariat of the European Council before he returned to Dublin and Martin O'Donoghue's ill-fated Department of Economic Planning and Development. Now he was in the Department of the Taoiseach. With all this diversity, Pádraig had a good deal of experience and I enjoyed his company. When Dick asked me to look at the question of local government reform, I decided to contact Pádraig because he had been in the Custom House with Pa O'Donnell, the Fine Gael Inter-Party Local Government Minister from Donegal, who had reformed the powers of the city and county managers in 1955.

Back in 1954, in order to get a comprehensive view of what new powers the councillors wanted to balance with what they regarded as the excessive powers given to the county manager, the Donegal minister went on a tour of the country. It was an adroit political move. Dublin was very far away and communication was slow. Pádraig was part of the minister's team, as was a very junior Gerry Meagher, now secretary of the Department of the Environment. With the scars of Kildare still fresh, I borrowed Pádraig Ó hUiginn's idea of visiting councillors and their officials on their own turf and I included side meetings with party activists. My overriding concern was to listen to and hear their concerns and priorities.

John Cullen, a principal officer in the department, prepared a comprehensive brief for each visit, which enabled me to quickly understand matters of concern to each local authority and the position in relation to representations made to the department about particular projects. I found the visits stimulating and enjoyable. I realised that we had public servants of great ability and the utmost integrity. Men, and they were all men, including Paddy Donnelly, Dick Haslam, Noel Dillon and Joe McHugh, impressed me with their dedication and commitment. Quite often, councillors, including some Labour councillors, told me they found the manager very tough, but invariably fair and decisive. Indeed we take for granted, at our own peril, the quality of our public service. Attacks from right-wing commentators on the level of public pay take no account of the commitment and honesty our nation has received from these public servants.

My visits gave me a good sense of the mood of local management and public representatives. The dual mandate was then a strong feature of local authority politics. Government deputies who were also councillors saw their role as mediating between government ministers and their own local backyard. Opposition deputies used the local authority as another platform from which to attack central government. The dual mandate was a distraction and did not, in my opinion, lead to good local government.

There was another level of disagreement between those councillors, of different political parties, who merely wanted to be in office and those who wanted local political power. The first group would hide behind the administrative and political skirts of the county manager. They would trade their votes, in support of his priorities, in return for receiving preferential treatment of representations for their constituency clients. In contrast, councillors with a policy-driven agenda could and did run foul of the manager. My own apprenticeship in local government made me sympathetic to this latter group, but now, as a Minister of State for the Environment, I was caught between the two positions. In these circumstances, the role played by, for example, Noel Dillon in Wexford or Paddy Donnelly in Kilkenny, was particularly attractive. They engaged the political energy of the policy-makers on the council, co-opting them to the political projects, while at the same time retaining the support of the more traditional and clientelist public representatives.

In contrast, Frank Feely, then Dublin city and county manager, frequently failed to bring his council with him and often appeared to be in competition with the councillors for public recognition. A different personality as manager might have had more success, but no other manager had to deal with such a difficult and diverse political body as Dublin City Council. Yet, the stories abounded of the manager upstaging the Lord Mayor on various occasions. Bertie Ahern, when Lord Mayor in 1986–87, in anger and frustration at the end of a busy day, hung his chain of office around the manager's neck, in the midst of the large domed central space in City Hall, proclaiming that since Feely had behaved all day as if he were the mayor, he might as well wear the chain!

At this time Ken Livingstone was the controversial leader of the then Greater London Council (GLC) and a major thorn in the side of Mrs Thatcher's government. My interest in local government reform and the metropolitan structures of the GLC prompted me to visit London with John Long and Frank Kelly. We had a series of meetings with different local government figures. In particular, I remember our visit to Livingstone's office. Beyond the initial pleasantries and political discussion about Northern Ireland, where I disagreed with his uncritical support for Sinn Féin, I found Ken to be knowledgeable and immensely focused on metropolitan issues. After I had expressed my proposals for a metropolitan structure for Dublin similar to London's, he posed sharp and clear questions. What was the population size and the independent local tax base? When I had answered, he dismissed the concept of a two-tiered metropolitan council for Dublin because the population was simply too small. Such a structure would be expensive and bureaucratic. Turning to the more detailed question of the self-management of council estates and the tenants' purchase of council flats, he was equally blunt. If middle-class, educated, local-authority public servants could not manage such complexes, what reason was there to assume that deprived and managerially ill-equipped local communities could do a better job. The self-management of estates was a copout by Thatcher's government. I was struck by the large gap between the naïveté of Ken's political rhetoric on national issues and his pragmatism and common sense on urban politics. I am not surprised that he has gone on to be a successful Mayor of London.

Though I was immersed in my own substantial departmental responsibilities, I was conscious of the political difficulties facing the government and the Labour Party. 'The Way Forward', Haughey's election manifesto, based substantially on extensive work done by the civil service, had promised a £120 million contingency fund for the Department of the Environment. When the new government saw the real financial situation, no provision had been made; the figures were a fabrication. Alan Dukes' tenure at the Department of Finance was firm, but he failed from the outset to appreciate the constraints under which Dick Spring and Labour were operating. As the contingency fund was quietly buried, political support,within the party in favour of coalition, began to fade. Arrangements to provide for the introduction of water rates and financial charges for planning applications took their place. Abolishing taxes is always easy and popular. Introducing new ones, or resurrecting old ones whose departure had been celebrated, is a much more difficult task. It fell to me to take the relevant legislation through the Oireachtas. The more I was convinced of the necessity of these new taxes, the more I realised the political damage that their introduction was doing to the party, but I did not feel that we had any choice but to proceed.

Some two years before I became Minister for State, a case was taken to the Supreme Court to test the constitutionality of rent control legislation on residential properties. This law had been enacted by the British government, as a temporary price control measure, at the onset of the First World War. Like many such temporary measures, it took on an air of permanence and remained on the statute book of the independent Irish state until, in the late 1970s, it was challenged by Paddy Madigan, a Fianna Fáil solicitor and property owner. He won his case and, overnight, thousands of tenants who thought they were secure with their low rents were exposed to very large increases. Rent control is a crude measure and the market distortions of more than sixty years had done great damage to the management of the housing stock. Landlords did not get an economic income from their properties and so did not maintain their buildings well. Tenants, some with substantial incomes, paid a ludicrously low rent for a property which they and their successors could continue to rent indefinitely. But there were also many tenants with very low incomes or fixed pensions who were vulnerable to big rent hikes.

The first legislative attempt to solve this issue was deemed unconstitutional when the president referred it to the Supreme Court. A Private Member's Bill, although it passed second stage in the Seanad, had gone no further. The problem was one of personal and political interest. Many of my constituents lived in rent-controlled properties and I had every reason to move quickly on this matter before the district courts were full of cases of potential evictions of tenants, unable to pay the full market rent, which a landlord was now free to set without let or hindrance.

Eddie Lewis, an energetic and able civil servant, helped me put together a Rents Tribunal Bill, structured on the model of the Employment Appeals Tribunal. The proposal was for the state to pay a rent allowance, bridging the gap between the market rate and the existing rent, subject to the income of the tenant. This concept was transposed into draft legislation. The bill, published in June 1983, had to be enacted as early as possible: I was told that my timetable for getting the bill through the Dáil and Seanad and signed by the president before the summer recess was unrealistic.

Nonetheless, I decided to chance my arm and phoned the leader of the opposition, Charles Haughey. I asked for his co-operation with the speedy passage of the legislation. As I made my case, he said little but agreed, abruptly telling me that I would have to persuade the Fianna Fáil Seanad leader, Mick Lanigan, to facilitate an early taking of the bill. I phoned Mick at his home in Kilkenny. He was open to my request but, until he saw a copy of the bill, he could not give any promises. I asked Joe Coggins to deliver the draft bill to Senator Lanigan in Kilkenny and then park the ministerial car outside his home. Lanigan's neighbours would realise that, even out of office, he still had influence. I was successful. After the bill went through the Seanad, we got all stages through the Dáil between 10 p.m. and 12 midnight on the last full-sitting day of the

House. By the end of August, the regulations to give effect to the bill and the composition of the Rent Tribunal, under the chair of Mary Laffoy SC, were completed. Personally, I was pleased that a small, but effective social market mechanism was now up and running in the difficult housing market.

I did not have much involvement in the Environment Council of the European Union, then known as the EC. On a couple of occasions, I attended some council meetings and got to know my British counterpart, William Waldegrave. In the course of a long and tendentious council meeting in Brussels, I spoke to Waldegrave about our domestic difficulties on local taxation. His government was about to introduce reforms to the UK rates system that would lead to the community charge, or poll tax, to replace the country's system of rates. Having given him a potted history of Ireland's experience, I cautioned him about the impact of the changes they were contemplating. His silent response signalled a political recognition of their difficulties, along with the realisation of the determination of his senior colleagues, including his prime minister, to implement them.

At the same time a separate issue arose. Many traditional right-wing members in Waldegrave's party were supporting demands to disenfranchise Irish residents in Britain. A consequence of Britain's 1949 Ireland Act, which saw the newly declared Republic of Ireland being forced out of the British Commonwealth, confirmed the right of tens of thousands of Irish people living in Britain to vote in general elections. The violence in the North since the late 1960s had led to demands for this right to be removed. To counteract this political alienation, the Irish government proposed reciprocating with British residents in Ireland being given the right to vote in Dáil elections. The legislative responsibility for this decision was with the Department of the Environment and the task of taking it through the Oireachtas became mine.

It was decided to widen the proposal and extend the franchise to include all EC member-state citizens who were resident in Ireland and to include European parliament elections. Greece had recently become the tenth member state and the entry of Spain and

Portugal was on the horizon. When taking the measure through the Dáil, I became aware of the interaction of the office of the president and the legal doubts about the constitutionality of the proposed law. A government cannot knowingly introduce legislation that the Attorney General deems to be unconstitutional. However, a well-prepared government can accept public queries about the constitutionality of proposed and desirable new legislation which could possibly be unconstitutional.

There were doubts, and extending the franchise under the Constitution to British citizens was one of those. While not allowed to request the president to directly refer a bill that has been passed by the Dáil and Seanad, a minister's open acceptance of a legitimate doubt is the code to achieve the same outcome. Accordingly, suitably briefed by my civil servants, I gave the appropriate responses on the floor of the Dáil and Seanad in response to questions put by opposition deputies, as well as government backbenchers. President Hillery did refer the bill to the Supreme Court, which deemed it to be unconstitutional. To keep faith with the government's commitment, an amendment to the Constitution to make such a provision was brought in and passed successfully in June 1984, alongside the second direct elections to the European Parliament.

There were tensions between Dick Spring and Fine Gael's John Bruton over the implementation of Labour's flagship proposal, the National Development Corporation. As Minister for Industry and Energy, Bruton was also coming under pressure from another quarter; the Dublin Gas Company, in private ownership, was a badly run utility now facing bankruptcy. Its collapse was simply unacceptable because of the widespread disruption it would cause, particularly to poorer households that were dependent on gas. However, Bruton's ideological opposition to public ownership brought him into conflict with Frank Cluskey. A large number of the company's workforce were members of the Federated Workers' Union of Ireland. Not only were their jobs at risk, but a substantial flow of secure union dues was also under threat.

Frank was Minister for Trade, Commerce and Tourism, a cabinet post for which he had neither the feel nor the flair. As the economic and budgetary difficulties unfolded over the early months of the new government's term in office, he became uneasy and uncomfortable in cabinet. His colleague, Gemma Hussey, recounted his brooding presence on more than one occasion in her subsequent memoir, *The Cutting Edge: Cabinet Diaries 1982–87*. By the autumn I suspect that he had had quite enough of being trapped in cabinet with a job he did not relish and a growing political storm over which he had little control. The Dublin Gas Company controversy gave him a pretext to leave. Essentially, the dispute between himself and Bruton provided Frank with a credible political platform: the public ownership and consequent survival of Dublin Gas. The European elections were due in 1984 and he had already spent a year in the European Parliament after losing his Dáil seat in June 1981. In retrospect, I feel his desire to run for the European Parliament was a tightly held secret, even from his closest colleagues.

That said, when Frank Cluskey announced his decision to resign from government in November 1983, on an issue of principle over the treatment of Dublin Gas, I was taken aback. However, not being party to the discussions among cabinet ministers, I had no sense of Frank's obvious discomfort. His resignation was a major news story and it generated a lot of coverage, which was soon followed by speculation among the political correspondents about who would get Frank's cabinet seat. My name appeared in the papers as the most likely prospect for promotion. I was perceived to be politically more senior than either Joe Bermingham or Michael Moynihan, the two other junior Labour ministers, or the Leas Ceann Comhairle, John Ryan of Tipperary North. I had been assigned more delegated powers and functions by Dick Spring than any other minister of state in that government. Nevertheless, twenty-four hours after Frank's resignation, I still had had no word from Dick and I became apprehensive about the resounding silence.

I warded off direct questions from friends and supporters who enquired about my promotion prospects by saying that changes were being contemplated and that the decision was about filling more than one vacancy. In truth, I did not know what was going on. It had, however, become clear to me that the workload in the Department of the Environment, combined with the position of Tánaiste and party leader, was an immensely demanding burden on Dick. Kerry was a long way from Dublin and his use of the government plane to Farranfore airport had attracted negative comment by those in the media who believe that Labour politicians should take a vow of operational poverty when in government. Few of the begrudging commentators made reference to the time it takes to travel between Dublin and Kerry, or the fact that Dick was still in severe pain from his accident. At the time, there was talk of Dick taking over responsibility for the Department of Energy and having less departmental responsibility. This would give him more time for his other duties and would clip the wings of the abrasive John Bruton by being able to deal in a sensitive way with the future of Dublin Gas.

Naturally, I assumed that this would logically open the door for me to become Minister for the Environment, and I began to hope that my long-held dream was in sight.

On the afternoon of 12 December, Dick phoned and asked if I would become Minister for Labour as part of a bigger and wider reshuffle. I was surprised and disappointed. I knew little about the Department of Labour and my head was already racing away with how I would advance my various projects in the Department of the Environment. Finally, I expressed great reluctance and asked for time to consider. At one point I even suggested that I might stay on as Minister of State in the Department of the Environment.

The following day Liam Kavanagh rang me. He urged me to accept his old job in the Department of Labour because he was being asked to move to the Department of the Environment. He spoke about the pressure on Dick and of the necessity to create a wider reshuffle so that the partial demotion of John Bruton, who was losing the Department of Energy, could be politically softened. Even as I listened sympathetically, wanting to accept what Liam was saying, I was reluctant to let go. After the call, I went to the outer office and told Frank Kelly that I was going out for a while. He looked at me quizzically, expressing concern because some people whom I had arranged to meet were already in the building. I told him they would have to wait.

I walked purposefully around the Custom House. Angry yet determined, I argued with myself about why I had entered politics and about the potential to achieve and fashion change at cabinet level, irrespective of the department. Being a Labour Party member meant implementing our values of democracy, equality and solidarity by harnessing the state and the public service to transform the quality of people's lives and specifically eliminating inequality, in all its manifestations, and reducing poverty.

Yet, the Department of the Environment was what I knew best and the Department of Labour appeared to be less specific by comparison. It seemed crazy to shift me from a portfolio where I had proven expertise and commitment to one in which I had little knowledge. Against that, the potential of a senior minister's job and the influence within cabinet began to reduce my attachment to the Department of the Environment. By the time I strode around to the front of the Custom House, looking out over the Liffey, I had gone through all the options and had decided to accept the offer. My head was beginning to explore the possibilities of the new post. What was the budget of the Department of Labour? What agencies or outside bodies reported to it?

As I arrived back, Frank Kelly pointed towards the room where my visitors were waiting and wondered if I would see them now. I beckoned for him to come into my office and asked him to get me a copy of the Book of Estimates. He immediately left the office and soon returned with the document. Then I asked him to give me ten minutes and to apologise to the visitors again for keeping them waiting. Straightaway, I opened the book at the Department of Labour section. As I scanned down through the subheadings I was surprised at the number of different activities that come under the department's aegis. I had not realised the size of the allocation to AnCO (the Industrial Training Authority) and to the Youth Employment Agency, or the amount of money that came from the European Social Fund (ESF). In fact, I became excited about the portfolio. My mind made up, I phoned Liam Kavanagh and told him of my decision. We did not speak for long but he said that he would tell Dick and that he was delighted with my decision. And then, finally, I asked Frank Kelly to bring in our guests.

Ken Livingstone and Phil Flynn came into my office. Ken was over to take a tour of local authority housing in the greater Dublin area and wanted to see how our tenant purchase scheme was functioning. I greeted them warmly, apologising for having kept them waiting for so long. I figured that Phil had a fair idea of what was going on. I explained to Ken that I had been speaking with colleagues about whether or not to accept a particular position in cabinet. I expressed my reluctance about the change but told them what decision I had reached. As Phil Flynn wished me all the best in my new position, Ken said that he hoped some day to be confronted with the same problem with which I had been grappling.

Later, when I was alone in my office again, the phone rang and I was soon speaking with Dick. A cabinet meeting was about to start, the Dáil was sitting that afternoon and the reshuffle would be announced at the order of business, after Question Time at 2.30 p.m. I went to Leinster House, having said my goodbyes to a number of senior staff who had heard the news. They came to my office and wished me well, expressing regret at my departure. I did feel quite a twinge as Brendan O'Donoghue, an assistant secretary, expressed his pleasure at having worked with me and complimented me on the contribution I had made – though he strongly supported my decision to take the cabinet job.

The formal reshuffle involved Dick becoming Minister for Energy, John Bruton reuniting the Department of Industry and Commerce with Trade and Tourism, Liam Kavanagh moving to the Department of the Environment and me to the Department of Labour. I met Liam in the ministerial corridor at the back of Government Buildings, which had recently been connected to the Leinster House complex. In the course of our talk, Liam asked me to keep on Freda Nolan, his private secretary, and to retain his special adviser, Veronica McDermott. I readily agreed and also confirmed that John Long and Denise Rogers would still be part of my team.

I then went into Dick's room for a private chat. It was the first time we had spoken face to face since the previous week. He was direct, positive and friendly. 'This job is going to change your life for ever in a way that you don't realise or appreciate,' he told me, and we then walked down the corridor to the office of the Taoiseach. The formality of meeting the Taoiseach, Garret FitzGerald, was offset by our friendship and the fact that we shared a constituency. But now I was going to be a member of his cabinet. As he welcomed me, I responded by thanking him and acknowledging, in a pointed way, that it was in reality Dick who was appointing me to the cabinet.

I made arrangements for a celebratory drink in the visitors' bar later that evening for my family, the constituency executive and friends. But first I told Denise that I wanted her to come to Áras an Uachtaráin when I received my seal of office. Hesitant, she enquired about precedence and protocol, but I was firm. This was only ever going to happen for the first time once and she had done so much to bring this preferment about that it was essential she witness the occasion. I suggested that she get into the car and wait until I and the other ministers who were receiving their new seals of office came out of Leinster House. Nashie Grady, to whom I had said a sad goodbye four weeks earlier, when state cars and drivers were taken from ministers of state, was now back as one of my drivers. With cars and garda outriders, we took off at an indescribable speed from Leinster House, around St Stephen's Green, through Cuffe Street and up to the Phoenix Park.

I had never been in the Áras before and I was taken aback by the dowdiness and old-fashioned air that clung about the entrance hall and public rooms. It seemed to me to be a cross between a convent and a museum. We were invited to sign the visitors' book and were then taken down a dreary passageway lined with busts of former presidents. There, in a large room, the Taoiseach, the four ministers and the secretary to the government were told that the president would come out of an adjoining room. The press photographers were instructed to take a certain position and then Dr Paddy Hillery entered the room. There was a flashing of cameras and requests to look in this direction and that as the president presented me with my first seal of office and formal appointment as Minister for Labour in the Twenty-Fourth Dáil. The seal of office was in a small green leather case that opened to reveal a metal medallion. The seals had to be returned when the photographs had been taken. I was offered a drink and relished a whiskey.

Paddy Hillery said that he had recently met my brother Declan at a conference in Japan. Declan was a psychiatrist living in Saskatoon, practising medicine in that small city on the Canadian prairies where he, the president, had been a doctor many years before. He spoke about his time as Minister for Labour, in the new department that Jack Lynch had established out of the old and substantial empire that was the Department of Industry and Commerce under Seán Lemass. We spent longer in Dr Hillery's company than had been anticipated. I got the impression that he was a lonely man in that large building.

Back at Leinster House, Kevin Duffy, chairman of the Dublin South-East Constituency Council, was the first to congratulate me. There was so much to do and I was, in his view, the person to bring freshness and new ideas to the department. I listened to Kevin with respect and affection. We had first met four years earlier when the extension of Dublin South-East as a four-seat constituency took in part of the inner city, including Cuffe Street, where the Bricklayers' Hall was located. Kevin, general secretary of the Bricklayers' Union, had been recommended to me by Senator Jack Harte when I made enquiries about suitable premises for a constituency clinic in what had previously been Frank Cluskey's bailiwick. I had invited Kevin into Leinster House for lunch and we got on well together. From that initial contact, we developed a personal friendship and close political collaboration. He was a local boy, brought up in the Iveagh Trust Buildings, and had rebuilt the union from near bankruptcy; he was now a rising star in the trade-union movement.

Tired, drained but excited, I went home a full cabinet minister in the sovereign government of the Republic of Ireland. My sense of joy and achievement was tinged with a wisp of sadness. I thought of my father, Malachi, who had in his own time and in his own way made his contribution to bring into existence the very government and parliament of which I was a member. I regretted that he had not lived long enough to see this day.

Chapter 12

The Department of Labour
1983–1987

S oon after I became Minister for Labour, I was informed of two meetings that I had to attend in Paris. The first was an informal Social Affairs Council meeting, being hosted by the French presidency on 2 February 1984. An OECD conference for Labour ministers was due to start the following Monday and would last for two days. I wanted to attend both meetings since they would give me an opportunity to immerse myself in a new set of policy agendas. But what to do with the time between the two meetings?

Five months earlier when I was attending an Irish tourism promotion in La Ferme Irlandaise, an Irish restaurant in Paris, I had met Brendan Dillon, Ireland's ambassador to France. During our conversation he told me that he had been at the centre of Ireland's negotiations to join the EEC, as it was then known. In 1973 he became our first permanent representative in Brussels. When the lunch was over and we were on our way to the airport, Brendan described how he had been private secretary to Seán MacBride during his term as Minister for External Affairs (1948–51), and how MacBride had dispatched him from Iveagh House to deliver the letter to Noël Browne on the steps of the Custom House requesting his resignation from the cabinet in that first inter-party government.

'Come back to Paris and we'll continue this conversation,' he said.

I remembered his words as I waited to have my telephone call put through. He greeted me and asked what could he do for the new Minister for Labour. 'Can five colleagues and myself stay in the Irish embassy for the weekend?' I asked.

'Certainly,' was his immediate reply, 'but I should warn you that the embassy is a building site at the moment. If you don't mind that disruption, then Alice and myself would love to have the six of you and we'll even feed you dinner on Saturday night.' I told Freda Nolan, my private secretary, that we would be staying for the weekend with Ireland's ambassador and his wife. The rest of the group comprised Cyril O'Riordan, the assistant secretary with European responsibilities; Maurice Cashell, a principal officer and adviser in the minister's office; Pat Hayden, who worked with Maurice; and Freda and Denise.

It was a very European dimension to the start of my tenure in the Department of Labour and it made me aware of the significance of the daily work of the department which membership of the European Community required. It took me some weeks to get a sense of the department's full duties. But that was the easier bit. Its amorphous management structure was more disturbing and difficult to comprehend. There were pockets of intense activity by individuals who were keenly involved in domestic or European Community-based issues. Freda Nolan, an immensely capable and diplomatic person, kept me fully briefed. The late Ian Finlay was the secretary of the Department of Labour. Tadgh Ó Cearbhaill had recently retired, having been secretary from the establishment of the Department of Labour in 1966, but his influence still haunted the place. None of this I knew at the time and it was only by piecing together bits of information that I assembled a picture that made sense. I met Ó Cearbhaill some months later at a function in the Irish Management Institute in Sandyford and took an immediate dislike to his bumptious manner and the way he treated his successor who was with me.

I was reminded of the story of when Michael O'Leary had become Minister for Labour in 1973. Arriving at the Department in Mespil Road, Ó Cearbhaill greeted Michael and took him to an office on the top floor. Michael was made to sit in front of a large desk behind which sat Tadgh, who proceeded to outline the activities and structure of the department. Very soon O'Leary interrupted and asked, 'Whose office are we in?'

'Mine of course,' Tadgh replied.

'Where is the minister's office?'

'Next door.'

'Right, let's go into that office now and continue this conversation.' And O'Leary took his place behind his own desk.

Ian Finlay succeeded to the number one post. It soon became clear to me that there were few management meetings and that the three assistant secretaries ran, at different speeds, the four sections of the department. The Labour Court existed outside the department. Effectively, it was an independent organisation, staffed by departmental personnel with an assistant secretary as its chief executive. I soon formed an opinion of what was required in this uncharted territory, with the help of some friends and allies from the previous coalition government.

Kevin Bonner, then principal officer, and Pat Hayden were people I had known when Michael O'Leary was minister. John Horgan, no relation to my one-time Leinster House roommate, was deputy chairman of the Labour Court. The Youth Employment Agency, set up as a Labour initiative in the 1981 short-lived Labour/Fine Gael coalition, had Niall Greene as its chief executive and Terry Corcoran, an economist, as one of his key staff. Central to all this was Kevin Duffy, whose knowledge of the terrain and its diverse personnel was central to my quick immersion course. As I began to understand the department's range and its European dimension, I became excited about the potential prospects for effective action.

New programmes and funding were substantially influenced by the European Social Fund and agencies such as AnCO. At the time Ireland was the poorest of the nine member states and we continued to benefit substantially from the financial assistance which the European Community gave to the poorer regions after Greece joined in 1981. The Social Fund, the source for a large part of AnCO's budget, had helped to build a network of training centres around the country, and supported many of the programmes run in those centres.

Domestic legislation awaited the outcome of draft directives initiated by the European Commission, such as the proposal for protecting workers' rights in insolvent companies, which had to be finalised before the drafting of final legislation could be completed.

The International Labour Organisation (ILO), part of the United Nations, had its annual conference in Geneva every June and Ireland had participated in the conference before our membership of the EEC. Established by the Versailles Treaty, the ILO was designed as a counterbalance to the rise of communism. It was hoped that by bringing representatives of capital and labour together with government officials, the raw corners of capitalism would be rounded and so reduce social friction. There was plenty of convivial mixing among the employers, trade-union representatives and civil servants, who all enjoyed their annual month in Geneva.

Many issues were coming to my desk from different quarters, in an unstructured way that was in marked contrast to the procedures in the Custom House, and I felt that shape had to be given to our work and activity. Ian Finlay had told me that the four senior civil servants had met as a management group, intermittently, without the minister.

I decided that, at 9.00 a.m. every Monday morning, I would have a half-hour meeting in my office with my minister of state, Fine Gael's George Birmingham, followed by an hour-long management meeting with a set agenda and a rolling review of the work of the department and the range of programmes and projects which needed attention. I liked George, he was a very able minister of state, and we got on well. The main issues we faced in that first year were health and safety proposals, the relaunch of the Great Southern Hotel group, a new industrial relations review and a White Paper on manpower policy.

The trip to Paris was informative and enjoyable. My introduction to the Social Affairs Council was different to my limited experience of the two Environmental Councils I had attended in Brussels. Pierre Bérégovoy, one of Mitterrand's senior lieutenants who later became prime minister, chaired the meeting. Bérégovoy was generous to me as the new member of the ministerial group of ten, some of whom were strong personalities – Ken Clarke and Lord Young from Britain, Gianni De Michelis from Italy, Jean-Claude

Juncker from Luxembourg and Dimitrius Yiannopoulos from Greece soon asserted themselves.

When the OECD conference started, I was well prepared having read the extensive briefing material. In addition, my first meeting with my European colleagues had given a good insight into the economic problems within the European Community at that time. I found myself seated between John Selwyn Gummer, then an Employment Minister in Margaret Thatcher's government, and the US Under Secretary for Labor, whose name I do not remember. But both were aggressive in their right-wing views. In the early 1980s, the growing certainty of radical conservatism was beginning to assert itself intellectually and politically with an arrogant self-righteousness which I would later encounter at home when Michael McDowell defected from Fine Gael to help found the Progressive Democrats.

Both Gummer and his American colleague rubbished the European social market economy with its high levels of support and protection for workers, consumers and women. It should all be scrapped, they argued, and free-market forces should be allowed to invigorate the sluggish economy. Protectionism, particularly that provided by government, was bad.

Knowing I was facing strong conservative forces, I could not leave their assertions unanswered. I argued at least for consistency in our international approach within the OECD. I was never a great fan of Europe's Common Agricultural Policy and now felt that it had long outserved its usefulness. The enormous subsidies, more than half the entire EC's budget, were mostly going to rich farmers, whilst European consumers paid high food prices. The closed agricultural markets of the European Community, along with the United States and Japan, were preventing Third World countries from developing their own agriculture and so possibly trading their way out of poverty. So as not to appear parochial, I referred to the British situation and how the contradictions of the CAP were making market efficiencies in one of Europe's most developed agri-sectors so difficult to achieve. If colleagues around the table wanted to introduce market forces into Europe's labour market, why should it be confined to that, surely agriculture could do with a similar blast of what they believe to be healthy fresh air? This exposed the hypocrisy of both countries; Britain and the United States wanted one set of economic rules for workers and a different set for farmers and employers. Over lunch, Gummer complimented me on my knowledge of the problems of British farming and wondered if I was an agricultural specialist. When I told him that I was an architect, he asked how I knew so much about the intricacies of Britain's agricultural problems. I calmly informed him that, for many years, I had listened to the omnibus edition of *The Archers* on BBC Radio 4.

Alice and Brendan were generous and interesting hosts. On Saturday morning, I took up Alice's invitation to go to the new markets at Rungis, near Orly Airport. The vacated inner-city site was the new dramatic cultural centre, named after de Gaulle's successor, Georges Pompidou. As the son of a grocer, I revelled in the large variety and range of the food halls at Rungis. Alice and I planned the evening meal which she was going to cook for her self-invited guests. Later I spoke at length to Brendan about his experiences of negotiating Ireland's terms of entry to the EEC. I urged him to consider writing all this down so that the events of the time would be recounted directly, but sadly he never did.

Coming back from Paris, and thinking about the work ahead in the Department of Labour, I realised that I knew very few of the general secretaries of the more than eighty-eight trade unions whose main point of contact with government was through the department. The senior members of the Irish Congress of Trade Unions – such as John Carroll, Dan Murphy and Billy Attley – were familiar figures, as was Donal Nevin, who had succeeded Ruaidhrí Roberts as secretary of the ICTU. Donal was very close to Frank Cluskey and was an influential, behind-the-scenes member of the Labour Party. While the bulk of the 640,000 membership of the movement was contained in three large unions, I was anxious to develop links and make contacts with as many individual unions and their general secretaries as possible. I knew that I needed help from someone familiar with the territory and the personalities, who could, by working with me in the department, provide a connection to these people. Reform of the current industrial relations legislation was a major item on the department's programme and I wanted to get to know as many of the union officials as I could.

I had met Stephen Tracey at a number of Labour conferences, heard him speak and liked what he had to say. Formerly the general secretary of the National Union of Sheet Metal Workers of Ireland (NUSMWI), he was now an official with the ITGWU. I got the Taoiseach and Tánaiste to agree that I could take on a trade-union adviser and I approached Stephen with an offer. He agreed to come and work with me after resigning from his post in Liberty Hall.

From the beginning Stephen Tracey was invaluable. A series of one-to-one meetings was set up with general secretaries of the small and medium-sized unions. Many had never met a Minister for Labour and none had had a meeting in the office of the minister where the one item on the agenda was the employment concerns of their members and their union. Stephen filled me in on the background of each individual. As well as Stephen, I often asked Kevin Duffy for his opinion about a union or a particular general secretary. That year I developed a comprehensive knowledge of the personalities of the many people who made up the trade-union movement in Ireland. A year later, as we were analysing the complex question of Ireland's antiquated industrial relations laws and the extraordinary legal logic of the 1906 British Act on which strike legislation was based, I had a good understanding of how the trade unions saw things, as a result of that protracted exercise.

On the employers' side, Dan McAuley was the director general of the Federated Union of Employers. His calm, professional manner was frequently contrasted with the abrasive personalities of some of the captains of industry who made up his council.

The organisational structures of the industrial relations machinery of the early 1980s were antiquated because they were partly run by the department. Many directly involved felt that the rigidities of the civil service were an inappropriate constraint on the operation of industrial relations law. My predecessor, Liam Kavanagh, had initiated the process of reform, and work was at an early stage when I became minister. New legislation would be required, because it was essential to supersede the original 1906 British act. Kevin Duffy explained to me the history of the act's birth and the tortured logic of its double negative legal basis.

To my surprise, I learned that in the Republic of Ireland there was no right to strike, but rather a guarantee of immunity from civil prosecution for damages incurred if a person, or persons, carried out industrial action. The question of ballots and notification procedures, along with single-person disputes, had also to be resolved. As a counterview to the prevailing conservatism of the department and Congress, Kevin advocated that a positive right to strike should be enacted in legislation, but with a set of procedures and conditions set alongside it to safeguard society, individual trade unions and employers alike. A right to strike existed in nearly every other European country, with the exception of Britain. I was attracted to the coherence of his arguments and, in due course, that fundamental change, along with many procedural and institutional changes, were put together in a discussion document that was published and circulated to the trade unions and employers. I was not to be the Minister for Labour to carry the process to its final legislative stage. My successor, Bertie Ahern, accepted nearly all the ideas put forward in the original discussion document with one major exception. He did not accept the concept of the right to strike and instead carried the conservative basis of the 1906 act through to the 1990 Industrial Relations Act.

I had known Bertie when we both served on the City Council in 1974 and had congratulated him when he was promoted by Charles J. Haughey to be the Fianna Fáil spokesperson on Labour in 1984. I asked Freda Nolan if she had a copy of the briefing document on the department that had been presented to me when I had become minister.

'Why do you want it?' she asked.

'Because I want to send it to Bertie Ahern.'

'Why would you want to do that?'

'First, as a deputy, he is entitled to it. Second, he is well able to get something similar himself, and, thirdly, if I send it to him, I will then know what he knows.'

She smiled as she gave me the substantial document to attach to the personal letter I had written to Bertie.

The reform of the manpower services and the creation of what subsequently became known as FÁS was another project on my agenda. It was decided that we should prepare a White Paper on manpower policy that would be a comprehensive review of the Irish labour market and its training needs; this led to the reorganisation of four separate bodies into one coherent organisation. AnCO, the Industrial Training Authority set up in 1967, was the largest body with a lot of staff and substantial resources, mostly drawn down from the European Social Fund. The Youth Employment Agency had a narrower remit, focusing on the very high levels of youth unemployment and financed by a 1 per cent levy on income. CERT was the specific training body for the hotel and tourism industry and it jealously guarded its independence from AnCO. Finally, within the department, a large section ran the National Manpower Service, the government's employment placement agency. Staffed by civil servants, with a network of offices around the country and its headquarters within the department, it was considered to be a rather lethargic agency.

I shared the emerging consensus that these four bodies should be integrated into one national organisation, operating as a semi-state body, removed from the department's day-to-day control. The energy and flexibilities that were the characteristics of AnCO would become the prevailing ethos. However, first we had to prepare the White Paper and this took much longer than anyone had anticipated. When it was published, it seemed to me then, and more so now, that it was quietly ignored as the preparation of the legislation for the new integrated organisation began.

It soon became clear that CERT did not want to be absorbed and a clever rearguard action to maintain its independence was mounted by the tourism industry and its board. I had lost about a year in the

White Paper phase and the government was now coming to the end of its term. I kept pushing for CERT's inclusion within the National Employment and Training Agency (NETA), the proposed name of the new organisation. Fianna Fáil, sensing my difficulties, slowed up the second-stage debate and I began to run out of time. Even my last-minute offer to exclude CERT did not get the co-operation I had got in 1983 with the Rent Tribunal legislation. The government, now in dispute with some Fine Gael backbenchers over other matters, did not have the time available to let the legislation proceed at the slow pace Fianna Fáil demanded.

I was deeply disappointed because I had put great effort into the project, but I did learn from the experience. Ten years later, as Minister for Enterprise and Employment, I had responsibility for implementing the recommendations of the Culliton Report on the restructuring of the Industrial Development Authority (IDA) and related agencies. I was aware of the frustration and the demoralisation that had affected the establishment of FÁS (Foras Áiseanna Saothair – the successor name to NETA), caused largely by the length of time between my announcement of organisational change and its implementation by my successor. I was determined not to let that happen again. In January 1993, the outline structure of three boards, Forfás, Forbairt and IDA Ireland, were quickly established and became operational that July. The legislation to give effect to these new structures was completed by December 1993. When Charlie McCreevy, as Minister for Tourism and Trade, strongly objected to the incorporation of Córas Tráchtála Teo (CTT), the trade marketing board, I remembered sadly the fruitless campaign to include CERT in the new organisation.

In 1993, at a meeting between Minister McCreevy and myself, facilitated by another cabinet colleague, Charlie recognised the organisational logic of including CTT in Forbairt, but pointed out that it was effectively stripping him of half his department. I did not push the issue and got on with the three organisations. I knew it was not ideal and said that in future someone else would complete the task. In due course, when Mary Harney added Trade to the Department of Enterprise and Employment in 1997, she

incorporated CTT into Forbairt, renaming the new enlarged organisation as Enterprise Ireland. Fighting other people's battles can be
a distraction for ministers, who sometimes take the strident advice
of their senior officials beyond the bounds of political reality.
Because the next general election seems to be at least four years
away does not mean that a minister has four years to complete a
project.

I was now living in a small, two-bedroomed, single-storey house in
Sandymount. Every morning on my way to work, I collected
Malachi and Síne and took them to school I always enjoyed this
daily contact. They usually stayed with me at the weekend. One
Sunday evening as my twelve-year-old daughter was completing her
homework, she said, 'Dad, you know the way you are the Minister
for Labour.'
    'Yes.'
    'Well, who is the Minister for Fine Gael?'
    I burst into laughter and Malachi started ribbing her about her
question. But naïve and all as it may have been, it was, on reflection,
perfectly logical.

There are some proposals that are on the minister's desk when he or
she takes office, or else are part of a programme for government. By
contrast, a minister's own initiatives can be difficult to introduce.
The issue of unemployment was dominant throughout my term in
that Fine Gael/Labour government. Structural long-term unemployment appeared to be the norm in Ireland, and also in many
European countries, including Spain and Portugal, both of which
were soon to become member states of the European Community.
At each meeting of the Social Affairs Council, unemployment was
always high on the agenda. Conscious of the theoretical work being
done on the Manpower White Paper, my mind increasingly focused
on the problem of the long-term unemployed. During one discussion, I suggested to the White Paper working party that we

should look at a country like Hungary. It had a government-directed centralised command economy, based on five-year plans, with some free-market forces operating within that economy. Even so, the Hungarians were making some interesting changes. *The Economist* magazine regularly ran articles about Hungary and what it described as its version of 'goulash communism'.

I wondered how the Hungarians dealt with their own unemployment problem and whether or not Ireland could learn from them. I mentioned this to civil servants in the department and I suspect that I secretly shocked some of the more conservative ones. Any suggestion that there were economic or social lessons to be learned from a communist state was to them proof positive of my true colour.

In fact, I was very attracted to the socialist concept of a structured labour market where everyone had a role and where being without a job, or social parasitism as it was called, was outlawed. I felt that excluding a person from the possibility of work was a denial of a basic human right, arguing that when a person first met another, three basic questions were often asked. What is your name? Where do you live? And what do you do? To be unable to answer the third question, or to have to reply 'Nothing', was and is demeaning. Everyone does something, even if they do not get paid for it. But the failure of a market economy to generate enough economic demand to create additional jobs should not be a punishment for unemployed people. Western Europe had developed a system of unemployment insurance, but its duration was short, and in Ireland unemployment assistance payments were low and means-tested against the household income. The result was poverty for people who could not get a job. Confronted with the issue of what seemed to be permanent long-term unemployment for significant sections of Irish society, I felt that we had to do much more than increase the amount of money paid out in social welfare. For me, the material poverty of the low level of income was compounded by the social exclusion which unemployment itself entailed. I found it unacceptable that there were homes where young children did not see their mother or father go out to work.

A fundamental value of a socialist society is full employment and it must remain a constant objective. During an informal Social Affairs Council meeting in Luxembourg, presided over by Jean-Claude Juncker, I stated that it had taken Europe two centuries to remove a dominant group in our society who did not associate income with work – the aristocracy. With all the resources that we now had, we should not push the long-term unemployed into becoming a new category of citizen who also saw no connection between income and work. I started to explore the active labour-market measures that had been developed by the social democrats in Scandinavia and we also did analysis of the Hungarian labour market. My proposal was then fleshed out further within the department.

A person who was unemployed for two years or more could be given work on a Social Employment Scheme, for a minimum of one year, and receive 20 per cent more than the unemployment assistance in return for a part-time week of twenty hours. The participants were free to take other small jobs such as they may have been doing anyway. The employers could be local authorities, schools, community groups, sports clubs or heritage and cultural bodies. The trade unions expressed genuine fears about displacement, fearing that local authorities would lay off existing workers to avail of what would be cheaper labour. In response to this genuine concern, a monitoring committee involving the unions was established to vet all projects. The Social Employment Scheme was formally adopted by the cabinet in 1985. A provision was made for 11,000 places in its first year.

The scheme was launched on a pilot basis in Wexford. Senator Brendan Howlin had been nominated to the Seanad by Dick Spring as one of the Taoiseach's eleven nominees. Furthermore, I was anxious to help Labour win back Brendan Corish's seat in Wexford and had made a number of visits to the constituency. Through Brendan, who was a county councillor as well as a member of Wexford Town Corporation, I met Noel Dillon, a dynamic county manager. As a result, the Model County was the obvious choice for the pilot project before we went national with the scheme. In addition to the local authority, a number of voluntary groups came forward as sponsors and employers. However, public liability insurance emerged as a major problem. The cost to voluntary organisations was prohibitive and no employer group, except local authorities, could afford the insurance – and it would not do to have all the participants employed by local authorities. As we sat around the table in Davitt House (the Department of Labour building), we were facing disaster because the scheme had already been launched. I then remembered an insurance broker whom I had met socially. I rang him and he joined the small working group. Together we produced a general arrangement for all groups and participants in the voluntary sector. Cyril Forbes saved the Social Employment Scheme.

The Social Employment Scheme was further developed by Fianna Fáil after I left the Department of Labour. It was a happy coincidence that I found the scheme back on my desk when I became Minister for Enterprise and Employment in January 1993 and I was able to alter some aspects of its operation. The name was changed to the Community Employment Programme and was run by FÁS. Since its launch over 250,000 people have participated in the scheme. For many, it was a second chance of getting into the labour market and they then went on to successful careers and full-time jobs.

'Work Worth Doing' was the slogan that Dave Holden came up with when we launched the scheme. I have seen countless projects successfully run throughout the country. While participants are able to stay for only a maximum of two years, the actual community projects provide ongoing employment and continuity with a wide range of services. The private sector would never have provided these in many rural areas or in inner-city, working-class communities where economic demand is low. Of all the political initiatives with which I have been associated, this is one that, to this day, gives me the a lot of political satisfaction. Progressive Democrat leader Dessie O'Malley denounced the schemes as being 'economically as valuable as swatting nettles in a graveyard'. His successor, Mary Harney, had a similar antipathy towards the Social Employment Scheme, but she could not abolish it because of its public popularity.

A few days after I became Minister for Labour in 1983, I met, at his request, Malachy Sherlock, the director general of AnCO. During the meeting, he extolled the virtues of the old Irish College in Louvain, just north of Brussels. Founded in 1607 and now no longer required by the Franciscan Order, it was being given to the Irish community in Brussels, provided they could do a major job of restoration on what had been a large residential college attached to the Catholic university in that historic city.

One of the training programmes run by AnCO was for construction apprentices. Work experience, essential to completing their course, was not always available in the private sector. To fill that gap, an imaginative, community, youth-training programme had been established. Voluntary organisations with building needs could avail of AnCO's supervised trainee workforce for free, provided that the organisation paid the cost of the construction materials. I knew of many sports clubs and community groups across the country which had been the beneficiaries of this programme.

Malachy was proposing an all-Ireland programme, involving trainees from North and South, in an innovative scheme. The trainees, the best from each training centre around the country, would live and work in the Irish College in Louvain for six months. Over two years, the restored college could become a centre for Irish learning and experience at the very heart of the new Europe; Brussels was less than half an hour away.

I knew of the college and its role in Irish history. After the defeat of Gaelic Ireland at the Battle of Kinsale and the subsequent Flight of the Earls from Ulster in 1607, that Irish party, including O'Neill and O'Donnell, passed the winter in Louvain before journeying south to Rome. The college had come as a gift of solidarity from the King and Queen of Spain during those times when Europe was divided between Catholic and Protestant.

But today there was one small problem which Malachy Sherlock outlined – the 1967 AnCO legislation did not state whether the training authority could operate outside Ireland. Back then such a possibility could never have been imagined. Now it rested with me as minister to decide, because the legal advice was neutral on the question. When I visited the complex of buildings in Louvain some weeks later, I was seduced by its history and future potential and had no hesitation in deciding 'Yes'.

Two years later as the date approached when Spain and Portugal would become full members of the European Union, in January 1986, I wanted to mark that unique event with a party of welcome for my Iberian ministerial colleagues on the Social Affairs Council. It was an appropriate time for Ireland to say thank you to her Iberian friends, 380 years later. Despite my senior civil servants' reservations about the protocols involved and concerns about a possible poor attendance, the event was a tremendous success. We organised a grand reception for the new Spanish and Portuguese European Commissioners, their Social Affairs ministers and colleagues. Peter Sutherland, the Irish commissioner, who coincidentally at that time had responsibility for Social Affairs as well as Competition, was present and the entire event,which had been organised by AnCO on my behalf, provided a wonderful and memorable evening.

On 21 December 1985, Des O'Malley, Mary Harney and Michael McDowell launched the Progressive Democrats (PDs). The superbly timed announcement resulted in a surge of support for the new party in the opinion polls. The roller-coaster of the PDs gathered strength as first Pearse Wyse and then Bobby Molloy joined, to be following by Michael Keating, a defection from Fine Gael. Labour Senator Helena McAuliffe was also enticed across the floor by her social friend Mary Harney, much to the party's disgust. Helena stood, unsuccessfully, for the PDs in the then Longford–Westmeath constituency but subsequently left the party and later returned to her natural home with Labour. Former Labour Senator Tim Conway also inexplicably decided to join the new right-wing party.

In February 1986 our weekly parliamentary party meeting was thrown into confusion when a colleague, arriving late, raised a question about the announced cabinet reshuffle. He told us that Garret FitzGerald had just announced to his parliamentary party meeting that same morning that there was to be a reshuffle involving both coalition parties. We agreed to an immediate adjournment while Dick Spring left the room to find out what was going on.

The previous autumn media stories had circulated about a cabinet reshuffle and I had raised the issue at one of our pre-cabinet ministerial meetings which were held in Dick's office in the Department of Energy on Clare Street. He said that Garret had spoken informally about the matter but no more had come of it. Dick referred to the letter that the Taoiseach had written to ministers when the government was formed. Since I had not received this letter, I asked what Garret had written and was told that the Taoiseach had informed all ministers on their appointment that he reserved the right to have a reshuffle of office-holders during the term of his government. Dick then asked the three Labour ministers – Liam Kavanagh, Barry Desmond and myself – along with the Attorney General, John Rogers, who was not directly involved, if we wanted to change our jobs. The response was a clear 'No' from all three of us and so the matter was dropped, on the understanding that any reshuffle would be confined to Fine Gael.

Now, some five months later, the situation appeared to have changed dramatically. Later that day Dick confirmed to his cabinet colleagues that Garret did intend making major changes on the Fine Gael side but, in the interests of solidarity, he also demanded Labour changes. Joe Birmingham, who was retiring from the Dáil at the next general election, had earlier indicated to Dick that he might stand down as Minister of State for Finance to enable the Labour leader to promote someone else and so help consolidate the party. However, confronted now with the reality of instant demotion, Joe was not a happy man.

In the event, Garret asked Barry Desmond to surrender his Health and Social Welfare portfolio and move to another department. Barry refused point blank. A crisis then broke out on two fronts. Garret had intended making Gemma Hussey the Minister for Europe, but had not thought through the implications of this before his offer to her became public. When she learned that she would not be in charge of a full, independent department, with its own financial allocation, separate from Foreign Affairs yet in some way subservient to it, she understandably declined the portfolio. Peter Barry, Minister for Foreign Affairs, had also blocked the division of Foreign Affairs into effectively two separate departments. But the genie was now out of the bottle and unless both parties could agree to a collective reshuffle, the future of the coalition was in doubt. As the hours passed, the crisis intensified.

In the end, Barry Desmond reluctantly agreed to relinquish Social Welfare while holding on to Health, and Liam Kavanagh came to the rescue by agreeing to give up Environment for the less important conglomeration of Tourism, Fisheries and Forestry. Dick told us the names of the three Fine Gael ministers who were being moved. He sought our agreement before returning to Garret to restore some stability to a weakened government caused by the Taoiseach's self-generated debacle.

What was now proposed was that Gemma Hussey would get the less glamorous job of Minister for Social Welfare, Alan Dukes was to move to the Department of Justice, Michael Noonan to the Department of Industry and Commerce, and John Bruton to the Department of Finance, with John Boland becoming Minister for the Environment. I asked what was to happen to the Department of Public Service, only to be told by a hassled Dick Spring that it was to be added to the Department of Finance. I pointed out that we had four cabinet ministers, but originally had been allocated five departments. By losing the Department of Social Welfare to Fine Gael, the strong anti-coalition sentiment in the party, both within and outside the Houses of the Oireachtas, would be strengthened. I also told Dick that John Bruton was anathema to the trade unions and we were in the middle of a confrontation with the teachers' unions, whose demand for a wage increase the previous autumn had been described by Gemma as 'immoral'. I went on to say that the combination of John Bruton and Paddy Cooney, the new Minister for Education, was not the best prospect for the resolution of a dispute that had brought the three teachers' unions resolutely together. With Liam Kavanagh's support, I pointed out to Dick that Public Service had originally been combined with the Department of Labour and that I was prepared to take it back.

'Garret would never agree to that,' a beleaguered Barry Desmond retorted.

'Just ask him,' I urged Dick, as he left the room to present Garret with our compromise response to his request for agreement to the now botched reshuffle. After a short period, Dick returned, relieved and relaxed. Garret had agreed to the changes, which Liam Kavanagh had made possible along with Barry Desmond's surrender of the Department of Social Welfare.

'And what about the Department of Public Service?' I asked.

'Oh that,' said Dick. 'That's no problem; he did not raise any objection about that.'

While I emerged enhanced from the whole fiasco, the damage to the cause of the coalition was almost terminal. The mood amongst government supporters was solemn and Labour Party members were angry. For my part, I could not see the benefit of a general reshuffle, even though by getting the Department of Public Service I was a beneficiary.

That early spring of 1986 did not generate a sense of renewal within the Labour Party, either in government or beyond. Despite being extremely busy in both departments and thoroughly enjoying the increased challenge, I knew that the public were indifferent and the electorate hostile. My entry into the office of the Minister for Public Service was immediate. While I had some previous experience of the building while John Boland was minister, I was now to occupy his office. Kevin Murphy, the wise and experienced secretary of the department, came over to Leinster House on the day I was appointed minister and soon introduced me to the priorities of the department. Mary Austin continued in the job of minister's private secretary which she had with John Boland. Top of the list of priorities was public pay and the teachers' dispute. Even though I had been Minister for Labour for three years, I had no direct experience of negotiating a pay deal. During the lifetime of that government, the employers' organisations – the Confederation of Irish Industry (CII) and the Federated Union of Employers (FUE) – had refused to participate in social partnership, or national understandings as they were then called. While I knew Gerry Quigley, Kieran Mulvey and Jim Dorney quite well, I had not negotiated directly with the leaders of the three teachers' unions. Soon I was to be introduced to a new world.

I was not that close to Paddy Cooney even though we had been colleagues in government for just over two years. I found him a rather old-fashioned man. We had shared a fascinating visit, as election observers, to Zimbabwe in February 1980, along with Bobby Molloy and Richard Townsend of the Department of Foreign Affairs. Such visits to far-flung places can bring diverse parliamentary colleagues closer together. Paddy and I now found ourselves charged with negotiating a resolution to a fractious pay dispute which had the potential to adversely affect the rest of the government's public-service pay strategy.

The three teachers' unions succeeded in mounting a very effective combined campaign entitled Teachers United. The general secretaries, despite their internal rivalries, played a great game in public. So good was their performance that the long-sought-for goal of a single united teachers' confederated union seemed to be a real prospect. Kevin Murphy and Billy Smith, along with Declan Brennan from Education, were the senior civil servants who led the discussions in the absence of ministers. We were negotiating, on and off, for the best part of three weeks. On the eve of May Day, Cooney, myself and senior officials stayed up all night in the department awaiting a response from the trade-union side. Nothing arrived.

Some days later, progress was made. At 3.30 in the morning Billy Smith phoned me at home to say there had been significant movement on the union side and that a response from government was required urgently. His advice was that if he could move a small bit beyond the line that had been laid down by the cabinet, a deal could be clinched. I listened to his persuasive arguments, enquiring if the proposed concession would have a knock-on effect on other public-service pay claims. Satisfied that it wouldn't, I told him that I would phone Paddy Cooney.

Well advised, I knew that this was the opportune moment. Judgement was required and a decision had to be made. There and then, Paddy Cooney and I decided to authorise our officials to conclude a deal, in principle, without reference to the cabinet. Both of us knew that the position would not get any better. So I phoned Billy Smith to give him the all-clear, telling him that I had spoken to the Minister for Education and that we would inform the Taoiseach.

However, the Taoiseach was not pleased with this turn of events and later that day he confronted Paddy and me – but we stood our ground, defended the decision of the official whom we had authorised to negotiate and told him that it was the best deal available. I went on to say that it simply was not possible, or practical, in the middle of the night, to involve him as Taoiseach.

As we entered the final lap of the government's term of office, a number of my policy initiatives began to mature. When I had taken office, the future of the Great Southern Hotel Group was an issue that had to be resolved. The parliamentary party had demanded that the Great Southern Hotel Group be held in public ownership. An orphan of the embattled CIÉ group of companies, this historic hotel chain had languished at the bottom of the agenda of the state's public transport company and seldom received the attention it desperately required. Some years earlier, the loss-making group had hurriedly sold two hotels at below their market value, following a departmental direction. The solid employment and good catering standards that the group represented would disappear if they were to go the way Minister for Transport Jim Mitchell wanted. They had accumulated debts, mostly tax arrears, of approximately £14 million and it was agreed that clearing these debts would be the sole capital injection that the state, through the Department of Labour, would make to relaunch the group.

My first task was to select a new board for the existing company, with its six hotels in counties Kerry, Galway and Wexford. It seldom falls to a minister to select an entire team for a semi-state company which is already in operation. I wanted to give the Great Southern hotels a chance to show that public enterprise could perform efficiently, provided it had a fair chance, reasonable finance and no political interference. Therefore, I decided, with the agreement of the Taoiseach and the Tánaiste, to select a group of people with a range of complementary skills, whose individual experience and combined co-operation could make a success of the hotel group. I wanted people who had never served on the board of a state company.

Eileen O'Mara Walsh was president of the National Tourism Council, a successful travel agent with her own business and also a party political supporter, having canvassed in a number of elections. A natural leader, she presided over a team of accountants, publicans, retailers, hoteliers and a property specialist, who, with two trade-union representatives, made up ten directors, including the secretary. At my first meeting with the board, I thanked them for giving of their time and promised them that their collective decisions would be respected and that there would be no political interference in their deliberations. The company's day-to-day management would not be second-guessed by the civil servants or myself.

One of their first tasks was to appoint a new chief executive, and some weeks later Eileen rang to say that the board had a difficulty in attracting a suitable candidate because of the constraints of the public service salary range. I told her to do the best she could. She came back and told me that they had completed their interviews and concluded that the best person for the job was the incumbent, Eamon McKeon. My response was not positive. Given the many previous difficulties faced by the group, I told Eileen that I found the decision most unusual, but that I would respect it.

At Eileen's invitation, I met Eamon for lunch in Bernardo's, a well-known Italian restaurant on Lincoln Place. I felt bound to tell him directly about the reservations I had articulated to Eileen and he was gracious in the face of my comments. It was, I said, up to him to prove me wrong – which is exactly what he did. By introducing

change into the moribund organisation, Eamon McKeon helped to
transform the company into a profitable enterprise. Sadly in later
years, the politics of Aer Rianta (which became the new owner of
the Great Southern Hotel Group in 1989 in a bizarre transfer from
the Department of Labour to the Department of Transport) meant
that the political interference I had disavowed returned with a
vengeance. As a consequence, the group's potential for natural
growth has been unnecessarily curtailed. Since 1984, other than the
original elimination of its arrears of tax and social-welfare
payments, it has not received a single penny of additional state
equity in the form of cash or capital injection. Sadly, it is now back
where I found it, losing money because of shareholder neglect.

There was a file on my desk soon after I came into the Department
of Labour with a curious acronym: COWSA, the Committee for
Welfare Services Abroad. It had a membership of about twenty, the
majority of whom were Catholic clerics, with a Church of Ireland
clergyman, a couple of nuns and some political appointees. COWSA's
remit was to help in a very minor way, because of its limited resources,
Irish associations in Britain which were assisting Irish emigrants who
had fallen on hard times. I made some enquiries about the committee
and was told that it was an old and somewhat redundant gathering,
even if the work with which it was charged was of growing
importance. I decided that a fresh start was needed, so I wrote to all
COWSA members, thanked them for their work and informed them
that I was replacing their committee with a new organisation.

Following some informal consultations with the Federation of
Irish Societies in Britain, with whom I had a previous contact, I
agreed with Seamus McGarry and Gearóid Ó Meachair, among
others, that what was required was a new group, representative of
the Irish bodies that were doing the work in many British cities,
such as London, Liverpool and Manchester. At my request,
Maurice Cashell came up with a new name for this body – Díon,
meaning roof or shelter. This new smaller body was to be chaired
by the Department of Labour official attached to the Irish embassy

in London, since most of the committee were based in Britain. Vicki Somers, a senior social worker with the Eastern Health Board and a long-time Labour Party activist in Dublin South-East was a particularly effective member and also kept me fully up to date. We significantly increased the financial resources and Díon began the excellent work that it still undertakes today.

Most Irish citizens who were forced to emigrate to Britain in the 1940s and 1950s had dramatically improved the quality of their lives over ten or twenty years, relative to the opportunities that existed for them in Ireland. Many sent back substantial sums of money, an economic lifeline, to the land of their birth. But sadly, for a variety of reasons a small percentage did not do well and, as they got older, they fell out of the system, ghettoised by their own isolation. Being Irish contributed to a life of poverty, alcoholism and cultural alienation. Díon supported those Irish organisations that had reached out to these people. They provided sheltered housing, welfare and health advice, along with a supportive daycare programme for the elderly in the Irish centres across Britain. When in London visiting Ken Livingstone in 1983, I had seen some of the work they had done and over the following years had several opportunities to visit centres in Britain and admire this important work.

In July 1984, Mary Manning, a checkout assistant in the Henry Street branch of Dunnes Stores refused to accept payment from a customer for South African oranges. She told her supervisor that she was acting in accordance with her conscience and a resolution passed at her union's annual conference in solidarity with the anti-apartheid movement, which had strong support in Ireland. Mary Manning was suspended and nine other workers walked out in solidarity. They were suspended from their jobs but were joined on the picket line by another Dunnes Stores worker from the Crumlin branch and were in turn supported by their union, the Irish Distributive and Administrative Trade Union (IDATU), which today is known as Mandate. Within weeks, the stand taken by these courageous and principled young workers became a

national and then an international story. But the importation of
South African fruit was legal. Dunnes Stores chief executive Ben
Dunne refused to stop selling the fruit. Although the issue was
fundamentally political, it had manifested itself as an industrial
relations dispute and so it appeared on my desk, needing a
resolution. In the weeks that followed, departmental officials and I
had many discussions with retailers and fruit importers.

Early on, I referred the dispute to the Labour Court; this required
the union and employers to enter into negotiations. These took
place but without success. The anti-apartheid movement wanted a
ban to be placed on the importation of fruit and vegetables from
South Africa, as part of its wider political campaign. I was in full
sympathy with the workers and supported them politically. For
many years I had been a member of the Irish anti-apartheid movement and as a student I had gone to Parnell Square to take part in
a protest march to Lansdowne Road where the Springboks were
playing Ireland.

Any effort to ban South African produce was deemed to be contrary to the terms of our EC membership and the various obligations
of the General Agreement on Tariffs and Trade (GATT). This was
the advice I received from Peter Sutherland, then Attorney General.
Attempts to obtain a voluntary ban from the various importers
and shop owners, which would have resulted in the end of the
prolonged strike, very nearly succeeded, but in the end the
voluntary ban was rejected. What the strikers required was a legal
government ban.

Peter Sutherland became Ireland's European Commissioner at
the end of 1984. The Taoiseach reluctantly picked him because
there were some ministers around the cabinet table who would have
liked to put their own hat in the ring. However, it was agreed that
the consequential constituency vacancy would have resulted in the
coalition government losing the subsequent by-election. Other
names mentioned were Dick Burke, Jim Dooge and Justin Keating,
but Sutherland's candidacy, initially suggested, I believe, by Joan
FitzGerald, Garret's wife, won the day. The announcement of his
appointment was made early that autumn, so as to give him a good

chance of getting a senior portfolio in the European Commission with President Jacques Delors, which he eventually did, receiving the Competition portfolio, as well as Social Affairs, for a short time.

However, between the announcement and the appointment of his successor as Attorney General, tension rose in the cabinet. Deeply frustrated at the prolonged absence of legal advice available to herself and to other government departments, Gemma Hussey petulantly asked at the start of one cabinet meeting why there was no agreement between the Taoiseach and Tánaiste about a new Attorney General. Her intervention was unexpected and there was an embarrassed silence.

'It's very simple,' Dick Spring snapped, before Garret could respond. 'Fine Gael can have one job but not two, and have to make up their mind if they want to have an Attorney General or a Commissioner.'

Despite Garret's efforts to persuade Dick of the merits of certain liberal Fine Gael senior lawyers, the Labour leader held his ground. Protests about the unique personal relationship between the Taoiseach and the Attorney General were dismissed. Finally, John Rogers, a close personal friend and political confidant of Dick's, was appointed the new Attorney General, the first Labour nominee to the office. In 1984 this was seen as a great breach of traditional protocol but has subsequently become the norm. Michael McDowell, a trenchant critic of Fianna Fáil, became Attorney General to Bertie Ahern's Fianna Fáil/Progressive Democrat coalition government when David Byrne succeeded Commissioner Pádraig Flynn in Brussels. John Rogers was an excellent Attorney General and soon won the respect of the Fine Gael cabinet members. Clear and decisive, he gave succinct legal opinions.

Meanwhile the Dunnes Stores strike continued. I asked Paul Cullen, who had replaced Maurice Cashell as special policy adviser, to help us to find a legal route to impose a ban on the importation of South African fruit and vegetables. His diligent examination of International Labour Organisation conventions revealed, amongst other things, that imported goods and services which were the product of forced or prison labour could be banned under international law. Providentially, he obtained evidence that confirmed that the prison authorities were hiring out some prisoners in South African jails, at a pittance, to white farmers. Then he assembled a comprehensive file and it was soon placed on the Attorney General's desk. I asked John Rogers to advise as to whether or not the cabinet now had the authority to introduce a suitably worded ban on the importation of South African produce which would be legal, while not compromising the country's commitments to free trade and international agreements. Subject to reasonable provisions of time and due notice to all participants, he informed me that the Irish government could impose such a ban, by invoking the relevant ILO provisions. It was very much a case of the legal bottle being half full rather than half empty, but John gave me the benefit of the doubt and his official advice to the cabinet could not be challenged on legal grounds.

All that I had to do now was to persuade the cabinet of the merits of such a measure. It finally came to a vote and, unusually, the measure to introduce the ban was narrowly carried, with the Taoiseach having a decisive vote in favour against the majority of his own party colleagues. The announcement of the ban was a triumph, and the dispute ended with the eleven workers being fêted nationally and internationally.

As we moved to the 1986 Christmas holidays and a recess, it was clear that the government's time was virtually over. The impasse on expenditure cuts in the Book of Estimates could not be resolved. Labour did not accept the demands being made by Fine Gael. At private meetings of the Labour cabinet members, which took place before the full cabinet, we came to the conclusion that after the Christmas and New Year break we would resign and face into the inevitable election as an independent party.

It was a sombre meeting in the cabinet room on 14 January 1987. Both Taoiseach and Tánaiste reported on the difficulties of finding agreement between the coalition parties. As the Taoiseach spoke, it was obvious where the discussion was heading. John Boland intervened. 'Taoiseach, I don't want to interrupt you but since you have your back to the window, you may not be aware that it is snowing.' I had been looking at the snowfall becoming heavier, lowering the pale midday light in the square of Government Buildings. It reminded me of the closing scene of James Joyce's short story 'The Dead'. 'I think that you may want to consider whether to call an election this week or wait until the weather improves,' Boland said with both humour and sadness.

An emotional cabinet meeting took place six days later. When I left the Department of Labour to go to that meeting, I told Denise that the Labour Party ministers would be resigning and that I would not be back to the department. She could not share this information with anybody and had to do her day's work waiting for the official news to break. Labour and Fine Gael ministers said their farewells, expressing appreciation for the work they had done together. Fergus Finlay came out of the communications room to meet us and outlined the media arrangements. The four Labour ministers – Dick Spring, Barry Desmond, Liam Kavanagh and myself – walked down the steps to the front door of Government Buildings. In front of an array of cameras and reporters, Dick made a terse announcement of our decision and the reason for it. We could not accept that the burden of economic readjustment, involving the reduction of public spending, was being placed on the backs of those people in our society least able to carry it. We were out of government and a general election was not far away.

Chapter 13

Survival in Opposition
1987–1989

The Labour Party organisation in Dublin South-East had no illusions about how difficult the 1987 election would be. The opinion polls for the party, at national level, were chilling. Labour had gone from 8 to 4 per cent between 1982 and 1986 and there appeared to be no light at the end of the tunnel. But we did not need the opinion polls to tell us that we were in trouble. In June 1984, Frank Cluskey had been defeated in the European Parliament elections. Labour had won four European Parliament seats in 1979, through Eileen Desmond, Liam Kavanagh, John O'Connell and Michael O'Leary. It was a remarkable achievement to win four of the fifteen seats but now, five years later, we had lost all of them. Following his defeat in that contest, Frank Cluskey played a less than constructive role within the Parliamentary Labour Party up to the advent of the general election.

Because of the political unpopularity of the coalition government in the spring of 1984, the cabinet decided to postpone the June local elections until the following year. It was hoped that our political fortunes would improve, but instead they were severely dashed and, in retrospect, we would have been better off linking the local and European elections and holding them on the same day in June 1984.

In Dublin we paid a heavy price for our political cowardice. Labour held only two seats out of fifty-two on the City Council – a loss of nine seats. In Dublin South-East, where I was not a candidate, we lost the three council seats we had won in 1979. The ballot boxes and the opinion polls were giving us the same clear message as we edged our way towards the end of 1986.

In the autumn of that year we began to plan meticulously for the forthcoming general election in Dublin South-East. The constituency executive reconstituted itself as the election committee. Caroline Hussey took on the responsibility of director of elections again and careful preparations were put in place for a campaign which we knew would be our toughest yet. The consensus of our election team was that, to hold the seat, we would have to stress the personality of our candidate and concentrate on the work that had been done in the constituency, as much as the party's record at national level. Fortunately, I had much to report because we had a considerable record of local achievement.

Soon after the Social Employment Scheme had been successfully piloted in Wexford and launched nationwide, I found myself with John Long travelling back from Mayo. In the early hours of the morning, as Nashie Grady drove us home, John and I discussed how small, apparently poorly resourced, local communities were able to utilise the various programmes, most of them under the aegis of the Department of Labour, to build community halls or establish local improvement projects. This was in marked contrast to Dublin South-East where little or nothing was happening. It seemed strange to me that as minister I would be travelling to different parts of the country to preside over the opening of various projects while I could not make that same journey within my own constituency.

That night I decided that we had to be proactive. We invited representatives from residents' associations to the Department of Labour on Mespil Road and informed them of the Social Employment Scheme and how it might be used to address local problems while at the same time help to reduce unemployment. Sadly, there was no constructive response to our invitations and we heard nothing from most of the residents' associations after they had availed of of our hospitality in the department. Hesitantly, I accepted that the Labour Party in the constituency would have to take the initiative. I simply could not contemplate a situation where, in contrast to most other constituencies, the range of active labour measures, which I had either introduced or for which I had responsibility, were not being effectively availed of in my own constituency. Within the space of a couple of months, a community hall project was begun in Charlemont Street, which when completed housed youth activities and a very successful meals programme for the elderly residents in the complexes of flats in and around Tom Kelly Road.

The Dodder Amenity Trust was established and employed nearly forty people, cleaning up the banks of the River Dodder and constructing a river pathway from Ringsend to Clonskeagh. Sandymount Community Services was launched, soon to be followed by Rathgar Community Services. Operating under the Social Employment Scheme, local residents, frequently elderly people, had essential household maintenance work done at an economic cost and in a secure manner by a locally managed and accountable workforce. A successful community newspaper emerged from Sandymount Community Services: *NewsFour* is still going strong and is economically self-sufficient twenty years later. The old Regal cinema in Ringsend became the base for the AnCO-run community training workshop. The energy of that group of locals, some of whom, like Mary Lawless and Charlie Murphy, were Labour Party activists, helped to transform their community and to bring hope and activity to areas that had given up. A Community Youth Training Programme (CYTP) scheme was used to refurbish the old national school building on Pearse Street and to this day St Andrew's Resource Centre is one of the most successful community projects in the city. In the run-up to the general election, which finally took place on 17 February 1987, we produced information brochures and party literature highlighting the extensive work which I had, with the help of Labour Party and community activists, initiated across the constituency. It was all very necessary.

The long campaign of four weeks started after 20 January: the day the four Labour ministers resigned from the government. The Taoiseach, Garret FitzGerald, had deliberately chosen the maximum length of time for the campaign to ensure that the realities of our economic situation could not be fudged by the populist rhetoric of the Charles Haughey-led Fianna Fáil party. However, Fianna Fáil won the election after a tied vote of 82 to 82 and Charles Haughey became Taoiseach on the casting vote of Seán Treacy, the newly elected Ceann Comhairle who, by convention, voted with the government. Labour lost four seats: Frank McLoughlin in Meath; Michael Moynihan in Kerry South; John Ryan in Tipperary North and Frank Prendergast in Limerick East. We had dropped from sixteen to twelve seats and were now ranked the fourth party in the Dáil, displaced by the ebullient newcomers, the Progressive Democrats.

That was bad enough but it was very nearly calamitous. Dick Spring, a deputy with a superb organisation at local level and a great political base, held on to the third and last seat in Kerry North by just four votes. I watched in shock the television coverage of that count from Kitty O'Shea's pub after my own successful election. I had fought a tough and good campaign in which one of my Fianna Fáil opponents was Mary McAleese, who won 2,243 first-preference votes. The star performer was the newly elected PD deputy Michael McDowell, a former director of elections for Garret FitzGerald. My own vote dropped by 40 per cent and I had to wait for the fifteenth and last count before I was elected.

The aftermath of the 1987 general election had dramatically changed the composition of the Dáil. On the right, the Progressive Democrats, led by Dessie O'Malley, won an astounding fourteen seats. On the left, The Workers' Party made gains and were poised to win more, which they did two years later when Charles Haughey, in a fit of pique, called a general election to take place alongside the European elections in June 1989. For Labour, that two-year period was difficult and for me personally a period of political crisis, as well as political self-doubt.

Days after Dick Spring survived his election count in Kerry North, the four former Labour ministers were gathered in the home of Fergus and Freda Finlay. Emmet Stagg's election to Joe Bermingham's seat in Kildare, combined with the return to the Dáil of Michael D. Higgins, had significantly strengthened the left wing of the party. The left argued that the coalition had been a disaster for Labour, that our alliance with Fine Gael had cost us votes. Furthermore, the emergence of the tightly disciplined Workers' Party further to our left meant that we were being badly squeezed from both sides. The solution, according to Labour Left – a faction led by Emmet Stagg, Pat Carroll, Jerry Shanahan and Sam Nolan – was to disavow participation in any future coalition government unless Labour was the dominant party. This meant no participation in government for the foreseeable future. However, the party had succeeded in 1986, under Niall Greene's skilful chairmanship, in producing a report on its future development. One of the key recommendations was that Labour would participate in a future government only if it had won a significant number of seats and so could have a major impact on direction and policy.

Meanwhile Joe Higgins and Militant Tendency were saying much the same thing as Labour Left, but in even harsher and more absolute terms. Militant's strategy was to join existing Labour parties throughout Europe and use its position in a concerted manner to gain control of the political programme of that party and to make it identical to their fundamentalist Trotskyist beliefs. Effectively a party within a party, Militant caused endless diversionary trouble both in Ireland and Great Britain. Their antics alienated potential members and supporters and took up considerable amounts of our time. But, whatever about the irritant of Militant, Labour Left was intent on a radical change of direction.

That evening in the Finlay home, the feeling was that in order to achieve change, Labour Left would try to ensure the new party leader was elected by the party's rank and file. Dick's tenure was currently secure, because he had been elected by the parliamentary party. Nevertheless, a Labour Left proposal to open future leadership elections to party members was an indication of the way they wanted things to go and the early months of 1987 saw a number of skirmishes that were damaging to Dick's morale.

The annual conference was to be held on the last weekend of September 1987 in the City Hall in Cork. Michael D. Higgins had announced his retirement as chairman of the party and Labour Left quickly nominated Mervyn Taylor to replace him. Reluctantly, I responded to Dick's request to stand against Mervyn as chairman. While I did a lot of canvassing, it was not enough. The party was so divided that I could not even depend on the votes of all the delegates from my own constituency. Militant had established a strong base in Dublin South-East, which had started when Joe Higgins had left UCD. He became a member of the constituency as a student branch member and dominated the Ranelagh branch. Even within the Sandymount branch, of which I was a member, there were intense divisions. John and Yvonne Fitzsimons, along with Michael Taft, had run a continuous campaign against the party leadership when Labour had been in government. Each month would see some challenging motion on the constituency agenda. No meeting passed without a silent counting of heads to ensure the presence of a supportive majority. A great deal of energy, mostly turned in on ourselves, was burned up during that time.

It could not go on indefinitely. Having recovered from the shock of his narrow election victory and the physical fatigue of more than five intense years in office, Dick Spring began to fight back. The main debate in Cork was a proposal to change the way the leader was elected. Moving the amendment from the Rock Street branch in Tralee, Dick deliberately spoke from the delegate's rostrum and not from the leader's one on the stage. In a display of spirited determination, he took off his jacket and laid down the gauntlet to his detractors. Many delegates had never seen him speak with such passion. Later I said that you do not get picked to play full-back for Ireland unless you possess courage and Dick had plenty of it. He carried the day and the first step in the struggle to regain control of the party had begun. However, the following morning, Mervyn Taylor was elected chair of the Labour Party. I lost the vote by 517 to 631. The one thing that was clear to me as I left Cork was the necessity to concentrate on rebuilding the organisation in Dublin South-East and to bring in new members who would be supportive to the traditional Labour message. In this, Dermot Lacey played a major role, along with others, including Ella Casey, Vicki Somers, Jenny Caulfield, Michael Coghlan, Kevin Duffy, Caroline Hussey, Ray Kavanagh, Mary Lawless and Ciarán O'Mara. All helped and things slowly began to improve.

In October 1987, Mervyn Taylor resigned as party whip, following some pressure from Dick, who saw a potential conflict in his being both chairman and whip of the party. It was agreed that Brendan Howlin would become the party's new whip. Before long, Emmet Stagg challenged Dick's efforts to retain control of the administrative council of the party by nominating the six ordinary members from the parliamentary party in the normal way. Emmet had obtained a legal opinion that challenged the existing method and stated that an election, rather than the leader's nomination, was required. The fact that Senator Mary Robinson was asked and had drafted the legal opinion was interpreted as a dig at Dick; many believed that she had wanted to become Attorney General and was annoyed at the decision to give the position to John Rogers. Over several months, the wrangling for control of future leadership elections continued until, weary with it all, a compromise involving an agreed list of names was formally voted on by the parliamentary party.

All these manoeuvrings were taking place in a changed political background outside the very inward-looking preoccupations of the parliamentary party. Charlie Haughey had succeeded in getting the trade unions and the employers to agree to a new pay deal, even though the employers were initially reluctant. Called the 'Programme for National Recovery', its intellectual basis had been set out in a report of the National Economic and Social Council published in 1986. Amongst other measures, enormous cutbacks in public expenditure were considered necessary in order to balance the public finances. What added insult to injury, as far as Dick Spring and Barry Desmond were concerned, was the acquiescence of the leaders of the major unions – Bill Attley of the FWUI and John Carroll of the ITGWU – to this new draconian policy. Barry, in particular, could not contain his anger and at one stage wanted the Labour Party to vote against the 'Programme for National Recovery' in the Dáil. The pay deal was agreed before the publication of the Book of Estimates, enabling union leaders to protest their innocence in not knowing the full extent of what was proposed. The subsequent details of the Estimates revealed what the euphemistic phrase 'reductions in public expenditure' actually meant.

In my view, Labour should have been asking itself why it had not been able to persuade the unions, instead of giving out about them, for acting on advice which we ourselves had accepted in principle. With hindsight, the employers' refusal to participate in any national understanding or pay agreement back in 1982–83 coincided with Fine Gael's reluctance to intervene directly in the macro management of the economy by the government, mainly because the economic theories of Thatcherism were strongly embedded in the minds of some of the younger Fine Gael ministers, including Jim Mitchell and John Boland.

Some years later I learned that Donal Nevin, the secretary of the Irish Congress of Trade Unions, had privately told Garret FitzGerald that the ICTU would not agree to modest wage increases in return for income tax reductions. This was something I had raised at cabinet and had got permission to explore the notion with senior trade-union leaders. John Carroll had indicated support for the idea if the government would agree. However, whilst I was looking into this, Garret was getting a totally different and what he considered to be a more authoritative response from Congress. But there is a time for everything. Donal Nevin's retirement and the arrival of Peter Cassells as the new general secretary of Congress in 1987 was a critical factor. Moreover, the arrival of fourteen Progressive Democrat deputies had raised the spectre of a Celtic Thatcherism which would have seen the trade unions banished from the steps of Government Buildings, as had happened in Downing Street after 1979.

The budget for 1988 was comfortably passed on 27 January. Fine Gael supported the budget on the basis of a policy proclaimed earlier by their new leader, Alan Dukes. Dukes had defeated Peter Barry and John Bruton when Garret resigned immediately after the 1987 general election. Known as the Tallaght Strategy, because Dukes delivered the speech outlining it to the Tallaght Chamber of Commerce, it stated that for as long as the minority Fianna Fáil government implemented Fine Gael economic and fiscal policies, they could rely on Fine Gael's support in the Dáil. While the ideological position had some clear logic, the political approach was baffling. In 1987, Ray MacSharry, the Minister for Finance, had implemented the revised Estimates and budgetary proposals which Labour could not accept and which had been the cause of our resignation from government. Alan Dukes had sought no political price or concession in return for this support for Fianna Fáil. Indeed, Dukes, we were subsequently told, did not consult or inform his own frontbench before announcing the Tallaght Strategy.

Knowing what we now know about Haughey's need to stay in office in order to sustain the secret flow of money to him from various businessmen, it is probable that he might have been prepared to deal. Could that have begun the process of bringing Fianna Fáil and Fine Gael closer together? This, after all, was the long-vaunted strategy of Labour, particularly its left wing. While such a coming together would have been highly desirable, Fine Gael loyalists asserted, on more than one occasion, that it could never happen. I recall Enda Marron, a Fine Gael activist, telling me, over a pint in Kitty O'Shea's, that Fine Gael would die as an organisation if it were to link up with Fianna Fáil, even as a separate party in coalition – a view Michael Noonan reinforced to me many years later.

Throughout the early months of 1988, the Labour Party began to improve its internal organisation and self-confidence. On the last weekend in March, Militant lost control of Labour Youth, through a combination of Stagg supporters and Labour loyalists, such as Pat Montague. Later that spring, Niamh Bhreathnach, a Labour loyalist, won the chair of the Labour Women's National Council and my partner, Liz Allman, was elected treasurer.

The public expenditure cuts were now beginning to take effect and public anger was growing. In June, Dick Spring published a major economic policy position paper that had been prepared by a group of sympathetic economists and party members, including Eithne Fitzgerald and Greg Sparks. It was well received in the media and there was a sense that Labour was slowly beginning to find its direction.

Early in 1989, we began to prepare for the European Parliament elections that were being held, in Ireland, on 15 June. I was given the responsibility of directing our Dublin campaign where Barry Desmond was to be our candidate. The impact of the savage cutbacks in social services was severely testing the popularity of the minority Fianna Fáil government. As election day approached, there was speculation that the Taoiseach, Charles Haughey, might also call a snap general election. Following a visit to Japan in April, he was facing a possible defeat on a Labour Party private member's motion, on the issue of the allocation of £400,000 to help haemophiliacs with AIDS. Haughey threatened a general election if the Dáil voted against him, but the opposition parties called his bluff and some days later, on 25 May, he finally sought the dissolution of the Dáil.

Barry Desmond was elected to the European Parliament and the number of Labour Dáil deputies increased from twelve to fifteen. The Workers' Party won seven seats and the Green Party made its first entrance to the Dáil when Roger Garland defeated the PDs' Anne Colley in Dublin South. With no clear majority after the results were declared, Haughey was eventually elected Taoiseach following the historic formation of a Fianna Fáil/Progressive Democrat coalition. Irish politics would never be the same again.

Chapter 14

The Fall of the Wall

The warm July evening had encouraged us to sit outdoors, even though it was close to midnight. We started singing, attracting the attention of the Parisian passers-by. We were an Irish group of forty and had gladdened the eye of the café manager as we sat down, adding considerably to his turnover. The waitresses taking our orders wore the emblematic red felt cockade, immortalised by Marianne as she stormed the Bastille on 14 July 1789. Two hundred years later, representing the Dublin South-East Labour Party, we were in France to celebrate the achievements of the French Revolution.

Earlier that day we had stood on the plinth of the Madeleine Church just off the Champs Elysées, and watched, enthralled, the swagger of the singing French soldiers as they marched passed. The day before we had gone to the Irish College, close to the Panthéon. By 1989, the Polish seminarians and priests, who had been tenants there since 1945, had started to go home as Solidarity and the Polish communist government came to a political understanding.

At a time of European political ferment, Paris was an exhilarating place to be. The Irish College was being reclaimed and, like its sister college in Louvain, would become an Irish cultural centre and accommodation resource in France.

For some time after the 1987 general election, I had wanted to strengthen our constituency group in Dublin South-East. We were in a difficult process of renewal and growth which required great time and commitment. As a consequence, I felt that an outing, away from the rigours of political meetings and conference intrigue, would be both interesting and enjoyable. It would also consolidate the constituency political team. I therefore arranged a constituency group visit to Paris in July 1989.

There were strong links between republicanism in France and in Ireland, and with the very origins of the left–right divide in democratic politics was synonymous with France. Through my father's interest in the period, particularly the life of Wolfe Tone, I had had a knowledge and an emotional bond with France from an early age. My 1961 summer in Lyons served to reinforce that sentiment.

I was the main organiser of the trip – arranged to follow the June 1989 European elections, which also coincided with France's bicentennial celebrations – and now know that I would not have made a successful travel agent! Our hotel, just off the Boulevard Saint Michel, was great value and when we got there we saw why. Beyond being basic, it was considered by some, particularly Liz Allman, as being a fire hazard: escape was by the roof, not the stairs. Some family members were also in the group. My brother Colm wanted to come on the trip despite working in London. My sister Moninne and sister-in-law Hilary, Conor's wife, were also coming with us, so Colm arranged to travel separately and he arrived late on the first night.

The following morning I duly went downstairs to check what time breakfast started but the night porter indicated that there might be a problem. He pointed to a man who was fast asleep on a couch in the restricted reception area.

'Is he part of your group?' he asked.

I assured him that he was.

'How do you know? Are you sure?'

'Yes, I am – he's my brother' was my reply.

We decided to let Colm sleep and soon set out for the day, leaving a note behind to say that he would find us at the Hôtel Villa Saint-Germain on Rue Jacob. This was a boutique hotel that had recently been restored by a leading French architect and designer, Marie-Christine Dorner, a student of Philippe Starck, and was a place both Liz and I very much wanted to see. Moninne, Hilary, Liz and I took the guided tour of the building and were sitting in the lounge when Colm arrived. He took in the elegant surroundings and pronounced as a greeting, 'Ah ha, the flight of the bourgeoisie!' Roaring with laughter, we explained that we had not changed hotels but had in fact come to look at the interior design. Then, in good spirits, we all went out to join in the bicentenary celebrations.

Late the following evening, as we sat outside the café, the singing paused and Alice Somers thanked me for making the trip possible and for inviting herself and Jimmy, both long-standing Labour Party activists, from Dublin Central, along.

'Where are you taking us next?' she asked.

'Budapest,' I replied. Then I told her that extraordinary things were happening in Central and Eastern Europe because of Mikhail Gorbachev.

'But why Hungary and not Poland?' Alice asked.

Next I found myself telling her, and the group that had gathered, about my first visit to Hungary.

In September 1985 a group from the Department of Labour finally arrived in Budapest, a year later than I had wanted, mainly to investigate how the Hungarians dealt with unemployment. My enquiries about the workings of the Hungarian labour market under communist control were dutifully, if not enthusiastically, pursued in the department. I was informed, nearly with a sense of relief, that contact could not be made because Ireland had no embassy behind the Iron Curtain, except in Moscow, and that there was no Hungarian embassy in Ireland. While I already knew this, I nonetheless suggested that we could ask our departmental officials, who were due to attend the June general assembly of the International Labour Organisation in Geneva, to make informal contact with their Hungarian counterparts.

The Hungarians responded with alacrity. They would be delighted for an Irish minister to visit their country. Since both ministers were due in Geneva in a few weeks' time, they asked if it would be possible for a meeting to be arranged in the Hungarian embassy there, to finalise the details of the visit to Budapest. It was. Once in Geneva, I met Dr Rácz, a member of the 300-strong central committee of the Hungarian Socialist Workers' Party but not a member of the party's politburo. The political structure, modelled on the Soviet system, was a duality of power and control. The normal government structures of prime minister, cabinet members and parliament existed side-by-side with the party organisation, which exercised real power. The party's leading role was formally recognised in the constitution. The secretary general, János Kádár, elected by the central committee, was the leader. Parallel to the various ministries of state, such as agriculture, education and labour, the party had its own departments. Their role was to develop policy and hand over its implementation to the government. Where the system became confused was when a member of the politburo, who had responsibility for, say, health, was also the Minister for Health. But this was not the case with my counterpart, who, I was told, was more of a technocrat than a politician. Within days of my return from Geneva, an official letter of invitation from the Hungarian government arrived at the Department of Labour.

Some days later, at an all-day government meeting in Barretstown Castle, County Kildare, I told the Taoiseach of the invitation and of my wish to accept it. The Taoiseach agreed to the visit and a few months later, I found myself checking in to the Forum Hotel, opposite the chain link bridge across the river Danube on the Pest side of this old city. Michael Keegan, Paul Cullen, Freda Nolan and myself made up the delegation.

That evening I went out for a walk on my own. My mind was full of thoughts of my father, the 1956 Rising and the crackling radio news broadcasts which were amongst my first political memories. Now, thirty years later, here I was in the centre of Budapest preparing to meet my counterpart in the Hungarian government.

I have always window-shopped in foreign cities and gone into supermarkets just to see what was for sale and at what price. You could say the legacy of the family grocer is strong within me. Peering into the windows of a music shop, which for all the world was like Mays Music Shop on St Stephen's Green, I deciphered from the posters and the display of LPs that it was celebrating the one hundredth anniversary of the death of Liszt Ferenc, or Franz Liszt. In my ignorance, I had not realised that Liszt was Hungarian and that there was a strong tradition of classical music in the country. Indeed the range of recordings was immense and a fraction of the prices at home: my large collection of Hungaroton records, purchased then and on subsequent trips, remains a constant reminder of that visit.

The following morning we had our first meeting with Dr Rácz and officials in his department, across the square from our hotel. We took our places on one side of the long narrow table in the conference room. Across the table from me sat the minister, flanked by ten officials. When the preliminaries were dispensed with and the strong black coffee served, Dr Rácz opened with a description of how the Hungarian labour market worked in a command economy that had no unemployment and consequently no unemployment benefit or assistance programmes. He invited his officials to describe the operation of their system. The sequential translation into English meant that the presentation took some time. Essentially, up to three-quarters of Hungarian school-leavers followed their own vocations, either into further education or employment. Those who had failed to get employment were placed with a range of nationalised public companies on a quota basis. When the exposition had finished, questions were invited. Out of politeness, we asked a couple of questions, seeking clarification or elaboration.

Then Dr Rácz caught my eye and leaned towards me, speaking more intensely than before. When he had finished, I listened to the translation while continuing to look directly at him. 'You must understand, Minister Quinn and colleagues, one important thing about what we have just described – it does not work!'

He saw the surprised look on my face and nodded confirmation. Along the table the smiles and nods of his officials indicated their agreement with their minister.

'So what does work?' I asked, intrigued at this public and comfortable admission of a systems failure in a communist state.

'Well,' he began, 'we have too many people in some enterprises and they can get in the way of effective and efficient production. New workers, who are surplus to the needs of the enterprise, are left alone. Many then take on another job. In fact, it is not unusual to have two informal jobs as well as the official one.'

Later, when the Irish delegation was alone, I marvelled at the openness of the Hungarians and how they managed to have a flexible economy within the strictures of the Soviet system, with its Comecon trading structure with other Soviet-style economies.

Following the brutal putdown of the 1956 Rising, János Kádár, the new Moscow-approved Hungarian leader, entered into a different type of political relationship with his people. The Hungarians would have much greater economic and private political freedom in return for publicly recognising the geopolitical relationship of Hungary within the Soviet Bloc. Turning a biblical phrase to his own advantage and changing its meaning, Kádár famously proclaimed that, 'He who is not against us is with us.'

Back in Dublin in 1989, I started working on a Labour Party group visit to Hungary. By the autumn there was intense interest because Central Europe was in turmoil. Moscow had informed the European communist governments that its tanks would no longer be available to maintain them in office. In Poland, Solidarity and the Polish Communist Party had begun negotiations on the formation of the country's first non-communist government since 1945.

Many German families, divided by the Berlin Wall, were united every year when they took their summer holidays on the shores of Lake Balaton, southwest of Budapest and Europe's biggest lake. Responding to a series of changes in the Communist Party, following the surprise ousting of Kádár as party leader at a party congress in 1988, the four new reform leaders made a number of dramatic announcements. Imre Pozsgay declared that, contrary to the previous official line, the 1956 Rising was not a counter-revolutionary fascist uprising. Furthermore, the four announced that the leading role of the party, set out in the constitution, was to be removed. This took away the legal basis of the Communist Party's monopoly of power. In an act of incredible poignancy and with great subsequent significance, Gyula Horn, the foreign secretary, was photographed applying heavy-duty wire cutters to the frontier barrier between Austria and Hungary. The Iron Curtain was literally being cut down by one of the four leaders of the Moscow party in Hungary. News of this event quickly spread, particularly to the campsites and hotels along the shores of Lake Balaton.

Soon there was a stream of traffic heading towards the Austrian border. East Germans, in their Trabant cars, were calmly leaving the Soviet empire and soon the flow of traffic developed into an exodus. Despite protests from the East German government, the Hungarians maintained their stance. Soon there was pressure on communist Czechoslovakia, and the Velvet Revolution in December 1989 saw the rebirth of democracy in that country as well.

It was against the background of these historic changes that in March 1990 I arranged for a group of thirty Labour Party members and supporters to fly to Frankfurt and then go by bus via Prague to Budapest. While change was everywhere, the apparatus of the old regime was still intact, including border guards and visas. The journey to Prague took longer than anticipated and we arrived late at night to an empty, fairytale-like city, devoid of western symbols, such as neon lights and advertising hoardings. From Prague, we travelled by bus, southeast to Bratislava and Budapest. 'Great tank country' was Brendan Walsh's observation as he looked out at the rolling plains on either side of the motorway unhindered by field boundaries between Prague and the Slovakian capital.

The visit was memorable in many ways. It was exhilarating to be there at that time of change, to meet the political activists and ordinary citizens, to have the tangible sense of a great movement occurring, though in what direction was still unclear. After a lot of pressure, I got to meet Imre Pozsgay in his ministerial office in the impressive parliament building on the banks of the Danube.

'What can a country like Ireland do to help you and the Hungarian people?' I asked.

'Make sure that Austria joins the European Community so that we can follow quickly,' was his instant reply.

I must confess that while I could foresee the entry of neutral Austria, the idea of Hungarian membership seemed very far away. Little did I dream that during Ireland's presidency of what became the European Union there would be a Day of Welcomes, at Áras an Uachtaráin on 1 May 2004, as ten new member states, including Hungary, were formally given membership.

The impact of the fall of the Berlin Wall in 1989 compounded the internal ideological difficulties within left-wing parties across many other countries within Europe. Despite the historic opposition of democratic socialism to communism, the collapse of the Soviet system, particularly in Central Europe, was claimed to be a triumph of capitalism and a defeat of socialism. Margaret Thatcher and Ronald Reagan had confronted the evil empire and had won. In a famous article, Francis Fukuyama proclaimed what he described as 'the end of history'. In other words, the ideological battle about competing political systems was now truly over. What few commentators in Britain and Ireland referred to was the end of the civil war within the left in Europe because of the failure of communism.

There was no communist party of any significance in Britain, but the collapse of communism clearly weakened the left within the British Labour Party. Because of the influence of British politics in Ireland, this had an impact within the Irish Labour Party. The existence of an alternative model of the economy was symbolic, even though most left activists in the West were unfamiliar with the actual realities of life in the Soviet Bloc. In a strange but important way, its very presence held out the prospect of a different future, even if such an alternative economic structure was inefficient and undemocratic. For a time, reforms did appear possible, with the programme of *glasnost* and *perestroika*, put forward by the Soviet leader Mikhail Gorbachev. Some on the left of the Labour Party began to question the future political direction of the party, caught as it was between the triumph of Thatcherism and the fall of communism.

What was not clearly seen or understood by many was how the failure of communism, as a socio-economic political model, represented a triumph for the forces of democratic socialism and social democracy within continental Europe. With two major exceptions, in France and Portugal, western European communist parties changed their names and their political programmes in a very short space of time. This was particularly so in Italy and, to a lesser extent, in Spain and the Nordic countries. An internal conflict on the left, which had raged from the 1920s through to the emergence of Euro-communism at the end of the 1970s, was now clearly at an end.

In Ireland, there was one direct political consequence of the collapse of communism in Europe. The internal cohesion of The Workers' Party began to disintegrate. The party, which some of its leading members described as being Marxist–Leninist, was affected by the continental contradictions that made their way to it across the Irish Sea. The continued existence of the Official IRA and its links to Sinn Féin, now renamed The Workers' Party, was undoubtedly a major additional factor. Even though the Official IRA had been on a prolonged ceasefire, the continuing violence of the Provisional IRA and loyalist paramilitaries was a major headache for The Workers' Party, particularly in the Republic.

In the 1989 general election, they had achieved the long-sought-for electoral breakthrough, winning seven seats in the Dáil, three of which were newly elected deputies to seats previously held by Labour. Natasha Weyer-Browne had worked as my director of elections during that campaign to ensure I retained my Dublin South-East seat. The Workers' Party now constituted a parliamentary group within the Dáil. In addition, Proinsias De Rossa, their new leader, had a spectacular dual victory: on election day in 1989, he won a Dáil seat and also took a seat in Dublin in the election to the European parliament.

However, the internal cohesion of his party's ideology was particularly affected by events in the Soviet Union and the party states of Central and Eastern Europe. Eoghan Harris, an influential current affairs television producer in RTÉ and a member of The Workers' Party, was regarded by many, particularly himself, as their main ideologue. In 1990, he wrote an internal pamphlet for the party, entitled *The Necessity of Social Democracy*. Its unauthorised publication initiated a major row within the party and led to Harris' departure, but his withering critique of where The Workers' Party was and where it had to go ultimately contributed to a split in the ranks and the formation of Democratic Left. What many Labour activists, particularly in the Dublin area, had seen as the inexorable rise of The Workers' Party was soon to come to an abrupt end in the most unlikely of circumstances – through self-destruction and not external factors or electoral rejection.

Throughout this time, I continued with my constituency work which, given the nature of Dublin South-East, was varied. For example, on 28 June 1988, I finally received, after eleven months, a definitive answer to a constituency query to the Minister for Justice, Gerry Collins. The reply angered me deeply and, despite much publicity, I was unable to change the decision, which I still find profoundly unjust and open to the accusation of racism.

As Minister for Labour I had responsibility for work permits. Before a permit was issued, the consent of the Department of Justice was required, more as a formality than for any other reason. At the time, there were enormous delays with the Department of Justice, even when there was no difficulty with the candidate's eligibility, so I proceeded to grant applications, provided other criteria were properly met. Work permit applications that came across my desk, either by way of appeal or through constituency representations, were mostly from the owners of Chinese or Indian restaurants, looking for qualified chefs and waiters. I was well disposed, in principle, to these applications because I believed that the presence of Chinese or Indian nationals in restaurants added to the integrity and authenticity of the cuisine and ambience.

Sometime after the 1987 election, a young Sikh woman came to my clinic in Camden Street with her infant child. They had been in Dublin for two months and her solicitor had advised her to go to a politician because they had been frustrated at the lack of progress on the question she needed answering. Her request was quite simple. If her husband, whom she had married in India and who was still there, arrived at an Irish airport, would he be allowed to stay with her and live in Ireland? She had been born in London and spoke with a London accent. Her family were orthodox Sikhs and she had married, within her community, an Indian national living in India. The existence of the child was sufficient proof to me that this was not a scam.

My initial letter to the Department of Justice produced an acknowledgment which I forwarded to the young woman. Some weeks later, she and her brother, who lived in London, came to the clinic. He explained that her family were anxious about her being on her own with a young child in Dublin. They were in the clothing business in London and, if her request was successful, they intended to open a business in Dublin. Genuinely, they thought she could have a better life in Ireland.

Before the child was born, her husband had been refused entry to Britain, since the authorities there suspected that theirs was a marriage of convenience. Because Ireland since 1922 has had a common travel area with Britain, we implement mutual restrictions on each other's behalf. What angered me most were the evasions, procrastinations and insensitivity of Minister Collins and his department. It took nearly two years for a definitive reply to be given to a straightforward question from an elected deputy on behalf of a constituent, and the answer was no. So much pain, effort and expense could have been avoided if the answer been given much earlier.

It was not my last brush with the Department of Justice. Some years later, I sat embarrassed and ashamed before a Sudanese doctor who had come to Ireland to work in our hospitals while doing postgraduate studies. His request to have his wife join him in Ireland had been refused, with no reason given. I was stiffly informed in a reply to a parliamentary question that the minister, in other words the department, was not obliged to give any reason. Anger and persistence finally extracted an informal explanation. Married couples living in Ireland for four years might have one or even two children. They could therefore, as the law was then, stay on in Ireland.

'Why was I not told that when I applied to study here?' the doctor asked. 'I have no intention of staying in Ireland. I am only here to complete my studies, since I could not do this at home. But had I known of this restriction, I could have gone to London or Edinburgh, where some of my colleagues currently are with their wives.'

His anger, combined with his contempt for the deception, stung me. Ireland's medical system, then and now, could not function without the assistance of foreign doctors, yet we have treated them outrageously. I had quite a number of similar cases, but was seldom successful in meeting the constituent's request to be joined by his or her spouse. Developments in this field since then have driven me to despair. The refusal of the Department of Justice, under successive ministers, but in particular under John O'Donoghue and Michael McDowell, to allow asylum-seekers the right to work after a limited period in this country, has directly, if not deliberately, contributed to the poison of racism in Ireland.

Chapter 15

The Robinson Campaign
and a New Approach

On 5 January 1990, Denise Rogers stood at the door of our first-floor Leinster House office. 'Dick has just announced on *News at One* that, if necessary, he will be the Labour Party's presidential candidate.' She asked if I had known that he would be making this announcement. I didn't.

What was Dick at? Was he really going to run for the Áras? If he won, what would happen? I could not see him leaving the stage of national politics, especially since he had become the real leader of the opposition after the 1989 election.

For the first time in the state's history, when the Dáil met on 29 June 1989 after that election, all the candidates for Taoiseach were defeated. Haughey attempted to stay on, but it was a politically determined Spring who forced him to resign and then, and only then, to continue in a caretaker capacity, without the full powers of an elected Taoiseach. Such was the impasse that it took more than three meetings of the Dáil before a new government was formed on 12 July 1989. In the end, Haughey was forced into a coalition with his former bitter enemy, Des O'Malley, and the Progressive Democrats, who now had six deputies, compared to the fourteen they had had in 1987.

A core value of Fianna Fáil had been shattered. Single-party government was really now a thing of the past. Dick had effectively led the political charge on the floor of the house, outwitting Alan Dukes, Fine Gael's leader, and outperforming the Workers' Party, the other opposition party. Proinsias De Rossa's success in winning a seat in the European Parliament had come at a cost: on many important political occasions the leader of The Worker's Party was not in the Dáil chamber.

On that January afternoon, as I looked out the window, I reflected back on the success of the 1989 Tralee national conference where the leadership had regained control of the party. At the conference, a short motion had been passed, with leadership approval, almost unnoticed by the delegates. It committed the party to contesting the presidential election when Paddy Hillery's second term expired in October 1990. The Labour Party had never before fielded a candidate. The last third-candidate challenge had been in 1945 when Dr Pat McCartan had stood as an Independent against Fianna Fáil's Seán T. Ó Ceallaigh and Fine Gael's General Seán MacEoin. The last two-candidate contest had been in 1973 when Fianna Fáil's Erskine Childers had defeated Fine Gael's Tom O'Higgins.

During 1989, Fianna Fáil and Fine Gael seemed certain to ensure that there would be an agreed, albeit Fianna Fáil, candidate for the soon-to-be vacant position, so that no tiresome and expensive election would be needed. The growing confidence of the Labour Party and its members wanted to challenge this cosy arrangement. It was seen as a unique opportunity to develop the party's profile and build on our support. The only problem was that we had no candidate and now our leader was about to commit himself, or so I thought. What Dick actually did was to commit the country to a presidential contest.

Barry Desmond's success in the 1989 European elections meant that the position of deputy leader of the party was available. I was nominated, unopposed, to the vacancy. While I had worked closely with Dick on different projects, this was the first time for us to be in a formal working relationship. But little changed. He had been leader since November 1982 and seemed to work in a solitary way, even when Barry Desmond was deputy leader, surrounded by his close advisers Fergus Finlay and John Rogers. While I was on good terms with Fergus and John, I was aware that I was not part of the inner circle which met and advised. Therefore, I did not fully appreciate the analysis that preceded his decision to give the *News at One* interview.

In the event, Dick's announcement had an explosive impact. Labour had set the charge. The soft promotion of the Tánaiste, Brian

Lenihan, as the Fianna Fáil candidate, now had to face the reality of a contest. A pre-Christmas *Late Late Show*, which saw Gay Byrne provide a major platform, enabling Brian Lenihan and his wife to talk about political life and his recent liver transplant operation in the Mayo Clinic in Minnesota, was interpreted as the unofficial launch of the Lenihan presidential election campaign. Fianna Fáil's strategists clearly hoped that the genuine sympathy wafting towards Lenihan, combined with his own geniality, would be a sufficient display of strength to ward off any electoral challenge.

From the moment of Dick's interview, the search for the Labour Party's candidate began in earnest. Emmet Stagg's Labour Left faction with the hesitant support of Michael D. Higgins, immediately came forward with the name of Dr Noël Browne, who was living in isolated retirement in Connemara. Their motivation in proposing Browne had more to do with thwarting Dick than anything else. But Dick had a different agenda.

Having dramatically caused a presidential election, Spring now wanted to redefine the role of the office before selecting an appropriate candidate. The lawyer in Dick asked John Rogers SC to look at the office of President of the Republic and suggest how the job could be expanded within the established legal and constitutional confines. The outline of a 'working presidency', as distinct from a sinecure or retirement perch for a senior Fianna Fáil politician, began to take shape.

During a morning coffee break the following day, when most of the Labour Party secretariat got together, Denise Rogers, dismissing the possibility of Dick's candidature because of the outstanding work that was still to be done in the Dáil, said that she thought Mary Robinson should be the Labour Party candidate. 'She is someone who would make a difference,' Denise declared

Fergus Finlay heard the remark and passed it on to Dick Spring and John Rogers. Following an initial approach, on St Valentine's Day 1990, and a subsequent meeting held in the utmost secrecy, Mary Robinson agreed to run. But all was not clear and some hurdles had yet to be crossed. I was not part of the group, which included Dick, Fergus and John, who first met in the Robinson's

Sandford Road home, but was soon brought on board. Following a parliamentary party meeting on 21 March, Dick announced to the media that he intended to propose Mary Robinson as Labour's candidate to the forthcoming joint parliamentary party–administrative council meeting on 26 April.

Labour Left reacted with a great flurry of activity, combined with intense bitterness. They wanted Noël Browne to be the candidate or, in truth, anyone other than Dick's choice. Essentially, it was all part of the challenge to his leadership, fronted by Emmet Stagg. Despite these early tensions, Mary Robinson was endorsed by a margin of three to one. Dick had asked me to take on the task of directing the presidential campaign and so I became closely involved in one of the most exciting and dramatic presidential election campaigns in the history of the state.

I knew Mary and Nick Robinson, since we were young students. While I was a bit cynical at the time of Mary's public reason for her resignation from the Labour Party in 1985 – the Anglo-Irish Agreement – I remained a political admirer. I thought that her refusal to rejoin the Labour Party, even though her candidacy was backed by the party, would be a difficulty. However, as I began my work on the campaign, I realised the advantages of having a prominent candidate, who was nominated by a political party but who remained outside that party's formal membership.

Bride Rosney, who I had not worked with before, was at the side of Mary and Nick Robinson from the very start of the campaign. Her loyalty to Mary knew no limits and she was ruthless in the pursuit of her candidate's objective. Brenda O'Hanlon joined us as an effective member of the team, with responsibility for press relations. In the midst of this was the diminutive Ann Lane, Mary's Oireachtas and legal secretary for twenty-one years. A motorcyclist, Ann's crash helmet and leather jacket became a familiar sight in Leinster House. Her understanding of politics was a bonus in helping to keep the diverse and sometimes fractious components in touch with each other, and so it was decided that Ann should be based in Mary Robinson's home for the entire campaign.

Fergus Finlay and Nick Robinson contributed at the campaign

committee. Ita McAuliffe, the parliamentary party's administrator, was co-opted as the efficient executive secretary, and others, such as Ray Kavanagh, the party's general secretary, and James Wrynn, its financial secretary, were also members of the team. Denise Rogers stayed in the background, working from my office in Leinster House. From the outset of the campaign, there were deep tensions and personality clashes which remained with us right through the count and on to the stage of the Olympic Ballroom in Pleasant Street, Dublin on the night of our celebrations.

From the beginning it was agreed that the campaign would be run and substantially financed by monies raised by the party, but not directly from party funds. Expectations of finance coming via the Robinson network proved to be grossly overestimated and the major financial responsibility fell on the party's shoulders. In the initial stages, this constant ambiguity drove the tension of the campaign because all participants, myself included, had their own agenda.

I wanted to use the campaign to broaden the appeal of the party beyond its narrow tribal and traditional confines. For that reason the campaign headquarters would not be in 16 Gardiner Place, the Labour Party's head office, but in a separate neutral location. We soon found ourselves in the basement floor of the sympathetic Manufacturing, Science and Finance (MSF) union at 15 Merrion Square. The senior official in charge of MSF, John Tierney, was an old friend of mine and a supporter of The Workers' Party. His assistant, Jerry Shanahan, was a strong Labour Left activist. I had participated in weekend political seminars that MSF had organised for its union activists, following the merger of TASS and ASTMS which had created MSF as a new white-collar union.

The physical separation from Labour's northside headquarters was symbolic and practical, as was the choice of logo that we would use for the campaign. The red plough and the stars logo that the party had been using for nearly a decade was dated and possibly counterproductive. A conversation one Friday evening in O'Reilly's pub in Sandymount with Tim Bird, an exotic individual from my childhood, focused this in my mind. He began speaking about politics and made some comments about the Dublin South-East constituency offices in Charlemont Street. 'All those flags and stars,' he observed, 'smack too much of Tiananmen Square and the fall of the Berlin Wall. It sends out the wrong image and the wrong message.'

On Dublin South-East literature, we had been using the Socialist International logo of 'the rose and the fist' and I was anxious to have this symbol incorporated into the Irish Labour Party's new image. The Robinson campaign gave us a perfect opportunity to introduce a new logo which, when the campaign was over, could be adopted as our own emblem. Sweden's Social Democratic Party had been helping Labour to develop our organisation and had, at that time, an attractive simple rose logo. In consultation with James Wrynn and Ray Kavanagh, I arranged for the committee to see preliminary artwork using the Swedish rose.

Meanwhile Bride Rosney, Nick Robinson and others had a different plan. Unbeknownst to me, and perhaps others, Eoghan Harris had become central to the Robinson family's thinking. Through Harris, and an RTÉ designer, they came up with an alternative rose logo. It was more terracotta than red and graphically looked more Japanese than the realistic Swedish rose. Nevertheless, it won the day. Although I was disappointed, we now at least had a rose logo. Besides, since we would be using the Labour Party's printing facilities in Leinster House, all the terracotta ink would be red anyway! The campaign committee met every Wednesday evening and the momentum slowly began to build. Just as Dick had wanted, we were the first in the field with a committed candidate.

Early in May, John Rogers returned from the remote village of Allihies in West Cork where he had suggested that the candidate might commence her campaign at a small local community function. I knew that Eoghan Harris, who had by now left The Workers' Party, had sent the Robinsons a ten-page memo outlining what he called a 'voyage of discovery of the country' as part of a wider and deeper strategy. While his recommendations contained much of what we wanted to do with an early start and a countrywide campaign, Eoghan's opinion had great credibility with Mary, Nick and Bride Rosney. But theory is one thing and reality something else.

'Something is happening out there, far away from Leinster House. This lady, our candidate, is connecting with the people in a way I would not have believed, had I not seen it myself,' John Rogers said on his return from Allihies. With his bent shoulders, and ponderous and serious demeanour, as perhaps befits a barrister who prematurely becomes a senior counsel, John is an astute political observer. His underlying message was very clear: we could win.

I must confess that until early June 1990, I did not believe that Mary Robinson would be the next President of Ireland. However, I always felt that we would do much better than the combined left vote of the previous general election. Taken together with this vote – covering the Labour Party, The Workers' Party and Independents such as Jim Kemmy – was less than 17 per cent. In the original pro-life referendum of 1983 and the 1986 divorce referendum campaign, approximately 30 per cent of the electorate voted for the left, and this figure was still ours to win in this election, if we could harness it in the first count. With that percentage there was an outside chance that we could come in second of the three candidates. With the elimination of the Fine Gael candidate, the second preferences would mostly come to Mary Robinson and so give her a real chance of victory.

Two factors would determine the outcome. Could Mary Robinson gather votes beyond the narrow left confines of our party, and reach out to that minority which had expressed itself so courageously in those two referenda? Second, would Fine Gael field a strong candidate? Fine Gael had showed no signs of wanting a presidential contest. I knew that neither Garret nor Joan FitzGerald wanted to be trapped in the Áras. It also became clear to me that Peter Barry, the party's second choice, was not prepared to stand after he had been rejected as their first choice for leader, when Garret retired in 1987. Towards the end of June, Mary's support was being continually reinforced by reports from the campaign trail. After a long and difficult political progress, Fine Gael opted for Austin Currie. From that moment, I knew that we could win, even though we would have to work very hard right up to polling day, 7 November. Then in June, the *Sunday Business Post* published an opinion poll that gave Mary a real chance.

The campaign gathered momentum, as people from diverse quarters began to surface with help and even money. Niall Greene, Greg Sparks and Donal Nevin were appointed trustees of the 'Fund to Elect Mary Robinson'. In consultation with them, we decided to put an early advertisement on the front page of a Saturday edition of *The Irish Times*, as much to announce our presence as to generate funds. Catherine Donnelly, a highly talented copywriter, had volunteered her services to the campaign and she came up with a great line for the advertisement, which caught the mood of the time: 'Put your hand in your pocket for a person who is not in someone else's.'

The National Commemoration Day ceremony takes place on the second Sunday in July each year. Since Dick Spring was in Kerry, I represented the party at this formal event to commemorate all Irish men and women in the Irish army serving with the United Nations or the British army who had died in wars or in the cause of peace. It is a solemn and evocative ceremony and one that Liz and myself enjoyed attending. In a flash of inspiration, Liz suggested that we ask Mary Robinson to come with us and she enthusiastically agreed, despite not having a formal invitation. We arrived early at Kilmainham and I went to take my place with other party leaders or their representatives. The person from the protocol division of the Department of the Taoiseach ensured that Liz and Mary Robinson were given a prominent position in the front row where, coincidentally, the television cameras would undoubtedly catch them. After President Hillery had laid the wreath for the last time as president, the party leaders filed in procession after him and the Taoiseach, from the central square back into the dining hall of the Royal Hospital. En route, I found myself walking with Peter Barry. Caustically, he remarked about our advertisement in the paper, 'I see you are going after our vote.' I said nothing of substance in reply, but was pleasantly surprised that our strategy was working. After the formalities, Mary mixed with the invited dignitaries, including the chairpersons of county councils from around the country.

Two weeks later, Liz and I took a special journey. We flew to New York and stayed with Dáithí Ó Ceallaigh and his wife Antoinette. Dáithí was Ireland's Consul General in the city and later Ireland's ambassador in London was of great help to us in finalising the arrangements for our marriage. Liz and I were married on 27 July 1990. My brother Lochlann was there and Gerry Burke-Kennedy, my nephew and our best man, was joined by Geri Dunne and her husband, Brian, who had travelled from Ottawa. Liz's friend, Máire Crowe, a journalist based in New York, along with Antoinette and Dáithí also joined us for a celebratory meal in Manhattan. After a brief honeymoon, there was a reception in Roundstone, County Galway, hosted by Lochlann and Brenda, at which many of our friends and family helped us to celebrate our wedding.

Back in Dublin I had to bring together Mary Robinson's supporters and campaigners who were, in some cases, antagonistic towards each other. The rivalry between The Workers' Party and Labour was now quite intense. Eamon Gilmore in Dún Laoghaire and Eric Byrne in Dublin South-Central had taken the seats of Barry Desmond and the late Frank Cluskey, who had died in May 1989, some weeks before the general election. While relations within the Dáil were civilised, if a bit cool, between the two parliamentary parties, the rivalry among activists in these constituencies was quite different. Dick had asked me to undertake responsibility for rebuilding the Labour Party organisation in the Dublin area. At the same time Bride Rosney and Nick Robinson were pushing me to involve The Workers' Party in the campaign more, particularly where Mary would be part of a public canvass, such as at a large shopping centre. This meant that activists from the Labour Party and The Workers' Party would have to campaign side by side. Outside Dublin there were similar difficulties. I can recall a very intense and heated discussion with Brendan Howlin about the logistics of Mary Robinson's visit to Wexford. In his view, far too much time had been assigned to Michael Enright, a Workers' Party local councillor and a bitter rival of Brendan for the left seat. After several conversations with Bride Rosney and Brendan Howlin, a revised schedule for the candidate's visit was reluctantly agreed. Eamon Gilmore was to be co-opted on to our election committee in return for The Workers' Party public support for the Robinson campaign, but I succeeded in delaying his arrival for eight weeks. We also targeted many other potential supporters. People from the liberal wing of Fine Gael were attracted to Mary Robinson but did not like elements of the 'hard Left'.

The final group we attracted was women. Women of different, or no, political allegiance became helpers, canvassers, workers and advocates for the concept of a 'working presidency' and the first female president.

After the election, I described co-ordinating these diverse components, in a conversation with the journalist John Waters, as like being in charge of a train with each carriage full of different passengers. While we were all travelling in the same direction, it was important, from my point of view, not to let the passengers from one carriage know who was on the train in the next carriage.

Quinn McDonnell Pattison was the advertising company for the Robinson campaign. Given our limited resources, an outdoor, forty-eight-sheet poster publicity drive for the last eight weeks of the election was considered to be the most cost-effective option. The professional fashion photographer Conor Horgan also volunteered his services. With a few assistants Conor, did a number of outdoor shots in the public park between St Patrick's Cathedral and the Iveagh Buildings. The people for the photographs – a group of old men for one poster and a young couple for the other – gave permission for the photographs to be used as part of the presidential campaign.

The images were excellent. We decided to use a mix of the old men and the young couple. After four weeks we would replace one image with another, so that the coverage was consistent. However, when the posters were printed, I got a message to say that the young woman in the photograph had phoned to withdraw her consent.

It seems that she was at the highly sensitive point of trying to end the relationship with her boyfriend when she had been interrupted by a smiling Mary Robinson and asked to pose for the photographs. The moment lost, it was some time later before the young woman did break the news to her boyfriend. Understandably, she did not then want her photograph displayed across the country, seated beside her ex-boyfriend and the potential next President of Ireland.

I was alarmed when I got the news. Nearly half our entire budget had been invested in these posters. I was annoyed with myself for not making sure that everything was watertight and that the undertakings were irrevocable. 'That is why we use professional actors,' was the sympathetic response from Steve Shanahan in QMP.

I phoned the girl's home and explained our difficulty to her mother. The mother liked the lad and hoped that her daughter and he would get back together. So did I and very soon at that! The mother and myself agreed to keep in touch; she admired Mary Robinson and was anxious to help. I nearly offered the services of a professional relationship counsellor for the young couple, but instead bit my tongue and decided to authorise a slight change of plan. All 130 sites now had an appealing image of Mary Robinson, seated on a park bench reaching out and connecting with the old men.

The reaction from the campaign team was similar, 'Yeah, a great image, a terrific message, but too much emphasis on old people. Can you not have her with young people as well?' I said nothing, hoping for the best. In one dark moment, I even sought legal advice as to how long an injunction would take if we went ahead with the young people posters. But our luck held, the romance was back on and, to celebrate it, an image of the happy couple was put on 130 billboards countrywide, seated side by side with our candidate.

RTÉ gave us details of the political broadcast timeslots that were being allocated to the three candidates. The campaign committee decided that Eoghan Harris' repeated offers of help should be accepted on this specific project and I arranged for him to call to my home in Sandymount, one weekday at lunchtime. I did not tell him, on the phone, the concerns within the Labour Party that his key presence in the campaign might discourage the now active involvement of The Workers' Party.

We agreed on the logistics of making the political broadcast. Eoghan was going to accompany the candidate for two days and use whatever film footage he could take. In addition, he wanted to spend a few hours with the candidate so that he could direct specially structured shots. He also wanted a person to act as a constituent whom Mary had canvassed, and who had taken pity on her and brought her in for a cup of tea. I contacted Theresa Westby, a friend and supporter of many years, who instantly agreed to my request. In fairness, Eoghan turned Theresa into a real professional actor and, by a clever use of lighting, staged an evening shot that had been taken first thing in the morning. In the Department of the Environment, Tim Sexton graciously agreed to accept Mary Robinson's nomination papers on a Saturday in the Custom House, and Eoghan was able to film this important event.

The following Sunday evening Eoghan rang to say he was up in UCD and could I come and join him because he needed a direction on the content of one of the political broadcasts. Liz and I drove to the UCD campus at Belfield and into the back entrance of the library. Inside a small studio with an editing room facility, Eoghan showed us the first film that was nearing completion.

He had taken footage of Mary surrounded by campaign workers and electors in different parts of Dublin. From time to time a close-up of Mary caught her characteristic hand gesture as the sound-track played the traditional tune 'Tabhair dom do lámh' ('Give me your hand'). It set the tone of what a working presidency might be and introduced the candidate to a wider public. But I was concerned that the film had no political content.

'That is for the second broadcast,' Eoghan said as he showed us a questions and answers session he had filmed in Ballyfermot Senior College between Mary and Leaving Certificate students. I had to select a number of questions and the replies from the footage. This formed the middle of the election broadcast, which was both introduced and rounded off by Dick Spring. It is amazing what tight editing can do in two minutes, but we had good, unrehearsed questions and Mary's well-honed replies.

When the second broadcast was completed, Eoghan started to talk in his intense way, about the third and final political broadcast. He wanted to take Mary around the country, but time and the budget prevented that. Instead, we did have a series of photographs, starting in Allihies, of the countrywide campaign. The outdoor market in Blackrock would be an ideal location where a young couple, coming to meet the next President of Ireland, would encounter her as she danced with a stall holder, beside an old-fashioned HMV gramophone with a 78 record on the turntable. Describing this, Eoghan said he wanted as a soundtrack the popular operatic aria 'Nessun Dorma' from Puccini's *Turandot*, which had been the signature tune for the television coverage of the soccer World Cup in Italy earlier that summer. He argued that the country had felt really good about itself during the competition and would remember the music. Ireland had got to the quarter-finals against Italy and the whole nation had come to a standstill to watch the match. Liz and I had watched it in the Barley Mow pub on Francis Street.

I listened to the energy in Eoghan's voice, as he described this broadcast, and I could sense the emotional appeal. When I subsequently saw the finished piece, I was dumbstruck. In between photographs from across the land were close-up shots of Mary's study and large index files of the many civil and human rights cases she had fought and won. Throughout the three-minute broadcast not a word was spoken until the very end as the camera closed in on the revolving HMV disc with its famous trademark and a simple voiceover saying, 'Mary Robinson, a great record.'

Over the years, I have been involved in many campaigns and participated in the production of a wide range of political material, but I do not know of anything better than those three broadcasts that Eoghan Harris produced.

Public interest became fully engaged in the last stretch of the campaign. The big question was whether or not Mary Robinson could overtake Brian Lenihan on the second count. Austin Currie turned out to be an even weaker candidate than I had thought and that frailty was ultimately to undermine his leader, Alan Dukes, who was ousted as party leader in December 1990, weeks after the election. On 22 October the campaign was thrown into confusion when Brian Lenihan denied, on the television programme *Questions & Answers*, that he had acted improperly in trying to persuade President Hillery to dissolve the Dáil some eight years earlier. The charge was led by Garret FitzGerald and it emerged some days later, at a press conference organised by *The Irish Times*, that Lenihan had lied on television. Jim Duffy, a research student, had taped an interview with Lenihan in which the Fianna Fáil minister openly talked about trying to contact President Hillery. This revelation caused a major controversy and questioned Lenihan's credibility. The Fianna Fáil presidential candidate was now charged with attempting to gravely abuse the very office to which he was seeking election.

Opposition parties put down a no-confidence motion in Lenihan. Reluctantly, Labour agreed to support this, feeling that it might galvanise Fianna Fáil support for their candidate. We did not anticipate the Progressive Democrat reaction between the tabling of the motion and its vote; they demanded a response from C.J. Haughey. Even though he had defended his friend and Tánaiste in the Dáil earlier that day, Haughey fired Lenihan from the cabinet before the vote was taken. As a result, Lenihan was forced to campaign as a backbencher for the final days of the campaign.

Another surprise boost came the Saturday before polling day. Contributing from a radio studio in Castlebar to the current-affairs programme *Saturday View*, Minister for the Environment Pádraig Flynn attacked what he described as Robinson's 'new interest in the family, being a mother and all that kind of thing'. This provoked a strong defence from Brendan Howlin and a vitriolic response from Michael McDowell, who were also on the studio panel. Charlie McCreevy subsequently told me that he was out with a team of canvassers in County Kildare and as they moved through a newly built housing estate, the spontaneous hostility which Flynn's remarks had generated forced them to end their canvass in the mid-afternoon.

I believe that Mary Robinson would have won the election anyway, but the controversies enlivened the last ten days of the campaign and increased her margin of victory. We were now confident that the presidency would finally be occupied by a progressive liberal woman, a political activist and decidedly not from the conservative Fianna Fáil party that had so dominated the presidency since 1938.

The scenes at the count centre in the RDS and later in the Olympia Ballroom are ones I will always remember. As chair of the campaign committee, I was at the RDS, equipped with a rented mobile phone, then a new piece of technology. It was the size of a large book, nearly as heavy and with a battery that lasted for two hours. Pestered by journalists and photographers about the whereabouts of the successful candidate, I made contact with Bride Rosney. Having confirmed the arrangements for Mary's triumphal arrival, I went outside to the waiting press corps.

'She's going to be here in twenty minutes. The car will come in at that gate and up to where I am standing. There will then be time and space, inside, for photographs and other interviews. Now please, make space for the car when it arrives and don't all crowd around her. Remember, lads, she is the president.'

It was only when I uttered that last sentence that I realised just what was happening and how much I, myself, was emotionally affected by all that we had achieved.

Some days after Mary Robinson's election, I attended a meeting of the Medieval Trust in the offices of Woodchester Finance Company in Dublin. Craig McKinney was the chief executive of Woodchester, a highly successful finance house, and a major supporter of the Medieval Trust and its project 'Dublinia'. Before the meeting began, he congratulated me on the Robinson success. Afterwards, I took him aside and tentatively said that, if he was happy to support Labour's presidential candidate, would he support Labour for government? His answer was clear. No. He thought our policies were too old-fashioned and not relevant to our present economic problems.

Instinctively, I felt that he was speaking for a much larger part of the population than just the financial sector.

The economic difficulties of the time and the high level of unemployment had given rise to much discontent, but there seemed to be little confidence in entrusting Labour with the reins of power. Mervyn Taylor was our spokesperson on Finance and he had adopted an old-style traditional leftist approach. In this, he was supported by Emmet Stagg and Michael D. Higgins. There was a comfort in reiterating a set of secure, if out-dated, policy positions. The globalisation of the world's economy was having an impact on traditional economic sectors. The European Community's internal market competition rules made impossible many traditional state intervention measures and financial subsidies. New policy measures were needed. While I was not clear as to what these might yet be, I knew that unless I got directly involved, the party would not begin to look for them.

Soon I outlined my thoughts to Dick, including taking on the job of spokesperson for Finance, if he was prepared to give it to me. He too had been in a reflective mood and outlined the plans he had been formulating since the successful Robinson campaign.

Early in January 1991, an all-day meeting of the administrative council and the parliamentary party was held in Jurys Hotel, Ballsbridge. A number of outside speakers were invited to address the gathering. Our first guest speaker was Dr Anthony Clare, a psychiatrist and noted broadcaster, famous for his BBC Radio 4 series of interviews with public personalities, *In the Psychiatrist's Chair*. Recently returned to Dublin as professor of psychiatry and director of St Patrick's Hospital, he spoke engagingly about modern society and the changes that were happening in Ireland and in the rest of Europe. Many people were challenging traditional attitudes, ties and patterns. This was a time when a political party should show that it understood these changes, while at the same time knowing where it wanted society and its members to go. A lively discussion took place after Anthony Clare's address.

Later, John Bradley of the Economic and Social Research Institute (ESRI), a friend of Eithne Fitzgerald, made a presentation on the macro-economic changes confronting Ireland. He spoke about the changed economic and regulatory landscape of the European Community of twelve member states and how the operation of the Single European Act would bring about the completion of the internal market. It was necessary to understand the nature of these changes and to formulate a political response to take account of them. Clearly, Bradley struck a chord with the meeting and caught the mood of many present. The local elections were to be held in June and many prospective candidates were in the room. The conference was a success and the relevance of what had been heard from both speakers motivated many of those present and reinforced their commitment to campaign vigorously following our Robinson victory.

One outcome of the conference was personally satisfying. Reflecting the desire for change and modernisation, the meeting took the decision to change the logo of the party, and the Swedish red rose emblem, which I had failed to have adopted for the Robinson campaign, was now enthusiastically accepted.

Finally, Dick made a number of changes in the parliamentary party. I became the party's spokesperson on Finance, but did not feel properly equipped to fulfil the task, despite having approached Dick about it. While experience in a large architectural firm had given me a good understanding of business, I did not regard myself as economically literate to the level the job required. Although I had subscribed to *The Economist* for many years, any financial knowledge I had was informal.

First I spoke to Greg Sparks and he agreed to help, as did Ciarán O'Mara. So early in 1991 we set about arranging a systematic course of briefings and meetings, designed to fill the many gaps in my own knowledge of economics and finance, and I intended to convey to those I would meet that the Labour Party and I were serious about our task. I started with the Department of Finance, phoning the secretary, Seán Cromien, and asking for a formal briefing on the entire work of the department. When I met him, in his office, he made a point of telling me that he had cleared our meeting with his minister, Albert Reynolds.

'That's what I would expect you to do,' I replied.

Celebrating with Joe Costello and Pat Upton, newly elected Labour TDs, 25 November 1992.

The Parliamentary Labour Party walking to its first PLP meeting in the Shelbourne Hotel after our dramatic victory in the 1992 general election.

A pictoral history of the Labour Party that I designed with the artist Brian Dennington. It was published to celebrate May Day becoming a public holiday, which I brought in as Minister for Enterprise and Employment in 1993, with effect from 1994.

Meeting photographers on my first budget as Minister for Finance, 8 February 1995.

Presidency press conference at the time of the successful negotiations
for the Stability and Growth Pact, 12 December 1996.
l-r: Commisioner Yves de Silguy, myself, Joe Lennon.

Trying to keep discipline on my cabinet colleagues to ensure
that Ireland qualified for the euro.

Walking with Liz and Brendan Howlin, TD, to the press conference
after being elected Leader of the Labour Party, 13 November 1997.

How the media
viewed the dual
victory of the two
by-elections,
February 1998.

Tom Halliday, *Irish Independent*

In pensive mood at an election press conference, 2002.

The day I announced I would not be seeking a second term as Leader of the Labour Party, 26 August 2002.

A family photo taken in 1985.
back row: Colm, myself, Declan.
front row: Lochlann, Mammy, Moninne, Conor.

A family photo taken in 2002.
l-r: Martin, Síne, myself, Conan, Liz, Sara Jane, Malachi.

Liz and Conan.

Before long he gave me a full description of the work and struc-ture of the Department of Finance. When he had answered many of my questions, I let him know that I was arranging similar meet-ings with the Revenue Commissioners and other state agencies. Kevin Murphy, who had been secretary of the now defunct Department of the Public Service, was still in charge of the public service management division of the Department of Finance, and I was familiar with that section of the house. Over the next few weeks I met with Cathal MacDomhnaill, chairman of the Revenue Commissioners, and Pádraig White, chief executive of the IDA, and asked them to outline the problems they saw affecting the economy and what should be done.

Next I turned my attention to the academics. I had known Peter Neary, the young dean of the Department of Economics in UCD, as a student many years previously. When I phoned, looking for a 'crash' seminar on economics, he invited me to meet members of his staff over a long and discursive lunch in Belfield. Some days later, I had the benefit of listening to analysis and opinions of a number of academics, thanks to Dermot McAleese. Dermot was a member of the board of the Central Bank and the Whately Professor of Political Economy in Trinity College. I knew Dermot and his wife and when I phoned with my request for a grind in economics, he generously invited me to his home for dinner and a discussion, with academic colleagues, about the problems of the economy and what the state should do.

Then Greg and Ciarán drew up a list of people in the world of finance and business whom they thought would be interesting, informative and probably sympathetic. We arranged to have a series of breakfast meetings, in the Mont Clare Hotel every Monday. There I met bankers, accountants, stockbrokers and economic commentators during the course of the year. After six months I felt that I was getting on top of the issues and beginning to develop proposals for the modernisation of our economy and the creation of additional employment. I knew that the perception of the Labour Party was changing among a significant group of professionals, who, in turn, would have a lot of influence within their own immediate communities. It was my opinion that Labour had to be seen as a serious political force which could be trusted to manage the economy well. My many meetings and discussions confirmed my political belief that there was a role for the state in direct intervention in the economy in ways that helped indigenous companies grow and increased exports and employment. But we needed new policy instruments in the hands of the state. The high cost of finance and the absence of venture capital was one example where state intervention was required at that time. Across the Irish Sea, John Smith, Labour shadow chancellor to Neil Kinnock, was beginning to look both credible and trustworthy as John Major struggled to keep the Tories in office. I thought that if Labour were to win the forthcoming British general election, then we could only benefit.

The Dublin campaign committee for the 1991 local elections was busy ensuring that we had candidates selected in every one of the thirty-two electoral areas in the Dublin city, county and Dún Laoghaire local authorities. Essentially, we were starting from a low base because Labour had done so badly in 1985. We had only two out of fifty-two councillors in the city, eight out of seventy-nine in the county, and just one out of fourteen in Dún Laoghaire. Various personality differences and local rivalries inevitably existed throughout the Dublin region, reflecting tensions from previous campaigns. For example, Joan Burton had clashed bitterly with Joe Costello in the City Centre ward during the 1989 general election. There were claims of campaign contributions to the Dublin Central constituency fund not being honoured, arising from commitments in a previous contest. If Ray Kavanagh could not resolve internal rows, my role was to knock heads together and negotiate agreements. The Burton–Costello row was solved with Joan's decision to stand for the County Council in the Mulhuddart electoral area; this was open territory, with no Labour Party presence or significant organisation in situ.

Slowly, but surely, our panel of candidates grew. After one

campaign committee meeting I got a call from Róisín Shortall, asking if we had a candidate for the Drumcondra–Ballymun electoral area. I said that we didn't, but knew that Bill Tormey was the candidate in the other electoral area of Finglas, which helped make up the Dublin North-West constituency. Bill had stood in the 1987 general election and again in 1989, polling extremely well. Fine Gael's Mary Flaherty's margin of victory had been a mere fifty-four votes over him for the last seat. His election to the City Council was perceived to be a prerequisite if he were to run again for the Dáil. In fact, the constituency organisation was dominated by Bill's voluble personality.

'Well, I would be very interested in standing in that electoral area,' Róisín said.

'But I thought that you were a central part of Joe Costello's team.'

'Yes, I've been actively involved with Dublin Central for a long time, but I live in Dublin North-West, in the Drumcondra–Ballymun area.' Certainly, Róisín was a good prospective candidate and Bill Tormey, whom I informally consulted, had no objection and so another slot was filled.

Meanwhile, I also had to make a decision about running myself in the South Inner City electoral area. It stretched from Inchicore to Pearse Street, including the large area between the Liffey and the Grand Canal, half of which was within Dublin South-East. While Mary Freehill and Dermot Lacey had been nominated for the Rathmines and Pembroke wards, we had no candidate for the South Inner City. I had deferred making a decision but soon realised that I would have to stand. I did not believe in the dual mandate, yet I felt that if I had stood for the local elections in 1979, instead of handing over the seat to Mary Freehill, I might have been re-elected to the Dáil two years later. Dick Spring and Brendan Howlin asked me to be a candidate, as did members of the constituency executive.

By Easter, all the Labour candidates were in place and work was well underway on the campaign material. After discussions with the candidates and their directors of elections, I got agreement for a Dublin-wide poster campaign, using commercial sites, such as bus shelters and DART stations. Our slogan was to be 'Let's make Dublin a city that works'. Printed in white, the poster carried a line drawing of the Halfpenny Bridge set against a red skyline. Some objections were made to the effect that the bridge was hardly a symbol of Balbriggan or Clondalkin. My response was that it had an iconic value because it featured in the opening shots of RTÉ's urban soap *Fair City*, which had recently started.

In the last stages of the campaign, between Easter and polling day, I reinforced the message to all candidates that the local elections would be regarded as 'primaries' for the next general election, which everyone felt would not be far away. Only successfully elected councillors would be considered as potential Dáil candidates. I stated this time and again. There was intense interest because eight constituencies were without sitting deputies.

The campaign produced its inevitable surprises and disappointments. One I remember well. Early in the campaign, I got a phone call from Liz O'Donnell, whom I had met during the Robinson campaign in which she had been active. She wanted to help Labour and was trying to make contact with Cllr Mary Freehill. Naturally, I phoned Mary to let her know that Liz O'Donnell would be phoning, but we did not hear back from Liz until we saw her name in print as the Rathmines candidate for the Progressive Democrats! It appears that Mary Harney had asked her and actor Jeananne Crowley to stand for the party.

On the day of the count, I got a phone call mid-morning from my Liz, who was part of our tally team at the count centre, to signal that all was going very well. Mary Freehill and I would be easily elected, as would Dermot Lacey; three council seats in the constituency, one for each electoral area, where previously the party had none. It seemed that the message was the same across the city. Liz rang Dermot with the news which got better during the day, so much so that his parents were invited to come in and see their son being elected, and his wife Jill, who had had her appendix taken out two days earlier, came out of hospital. Yet despite leading for a number of counts, Dermot was not to be a winner. A transfer of votes when Jeananne Crowley was eliminated to another candidate in the Pembroke ward resulted in Claire Wheeler beating Dermot by thirty-seven votes to win a seat for the Green Party. She joined her newly elected colleague John Gormley, who had gone home earlier believing he could not win.

The election had taken place on 28 June and by the end of the following day when the count was over, Labour was seen as the main victor, particularly in Dublin. Bill Tormey did not win, but Róisín Shortall did, which was to have consequences later. In the city we had gone from two seats to ten and in the county from eight seats to fourteen. Around the country, figures were also good, but the focus of the media attention was on Dublin and here, more than anywhere else, Labour was the major winner.

After the election, Joe Costello, the only other Oireachtas member of the newly elected group of city councillors, called to my office in Leinster House. We discussed how we should work with other parties on the new City Council. I asked him to draft a policy position paper which could form the basis of negotiations we might have with the other parties or groups elected to the City Council. The basis of the draft would be our manifesto, but he should look at the platform of The Workers' Party and the Greens to explore common ground.

At that stage I was open to a possible electoral and policy deal with Fianna Fáil, but I kept that view very much to myself. Back in 1989, when Pádraig Flynn was famously describing single-party government as 'a core value' of Fianna Fáil, he did not know that C.J. Haughey was negotiating its abandonment with the leader of the Progressive Democrats in a move that opened up the potential of a coalition between Fianna Fáil and the other parties.

At our first meeting of the newly elected Labour councillors on 3 July, the mood of the group was opposed to any deal with Fianna Fáil, even if it was by far the simplest and easiest one to negotiate. John Stafford, leader of the Fianna Fáil group on the council, had already been in touch with me on the same topic. Stafford was a deputy for Dublin North-Central and I knew him well. I had been a member of the City Council in 1974, when his father was an Independent councillor. At first, I stalled John with my responses while awaiting the discussions of our own group.

Later I was unanimously elected leader of the Labour group and informed them that I had asked Joe to prepare a draft document that would form the basis of our discussions with the other parties. The group then elected Joe Costello, Seán Kenny and myself as the negotiation team. We met with Fine Gael and the Community Group on the Sunday, having had preliminary talks with The Workers' Party and the Greens over the previous days; these had gone very well.

From the beginning I had persuaded my colleagues that it was important to get an agreement on policy objectives before any discussion could take place about which party got what position among the many committees and external bodies, to say nothing about the position of Lord Mayor. We had nearly ten days before the City Council would meet to elect the Lord Mayor and begin the process of filling other posts. My memory took me back to 1974 and the negotiations in one of Paddy Belton's pubs, close to Busáras. Then, the discussion had been solely about posts and, as issues, such as Wood Quay, arose over the next few years, there was no coherent reference point on which Labour and Fine Gael could agree. I also knew that a discussion on a common policy position among the five groups, some with distinctive political positions, would take time. But as the discussion unfolded, there was a bonus which I had not anticipated.

Our move to open discussions with four other groups effectively blocked off a majority of councillors more than a week before the City Council was scheduled to meet. Once engaged in the process, Fianna Fáil could not approach any of the smaller groups in an attempt to put a deal together with them, including Tony Gregory and Christy Burke. After much discussion, a document emerged and twenty-nine councillors put their signature to it. Some weeks later, after the new City Council had held its inaugural meeting, it was also formally supported by Liz O'Donnell, the only elected Progressive Democrat councillor. In time the document became known as the Civic Charter and attracted a considerable amount of publicity. It was clear that we had caught the imagination of many members of the public. Earlier, my suggestion that the five-party group be called the Civic Alliance was adopted and met with general approval.

When the Civic Charter was agreed, and only then, did we turn our attention to the allocation of posts, starting with the Lord Mayor. With five groups and a five-year term, a chance and opportunity for each group to have its turn with the mayoralty was reasonable, if overgenerous from Labour's point of view, having regard to the size of our group. In recognition of this, it was agreed that Labour would have the sixth term, should the life of the council be extended by another year, as had often happened in the past.

Privately, I had told Joe Costello that I would be supporting him for Lord Mayor since the first term would come to Labour. Earlier the group, at my suggestion, had accepted that Labour should nominate only prospective Dáil candidates for the Mansion House position. We simply could not, at this stage in Dublin, with only three deputies, use this important post in any other way. Seán Kenny, the only Labour member of the previous City Council, was the other Labour candidate. After two secret ballots, both of which tied five all, Kenny's name came out of the hat.

One day soon after the local elections, Mervyn Taylor, who had been successfully re-elected to Dublin County Council, stopped me in the corridor of Leinster House, expressing surprise that I was not seeking the position of Lord Mayor. I explained our thinking *vis-à-vis* using the position to maximise prospective candidates in the forthcoming general election. 'Besides, Mervyn,' I continued, 'I want a four-year job with a real car!'

Connie Walsh, a great friend of my mother for many years, was buried the day after Seán Kenny became Lord Mayor of Dublin. I stood in the church remembering a story my mother used to tell of how Connie had expressed delight when her fourth son was born. 'Now they'll be able to carry my coffin from the church.' I looked at Connie's four sons doing just that, followed by their sister, as they went out into the summer sunlight that surrounded St Theresa's Church in Mount Merrion. I knew all four boys and was particularly friendly with Brendan, a contemporary of my brother Lochlann. As I stood beside Lochlann, outside the church, looking at the large attendance expressing their condolences to the Walsh family, he turned to me. 'Well done. I see you got your man safely elected last night.'

Chapter 16

In Government Again
1993–1994

Ray Kavanagh was in Dick Spring's Leinster House office in early January 1993. It was proving difficult to get a venue at short notice for a special conference to accommodate 1,200 delegates.

'Have you tried the National Concert Hall?' I asked him.

'Yes,' he replied, 'but it's not available on the Saturday.'

'Why not see if you can book it for the Sunday.'

Ray turned as he moved towards the door. 'Ruairi, why are you so keen on the National Concert Hall?'

'Because, Ray, when our delegates arrive there for a special conference, they'll know that they're going into government.'

It had been an exhilarating eighteen months since the local elections and the formation of the Civic Alliance. The City Council formally adopted the Civic Charter as policy, notwithstanding the reluctance of senior management in City Hall and the clear discomfort of the city manager, Frank Feely.

My time on the City Council was occasionally frustrating. Resources were very tight and it was difficult to drive an agenda that did not originate within the management. The abolition of residential rates effectively removed control of their resources from the councillors. I knew, then, that I would not have been able to raise funds again in the way I had to rescue the Olympia Theatre.

Elsewhere, political attention was moving to a very different stage. It was clear that an election would soon be called, and certainly before the end of the government's five-year term in 1994. In January 1992, revelations by Seán Doherty, a former Minister for Justice, on a TV programme, *Nighthawks*, blew the whistle on Haughey's control of Fianna Fáil and he was ousted. On 11 February, Albert Reynolds, the new Taoiseach, was now leading a government with the Progressive Democrats as junior partners. At a Fianna Fáil meeting in Kanturk, two years earlier, Reynolds had dismissed this partnership as a 'temporary little arrangement'.

I was responsible for Labour in Dublin and it was time to select our Dáil candidates. In most cases, they selected themselves, by virtue of their election to the city or county council. Bill Tormey used his influence with Dick Spring, through Fergus Finlay, to be added to the ticket in Dublin North-West, but to no avail. I had stated that the local elections were a 'primary' and held out for Róisín Shortall to be our sole candidate in that constituency. Bill never forgave me and has written bitterly about it since.

My hunch was that the general election would take place in the spring of 1993 but Fergus Finlay repeatedly predicted that once Albert Reynolds and Dessie O'Malley had given their respective testimonies to the Beef Tribunal, it would be all over. Unlike Fergus, I had taken a limited interest in the proceedings in Dublin Castle. But Dick was deeply involved, having been the main politician in the Dáil debates which led to the inquiry being established. That meant that Fergus was immersed in the detail of the tribunal. Fergus' prediction was correct and the PDs voted with the opposition motion of no confidence in the government from which they had resigned the night before, 5 November 1992, because of the major clash between Albert and Dessie at the tribunal.

Within hours, our election posters were up and we hit the ground running. During the campaign I did a *Morning Ireland* radio interview with David Hanly, when a poll showed Labour up five points, at 19 per cent. When he pressed me to predict what this might mean in extra seats, I answered that, on the basis of those figures, we could get more than thirty. Back in Leinster House, Fergus told me that I had been irresponsible and had set an impossible mountain to climb. When the polls closed on 26 November, the Labour Party had thirty-three seats, a gain of eighteen new deputies and our highest ever vote at 19.3 per cent.

The euphoria was uncontainable at a celebratory event in the Riverside Centre on Dublin's City Quay. The venue was packed with old and new deputies, supporters and Labour Party members. Dick Spring and I had to physically force our way through the surging crowd of well-wishers to the platform where Dick was to make his speech as leader. I started the proceedings, asking for calm and calling on all the deputies to join us on the platform; they were with their own family members and supporters in different parts of the hall. I requested loudly that the deputy for Dublin North come to the platform. There was a great cheer as Seán Ryan made his way through the crowd. As I named each constituency, I realised that I had started a triumphant roll call, because the crowd chanted the name of the deputy. When I got to Dublin North-East, I was loudly corrected by the jubilant cry 'the deputies, the deputies', because here to the surprise of nearly everyone, Tommy Broughan had joined Seán Kenny by winning a second seat for Labour.

From the beginning, I was in favour of a grand coalition with Fianna Fáil. This was because the country's economic crisis required Fianna Fáil's strength inside the tent, and we could not complete the liberal agenda without them. Labour had to define a new relationship with Fine Gael, but I knew that we would have to exhaust other possibilities in order to make a coalition with Fianna Fáil acceptable and even inevitable. On Dick's instructions, Fergus moved quickly to protect our left flank and to draw a common policy document with Democratic Left. They had four seats, having lost two, while the sole remaining Workers' Party TD, Tomás Mac Giolla, had lost his seat to Labour's Joan Burton.

There was a much-publicised meeting between Dick and John Bruton on Sunday morning, 6 December, in the Constitution Room of the Shelbourne Hotel. After the meeting – even though he told me very little of what had been said – I knew that Dick was effectively ruling out Fine Gael, but they in turn made it easy for him by emphatically ruling out Democratic Left in any future government of which they were a partner. The question of a rotating Taoiseach was also rejected. When Eric Byrne of Democratic Left lost his seat to Fianna Fáil's Ben Briscoe in a marathon ten-day

recount in Dublin South-Central, the majority of one seat for a
coalition of Labour, Fine Gael and Democratic Left – a total of
eighty-three – also disappeared.

In the rest of the world, the European currency crisis continued to
rage. It had started in September with Britain's exit, on Black
Wednesday, from the exchange rate mechanism of the European
Union. Despite enormous currency speculation and increases in
interest rates, combined with a number of devaluations in other EU
member states, Ireland was battling to maintain the value of the
punt within the system. The absence of an effective government
since the beginning of November prevented any decision being taken
on the question of devaluation other than the continued expensive
policy of 'no surrender'. Interest rates for homeowners and small
businesses were rising relentlessly, shattering business confidence
and damaging the economic morale and sense of security of
ordinary people.

Added to this was the looming crisis in Aer Lingus and its
associated company Team Aer Lingus, where the need for major
structural reforms, combined with a huge capital injection, was
meeting substantial resistance from the workforce and their unions.
Whatever small chance we had in government of dealing with these
major issues, we had none if the PDs were our partners in government and Fianna Fáil had reverted to their irresponsible oppor-
tunism in opposition.

Dick Spring had sent a copy of the joint Labour/Democratic Left
document, 'Policy Proposals to Build Social and Economic Justice
in Ireland', to all party leaders, including Albert Reynolds. Two
days later, as the talks with Fine Gael and the PDs were clearly
faltering, Fianna Fáil responded with a twenty-page position paper;
which largely met Labour's main concerns. Reynolds was on his
way to an EU summit in Edinburgh, so a meeting was arranged for
his return.

Fine Gael and the PDs broke off any pretence of further talks
when this became known. For my part, I was taken aback at the
extent of the Fianna Fáil paper and described it to a journalist in
the visitors' bar as akin to receiving not only a free ticket to a dance,

but the guarantee of a good time as well! On 13 December after a private meeting between Dick and Albert in the penthouse of the Berkeley Court Hotel, the Labour leadership heard Dick's report and took a decision by an open vote to start serious negotiations with Fianna Fáil with a view to forming a government. Fergus Finlay and John Rogers were among a minority opposed, but Brendan Howlin, Pat Magner and myself were part of the small majority in favour.

The first meeting of the two negotiating teams was scheduled for the following Wednesday. It was agreed that the two leaders would decide the shape and composition of the cabinet. The policy platform that would form the basis for a programme for government was the starting point for the negotiations. In the event of a dispute or failure to reach agreement, the matter would be referred for resolution to the two leaders. Dick asked me to lead our team, flanked by Brendan Howlin and Mervyn Taylor. Seen as being perhaps anti-coalition, Mervyn was our 'joker in the pack' because he was hardly known to the other side. The outgoing Finance Minister, Bertie Ahern, led the Fianna Fáil team with Noel Dempsey, who, as government chief whip, had a good working relationship with Brendan Howlin, and Brian Cowen, who filled their slot as the hard man and stubborn negotiator. Mervyn and Brian, both solicitors, had a legal sense of precise drafting. Greg Sparks, with the assistance of Fergus Finlay, Finbar O'Malley, the legal adviser to the parliamentary party, and occasionally Richard Humphreys, another lawyer, became our support team and moved into Government Buildings, occupying the room vacated by the PDs' assistant government press secretary, Stephen O'Byrnes.

Before our first meeting began, I spoke privately to Dick. I told him that I was confident that I could negotiate a good, comprehensive programme for government, based on our party policies, but I could not factor in the unexpected that was sure to turn up.

'What do you mean?' he asked.

'Basically this, Dick. Can you do business with Albert? Do you trust him?'

'Yes' was his reply.

To this day I can still feel the tension of the negotiations and the
suppressed air of excitement which surrounded them. The rest of
Dublin city seemed to be preoccupied with Christmas shopping and
the usual round of office parties as we talked for hours on end in
the Sycamore Room in Government Buildings. Brendan and Noel
were efficient in dispensing with those items that had been quickly
agreed and referred them to Greg Sparks and Martin Mansergh,
Fianna Fáil's special adviser, for the final drafting and inclusion in
the programme for government. The Fianna Fáil team were caretaker ministers and so had access to government departments for
advice on the policy proposals that were put on the table.

In effect the Labour team was negotiating indirectly with the civil
service, not on the principle of our measures but on their
practicality. This subsequently turned out to be quite beneficial,
although we did not think so at the time. Naturally there was disagreement on a number of proposals. Labour had been in favour of
freedom of information legislation and had prepared a bill that had
been debated in private members' time. When we reached that item
on the agenda, Brian Cowen flatly rejected it. After some intense
discussion, Bertie and I agreed that we should refer this to our
respective leaders. However, the caretaker office-holders would not
budge and the compromise that ultimately went into the programme
was a weak commitment to simply look at the introduction of
freedom of information legislation. While we were negotiating,
Dick, Fergus and Greg were examining the structure of government.
Pat Magner was very clear that if Labour were to go into government this time, all sections of the party should be involved, to avoid
the divisions that had plagued us during the 1980s. It was only at
this time that Pat Magner told me about Dick's unsuccessful efforts
to persuade Mervyn Taylor to fill the cabinet seat vacated by Frank
Cluskey in 1983. That certainly explained the delay in my appointment to the Department of Labour. Initially very annoyed, I realised
that Dick was trying to maintain a balance that would have reflected
the party's mood at that time.

Close to Christmas we were nearly finished, but we had to bridge
the ten-day holiday period while maintaining a sense of urgency. Liz

and I had rented a cottage in Roundstone for a few days around the New Year. Since a day of negotiations was arranged for the end of December, I travelled up from Galway, nearly missing the early morning train because of the wintry conditions on the Connemara roads. After a long day, we successfully completed our programme for government and I returned happy, if tired, to Connemara that evening.

The mood in the National Concert Hall on Sunday, 10 January 1993 was one of pride, satisfaction and celebration. Moosajee Bhamjee, not known to most people, got a rapturous reception and a roar of applause and cheers when he repeated his campaign slogan, 'We've had enough of the cowboys; 'tis time for the Indians', turning his South African birth and Indian race into an effective electoral asset.

The conference delegates endorsed the programme for government by an overwhelming majority. When the conference ended, Tom Ferris and his wife, Niamh Bhreathnach, went with Liz and myself to Eastern Tandoori, our favourite Indian restaurant, for a celebratory meal. I told them that we had not finalised the figures for the Estimates and that the preparations for the budget were not going to be easy. And it was this subject that occupied us the following day.

Dick and Albert joined the six negotiators and we went through the sums again. We did not reach agreement. That evening I went home, not sure if we would be in government in twelve hours time, such was the gap between our positions. Ominously, when I left Leinster House that night, it was snowing; just as it had been six years before when we had left government.

On the Tuesday morning there were further negotiations between Dick and Albert and the parliamentary party meeting was delayed for an hour. During that time I spoke with a number of the new deputies. Róisín Shortall, Tommy Broughan, Breeda Moynihan Cronin and Moosajee Bhamjee were all prepared for government, despite not knowing how tough it might be. When the party did meet, a lot of time was devoted to saying farewell to Senator Jack Harte, who was retiring. This preoccupation on the eve of government was quite surreal and I grew increasingly impatient, thinking of all the hours of negotiations that had been put in. But when Dick outlined the position, including an indication of what a very difficult first budget would contain, though the medium-term prospects were good, the parliamentary party accepted the proposal to enter government. On 12 January, after a rambling speech in the Dáil from John Bruton and a speech from a shattered Dessie O'Malley, who seemed clearly distressed, the House voted 102 to 60 for Albert Reynolds as Taoiseach. We were once again in a coalition government but this time with Fianna Fáil.

Earlier that Tuesday morning Dick confirmed that there would be a new department merging Industry and Commerce and Labour. It was to be Employment and Enterprise and I was to be its minister. The new Department of Equality and Law Reform was temporarily located in the Department of Labour. In his inimitable laconic style, he offered me the following advice: 'Keep in touch with the backbenchers, do not abuse the car and be careful about foreign travel.'

The five Labour ministers gathered in Dick's office at 6.45 p.m. and walked across the bridge into Government Buildings to meet our Fianna Fáil colleagues. On the way, Brendan Howlin told me that he was to be Minister for Health, the portfolio which he had shadowed so well in opposition. Michael D. Higgins, the new Minister for Arts, Culture and the Gaeltacht, embraced David Andrews, his colleague in many a Third World campaign. Briefly I spoke to Brian Cowen, outgoing Minister for Labour, about some FÁS appointments as Ballygowan water was poured and we got in line before proceeding into the Dáil chamber in the rank order of Oireachtas seniority, but not necessarily cabinet importance.

At the last moment that morning, it emerged that Mervyn had swapped jobs with Niamh Bhreathnach, with Dick's agreement. She got Education and he was given Equality and Law Reform because, as he subsequently told me, he felt there was a potential conflict of interest because his wife was a teacher. Mervyn is shrewd and I suspect that his legitimate reservation was combined with his own instinctive distrust of the conservative Catholic ethos which to this day imbues the Department of Education. As the first orthodox Jew in an Irish cabinet, he knew where he did not need to be, having regard to the difficulties that the liberal Gemma Hussey had encountered in Education a decade before.

As we waited for the debate on the formation of government to take place, Liz, Denise and I had a light meal before the vote of 101 to 59 sent me up to Áras an Uachtaráin to meet a delighted Mary Robinson. She greeted us warmly. Likewise Bride Rosney was clearly pleased to see us Labour ministers receive our seals of office. Then we conducted our first formal cabinet meeting, something that I had not previously attended. Joe Coggins and Nashie Grady were now back as my drivers. The first stop after leaving the Áras was to James and Loretto Wrynn's home in Ranelagh, where Anne Byrne had organised a celebratory party for many activists close to the leadership. These are evenings you do not forget, but I soon wanted to be at home with Liz, where in the warmth and comfort of our own home we had our own celebration.

The next day I had the difficult job of deciding who would be the secretary of the newly merged department. I had met Seán Dorgan, the secretary of the Department of Industry and Commerce, but did not warm to him, although, in fairness, I did not really know him. Informed by my experience in the Department of Labour and the brevity of political timescales, I asked Kevin Bonner to take the job. I knew him well and could work with him. When I rang Kevin in the Department of Labour building on Adelaide Road, he told me that Mervyn Taylor had just moved into the minister's office, and so I had to slink in the entrance door of the building. I was on my way to a funeral, in Wicklow, and was in a rush. Straightaway I told him that I wanted him to become the secretary of the new department. He accepted.

That afternoon I went officially to the old Industry and Commerce building on Kildare Street and met Seán Dorgan. I did not have the courage, there and then, to tell him of the decision regarding the secretary's position, but instead said that I wanted to change the private secretary and invited him to nominate a suitable woman for the job. In reply he said that the Department of Industry and Commerce had never had a female private secretary, to which I responded, 'That's exactly why I want one now.' Eileen O'Carroll became my second female private secretary. Some days later, Seán Dorgan, expressed his disappointment when I told him that Kevin Bonner had got the job.

'This was a position I really wanted,' he said.

'And I would have liked the Department of Finance myself,' I replied.

The ambiguity surrounding the name of the new department persisted for some days. Which should come first: Employment or Enterprise? Some wanted the focus on employment, in deference to the old 'Labour' rubric. Ten days later, at a reception for a new insurance company which was to be established in the Financial Services Centre, I brought the debate to an end.

'We are the Department of Enterprise and Employment,' I asserted, 'because without enterprise there is no employment.'

The minister's office was on the first floor of a fine building in Kildare Street. Pádraig Flynn had been the minister immediately before me, after Des O'Malley's long tenure. The room had wooden panelled walls, flowery curtains, a pink leather couch and two pink leather chairs. Immediately, I organised the refurbishment of the office. I asked Bríd Dukes, a friend and gallery owner, to purchase paintings and these were put up in the offices and along the corridor. Ten years later, watching the Minister for Enterprise and Employment conducting television interviews from the minister's office, I noticed that my office design, furniture, including the Tricolour and European flag, and even the desk filing trays, are still in place.

The ministers of state were announced the day after the government was formed and, in accordance with Pat Magner's advice, Dick had chosen a new wave of anti-coalitionists, such as Emmet Stagg and Joan Burton, as well as a new deputy Eithne Fitzgerald, and stalwarts such as Brian O'Shea and Gerry O'Sullivan. Other old loyalists like Toddy O'Sullivan, Michael Ferris and Liam Kavanagh were passed over, but the choices of leadership are never easy.

The chefs de cabinet, or programme managers, got their titles soon after the cabinet agreed to their establishment. On Michael Woods' suggestion, it was also agreed that each minister should have a special adviser as well. Dick's and my experience of government in the 1980s profoundly changed the structure of the new partnership coalition. The separate office of the Tánaiste was established, to be on a par with that of the Taoiseach, at the top of the information chain, receiving at the same time all proposals requiring a cabinet decision. Previously, it was merely a title with few functions and no resources. The chefs de cabinet and the advisers would represent the political corpus of the minister between departments, when the minister was in the constituency or away, for example in Brussels. The constant negotiating and bargaining between ministers and departments over resources, policy and areas of responsibility meant that the chefs were vitally important. These political gladiators would, up to a point, bargain on behalf of their political masters, in a way that was impossible for a civil servant, whose loyalty was to the department first and then the minister.

The frayed nerves and the hurried compromises, which had characterised the 1982–87 Fine Gael/Labour government, were to become a thing of the past. The new structure that Greg Sparks refined in management terms would enable ministers to take strategic political decisions with a minimum of damage to the cabinet's operational morale and cohesion. But at the insistence of Frank Murray, the secretary to the government, a change of title was made. These individuals would be called programme managers and they were responsible for implementing the programme for government. In truth, Frank Murray was the real chef de cabinet.

I asked Greg Sparks, who became programme manager to Dick Spring as Tánaiste and Minister for Foreign Affairs, to suggest someone as my programme manager. Given the turmoil in the economy, I knew that I needed a person who would be acceptable to the business community; there was still a suspicion abroad about Labour's ability to manage the economy. After some reflection, Greg Sparks proposed Dr Frank Roche, a major figure in the UCD Smurfit School of Business and a respected consultant. When we met, I knew he was the man I wanted. Some months later, Ciarán O'Mara accepted my invitation to become my special adviser. To this day I do not know what Frank Roche's politics are; but working with Denise and Ciarán I did not need another political person, yet I did require a trusted and innovative technocrat who would be creative and reassuring, and Frank fitted the bill.

After the second ordinary meeting of the cabinet, Albert Reynolds gave a clear signal that effective action had to be taken on the value of the punt. A day later Bertie Ahern, Minister for Finance, asked me as the economic minister from the Labour Party to come round to his office. His news did not surprise me and I told him that I agreed with the devaluation decision, which the Taoiseach and Tánaiste had made earlier on the advice of officials. After he described the steps that were being taken to implement that decision, Bertie turned to more general matters.

He wanted to know how I was doing in Enterprise and Employment and how I was getting on with the Taoiseach. After my initial positive response, he gave me the following advice. 'Don't presume that if you have written to Albert, you have communicated with him. You have to write him a memo with a covering letter. But a few days afterwards, ring him and ask if you can come to discuss the matter. It is only when you have talked over the topic, face to face, that you can be sure you have got through to him. If he asks you any questions, better still.'

The new system of programme managers and advisers, combined with the establishment of a separate office for the Tánaiste, soon generated much media criticism from those journalists who felt betrayed by Labour's entry into government with Fianna Fáil. Niamh Bhreathnach's decision in December to nominate her daughter as constituency secretary was deemed to be an act of nepotism when Niamh became Minister for Education in January. A cousin of Emmet Stagg, hired as one of two drivers for the new Minister of State, was evidence of 'jobs for the boys'. When the six Labour cabinet ministers completed their teams, many prominent Labour members, such as Anne Byrne, Pat Keating, Paul Mulhern, Colm Ó Briain, Tim Collins, Kevin O'Driscoll, Ciarán O'Mara, Kathleen

O'Meara, Betty Rock, Willie Scally and James Wrynn were involved and would go on to play critically important roles in maintaining the reforming drive of the government and the implementation of its programme. But for elements in the media, the story was one of nepotism and self-aggrandisement. Some Labour members, including deputies and senators, were very uneasy. They were not used to being under this kind of attack, particularly when it was ill-informed and biased.

Of the nine Fianna Fáil ministers, only David Andrews took on a programme manager from outside the civil service: Liam Cahill, ironically a former Labour Party member. The civil service was essentially Fianna Fáil's recruitment ground. This was not unusual, given that the party had been in government for five years and was already working with many of the people who became their programme managers and advisers. Yet, it did imply that perhaps they did not have a similar level of senior party activists to that of the Labour Party who were anxious to become involved. More crucially, it may indicate that Fianna Fáil is not a party of ideas. A pragmatic party concerned with holding on to power relies heavily on the civil service to develop policy. But Labour certainly failed, in my view, to sell the positive benefits of the new decision-making structure. When it was finally established, it worked effectively and at a very competitive cost, relative to the subsequent large-scale hiring of consultants and media companies that Bertie Ahern's administration would engage in after the 1997 election, when the emphasis appears to have been more on presentation and less on content or efficient government.

The fourteen Labour programme managers and advisers used to meet on Monday afternoons when the *clár*, or agenda, for the cabinet was circulated. They would identify any issue with which they had a problem, or wanted to ensure was agreed upon at the next cabinet. Early on Tuesday morning, the Labour ministers, along with Fergus Finlay, Willie Scally and Greg Sparks, would gather in the Tánaiste's office and prepare the party's response to the agenda for cabinet that would take place later that day. They would know the outcome of the Monday evening programme managers' meeting and be aware of reservations about issues between departments and sometimes between Labour ministers.

When I became Minister for Finance in December 1994, Ciarán O'Mara would read all the papers for the Tuesday cabinet meeting over the weekend in advance of the Monday meeting of programme managers and advisers. After this meeting, he would let me know what problems had arisen, what had been resolved and what remained for me to deal with. If these could not be solved in Dick's office then, by consensus, we agreed not to bring them to cabinet but to postpone them for another day. Dick noted outstanding items that were still the subject of a dispute.

Finally, Dick would then go along to the Taoiseach's office and talk with him for thirty minutes before the start of the cabinet meeting. Both men had a similar attitude to a business-like executive, equipped with a large secretariat and support management. As far as they were concerned, a cabinet meeting was not the place for long, inter-departmental exchanges. These should take place between the pages of a memorandum for government. The cabinet's role was to make decisions on those recommendations. If the Taoiseach and Tánaiste felt that a decision would not be taken on a particular matter between two disputing line departments, it would be noted at the start of the cabinet meeting. Sometimes Albert would say that if the ministers involved could not reach agreement, then the cabinet would do it for them at the next meeting.

The items that cabinet had agreed were presented to a full meeting of the programme managers the following day, with directions and instructions to proceed to the next stage without delay. On Fridays, the chief whip, the attorney general and the programme managers of the Taoiseach and Tánaiste would review the legislative programme in the light of that week's cabinet meeting. Priorities, new measures and changed circumstances had to be taken into account in adjusting the passage of legislation for which the chief whip had the major responsibility.

In time, the departments of state got to understand the role of the programme managers and advisers. The civil servants became allies and not competitors. Critically, they realised that when the minister was away from the department, the civil service could get a political response to an issue, secure in the knowledge that the minister would endorse it on his or her return. Over time, genuinely held differences of policy could be resolved, leaving just a few net points for determination at the cabinet table. At this point, the two cabinet colleagues would meet and arrive at a compromise, having expended little emotional or political capital on the issue.

This was in marked contrast to my experiences in the 1980s. It was not only more efficient but less bruising on the collective solid- arity that a cabinet must maintain, and was also a very effective filtering system which ensured that no half-baked proposal could be sprung on a government. The budget and taxation measures had been abused in this way in the past. Good ideas that are not fully thought-out, particularly late at night, can frequently lose their attraction in the calm light of day.

Having worked so closely together, with an increasing intensity through the 1992 election and the formation of government, the Labour ministers now found themselves turning to their own new departmental responsibilities and getting on with the day job. My task was to integrate two large departments, and in the process create a new operational and management culture. In the past, both departments reflected, in part, the adversarial nature of the relationship between employer and employee. While social part- nership was beginning to change this, at representative level between the ICTU and the newly merged Irish Business and Employers Confederation (IBEC), the same could not be said for the line departments. This was because the Taoiseach's department and Finance dominated the government side in the triangular relation- ship of social partnership. In the new Department of Enterprise and Employment, colleagues who were used to writing submissions against one another's memoranda now had to work together. In this new context, many people expressed fears about who within society would lose out.

I had the help and political assistance of two Fianna Fáil ministers of state. Seamus Brennan had been a cabinet minister from January 1992 and Mary O'Rourke had been in the cabinet from 1987 until 1992, when Albert demoted her to Minister of State for Trade and Marketing in the Department of Industry and Commerce. Now she had been moved sideways to Labour Affairs and Seamus had responsibility for Commerce and Technology. Both were seasoned politicians, but that was all they had in common, as far as I could see.

Quickly, Mary installed herself in the ministerial office in Adelaide Road, after Mervyn and his new department had gone off to a new building, Dún Aimhirgin on Mespil Road, which also housed Michael D. Higgins and the new department of Arts, Culture and the Gaeltacht. Mary had been a teacher before becoming a politician and was Minister for Education under Charlie Haughey from 1987 to 1991. This gave her a particular feel for the educational and training role of FÁS. Soon she was immersed in the large volume of work which that organisation generated and she travelled the country extensively. She was bright, sharp, direct and decisive and an early starter like myself. I got on well with Mary and admired her way of working with people.

On the other hand, Seamus was quite different and very difficult to know. His job was less specific than Mary's and he was frequently vague about what he was actually doing. Moreover, he seemed to take ages to decide on anything, even the draft of a press release. He was habitually out of the building and my office often had difficulty in making contact with him. Frankly, I did not have the same regard for his abilities as those of his party colleague.

Seamus did however suggest to me that we needed to do something about the concerns of small business. The merger of the Confederation of Irish Industry and the Federated Union of Employers into IBEC in 1993 had raised fears in the business community that the agenda of the Small Firms Association, a component of the CII, would be disregarded. An uncertain economic climate and the collapse of business confidence were affecting that sector in a strong way. On 21 April 1993, I was the guest speaker at its annual meeting and lunch in the Burlington Hotel. 'Fellow risk takers' was my opening remark, which definitely caught their attention, and I proceeded to draw comparisons between the worlds of business and politics. I shared my concerns about the lack of confidence in the indigenous business sector, which the policy drift of the previous administration had allowed because of tensions within the coalition government. Furthermore, I referred to the damage caused by the currency crisis, with its aftermath of high interest rates. It was clear that small business needed a particular boost in order to relaunch itself. I then announced that I was setting up a task force to chart the way ahead. But of more relevance to the delegates was my proposal that it be comprised exclusively of small business practitioners who would, unhindered, identify all the obstacles in their path and make explicit recommendations for their replacement. This was greeted warmly and, when established, did very effective and constructive work.

Within days of the new government coming into office, a major crisis began to break. I watched it unfold initially, more as an observer than a participant until, after a phone call from Taoiseach Albert Reynolds, it became clear that I was directly involved and should be seen to intervene. The large Digital Equipment Company, usually called Digital, a computer company with its headquarters outside Boston, had a major plant in Galway, as well as facilities in Scotland and Singapore. It had been in Ireland for decades and Galway was like a company town, with Digital as its largest employer. Because it was an anti-trade union company, it had a very extensive and elaborate human-resource section and the employment conditions were extremely good. But innovation and new technology had overtaken the company's complacent culture and, losing money as well as stock market value, it had to implement drastic cost-cutting measures.

The upshot was that one of the plants in Europe – Scotland or Ireland – had to close. Without delay the IDA made contact with Digital's headquarters in the US. Kieran McGowan, the chief executive of the IDA, Séamus Keating, the Galway city manager, and Pádraic McCormack, the Fine Gael mayor of the city, flew with me by government jet into the wintry snows of Massachusetts to plead our case with Bob Palmer, Digital's beleaguered chief executive. As we were leaving after making a detailed presentation in support of the Galway plant, he said philosophically that someone had to make these hard decisions and, if he did not, then his successor would. Digital duly announced the closure of the Galway plant in February 1993. The city was in shock and we moved, with the full support of the local community, to establish a task force to replace the lost jobs. As it turned out, this was successful and many more and diverse jobs were created by ex-Digital employees or were brought to the city by a very active IDA.

This was my first close-up encounter as a minister with the IDA and I was impressed. In time, I did a number of promotional trips with them. For example, an IDA team, led by Paddy Gallagher and based in San José in the middle of California's Silicon Valley, were like hunting hawks, with a sharp eye for spotting companies that one day would have to expand into Europe. Before a computer company had even considered such a venture, the IDA team would be selling Ireland. With a minister in support, they would get to see the company president. My presence on one visit opened the door to Lew Platt, chief executive officer of Hewlett Packard. For twenty minutes, in March 1994, I told him about the coming success story that Ireland would soon be and why Hewlett Packard should be a part of it. As I was leaving his office, I asked if the local IDA lads could come back and make a full presentation. He agreed. Paddy Gallagher was jubilant. They had been trying to scale the barricades of this company for five years and told me enthusiastically that my sales pitch had at last opened the door.

One of the more memorable visits I made was to Japan, organised by FÁS and the IDA. These organisations and their personnel had a very clear idea of their task, an enormous commitment to the job and Ireland, and a great feel for what they were doing. Later, when I became Minister for Finance, I continued to work with the IDA, but this time promoting the International Financial Services Centre (IFSC) in Dublin, which had been established in 1987. It was intensive work, but I loved it because, together, we were making a good impression for the country and achieving tangible results. At the same time, I was restructuring the semi-state support agencies for job creation. I am glad to say that the structures have stood the test of time.

Reading back over my journals for that period, I had forgotten just how intense and time-consuming the life of a government minister can be. The range of issues, combined with the speed at which they arrive on your desk, is enormous. I suspect that part of the satisfaction of being in power is the constant challenge of decision-making, but the other side is the fear of defeat, of public reproach and intense opposition within your own ranks. But I had settled into a large department convinced, or so I thought, that with our substantial Dáil majority I would be in the job for four or five years. One year on, weekend polls at the end of November 1993 gave our party strength, including undecideds, at 16 per cent and the core vote at 14 per cent. Unlike the difficult and intense times of the mid-1980s, this was a government which, despite a number of conflicts, in themselves not abnormal, was secure with itself.

By contrast, the opposition were in real trouble. Dessie O'Malley had resigned as leader of the Progressive Democrats on 5 October 1993. At the time I noted that, while I thought that Pat Cox would win the contest, Dessie's timing of his announcement was skewed in favour of Mary Harney. When elected, she was not impressive in opposition, which is not a flattering place for any party leader to be, as I was to learn myself later. Added to this, John Bruton was really floundering. Towards the end of that same month, there was confusion in the chamber as Fine Gael could not make up its mind what action to take on the order of the business that was before them. The Progressive Democrats were furious. Pat Cox observed quietly to me afterwards that it must be great playing against a leader of the opposition who wore slippers rather than boots!

But we were not without our own difficulties. The first was the revolt of five Labour deputies, who voted against the government on the issue of Team Aer Lingus and its restructuring package. This revolt had been brewing for some time. I thought that my last-minute compromise, in my contribution to a private members' motion on the issue, would have kept them on side, but I was wrong. The vociferous and belligerent leaders of the craft workers' unions led Seán Ryan, the Dublin North Labour deputy, a merry dance. They refused to accept changes in work practices in order to meet the challenges facing their state-owned company.

Meanwhile in Cork, the future of Irish Steel seemed to be a hardy perennial, going back to the mid-1980s when the Fine Gael/Labour coalition, at the insistence of local government deputies, kept the company afloat even though it was loss making. It was not in any better position when I became minister but, in addition to the traditional Cork lobby to keep Irish Steel open, we now had, for the first time, a Labour deputy newly elected from the town of Cobh, which was right across from the large steelworks.

John Mulvihill had been elected to the Dáil in 1992. As a former worker in Irish Steel, keeping the steelyard operating was a major plank in his election platform. On my first visit to the plant, on an island immediately in front of the incredibly beautiful town of Cobh, I was struck by the ugliness and the environmental pollution of the plant. Ciarán O'Mara was even more direct, 'This,' he said 'is a dire place and these are lousy jobs that belong to another age.'

But the pressure to keep Irish Steel open was immense, as was the push from Brussels to close it, and indeed the many other loss-making steel plants in Europe at that time. At an Industry Council meeting in Brussels, in November 1993, the matter received major attention. The message I got from the European Commission was clear – either eliminate the loss-making trading figures or close the plant.

By February 1994, we made one last major effort, but to no avail. Over seven months many attempts were made to turn the company around. First a new chairman, Pat Dineen, was appointed to the company. Then a major cost-cutting exercise was introduced, alongside an extensive work-restructuring proposal, negotiated by the ICTU and the trade unions and subsequently put to the work-force. This was narrowly rejected by a workforce ballot. In September

1994, at a committee meeting of cabinet ministers, consisting of Bertie Ahern, Brian Cowen and myself (in the absence of both the Taoiseach and Tánaiste) we took the decision firmly, but sadly, to close the plant. However, at the insistence of John Mulvihill, Fergus Finlay and the Bishop of Cloyne, the workers were persuaded to change their minds; later that evening, they grudgingly accepted the new working arrangements.

It was presented as a miraculous salvation, but I was far from impressed. Later, Richard Bruton, my successor in Enterprise and Employment, managed to sell Irish Steel as a going concern, for one Irish pound, to an Indian steelmaker who specialised in buying clapped out state-owned steel companies. Ispat ran Irish Steel for a number of years, but closed it as soon as the conditions of sale had expired.

In 1997, when Irish Steel was still in operation, John Mulvihill was canvassing in the general election. Having received a verbal battering on a number of doors in Cobh, he anticipated a warm reception when he knocked on the door of an Irish Steel worker. But the reception was very cool.

'But sure didn't we save Irish Steel for you?' John protested.

'Yeah you did, but it's a shite job and we all would've been better with a decent redundancy package.'

All of which shows that Ciarán O'Mara's first observations were correct and, unfortunately, John Mulvihill lost his seat in that election.

The first annual dinner of IBEC took place in the Burlington Hotel on 7 July 1994 and I was invited to be the guest of honour and main speaker. I took the opportunity to give a strategic speech on Ireland's economic future which I had been wanting to make for some time. Frank Roche did the research and provided me with plenty of material, but the draft and the final text were my own. In implementing the Culliton Report and restructuring the semi-state job-creation agencies, I had become very aware of the government's lack of a strategic plan. Back in 1989, Des O'Malley had set up a

task force, chaired by eminent businessman Jim Culliton, to review
the impediments to the efficient working of the Irish economy, and
in 1991 its comprehensive report was completed. At the time I was
conscious of the long-term thinking of the Japanese and how both
Singapore and Malaysia, with their 2020 plans, were also thinking
twenty-five years ahead. I felt Ireland needed to do the same.

France, after the Second World War, had modernised its economy
with a unique form of indicative planning or direct state guidance.
Despite Ireland's earlier attempts with the programmes for economic
expansion and a limited short-term document *Building on Reality*,
produced in 1984 by the Fine Gael/Labour coalition, Ireland had
nothing comparable. My training as an architect and my time with
Doxiadis in Athens had given me a sense of long-term strategic
planning where goals were set and clear objectives defined with a
programme of action prepared to achieve them. At the Magill
summer school of 1992, I had addressed some of these issues in a
paper entitled 'A Strategy for Job Creation'. Now with the Culliton
Report in place, a new initiative was required and the IBEC dinner
with nearly 1,000 guests was, I thought, the place to launch it.

Entitled 'A Strategy for Ireland 2010', my address set out five clear
goals to be achieved within the fifteen-year timeframe.

1. *Per capita income to be the EU average.*
2. *Full employment for all seeking work.*
3. *The best-managed and preserved environment in the
    European Union.*
4. *The best location to do business in Europe, because we
    had the best public administration system in the EU.*
5. *The best entrance into Europe for English-speaking
    business outside Europe.*

*I want us to be the model state of the European Union, which
is, as Jacques Delors has said, based on social democratic
values. Ireland must become a nation at ease with itself and
confident of its future; a nation in which every member of the
family belongs and from which no one was excluded. I wanted
to see a people culturally creative and active on the world*

stage, while drawing from the deep and rich wells of our own traditions. The five goals which will, if achieved, provide us and our children with the resources for the next century.

My speech was well received, even if the document was long. The fact that in 2005, five years ahead of the target date, we had already achieved the first two goals is now taken for granted. Yet we still have a great deal to do before we can reach the other three goals. Looking back now, a decade or more from the formation of the Fianna Fáil/Labour government, it is easy to forget just how difficult our economic situation really was. Unacceptably high levels of unemployment, both short-term and long-term, were matched by high interest rates. Investment and business confidence were low. In hindsight, my proposal was a necessary vision at the time and an essential part of the type of politics to which I am committed.

In July 1994 Mr Justice Liam Hamilton was putting the finishing touches to the Beef Tribunal Report. For some time Fergus Finlay had been indicating that the coalition would face a major crisis when that report was published. I paid heed when he voiced these concerns because he had been correct in his forecasts about the clash between Albert Reynolds and Dessie O'Malley in 1992. Joe Walsh, the Minister for Agriculture, told the cabinet that he expected to get the Beef Tribunal Report at the start of the August bank holiday. The ministers knew just how sensitive its conclusions could be for the cohesion of the government. How its publication was to be handled was a matter of great importance to us all. I made arrangements for Ciarán O'Mara to get me an advance copy, so that we could analyse it. Agreement was reached about how the government would respond publicly, but in the event this understanding was broken by the Taoiseach.

The evening the report was delivered, Dick Spring and Fergus Finlay could not make contact with Albert and his advisers. Fergus then tried to enter the Taoiseach's suite of offices in Government Buildings but was thwarted. Meanwhile, behind closed doors,

Albert and his close advisers were hell bent on spinning a self-serving interpretation of the report to the media. The truth is that Albert broke our understanding by rushing out a statement claiming that he had been vindicated by Justice Hamilton. Egged on by Fergus, Dick asserted that Albert had not complied with their original agreement.

The Hamilton Report was badly written and considered by many to be fudged in order not to embarrass the government. Its conclusions, combined with Albert's immediate reaction, opened a major division between the Taoiseach and the Tánaiste. That division may have been there for some time but, if so, I was not aware of it. Too busy in my own department, perhaps I did not want to think that there might be problems. Nonetheless, the government agreed that the Dáil would meet on 1 September to debate the report.

In the meantime other historic events were unfolding. On 31 August 1994 the Provisional IRA announced, with effect from midnight, an indefinite ceasefire. At the cabinet meeting, which took place in response to this historic breakthrough, there were champagne toasts and congratulations to the Taoiseach and Tánaiste. When we cleared the text of the statement of response, Brendan Howlin turned to Charlie McCreevy and said, 'I never thought twenty months ago that I would be applauding Albert Reynolds on the day the Dáil would debate the Beef Tribunal Report.' There was a real sense of history and of a unique achievement. And naturally the media was full of the ceasefire story.

Looming over the Beef Tribunal Report was also the question of who would succeed Tom Finlay, the Chief Justice, who was due to retire at the end of September. Some time before I had bumped into the journalist Geraldine Kennedy, who told me that Liam Hamilton would be Finlay's successor. When Ciarán O'Mara relayed this to Willie Scally, Dick Spring was incensed. As far as the Tánaiste was concerned, the matter had not been agreed. This was yet another example of Albert Reynolds' bad faith.

The debate on the Beef Tribunal Report commenced on 1 September 1994 and was to be concluded the following day, the first time the Dáil had sat on a Saturday since the Arms Crisis in 1970.

Almost immediately Dick Spring flew to New England where Bill Clinton was on holiday, so that he could brief him on the IRA ceasefire. Albert Reynolds, John Hume and Gerry Adams posed for photographs outside Government Buildings on 6 September. They shook hands, signalling the start of the peace process talks, which would eventually conclude with the Belfast Agreement on Good Friday 1998.

But the optimistic mood concealed a simmering political crisis which soon erupted with an intensity that surprised most people, myself included. In retrospect, the handling of the Beef Tribunal Report had badly damaged the trust between Spring and Reynolds. What had begun as a positive relationship had slowly but surely deteriorated.

At the weekly pre-cabinet Labour ministers' meetings, we would discuss the agenda and then, having taken note of our concerns in his green hardback notebook, Dick would go down the corridor to discuss these matters with Albert, before the cabinet proper began. The Taoiseach had no notebook and did not write anything down, relying on his memory, according to Dick. By contrast, Dick, who had trained as a lawyer, noted everything in his book. It now seems to me that the differences that began to arise between them had in part being influenced by this conflicting way of doing business.

The two men had discussed filling the judicial vacancies. At that time the convention was that the attorney general, the government's legal adviser, had first call on a vacancy on the bench, if he wanted it. Harry Whelehan had been appointed attorney general when his predecessor, John Murray, resigned to become a member of the European Court of Justice in Luxembourg in 1991. Whelehan was a quiet and amiable person who did not have his predecessor's political edge or experience, and his appointment surprised many. When he entered cabinet in 1989, he had survived the crises which had seen Reynolds and others depart in November 1991, only to return in 1992 when Haughey resigned and Reynolds became Taoiseach. He confined himself exclusively to legal matters and seldom spoke in cabinet. Both in manner and behaviour, Whelehan was very different to Peter Sutherland and John Rogers. If Harry had a political side to him, I never saw it. It is not clear to me if he personally asked for the position of President of the High Court or if the Taoiseach promised it to him, but it soon became clear that he certainly was determined to have it. When Whelehan's name was first mooted, Dick Spring and John Rogers expressed concerns about his suitability, but the Labour ministers knew that this was really a matter for the Tánaiste, himself a lawyer, to decide. The final appointment would be made when Dick and Albert had agreed a name.

On 13 September 1994, Brendan Howlin rang me late in the evening at home, to say that he had had a call from Dick, then in Japan. Dick was very anxious to ensure that at the government meeting the following day, which naturally he would not be attending, the Taoiseach would not nominate Harry Whelehan to the High Court because the matter had not been agreed between the two of them. The following morning the Labour ministers met, as normal, in Dick's office at nine. Niamh Bhreathnach was away, but I had briefed the three others and got their agreement that if Albert pushed for the appointment, we would leave the cabinet meeting. Dick then rang and I confirmed our approach with him. He was very clear in his message: under no circumstances could he accept Harry Whelehan's appointment.

I left the meeting to talk to the Taoiseach in the normal pre-cabinet consultation. At Dick's suggestion, I asked Brendan Howlin to come with me and I was very glad that I did. When we arrived in his office, the Taoiseach had with him Bertie Ahern, Michael Smith, Máire Geoghegan-Quinn and Joe Walsh. We stated our case clearly: we were not prepared to have the appointment of the President of the High Court discussed or decided on that day and if the Taoiseach insisted on going ahead with Whelehan's appointment, we would leave the meeting. Albert responded that the appointment had been agreed between him and Dick, but we rejected this emphatically. The matter was now one for him and his colleagues to decide. As Brendan and I returned to the Tánaiste's office, in a parting shot we told the Taoiseach that we would not attend cabinet until he assured us that the item was off the agenda.

Back in Dick's office, we were joined by Greg Sparks, Fergus Finlay, Ciarán O'Mara, Willie Scally, James Wrynn, Pat Magner and John Foley, the assistant government press secretary. The mood was tense, but calm. From nowhere, it seemed, we were now in a major political confrontation. As we waited for a response, our conversation drifted. At one time Michael D., Greg and I engaged in philosophical speculation as to whether or not Conor Cruise O'Brien had become a modern-day Edmund Burke, having regard to the commentaries that he was writing at that time. Someone in the room, Willie Scally remarked with laughter that it was typical of the Labour Party to be debating philosophy at a time like this, when the other side was probably on to their printers and ordering their posters for a general election!

Two hours after we had left Albert, Frank Murray came to Dick's office to inform us that the Taoiseach wanted to see me. As I was approaching the office, on my own, Máire Geoghegan-Quinn came out, but we did not speak. Inside, Albert told me that the item was off the agenda and that the government would only be appointing Liam Hamilton as Chief Justice. We would not be dealing with the appointment of the President of the High Court – that vacancy would be dealt with on another day. I told him that I, and my colleagues, would consider the position, having got his clear word on the matter. Back in Dick's office, the Labour ministers present agreed that we should proceed with the cabinet meeting, which turned out to be a productive one.

Later John Foley, the Labour-nominated assistant press secretary, told us that Albert had remarked to Seán Duignan, his government press secretary, that he was surprised at our firmness. In addition, John Rogers rang me to compliment me on the way the Labour ministers had stood up to the Taoiseach. He believed that Albert had tried to bully us, but it had not worked.

Yet the Taoiseach was not about to let it go. Three weeks later, the issue became a real crisis. On 4 October, the six Labour ministers met in Dick's Iveagh House office. We were clear about one thing – this was not an election issue. Then we were joined by John Foley, John Rogers and others and a debate ensued. At one stage,

Brendan got quite angry with John Rogers when John tried to speak for Dick. Later Fergus became passionate about the need for an election, if necessary on the issue. Both Pat Magner and I tried to cool things down. I suggested that we all should leave the room to let Dick rest since he had come back from Luxembourg earlier that day. But as the ministers left, John Rogers and Fergus Finlay stayed, still trying to persuade the Tánaiste to go to the country, much to the annoyance of the ministers. On 5 October, a compromise began to emerge at cabinet. Brian Cowen, Noel Dempsey, Brendan Howlin and myself were asked to devise a formula, including a change in the method of judicial appointments which would give us cover for the eventual appointment of Harry Whelehan to the judiciary.

The media had now picked up what was happening and, the following day, when anonymous, but anti-Fergus Finlay comments appeared in the press, a meeting was convened in Dick's office at short notice. The Labour ministers expressed their concern about what they felt was their marginalisation, the heavy hand of Fergus Finlay and the need for better communication between us all. There was no question of us being disloyal to Dick, but clearly there was a feeling that, while all the Labour ministers were getting on with their respective portfolios, the political train had begun to come off the rails. What I also found most unsettling was that I did not fully understand why.

On 11 October, the cabinet accepted the report of the so-called 'four wise men', largely prepared by Noel Dempsey and Brendan Howlin and presented by Brian Cowen. The following week the cabinet had a day and a night away in Tinakilly House, a hotel outside Wicklow town, to review progress and prepare for the year ahead. Yet, beneath the surface, the real problem had not gone away, nor would it.

In the midst of all this political turmoil, Liz gave birth to our son, Conan, on the afternoon of 27 October 1994. On 11 November, as the cabinet met, the results of the two Cork city by-elections were coming in. They heralded victory for the opposition parties, Fine Gael and Democratic Left, and disaster for Labour. Then, to our amazement, Albert Reynolds proposed the name of Harry Whelehan to be the next President of the High Court. The thin, gaunt frame of Dick Spring rose slowly from the cabinet table, followed by the five Labour ministers and together we left the room. We did not return for the duration of that ill-fated government.

Back in Dick's office we waited, like relatives between the death and the funeral, suspended in time and no longer in control. Then word came through to us that the cabinet meeting had continued and that the government cars were taking the Taoiseach, the Minister for Justice Máire Geoghegan-Quinn and the Attorney General to Áras an Uachtaráin to obtain presidential confirmation of Harry Whelehan's appointment to be the next President of the High Court. Máire Geoghegan-Quinn is reputed to have turned on the new judge and said that when she would be traipsing the boreens of Galway West, in the midst of a winter election, answering the questions of bewildered voters as to why there was an election at all, she would tell them Harry Whelehan. 'And do you know what the people will say? Harry who?'

No election was called, but for days it seemed likely. Over the weekend, the parliamentary party met and gave Dick its full support. Furthermore, we did not fear a general election. If Albert Reynolds had gambled on this factor, he had made a major mistake.

Now Fianna Fáil panicked, realising that Albert had to undo the damage of his extraordinary stubbornness. Contacts were made, meetings took place, formulas were suggested, all aimed at getting back to where we had gloriously been at the beginning of September. The thirteen Fianna Fáil and Labour ministers had got on well and wanted to continue their work in government. With Dick's agreement, Brendan Howlin and I went to see Michael Smith in his house in Donnybrook. We told Michael that a major apology and the eating, in public, of humble pie by Albert Reynolds was essential. At this stage, after all that had happened, it was the only course of action that would bring the Taoiseach and Tánaiste back together. The truth and perception as to who knew what and when, combined with the complication of the case of the notorious sex offender, Father Brendan Smyth, along with the emergence of a similar case which became known as the Duggan case, added high octane fuel to an already inflamed relationship.

On 16 November at 9.00 a.m. we had the prospect of a new deal with Fianna Fáil and an agreement was initialled at 10.22 a.m., based on the wording of an apology from the Taoiseach to the Labour ministers. Dick then left his office and went down to the Dáil chamber. When he arrived, Michael Bell gave him a name and a telephone number and told him to ring it. On his return to his office Dick made a call to Eoghan Fitzsimons, the new Attorney General, and all hell broke lose.

It emerged that not all the facts had been revealed about the Duggan case when Albert had spoken in the Dáil the day before. The Labour ministers hurriedly convened and agreed with Dick that we could no longer support Reynolds as Taoiseach. As he rose to go down the corridor to the Taoiseach's office, I asked Dick if he wanted company. He said yes and so Brendan, Mervyn and I walked with him. When we got to the office, the Taoiseach was accompanied by a number of ministers, including Máire Geoghegan-Quinn.

As Dick was speaking from his notes, Albert interrupted him a few times and I could see the clock moving relentlessly to 11.00 a.m., the moment when the Dáil would reconvene. I intervened on Dick's behalf, saying forcibly to the Taoiseach, 'It is very fucking simple: we either have your head or Harry Whelehan's.'

It was hard, blunt and brutal. As we left the room, the bells were ringing for the Dáil session to begin and Máire Geoghegan-Quinn was urging the Taoiseach 'to do it, simply to do it' and get rid of Whelehan, but it was not to be. Later that day, Dick Spring rose to speak in the Dáil, not from the usual frontbench government position but physically as far away as he could, emphasising the gap between him and Albert Reynolds. Live on the RTÉ evening news, Dick grabbed the attention of the Dáil and the nation, informing all, that in view of the unsatisfactory nature of the Taoiseach's explanations, the Labour ministers would be resigning from government the following day. The next morning I wrote my resignation letter, left the Department of Enterprise and Employment and moved into temporary office accommodation on the ministerial corridor of Leinster House.

Later that evening, the knives were already out. Albert Reynolds was soon gone, replaced by Bertie Ahern, amends made and the show was back on the road. Albert resigned as party leader but remained in office as Taoiseach. Swiftly, Bertie was elected leader of Fianna Fáil on 19 November 1994. The tension between Albert, still Taoiseach, and Bertie, not yet Taoiseach, created additional difficulties which were not immediately apparent. Dick was persuaded to open up new negotiations to prepare a programme for government between Fianna Fáil and Labour. Fergus Finlay and John Rogers, we were told, had made some efforts to resurrect a deal with Fine Gael, but nothing had come of it. Brendan Howlin and I met with the Fianna Fáil negotiators – Brian Cowen, Noel Dempsey and Mary O'Rourke – in Room 741, the Parliamentary Labour Party meeting room in the Leinster House complex. By the evening of 26 November, we had completed and agreed a new text for the programme for government.

Brendan Howlin met with Dick in Kites Restaurant in Ballsbridge to finalise the arrangements. At first Dick was not so enthusiastic about the project, but accepted that, with a new leader, a renewed coalition was possible. Monday morning's *Irish Times* carried a story by Geraldine Kennedy which cast strong doubts on the bona fides, not just of Albert Reynolds, but of the other Fianna Fáil ministers. Dick now wrote to Bertie, seeking to have the Attorney General conduct a full inquiry into the Brendan Smyth affair. However, the following day, given what was considered to be a wholly inadequate reply from the new Fianna Fáil leader, the Labour ministers came to the conclusion that a new deal with Fianna Fáil was just not possible.

On 11 December, talks began with Fine Gael, after preliminary discussions with John Bruton and Dick Spring had taken place during the week. Once more Brendan Howlin and I were negotiating a programme for government, but this time with Richard Bruton and Michael Lowry.

On that Sunday afternoon, we agreed the framework for the structured talks and presented Fine Gael with Fergus Finlay's comprehensive document. We met, again in Room 741, on the Monday and were joined by Pat Rabbitte and Eamon Gilmore, representing

Democratic Left. They were assisted by Paul Sweeney, an economist with SIPTU, the union born out of the amalgamation of the ITGWU and the FWUI in 1990. The economist Jim O'Leary joined the Fine Gael team and Willie Scally and sometimes Greg Sparks were present for us. On Tuesday, I knew it was going to be a long session: we had to conclude our negotiations that night because Democratic Left had called a special delegate conference for the next day to decide on their participation in a Rainbow Coalition – as the coalition was subsequently dubbed.

As we worked our way through the programme for government, it now seemed to me to be quite repetitious. Brendan Howlin was the notetaker, I was chairing the session and Fergus, ensconced in his office, was in control of the draft programme which was typed on his computer. Good progress was being made when Richard Bruton raised a set of questions about a particular policy item. I replied testily that we had already discussed and agreed that matter. He insisted that we had not, so I raised my voice, asserting forcibly that we most certainly had. Then Brendan, kicking my leg, quietly told me that I was both right and wrong.

'We did agree the matter,' he whispered, 'but with the other crowd, not these guys!'

On 15 December, the Dáil elected John Bruton as Taoiseach and later that day, just under two years from the last time, I found myself back in Áras an Uachtaráin to receive a ministerial seal of office. As we travelled back down the northside of the Liffey I was more conscious of fatigue than any sense of elation. It had been a gruelling five weeks from the time Harry Whelehan had made the same journey to the Park, but it felt more like five months. It had been extremely hard for Liz, who had barely seen me during that precious time after Conan's birth. All I wanted now was to be at home with them both, to close the door and spend Christmas and New Year together. There would be time later to reflect, to explain, first to myself and then to others, just what had happened that last weekend in November to change Dick's mind. I did not know then what it was, and I'm not so sure that I do even now.

Chapter 17

The Many Sides of the Department of Finance

Dick Spring stood facing me, in his Tánaiste's office, in front of his mahogany desk, while I had my back to the window, which overlooked the front yard of Government Buildings. We were alone. Negotiations with Fine Gael and Democratic Left were well advanced and I was briefing him that morning, 13 December 1994, on their progress. There was no doubt that a new Rainbow Coalition government would be formed when the Dáil assembled three days later, notwithstanding the remaining difficulties.

Dick looked at me, with an expression that conveyed both remoteness and intimacy. 'We can't get the rotating Taoiseach, but Finance is possible. Could you do it?'

'I could now,' was my immediate reply, adding that I felt I had the self-confidence to do the job on my own terms.

'Good,' he said. 'Well then, we'll take it, but I want you to do one thing.'

'Yes,' I said, as my mind raced across all that had happened in the previous weeks.

'I want you to take Brendan Lynch with you as a special adviser and to work closely with Greg Sparks.'

I readily agreed, knowing that, despite his many economic talents, Brendan's presence in the early days would be a guarantee, not to Dick, but to Greg Sparks, Fergus Finlay and Willie Scally that they had a direct presence in the Department of Finance. As it turned out, Brendan, a Labour party activist who worked at the time for a stock-broking company, maintained that contact of comfort and became a central member of my team.

Some other changes in my office now had to be made. Frank Roche went back to UCD and Ciarán O'Mara became my programme manager. Gerry Ashe replaced Paul McDonnell in the constituency office and did a superb job working alongside Denise Rogers. I asked Hannah O'Riordan, Bertie Ahern's outgoing private secretary, to stay on in the position. Furthermore, I phoned the Department of Enterprise and Employment and soon was having coffee in the visitors' bar in Leinster House with Joe Lennon, the departmental press secretary. He too agreed to come across to the Department of Finance and take on the new post of press officer.

In the days immediately after the formation of the government, there was not much that could be done because we were heading into the holiday season. Some substantial work on the Estimates was completed before Christmas but the most important decision that was taken was to postpone the budget until 8 February. This gave us a few weeks to review fully the Estimates and to allow the new Fine Gael and Democratic Left ministers to take charge of their departments, review expenditure and finalise their suggestions for the budget. The six Labour ministers were now experienced in government and knew clearly what they wanted.

Before the much-needed Christmas break, I accepted an invitation to be the guest speaker at the annual general meeting of the accountancy graduates who had come through the large KPMG Stokes Kennedy Crowley firm in Dublin. When I had made my speech, there were questions from the floor. One came from a middle-aged man with a plummy British accent. Did I think the financial markets might be nervous of me becoming minister, since I was the first Labour politician in the state to hold that office. I acknowledged that, yes, there might be some concern, but that I liked to think that I would be following the tradition of other Labour and Social Democratic ministers for Finance, such as Helmut Schmidt in Germany, Roy Jenkins in Britain and Wim Kok in the Netherlands. 'But,' I concluded, 'I can give you this guarantee. I will not screw up the Irish economy the way Nigel Lawson did the British.' There was a burst of laughter, mixed with some applause, which quickly put an end to the questions.

Early in January the real work began. More aware than ever after my two years in Enterprise and Employment of the short time that is open to office-holders to implement changes, I recognised that I had, at best, three budgets – about two-and-a-half years – before a probable general election in June 1997. The budget decision-making process was accelerated, and ministers revised their departmental estimates after Ciarán and Brendan had identified additional real savings which the new ministers were slow to see. We knew that we would get only one year at this, but even that was important. The economy was slowly starting to come right, compared to 1993, but we still had problems with the deficit of 2 per cent and high levels of unemployment at 14.7 per cent.

On a Sunday evening in the middle of January 1994, when I had finally got my study at home organised and ready, I began to write the first draft of the budget speech. I wanted it to be concise and self-explanatory, in contrast to the previous budget speech which had gone on for nearly two hours, since every section of the department had insisted that its precious paragraphs were included. What the budget objectives should be and how best to express them pre-occupied me for some time. In the end, I wrote that my budget aimed to reward work, promote enterprise and strengthen solidarity.

Then, over a number of pages, I elaborated on what these objectives meant and how they were reflected in the body of the speech. Three sections of the speech spelled out in detail the measures that were to be taken in each area. Leaving large blocks to be filled in by civil servants in the department, I then drafted the concluding sections, inserting, in the final section, the five goals of my 2010 speech from the Department of Enterprise and Employment. Pleased with myself, I went to bed. The following morning I presented the draft to Michael Tutty, the second secretary with responsibility for the budget and economic division.

'This is the first draft,' I said.

'Of what?'

'The budget speech.'

'But ministers do not write budget speeches, we do… well, we have in the past.'

'But you don't mind if I do now, with your help.'

'No, no,' was his quick reply. 'It's terrific to have a minister's input.'

In a way, I was reminded of Jimmy Molloy and the housing committee of Dublin Corporation many years previously. The job had to be done by officials until such time as a minister took on the job, then the same officials would be more than happy to work with and add to the energy and ideology of the office-holder.

However, the final budget would not be completed until the expenditure items, which would be announced on budget day, had been negotiated and agreed. This meant completing the amounts to be added to social-welfare payments. Proinsias De Rossa, the enigmatic leader of Democratic Left, was the Minister for Social Welfare, but it was Rosheen Callender – a senior official in SIPTU and a Democratic Left political activist who had become an adviser to De Rossa, and the departmental officials – that Ciarán O'Mara, Brendan Lynch and other Finance officials had to deal.

Progress was slow and no concessions were coming from De Rossa's side. Throughout my experience of being a line minister, successive meetings usually produced gradual progress, but it didn't happen this time. When we got to the final ministerial meeting, Proinsias suddenly and substantially changed his requests, making it possible for me to meet his demands. It was a negotiation style with which I was not familiar and I knew that I had to do two more budgets with him. This experience was difficult but gave me a great insight into how he negotiated – something that would prove very useful in a few years.

Some weeks earlier, I had had a meeting with John Bruton, the new Taoiseach, at his request. From the outset he made it clear that he was anxious to make things work for all of us, referring, I assumed, to his difficult relationship with Dick from the Fine Gael/Labour cabinet of the 1980s. But he was particularly keen that the Taoiseach and Minister for Finance had a positive and clear relationship. This was especially needed, since for the first time in the history of the state, the two office-holders would be from different political parties. Notwithstanding my loyalty to my own party leader, John Bruton stressed that we ourselves had to have a special bond of trust which he would totally respect and protect. 'I don't want what happened to another Finance Minister to happen to you, when the Taoiseach had conflicting loyalties.'

I looked at him quizzically at which point he mentioned Alan Dukes. Although I only knew part of what had happened back in 1982, I understood clearly that he was telling me that, for his part, past events would not determine future behaviour. Certainly, I was pleased with his approach and we subsequently went on to have a good and constructive working relationship.

My first budget, on 8 February 1995, was well received but was partly overshadowed by an embarrassingly accurate leak. Phil Hogan, the Fine Gael Minister of State in the Department of Finance, resigned at 12.45 p.m. the following day, when it emerged that faxed messages from his office to the *Evening Herald* were the source of the leak. Clearly, he was deeply upset at what had happened. Jim Higgins subsequently replaced him as Minister of State with responsibility for the OPW.

Now that the primary task was behind us, I was able to take stock of the department and set out my own priorities. Truly, I was blessed with the staff in Finance: Maurice O'Connell had recently become governor of the Central Bank, Kevin Murphy had become Ombudsman and Paddy Mullarkey was the new secretary of the department, while Michael Tutty took over Paddy's old job. Bob Curran remained in charge of the public expenditure division where he had been for many years. At the time, I felt that I was lucky to have such a team and from the very beginning I was comfortable with them.

Once installed in the Department of Finance, I took stock of the ambience too. The offices of the department were dowdy and greatly in need of renovation. To begin with, there was no cafeteria within the building, which seriously hampered casual interaction and networking among staff. Few changes had been made since the 1960s and it certainly showed. I wanted to modernise the ground-floor ministerial suite of offices to bring it up to the same standard as that of the main part of Government Buildings. Barry Murphy, chairman of the OPW, came to discuss my proposals for renovation, including the addition of a cafeteria on the top floor. He then revealed that the OPW had a plan to bring that whole corner of the Government Buildings complex up to the new standard of the Taoiseach's office, and perhaps this was the right time to begin it. Within eighteen months, the entire ground floor had been transformed and the cafeteria installed.

New legislation to modernise the public service and reform the 1924 Ministers and Secretaries Act had started to take account of the need to give the civil service a greater autonomy and flexibility while maintaining accountability in the day-to-day management of their departments of state. An incident which occurred during my visit to Japan the previous year had now fed its way into the process of drafting legislation.

When the Irish delegation, which I led, met the Minister for Industry and Trade in Tokyo, the translators requested the name and responsibility of each member as we took our places opposite our Japanese colleagues. Kevin Bonner, introducing himself in his clear Donegal accent, explained that he was the 'Secretary of the Department of Enterprise and Employment' or, as they might know it from Britain, the permanent secretary. As the names and positions were being translated, an expression of bewilderment appeared on the Japanese faces, when the translator had got to Bonner-san. He was carefully described as the 'everlasting typist in the Department of Enterprise and Employment'. Back in Dublin and, after much ribbing, he wrote me a note expressing the need, as the country extended its international activities, for more self-explanatory titles for senior civil-service staff. In 1997, the Public Service Management Act introduced the more descriptive title, secretary general, to avoid any future confusion.

Based upon my experiences in the Department of Enterprise and Employment, I began to look at new, far-reaching and more inclusive practices. There, Frank Roche had correctly observed that there was very little contact between business people, entrepreneurs and senior civil servants. The various representative bodies and their officials met department officials, of course, but it was not the same thing. Frank's argument made sense and we soon established weekly breakfast meetings with five or six active businesspeople and senior department staff to discuss, face to face, the concerns and needs of the business community, as well as providing them with an opportunity to tell us what they thought the government and public service should be doing to help develop the economy.

When I proposed the idea, some doubts were expressed and Bob Curran thought that we would get a litany of complaints. 'Besides, didn't we meet with IBEC and Congress on a regular basis?' However, the initiative proceeded and soon these meetings confirmed their value. This was a two-way exchange and it developed confidence among business people who felt that the government was listening to them. Finance mandarins were hearing, at first hand, of the barriers and obstacles to economic growth from the players on the pitch and not from a paid lobbyist. The spectre of volatile currency movements and sudden shifts in interest rates were still around, and business confidence needed to be consolidated.

Dave Simpson, a successful chartered accountant who was prominent in the Institute of Chartered Accountants in Ireland, turned out to be as enthusiastic and constructive, when I moved to the Department of Finance, as Kevin Duffy had been ten years earlier when I had gone to Labour. Soon after Christmas I met with Dave. Coincidentally, his wife Catherine and Liz had been at school together and remained friends. In fact, Dave was one of the first people to whom I had turned when I became Finance spokesman some years earlier. Now he had an idea that he wanted to put to me before the budget: tax consolidation. He explained that each year, since 1967, the new Finance Act that followed the budget made the necessary changes to the tax laws. However, there was no integration of these changes and practitioners had to connect each section across many different acts. It was inefficient, costly and prone to errors. A Consolidation Act, which itself would be amended, after every budget, could contain in one document all the corporation and company tax law and so provide simplicity of access and certainty of accuracy.

The idea appealed to me. In a market economy, one of the real benefits that a government can provide is certainty and transparency. This, in turn, reduces arbitrary risk and encourages investment. Without hesitation, I announced the commitment to consolidation in the budget speech.

Some weeks later, the chairman of the Revenue Commissioners, Cathal MacDomhnaill, came to see me to discuss the commitment. 'It is a wonderful idea, Minister, and something that we've been planning for some time.'

'Good,' I replied. 'How long will it take?'

'Ah, Minister, we believe between five and six years.'

'That is a pity,' I said, 'because I need to have it done by spring 1997, but if you cannot do it, within that time, never mind.'

'What do you mean?' he asked, taking sharp notice of what I was saying.

'Well,' I said, 'it's only a work of consolidating existing legislation, not new law. It is a complex but nevertheless a cut and paste job. If the Revenue Commissioners cannot do it within that time, then we'll go out to tender on it.'

'Please, Minister, let's consider this. Give me a week and we'll come back to you with a proposal. I know what you want.'

Cathal MacDomhnaill was true to his word and a joint public/ private project began the task about a month later. The project was run by Revenue with the participation of Butterworths, the business and legal publishers, and the engagement of a special consultant. A special unit was established in Dublin Castle and the project manager was an energetic young Revenue official, Liam Hennessy. The final draft was completed some weeks before we left government in June 1997.

One of the dominant issues which had ensured Kathleen Lynch's by-election success for Democratic Left in Cork North-Central in

November 1994 was the payment of arrears owed to thousands of women, arising from an EU Equal Treatment Directive and a subsequent court ruling. Approximately 70,000 married women who had paid into the social-welfare system, as employees, had been discriminated against, in comparison to married men, in relation to the receipt of payments for dependent spouses and children. On the day she entered the Dáil, Kathleen Lynch said during an interview that the party's minimum demand in any future government would be the payment of the arrears without delay. Estimates of the costs varied, but in the end the state paid out £360 million, over eighteen months – the biggest payout at that time.

Although I agreed with the principle behind the payment, my problem was how to finance it. The commitment had been made but was not included in the 1995 budget, so extra resources had to be found, in a manner that did not make a nonsense of delicately constructed budgetary arithmetic. One of the first official functions I attended, after Christmas, was the publication of the end of year results of the National Treasury Management Agency (NTMA), which took place in Treasury Buildings on Lower Grand Canal Street on 30 December after the close of business on the last trading day of the year.

The NTMA was established in 1990 as a separate financial body, reporting directly to the Minister for Finance, and charged with managing the national debt in the most effective a way possible, to reduce the substantial annual interest charges. The brainchild of Dr Michael Somers, a senior civil servant in the Department of Finance, it came into existence in response to a major problem that had confronted his section. Major changes had taken place in the world of finance, and Irish banks were now headhunting experienced officials in the debt management section of the department, who had expertise in international financial transactions. Somers could not keep his team together and the department obviously was not able to pay the market rate for the limited pool of expertise. His proposal for a separate semi-state agency, reporting to the minister, but able to compete on the open market for talented individuals, was readily accepted by the then Minister of Finance, Ray MacSharry.

Sadly, Michael Somers was regarded with considerable suspicion by his former colleagues because he had helped to create an independent NTMA and reduced the power of the Department of Finance. By 1995, the NTMA was an extraordinary success and has since been examined by many nations across the globe.

In trying to find the £360 million, I remembered a meeting with Ken Phillips, a senior finance consultant with Lehmann Brothers, on my first visit to Boston to visit the Digital headquarters back in February 1993. Ken was a specialist in securitisation, a form of financial engineering about which I knew nothing. Ken Phillips' idea stayed with me during my time in Enterprise and Employment, but now it had a direct relevance. I asked Michael Somers, after the official press conference had concluded, if the idea was practical. Could we use the Department of the Environment's loan book of tenant purchase dwellings to raise cash? The conservative value of the loan book was close to £700 million. The risk of defaulting payments was low, because most tenants had received a substantial discount on the purchase price. Besides, market values had risen considerably and there was a comfortable ratio of cover between the asset value and the outstanding loan. Dr Somers was open, helpful and enthusiastic. Yes, it could be done, but the idea should come from myself as minister and not from the NTMA, and he explained why as he outlined the history of the organisation.

In the following days, as I began to formulate my approach, I remembered the fate of my Roads Finance Agency project and the reaction of the Department of the Environment. I had since met with John Loughrey, who was now the secretary of the Department of Transport, Energy and Communications. In the course of a casual conversation at a social function, he confirmed my suspicions about what had happened to my 1984 proposal. I would not make the same mistake this time – besides, since I was the actual Minister for Finance, it would not be a problem.

But it was. Firstly, the idea had not originated from within the department. Secondly, it had the appearance of being easily accessible money and could be a temptation to cash-strapped ministers. The senior Finance official responsible for the securitisation project, Jim

McCaffrey, was not happy with his mission. Nor was Brendan Howlin, now Minister for the Environment, until I explained it to him in terms other than those used by the civil servants in both our departments. In 1995 the necessary legislation was enacted. A separate company, Ulysses Securitisation plc, was established by the NTMA and the successful bidder for the project was a consortium of banks led by Union Bank of Switzerland. All Kathleen Lynch's women received their arrears and Proinsias De Rossa was a happy man.

Before I moved to Finance, the idea of abolishing third-level fees had begun to be discussed among the Labour Party ministers and their advisers. The measure now took on real momentum. The ideology was very clear and the logic was very simple. In the mid-1960s Donogh O'Malley had transformed Irish education by introducing free secondary education, the subsequent benefits of which were apparent. A new generation was able to achieve their personal potential, and it changed the quality of the well-educated Irish labour force. The IDA was now successfully promoting the pool of Irish labour to mostly US-based corporations. Indeed the foundations of the Celtic Tiger owe their origin in part to O'Malley's initiative.

Most other European countries also had free access to third-level education. Abolishing the Irish fees would bring us into line, and would be a clear implementation of a basic Labour value – equality of access and universal service. But why now?

As the situation stood, the European Social Fund was already providing free access to some, but not all, third-level courses in our Regional Technical Colleges. In addition, an old provision in our personal income tax code was being vigorously exploited by the wealthy and middle class to effectively fund, for free, the university education of their sons and daughters. The tax covenant provision enabled a parent to assign 5 per cent of his or her gross income to a child, free of tax, and to have their net income assessed for personal income tax. However, there was no limit on how much could be covenanted to a non-relative. So two friendly families, trusting each other, could do back-to-back covenanting for their respective children, for as much as the gross income could bear. The wealthier the family, the bigger the tax-free sum that could be covenanted away from the Revenue Commissioners and into the bank accounts of the young fee-paying students, who could therefore easily pay the college fees. But average families, above the low threshold for means-tested student grants, simply could not afford to covenant large sums of the household income, and so, in order to pay for their children's education, either went without or, in many cases, remortgaged their homes.

Most parents realise that assisting their children to obtain a good education is one of the few ways they can help them into the future. The small covenant tax provision had become a major loophole and had grown rapidly. Tax foregone on covenanted income had run at about an average of £3 million–£4 million in the early 1990s. By the end of 1994 it had mushroomed to £36 million and was climbing. Against that, the cost of abolishing college fees was £41 million. Labour's objective could be achieved for a net cost of £5 million, provided the Minister for Finance introduced legislation to tightly control the operation of tax covenants.

I was easily persuaded by both positions, but soon two contradictory noises could be heard from within Labour's ranks. The first was an attempt, in our presentation, to suggest that this measure would improve access to third-level education for disadvantaged communities and their children. The second was an insistence that we should not highlight the scale of the tax foregone by way of covenants since this made our measure seem less bold than it otherwise appeared. In retrospect, it was a bad strategy and a timid approach. The measure was fundamentally about equality of access for people eligible to go to third-level college. It was not about educational disadvantage. That commenced at primary level and there were many reasons for it. Niamh Bhreathnach's pilot scheme entitled 'Breaking the Cycle' was concentrated on that issue. The results, if successful, would take years to manifest themselves. But our nervous ranks remained and I was amongst them.

Ciarán was strongly in favour of a vigorous publicity campaign, but the caution of presentation articulated by Fergus Finlay prevailed. When introduced, our measure was silently welcomed by many beleaguered middle-income households but denounced by some commentators, who claimed that it would not improve access for the poor to our universities. Disadvantaged children were not even making it into second level or, if they were, they dropped out of school before sitting their Leaving Certificate. Labour's critics, particularly within the Fianna Fáil opposition, frequently attempt to ghettoise us as the party of the poor and to judge us accordingly. Unfortunately, some of our supporters and members accepted this caricature. Their response made me think of an interview with Madame Mitterrand in 1981 after her husband had been elected president of France. In response to a question which contrasted the manifest wealth of her left-bank Parisian townhouse with the ideology of her party, she tersely replied that 'socialism was not the politics of poverty'. The abolition of fees was in my view a good decision. The issue of extra funding for our third-level education system is now a big one and should be primarily solved with extra state investment.

At the time of its publication in August 1994, the Beef Tribunal Report, prepared by Mr Justice Liam Hamilton, made one explicit recommendation which was accepted by the government – all financial advisers would, in effect, be required to act as whistle-blowers, if they knew that their clients were breaking the law. My predecessor, Bertie Ahern, had given a commitment to implement this in the next Finance Bill and I maintained that position in section 153 of the bill. The Institute of Chartered Accountants was, on behalf of its members, prepared to accept this additional requirement and would not oppose it. However, they pointed out that accountants were not the only professionals to offer financial and investment advice. Insurance brokers and solicitors did so as well and therefore any legal requirement could not single out accountants alone, as Hamilton's report seemed to imply. I thought this to be fair and reasonable and the section reflected such a comprehensive approach.

When the Finance Bill was published, members of the legal

profession were outraged. Ken Murphy, the Director General of the Law Society of Ireland, went on *Morning Ireland* and roundly denounced this draconian measure which got to the very heart of the confidential relationship between lawyer and client. If it was not actually unconstitutional, he claimed, it was close to being a breach of fundamental liberties in a democratic republic! When the item came up for detailed debate, presentations were made to the Joint Oireachtas Committee on Finance. To my ears, a less than convincing case was made by the legal and investment community. Among the vociferous defenders of their position were Michael McDowell and Charlie McCreevy. With pressure now mounting through the government backbenches, some second thoughts were publicly aired from within a divided accountancy profession.

Because the Attorney General's office thought it to be possibly unconstitutional, a watered down version of section 153 was finally enacted. Had all the public representatives known then what we know now – about the widespread abuse of the tax system by so many people, aided and abetted by lawyers, accountants, brokers and banks – we would, of course, have held our nerve. At least, I like to think we would have, but retrospective wisdom is easily proclaimed.

An amusing question was posed to a group of us, by a distinguished visitor, in whose honour a state reception and dinner was held in Dublin Castle on 31 May 1995. Prince Charles, the heir to the British throne, was on an official visit. It was the first such visit by a senior member of the British royal family since the British army had handed over Dublin Castle to Michael Collins, seventy-three years previously. Developments in the North, the Downing Street Declaration and the Sinn Féin/IRA ceasefire had helped to create a new climate and the royal visit was seen as recognition of the progress made and also as a confidence-building measure, designed to encourage all the participants to go even further.

The throne room of Dublin Castle is on the first floor, above the entrance hall, and accessed by a pair of ceremonial stairs. To either side of the throne room are two long galleries, overlooking the courtyard of the Dublin Castle complex. Behind the western gallery is St Patrick's Hall, the main ceremonial room in the building. With the two galleries being used as the reception room for the invited guests, the throne room between them was kept for the VIPs. It was here that ministers and their partners were gathered with some senior civil servants.

We were to be introduced to the Prince of Wales before dinner. Liz and myself were together with others, including Niamh Bhreathnach and Tom Ferris, Mervyn and Marilyn Taylor and Michael D. and Sabina Higgins. The double doors from the hallway opened and the Taoiseach, Tánaiste and Minister for Social Welfare came in with their wives and our guest of honour. John Bruton guided him over to the group of us in the centre of the room and proceeded to introduce us as we stood around in an informal semi-circle. When he heard the name Michael D., Charles reacted by saying, quite loudly, 'Oh, you are the Minister for Culture who has done so much for your film industry with all those tax breaks.' The socialist republican deputy from Galway West positively levitated with delight at this regal recognition.

When we had all been introduced, Charles turned and gazed around, taking in the space and proclaimed, 'Isn't this a wonderful building? What a beautiful room.'

Standing beside him, Liz replied, looking straight at him, 'And haven't we kept it well?'

With a twinkle in his eye, he pointed to the large empty throne beneath its canopy to the left-hand side of the room. Looking back straight at her, he said, 'Do you think I might sit upon it, even for a few minutes?'

'Don't even think about it' was her instant response, much to the delight of all present.

The formation of the Department of Equality and Law Reform was, along with Arts, Culture and the Gaeltacht and the Department of Enterprise and Employment, part of the radical restructuring that

Dick had agreed with Albert Reynolds back in 1993. While Fianna
Fáil apparently did not object to these proposals, it was Labour that
had initiated them and Labour ministers were appointed to the new
departments. Mervyn Taylor, after a hesitant start, turned out to be
an excellent minister and a good cabinet colleague. Government
departments are temporary task forces, established to deal with a
particular problem, staffed by permanent civil servants and, sometimes, availing of the help of outside consultants. When their
mission is accomplished, or superseded by new agencies, they are
stood down by a sensible government and their permanent staff re-
deployed. Seán Lemass' Department of Supplies during the Second
World War was the classic prototype of this kind of government
response. The departments of Lands, the Gaeltacht and latterly
Labour all followed in a similar vein.

The job of Minister for Justice is hard at any time. The attitude
of the department and many of its officials, who in my experience
are very inward-looking, is that all citizens are criminals, and if not
now, then will be at some time in the future. That mindset, combined with the dual problems of paramilitary violence and serious
criminal activity, sets the agenda for the day job. The Labour Party
assessment in opposition, and Dick's proposal at the formation of
the new government, was that Equality and Law Reform had to be
removed from the Department of Justice. Labour, in opposition,
had driven the equality agenda, not just on the general issue of
freedom of information and ethics in government legislation, but
also on the decriminalisation of homosexuality. The disabled had
been a forgotten community within our midst. In fact, successive
governments had scandalously ignored the problems of disabled
people and their families. Now we were committed to making
changes. Two different, but complementary, tasks had to be undertaken and Mervyn got stuck into both of them with great tenacity.

The provision of civil divorce in our increasingly pluralistic
society was a political objective to which the Labour Party had been
committed for nearly two decades. To achieve it, the prohibition
inserted in the 1937 Constitution by Éamon de Valera had to be
removed. But, deep-rooted prejudices and fears among the public

had to be tackled before a second referendum could be successful. Garret FitzGerald's hurried attempt in 1986 failed because we didn't do our homework. In addition, Fianna Fáil under Charles Haughey orchestrated the opposition with consummate opportunistic cynicism, given his own personal position at the time.

The Fianna Fáil/Labour government was committed to the divorce project and now, in opposition, they could not renege. Besides, Fianna Fáil's new leader, Bertie Ahern, separated from his wife and openly with a new partner, could not emulate his previous boss, C.J. Haughey, who had seen no contradiction in being married, having a mistress, Terry Keane, and opposing civil divorce.

Really the issue was not about Catholic Church dogma, true love and happiness – much as many of the anti-divorce protagonists would have liked to maintain that it was. The regulation of property rights, the safeguarding of the position of the first wife and family, including pensions, against the intrusion of the new partner and the possibility of additional children, were issues which engaged the minds of those who participated in the debate. Another question was how to secure the family business or family farm, if you allow the family to be divided and the marriage dissolved.

Since the debacle of 1986, some of these questions had been answered. Alan Shatter of Fine Gael had successfully moved a Private Member's Bill on family separation, which was broadly accepted and enacted by the government. Marital breakdown and second unions were now quite common across the country and all sections of society. The messy particulars of dealing with the consequences, rather than moralising over the causes, now demanded the attention of law-makers, irrespective of their own personal religious beliefs.

Mervyn Taylor was in the right place at the right time. He was, for all the world like a reliable country family solicitor, and quiet demeanour concealed the commitment of a passionate radical. During the five years he was minister, Mervyn enacted seventeen acts in family law reform, as well as two major pieces of equality legislation. Dermot Gleeson, the new Attorney General, complemented Mervyn's skills. An eminent senior counsel, Dermot's crafting of the wording of the constitutional amendment went through numerous draftings, and was honed and polished by a review group, of which I was a member. Nothing was left to chance. All possibilities had to be examined and all risks assessed before it was finally put to the people in a referendum. The people did vote yes, but only just, by a majority of less than half of 1 per cent. Who says change is easy?

I had flown to Athens on 26 June 1996 to attend the funeral of Andreas Papandreou, a former prime minister and the founder of PASOK, our Greek sister political party. On my way back, the flight attendant told me that the journalist Veronica Guerin had been murdered, in retaliation, we presumed, for her fearless, investigative journalism. She had been exposing Dublin criminal chiefs and their families to the enthralled middle-class readership of the *Sunday Independent*, and the entire nation was now in shock over her brutal murder and the manifest desolation of her husband and young son.

About ten o'clock the following morning, I was in my office when I took a phone call from Taoiseach John Bruton, who was en route from his home in Dunboyne to the order of business in the Dáil. He asked my advice on what to say in response to the inevitable questions which would be raised. Did I have any suggestions? As it happened, I did. Joe Costello and Róisín Shortall had been speaking at the Parliamentary Labour Party meetings about problems caused by drugs: the damage being done by traffickers and, to add insult to injury, the display of conspicuous ill-gotten wealth that the local drug barons flaunted in their neighbourhoods. The parliamentary party sympathised with their stance and Joe Costello and Róisín Shortall proposed a system to confiscate the illegal gains and a method whereby the confiscated money would be channelled back into the damaged communities by way of partial compensation.

Immediately, John Bruton was interested in what I had to say and responded vigorously in the Dáil during the order of business, using many of the ideas I had mentioned to him. As the horrific details of

Veronica Guerin's death emerged, an intense level of government activity took place.

This was not the first time that the Rainbow Coalition had attempted to deal with the growing drugs problem in Dublin. Nearly a year previously, on 20 July, a meeting had taken place in the Sycamore Room in Government Buildings when ministers, officials and representatives of the Garda Síochána gathered to examine the response to the trafficking of drugs and the poor levels of co-operation between the various arms of the state. Deputy Commissioner Pat Byrne gave a virtuoso performance on what should and could be done within the existing structures and so was given the task of co-ordinating the different state authorities. However, a year later, the hoped-for improvements had not happened – if anything, the situation had got worse.

The time of the Criminal Assets Bureau (CAB) had come. Within days, basic decisions were made and, at Liz's suggestion, Barry Galvin, the state solicitor for Cork, was proposed as the person who had the personality and the courage to take on the job of an Irish Eliot Ness, the legendary US FBI agent, who in the 1920s had successfully pursued Al Capone in the gangster-ridden city of Chicago. While at a meeting in the European Parliament in Strasbourg on 17 July, I asked Ciarán O'Mara to get Barry Galvin on the phone. I did not know him, but Ciarán did. Like Liz, he had seen his appearance on *The Late Late Show* where he talked to Gay Byrne on the issue of pursuing drug traffickers in the Cork area. Ciarán dialled his number and handed me the mobile phone in a corridor in the parliament building. Without delay, I told Barry Galvin what we were proposing to do, which he welcomed, and then asked him would he take on the job of running the new organisation. Straightaway he expressed an interest and said that he would come to Dublin to discuss the details.

Some days later, I got a call from Pat Byrne, now the Garda Commissioner. Having some real worries about the new agency, he wanted to discuss them urgently. When Byrne arrived, he was full of flattery and knew exactly what he wanted as he expressed his concerns to me, Ciarán O'Mara and a number of officials from the department and the Revenue Commissioners.

His main concern was that he didn't want the new body – which would combine members of An Garda Síochána, the Revenue Commissioners, including Customs and Excise, and officials from the Department of Social Welfare – to be called the Criminal Assets Agency. He felt that the members, particularly those from An Garda Síochána, would inevitably be called 'agents', with undertones of the FBI in the United States. More crucially, the other issue was the idea of a non-garda being chief executive. In effect, the problem for An Garda Síochána consisted in taking instructions from a civilian, whom Byrne already knew informally was likely to be Barry Galvin. I had no difficulty with the first issue and so the agency, there and then, became the bureau. The other question was a bit more complex. It was finally resolved with a compromise, whereby Detective Chief Superintendent Fachtna Murphy was the chief executive officer and Barry Galvin the chief legal officer.

Two pieces of legislation were enacted in 1996. The Proceeds of Crime Act was based in part on a Private Member's Bill, initiated by Fianna Fáil's John O'Donoghue and adopted by the Department of Justice. The other was the Criminal Assets Bureau Act, introduced by the Department of Finance, which became law in October.

On 30 July, there was a photo call at which Minister for Justice Nora Owen, Pat Byrne, Barry Galvin, myself and others were present. It was less than four weeks since Veronica Guerin's murder. As we chatted, I reminded Nora of the intense meeting we had attended in her department on 19 July when a working party of the relevant departments had been assembled to proceed with the government's intentions. Nora had suggested that, in order to add importance to their work, we should both attend the inaugural meeting, which was being chaired by Frank Dunne, an assistant secretary in Justice. She asked if they should meet in the Department of Finance or would it be possible for me to come over to St Stephen's Green. When I readily agreed to the latter, she expressed surprise because the convention was that while ministers went to the Department of Finance, the Minister for Finance did not go to line departments.

At the meeting in the Department of Justice, Nora Owen and I were seated at the top of the table on either side of the chairperson, and the two of us made brief, encouraging remarks, stressing the importance of the group's work. In reply, Frank Dunne thanked us and continued to say that if the working party came to the conclusion that a new body such as that proposed was required, then they would proceed to develop the concept. Before he had finished, however, I erupted. 'Excuse me. You will fucking come to that conclusion. The decision has already been made. If you don't fucking understand that, then we'll get someone else who does. Is that clear?'

I don't know which of us – himself, Nora or myself – was the most surprised at the vehemence of my outburst.

Of the many things that I did in Finance, establishing the Criminal Assets Bureau is one of which I am very proud. The irreparable damage that the drug traffickers had inflicted on families and communities was something I had seen at first hand in my own constituency. Imprisonment and the consequential social shame meant nothing to these rapacious gangsters. Only their impoverishment and that of their extended families, who while not directly involved, clearly enjoyed the associated high lifestyle, was the real sanction which would have effect. Imitation is a great form of flattery and Britain and Northern Ireland have followed our experience in relation to the Criminal Assets Bureau.

Looking back, it seems that a number of measures that I brought to fruition in Finance originated in Enterprise and Employment. The Dublin Docklands Development Authority is certainly one of the big ones. It all began as a reaction to the signals we were receiving during IDA working trips to the United States, along with the derelict condition of the old Dublin Gas Company site, right in the heart of my own constituency. The new types of information technology jobs, which were coming through the IDA, such as with Sun Microsystems, were attracting graduate employees. These companies wanted stylish but low-rent offices which would attract top-quality employees. They certainly did not want to be out in industrial estates amongst old-fashioned factories which the IDA had on the outskirts of the city. On the other hand, the existing downtown, office-rental market was simply too expensive for the operating costs of these new companies. Medium-rise, city-centre or close by, simply constructed office-type accommodation was what was required.

The late Dermot Pierce had an idea for such a development, now called East Point, on a brownfield site in the north Dublin docks area, but he had difficulty making the finances add up. On the southside, the contamination from the old gas works on the Grand Canal site made environmental cleaning highly problematic, legally uncertain and very expensive. Earlier efforts in the form of special tax designation for IDA-approved companies had not worked. I wrote to Brendan Howlin, Minister for the Environment, to ask if his department had any ideas as to how we could tackle the range of issues on the problem outlined to him. It was a long letter that I received in reply.

The Custom House Docks Development Authority had originally been set up by the Fine Gael/Labour government in 1986 and was the vehicle into which C.J. Haughey had set the highly successful Financial Services Centre. Confined to a small compact area of 28 acres (11.3 hectares), its remit was soon to run out.

Howlin now proposed to extend the remit to include the entire docklands hinterland (excluding the territory of the working port). The new area, comprising 1,300 acres (526 hectares), stretched from East Wall and Fairview on the northside to Ringsend and Irishtown on the south, running from City Quay and the Custom House right down to the mouth of the river.

However, we were also now proposing a more comprehensive and holistic approach to the development in contrast to the narrow remit of the Custom House Docks Development Authority. A social democratic model, incorporating integrated, sustainable, economic, social and physical development was the objective. I sponsored the project by announcing, in the 1996 budget, that a working party would be established to investigate the rejuvenation of the Dublin docklands area. After considerable innovative contributions and proposals, a new act became law in 1997 – the Dublin Docklands

Development Authority Act – and the authority came into existence on May Day 1997. Even though it was Brendan Howlin's responsibility, and he guided the legislation through the Houses of the Oireachtas, he generously recognised that it was my initiative and allowed me an enormous input into the drafting of the legislation, and the selection of both the members of the executive board and the community council. Lar Bradshaw was an excellent chair and, with the enthusiasm of Joan O'Connor and others, a master plan was completed in record time. Peter Coyne was appointed chief executive officer and Gerry Kelly took on responsibility for the social regeneration of the community. Gerry was familiar to me from the time he worked with Malachy Sherlock in AnCO. Today his achievements in Docklands are impressive.

The authority's successes have exceeded all my hopes. Anyone who knows that part of the city will agree that the transformation which has been achieved in less than ten years is truly remarkable. Its equal emphasis on physical, economic and social development is the epitome of the application of social democratic values at work. It combines the rigours of the commercial marketplace with the intelligent intervention of the state to achieve desirable social and environmental results. It was in that context that members of the community council, led by Charlie Murphy and Dolores Wilson, two Labour activists from my constituency, with support from Betty Ashe, first proposed the concept of a 20 per cent social housing component in all residential developments. What was seen as a risky pioneering objective has now become the national norm in Part V of our planning legislation.

Many other projects were dealt with during my thirty months in the Department of Finance. The next chapter is devoted to one substantial and important matter. For most people, civil servants and public alike, the primary task of the Department of Finance is the gathering of revenues, by taxes, and the distribution of that money by the Estimates through the various departments to the public. Such a central and important activity constantly attracts attention and proposals. Organisations, business interests, social bodies and many sectoral groups all make regular representations to the minister.

These pre-budget submissions, as they are known, had taken on a frenzied activity by the time of my first budget. I was appalled at the number of them, including those who expected and got a meeting with the minister, and the efforts that departmental officials put into reading and analysing the submissions and drafting elaborate briefing notes. It was, in my view, a terrible waste of time and a cynical exercise designed primarily for consumption by the members of the lobbying organisations. Before my first budget I had no option but to meet the interest groups, but to demonstrate my attitude to this process, I saw more than twenty groups in twenty-minute slots over two days. In the budget speech, I announced that in future such submissions would be made in public by each group, not to the minister but to the members of the Joint Oireachtas Committee on Finance. There, the supplicants for more cash or less tax would have to justify in public why such favourable treatment should be given to them and what return there would be for the wider community.

In the main, this kind of lobbying did not work, but there were two exceptions I can think of. In my first year, I announced my intention to progressively reduce corporation tax from 40 per cent by 2 per cent each year, to bring it closer to the 10 per cent tax on manufacturing and internationally traded services. However, when we completed the post-budget analysis, we found that most of the real benefit had gone to the large domestic corporations such as the banks and the insurance companies. Conscious of this, I was open to suggestions as to how to better target the tax reduction in my next budget. Lorraine Sweeney, chairperson of the Small Firms Association, came to see me before the budget. 'We could have given you a list of twenty things we would like you to do,' she said, 'but there is one thing we want you to do. Please target corporation tax relief on small businesses.' It was clear, precise, well presented and in line with my objectives, so I did it.

The other initiative was the £1,000 scrappage scheme for old cars. Cyril McHugh, chief executive officer of the Society of the Irish

Motoring Industry (SIMI), had publicly articulated this proposal but it had been rubbished by many people, including Finance officials. It was, McHugh argued, a win, win and win proposition! Give a person a £1,000 grant and they buy a new car – the government got tax revenue, the car dealer got a profit and the environment had an old and fuel-inefficient car removed from the road.

These two proposals, like all others, were taken in by the department and restated in an objective way. They were then assessed for the pros and cons and a conclusion drawn, with a recommended decision to be made by the minister.

To facilitate an easy comprehension of the vast range of proposals received by the Department of Finance, the format is the same for most measures. In order to identify these proposals when sent down to the minister's office for a decision, the folders have a red dot on the top right-hand corner. I can still remember opening the one that contained the response to a SIMI proposal and reading the concluding words, whose formulation says much about the official mindset. 'On balance, Minister, we can find no good reason to recommend against this proposal.'

Chapter 18

The Politics of the Single Currency

The bedside alarm went off at the unusually early hour of 5.00 a.m. Liz woke up drowsily and asked me to remind her where I was going and why. The first ECOFIN meeting under the new French presidency had been set for 16 January 1995. The ECOFIN Council, involving the Economic and Finance ministers of the twelve member states, met monthly, usually in Brussels, and once a year in Luxembourg. As I got dressed, I explained that this was my first meeting and how much I was looking forward to it. From 1992, I had followed with a keen interest this European project from the sidelines. Now I was directly involved. Then I came round to her side of the bed and kissed her goodbye. I leaned over to my eleven-week-old son, caressed his head, and told him that I was off to negotiate the construction of the currency in which he would be paid his first pocket money. Sitting in the car beside Nashie as we drove through the silent streets of Dublin, I thought about the agenda of the meeting but didn't think at the time that I would be giving Conan a €2 coin to spend in Michael and Catherine Ferron's shop in Roundstone on 1 January 2001.

When we got to Baldonnel, five officials were already there, with Paddy Mullarkey, Ciarán and Brendan and we were soon in the air in the government jet. Some of the hour-and-a-half flight time was used after breakfast to brief me on the issues to be discussed, but there was little of great complexity. We were met in Brussels airport and taken directly to the large new Justus Lipsius building of the European Council, built directly across from the old European Commission headquarters, the Berlaymont, on the side of Place Schumann. This was the heart of the European quarter in Brussels and an area I knew well. Pádraic MacKernan, the Irish permanent representative to the commission, joined us in the Irish representation suite of rooms. I had known Paddy for many years and he wished me well with my new responsibilities. He had little to report from the Committee of Permanent Representatives (COREPER), the regular meeting of his fellow perm reps, as they were known, who prepared the agendas of the various council meetings for their ministers.

However, Paddy indicated that there would be an official welcome extended by the French Minister for Finance, Edmond Alphandéry, on behalf of the ECOFIN Council to the Finance ministers from Austria, Finland and Sweden, the three countries that had become full members of the European Union at the beginning of 1995. The work for the next six months would then be set out and a discussion on it would follow. We went down to the main floor which contained a number of meeting rooms. Not surprisingly, the enlargement to fifteen member states and the probability of more in the near future required greater accommodation. Everything, including the council meeting room, was larger than the old building with which I had been familiar – and the intimacy of the past had been lost.

The octagonal layout of the council meeting room accommodated the ministers with two advisers and officials on either side. Behind this front row were two more rows of seats and desks for the member states. Directly opposite the President of the Council was the President of the Commission, Jacques Santer, the former Luxembourg prime minister. Seated on either side of him was Yves de Silguy, Commissioner for Economic and Monetary Affairs, and Erkki Liikanen, Commissioner for the Budget. Sometimes the commission team might be joined by another commissioner, if a matter related to their responsibilities was on the agenda. Commissioner Mario Monti was frequently present for economic issues directly connected to his Competition portfolio.

Every six months, the presidency of the council changed and, as it did, the location of each member state at the table moved to the left, with the presidency and the commission remaining always in the same two positions.

The meetings started usually before 11.00 a.m. and went on through the afternoon, ending no later than 7.00 p.m. Leftover business could be dealt with by the perm reps or was left on the agenda for the next meeting. As happens at many conferences, the break for lunch was an opportunity for a meeting within a meeting. The press were not at the council meetings, but ministers and officials regularly went out to brief their own press secretaries on the progress of an agenda item that was newsworthy at home.

However, lunch was different. Only ministers, commissioners and one or two senior EU officials were included in the pre-lunch drinks before the three-course meal was served in a designated dining room. Interpreters, housed behind the glass screens of the booths, facilitated the dialogue of the informed discussions on sensitive issues which took place. These issues may be ones already on the agenda or else on the horizon. For most of my time, over the thirty months and five presidencies I attended ECOFIN meetings, lunch was where the politics of the single currency were fully aired.

The idea for the single European currency all began with the Werner Report back in 1970 and spluttered along during the currency crises of the 1970s and the 1980s. As President of the Commission in 1977, Roy Jenkins gave an influential speech in Venice which relaunched the idea of Economic and Monetary Union (EMU) for the European Community.

When Jacques Delors became President of the Commission in 1985, the project took on a new momentum. He had been Minister for Finance in President Mitterrand's 1981 socialist government and brought to the European Commission a vigorous leadership and a vision of a Europe that would enable member states to achieve the social and economic goals which they had set themselves. His own national experience between 1981 and 1984 convinced him, and others, that the individual states could not make sufficient progress on their own. Instead, the full potential of the European economy of the ten, and soon to be twelve, member states had to be realised by all member states working together.

In response to a request from the European leaders in March 1985, the commission identified over 300 legislative decisions that, if taken by the member states, could unleash the full capacity of Europe's economy to grow at its natural potential. However, for this to happen quickly, the current decision-making process, which in effect gave each member state a veto, would have to change. The 1987 Single European Act (SEA) changed the rules, allowing for more qualified majority voting on those matters where the member states had voluntarily conferred their sovereign national powers to the European institutions.

Delors seized the opportunity which the SEA provided to re-ignite the whole European project. While there had been a brief reference to economic and monetary union in the preamble of the SEA, the real work on the project began in 1988. Soon known as the Delors Report, it culminated in a new treaty, agreed in Maastricht in 1991, which came into force in 1993.

From the public point of view, the politics of the day were focused on the single currency. John Major, who had succeeded the Margaret Thatcher a year earlier in November 1990, argued belligerently and successfully that Britain could not be coerced into a single currency. Consequently, both Britain and Denmark won the right to remain out of the single currency, the treaty's main provision. Major's political difficulties in Britain were compounded by the deep division within his own Conservative Party in the House of Commons. He continued to struggle with them through the winter and, to his, and other people's, surprise, won the June 1992 general election, the fourth Tory success since 1979. However, the sweet smell of victory turned very sour on 16 September 1992. Forever known as Black Wednesday, it was the day Britain crashed out of the currency exchange rate mechanism of the European Union. The Chancellor, Norman Lamont, was humiliated and limped on in office until he was replaced by Ken Clarke the following year. The British Conservative Party's reputation, always unwarranted in my view, for sound economic management took a hammering from which it has yet to recover. Its attitude to the European Union generally, and the single currency in particular, is now a faultline within the party which appears to be unbridgeable.

The broad outline of the journey to the single currency was set out in three stages in Maastricht. Stage I began on 1 July 1990, with the removal of exchange controls in two-thirds of the member states, and the remainder following. In addition, the currencies were now to be clustered into a narrow band of relative values in the exchange rate mechanism. There were also measures set out to encourage the different twelve economies to slowly converge so that, ideally, the business cycle would be synchronised across what the Maastricht Treaty now called the European Union.

Stage II started on 1 January 1994. A new body, the European Monetary Institute, was established in Frankfurt. Its task, as the forerunner of the European Central Bank, was to develop a co-ordinating role for the ten participating member states. With the exception of the UK and Denmark, the others were required to prepare their economies for convergence. This required some countries, such as France, to make their Central Bank independent of the government, in a manner similar to the German Bundesbank. Subject to achieving the standards set out in the convergence criteria, the European Council had to decide at the end of 1996 if it was possible to move to the third and final stage.

Stage III was the irrevocable locking together of the value of the national currencies and providing for the European Central Bank to take over the sole responsibility for setting the interest rate of the single currency for the participating member states. In the event, all that was not ready in time for the third stage to start in January 1997. Consequently, the council set 1 January 1999 as the definitive date when the project would go ahead with whatever countries qualified to meet the criteria.

In the early days of 1995, there was constant speculation in the media as to which countries would participate in the new currency. The core group was clear: France, Germany, Austria and the three Benelux countries. However, outside this natural grouping of close and even contiguous neighbours, speculation raged about who else might qualify to join them.

For my first six months on ECOFIN, the single currency was a slow burner politically. Perhaps this was because domestic French politics frequently intruded on to our European stage. It has always struck me as ironic that while the Fifth Republic strives to dominate the European agenda, France does a bad job when it has the responsibility of the presidency. I have had direct ministerial experience of two of them and, as a senior politician, observed in 2000 the French presidency that delivered perhaps the worst inter-governmental conference of all time, the Nice Treaty.

The 1995 presidency was up to form. We had three French Finance ministers in the course of six months, and because of the political turmoil in France no informal ECOFIN Council was held during this French presidency. My affection for all things French was severely tested so that, by June and after a number of ECOFIN meetings, I looked forward to seeing the baton pass to Spain in July 1995.

By now, I was developing a personal relationship with some of the politicians whom I met monthly. Ken Clarke, I already knew from the 1980s when, along with Lord Young, he was my counterpart on the Social Affairs Council. Jean-Claude Juncker of Luxembourg was now, with the departure of Santer, prime minister and Minister for Finance. Meeting him again was like resuming a conversation with someone who had temporarily left the room. The issues were still the same; only the agenda had changed. But the other ministers took more time to get to know. Nonetheless, slowly I came to like the energy and directness of Gerrit Zalm of the Netherlands and Pedro Solbes of Spain. Goran Persson, a social democrat from Sweden, was solid with cautious common sense, and Yiannos Papantoniou of Greece was another socialist colleague with a sharp intellect and an attractive personality. Two other characters impressed me during that time: Viktor Klima from my sister party in Austria and António Sousa Franco, who subsequently arrived when António Guterres led the socialists to a great political victory in Portugal.

My awareness of the other socialist ministers led me to think about how to harness, or at least harmonise, our approach to the issues in front of us. At Dick Spring's request, owing to pressure of business elsewhere, I attended the leaders' meeting of the Party of European Socialists (PES), which took place outside Cannes two days before the formal European Council meeting commenced. The meeting is still clear in my memory and my journal notes are extensive.

It was the first time for me to meet Tony Blair and John Prescott: the former was not interested in small country representatives, the latter was more than curious about the experience of actually being in government. I led the Irish delegation to the PES meeting, which included socialist parties both in office and in opposition. In the latter category were the Germans, French, British and Portuguese, who were frustrated in being out of power. In response, the presidency of the PES, chaired by Rudolf Scharping of the German SPD, bent over backwards to accommodate their concerns. All proposed press statements were carefully vetted to make sure that no domestic feathers were ruffled by what the sister parties, meeting together, might proclaim. Andreas Papandreou, clearly ill and feeble, made a spirited and sharply focused intervention during one of our discussions. Regrettably, he was regarded as an old-fashioned politician out of touch with the post-Cold War world. Colleagues failed, in my view, to understand the struggle he had undergone to steer his country to democracy and Europeanisation. He was certainly no saint, but look at Serbia and Greece today and draw your own conclusions. An ignorance of history is a real handicap for politicians, and sadly there were too many of those around the table that day. But the Spanish and the Portuguese listened to Papandreou with respect and recognised the historical similarities of their experiences.

Progress was made, however. My proposal for a new grouping of socialist finance ministers and opposition finance spokespersons across the union, to gather every two months on the eve of the ECOFIN meeting to discuss and review the agenda of the day and report back to our respective parties, was enthusiastically received. This informal arrangement enabled me to develop a close understanding of the domestic constraints which confronted colleagues, both in and out of government. It also helped me to get to know the personalities involved and for them to know and trust me. Towards the end of the Irish presidency in 1996, that gave me a considerable advantage when seeking to propose compromise solutions.

The doubts surrounding Ireland's ability to qualify for member-ship of the euro were centred, in a large part, on whether or not Britain would remain outside the currency. While we knew the Tory government's attitude, the British Labour Party remained less clear. John Monks, the TUC general secretary, made no secret of his support for the single currency.

I first met Gordon Brown in Atlanta, Georgia, in July 1988. We were guests at the Democratic Party convention which confirmed Michael Dukakis as its presidential candidate to run against the Republican outgoing vice-president, George Bush. I liked Gordon. He was open, direct and amazed at the level of connections that the Irish had throughout the American political system. Now seven years later, he was the chancellor in waiting and I was Minister for Finance. I wanted to make contact with him. Ciarán O'Mara got in touch with Ed Balls, then Gordon's close and influential adviser. Soon after I became Minister for Finance, they eagerly accepted our offers of assistance to our sister party.

Could we keep them up to date on what was happening at the ECOFIN meetings, including the single currency project? Our response was to send to Gordon's office copies of all the ECOFIN meeting papers immediately after the meetings had concluded. When Ken Clarke stood up in the House of Commons to speak on the topic some days later, his Labour opponent had full access to the relevant papers if not the conversations which accompanied them. Ciarán went over to see Ed Balls and he, in turn, made a return visit to observe how a finance department worked from the inside and the relative relationship of programme managers to the permanent departmental staff.

On 20 January 1996, Scotland were playing Ireland in Lansdowne Road. Gordon, a keen rugby fan, accepted my invitation to come over to the match and to join a group of us for dinner afterwards in the Institute of European Affairs in North Great George's Street. Lochlann and Brenda were having their traditional pre-match lunch. Gordon was well known to many people there, if only by sight, and he was delighted with the warm welcome he received in their home. Over dinner that evening, he was introduced to a thorough analysis of the currency project, the future evolution of the European Union as the Irish present envisaged it and a broad discussion on a wide accompanying range of issues.

Contact with Gordon Brown was maintained directly and indirectly through the Party of European Socialists pre-ECOFIN meetings that took place over that time. Some weeks before the 1997 British election, Ciarán O'Mara received a phone call from Ed Balls to see if it would be possible to get the full details of the legislative structure of the Irish Central Bank and how its independence was exercised. The full text of the legislation was sent by return, but it was not until some days after he was made chancellor that we realised the significance of Gordon's chief economic adviser's request to Ciarán. The newly elected chancellor announced that the Bank of England was to be set free of government control. Henceforth, that venerable institution, and it alone, would determine interest rates, just like the Federal Reserve in Washington or the Bundesbank in Frankfurt and even the Central Bank in Dublin!

I had a political motive, of which Gordon was aware. It was very much in Ireland's interest at that time that Britain would join the single currency. While participation at the beginning was clearly impossible under the British Tories, a new Labour government might be able to move quickly. Blair's enthusiasm was matched by Brown's caution. Britain's imminent arrival into the EMU would, I believed at the time, send a signal to the markets, stabilise the relationship between Britain and the Irish/euro currencies and enhance our respective trading activities.

When Pedro Solbes assumed the presidency of the ECOFIN Council in July 1995, the contrast was electric. Almost immediately, he brought energy and clarity to our meetings. During the Spanish 'informal' in September, held in Solbes' home town of Valencia, I met for the first time Hans Tietmeyer, Jean-Claude Trichet and Eddie George, the heads of the three most important central banks in Europe. A unique aspect of the informal councils was the full participation in our discussions of the governors of all the central banks. By now familiar with the agenda and on top of the brief, I enjoyed participating fully in the various discussions and dispensed with simply reading aloud a prepared speaking note, as was the case with some of my colleagues.

At the ministers' lunch in Valencia, which did not include the governors, an impassioned debate took place about the name of the new currency. The Treaty of Maastricht had used ecu, a word in French but an acronym in English, for the European currency unit. Many of us realised that it simply did not translate and so it was agreed, reluctantly by some, that we needed a new name to ensure the credibility of a new currency. There were various suggestions, but only one real runner, the euro. It was pronounceable in all languages and self-explanatory. Ken Clarke, a pro-European but a prisoner of the divided British Tory cabinet, was very vocal. He wanted any name but the euro. With classic British ingenuity, he floated the name of the florin, an old European unit of currency, but got no takers. Later in December 1995 at the European Council in Madrid, John Major ran a rearguard campaign to challenge our informal ECOFIN proposal to change the name from Ecu to euro. He was confronted by a no-nonsense Helmut Kohl. Sitting beside John Bruton and Dick Spring in the large conference centre outside Madrid, I watched Major, the beleaguered Conservative prime minister, struggling to explain to Kohl his ideological and political problems. The name euro would be seen in Britain as overtly political, he argued, and not just common-sense market economics. Kohl's response, even through the modulated voices of the translators, was blunt and brutal. 'John, this project is political. The single currency is the necessary bridge to a united Europe and we all have to cross it. It will be called the euro!'

Throughout 1996, at our monthly ECOFIN lunches, when the topic was discussed, the conversation frequently turned to 'the ins' and 'the outs'. This was the shorthand reference to which countries would qualify or choose to join the single currency from among the fifteen member states. It was Yiannos Papantoniou who coined that phrase. Few people at that time, including perhaps himself, believed that Greece would be with the first group of countries to join. On occasion a slight tension was perceptible between the Ins and the Outs groups, but Ken Clarke cleverly and definitively resolved it.

'Look,' he argued, 'we may probably not be part of the new currency and you all know my personal views on that, but it still remains critically important for Britain that this project, in itself, is a success. Failure would damage us all.'

It was at one of these luncheon exchanges that, I recall, Theo Waigel first introduced the idea of the Stability Pact. This was a set of tight, national budgetary rules for all countries using the single currency. At the time, the prospect was beginning to emerge, notwithstanding the convergence criteria, that other countries outside the core group would be admitted to the new currency. Waigel did not explicitly refer to Italy, but we all knew that this was the only large economy whose domestic economic mismanagement could seriously affect the rest of the single-currency partners.

I have no doubt that there was some Franco-German preconsultation on the idea, and Gerrit Zalm's instant supportive intervention could not have been entirely driven by his own clear views on the matter. In principle, none of us around that table disagreed with the concept. If the Germans needed the Stability Pact, politically, to persuade their now united citizens to give up the Deutschmark, then we would facilitate them, as far as possible. Closer to home, I could also see the benefits. The budgetary rules of the Stability Pact would help any Irish Finance Minister to curtail the excessive demands of line ministers for more cash.

In Verona, the Italians hosted the informal ECOFIN over the second weekend of April 1996. The city was renowned for its opera but we had some music of our own at the meeting. Alexandre Lamfalussy, President of the European Monetary Institute, the forerunner of the European Central Bank, had just given an update on the logistics concerning the design, printing and distribution of the bank notes. Following that, Yiannos Papantoniou indicated to the chair that he wished to speak and, when called, enquired about the wording and the lettering that would be printed on the notes. When asked to clarify, he bluntly stated that he assumed the word euro would be spelt in both the Roman and Greek alphabets. Before anyone else could speak, Waigel exploded. Leaning forward over the long refectory table at which we were seated, so as to look his

Greek counterpart straight in the eye, he continued in animated terms. 'Look,' he said, 'for fuck's sake, I am having more than enough bloody trouble trying to sell this project to my own people, as it is, and now you want me to put funny lettering on the notes as well. It is just simply not fucking on, and anyway, it is entirely academic. You guys are never going to qualify to join!'

I had never seen such energy in the man and the rest of us were more than stunned, but Yiannos was not a bit cowed. He held his ground, saying quietly but firmly that if ECOFIN could not agree to his position, then his prime minister, Costas Simitis, would raise it at the forthcoming June European Council in Florence. As it happened, he did, and if you look at any euro note today you will see what the outcome was.

While there was to be one set of designs for the bank notes, to be determined by an independent competition run by the European Monetary Institute, the ministers at ECOFIN had the final say on the design of the coins. The values of the units were readily agreed. One side of the coin would have a common design indicating its value and the other side would reflect the member state in which it had originated – in Ireland's case, our national emblem, the harp, was the obvious choice.

Throughout 1996, including during the Irish presidency, I found myself frequently being asked to speak at various functions and to explain the currency project. This was not an easy task, but having spoken to many people, some whose eyes occasionally glazed over, I developed a metaphor. The three stages were like building a pontoon bridge across a turbulent river. Each pontoon represented the national currency. The flow in the river, different under each pontoon, reflected the separate performance of each economy. The first phase was to get the rhythm of movement of each pontoon in tune with the others. This involved converging the performance of the different economies. The second stage was to connect the pontoons so that they moved as one. The final stage was now to lock them together, secure them to the riverbanks on either side, and erect the railings of the permanent bridge.

Many commentators, including lots of economists, argued that

Ireland should not join the single currency if Britain chose to stay out. Too much of our trade, in particular our domestically owned, small-business sector, was critically dependent on the British market. Some commentators were Eurosceptics and took their opinions from a lot of the London-based print media. There was some merit to the argument that if the euro was simply going to be the Deutschmark zone renamed, then we would have a problem. But increasingly, Italy, Spain and Portugal began to look like possible candidates. Much ink and paper was used in debating the operational merits of the project and the technical problems of this unique, and as yet untested, major political initiative. I spoke to many a doubtful gathering of business and finance people, both at home and abroad, particularly in the second half of 1996. Frequently I said to them, remembering Kohl's intervention in Madrid, that the single currency was first and foremost a political project.

The single currency was something to which the vast majority of European leaders were politically committed. Our job, as financial engineers, was not to query the design but to make sure that it stood up. With many audiences, I compared the European Union's single internal market to an arch, but I would add that it was incomplete at the top and so inherently unstable. Until such time as we fitted the keystone at the head of the arch, our entire structure would never be secure. That keystone was the single currency and its precise insertion would secure the satisfactory working of our internal market.

Ireland took on its fifth EU presidency on 1 July 1996. In the preceding months a great deal of preparation had been done. I recalled my time as President of the Social Affairs Council back in 1985 when the task was less onerous and there were only ten member states. Now it was quite different. I had seen what my three ECOFIN predecessors had done. I wanted to do the business of the day job and to make a good impression for the country. Therefore, I took a direct personal involvement in the arrangements, including the hospitality of the informal weekend.

The main informal meeting was to take place in Dublin Castle on 21 September. A reception was to be held on the Friday and a dinner on the Saturday evening. It was still the early days of the Celtic Tiger and many visitors who came to Dublin enjoyed a visit to the pub. So I decided to bring the pub to the visitors. I hired Kitty O'Shea's, as I had done in 1985, for the Friday night. Extensive discussions had taken place directly between publicans Kevin and Brian Loughney, myself and officials in the department. There were to be no formal seating arrangements and no speeches. As was normal, many of the ministers and central bankers brought their wives or partners and the informal nature of our arrangements more than suited their mood.

Since I could not bring them to an empty pub, we provided a genuine local atmosphere by inviting constituency members and friends. Towards the end of an enjoyable night, Ken Clarke was the last of my main guests still in the pub. He was surrounded and deep in conversation with a number of young men, including my son Malachi who had asked Ken to join them. As I looked at them crowded around the table in the extension of the pub, I asked his wife if I should go and rescue him. 'Not at all,' was her reply. 'He is fully enjoying himself because he wouldn't be able to do this at home.' I was told later that when he joined the company, he was bombarded by a series of heavy questions about Northern Ireland and the relationship between Dublin and London. When the tirade had subsided and he had a chance to respond, he opened by saying, 'I support Nottingham Forest. Who do you fellows follow?' An hour later he was still there and it was after midnight before I finally got him away and so could go home myself to prepare for the following long day.

Sir Nigel Wicks and his Monetary Committee, an official-level advisory body, had been working strenuously to put flesh on the bones of the Stability Pact. A number of net issues had been identified but their resolution required clear political decisions from ECOFIN. The most important part of our meeting would be doing exactly this. Later, Sir Nigel's committee could proceed with the detailed work. Then we would be able to complete the job in December. The heads of government would finally decide on this controversial measure at the European Council meeting in Dublin. Like highly detailed replies to college examination questions, I can no longer remember the precise content, but I will never forget the intensity which surrounded them. As Wicks posed each question, preceded by a short explanatory comment, I asked him to outline his proposed solution. Then, because we were fifteen ministers, I confined the floor only to those who had a specific objection.

If a discussion opened up, I kept a tight rein on it. The personal relationships that I had developed, both within the PES pre-ECOFIN bi-monthly meetings and with other ministerial colleagues, now became very valuable. We were not at a seminar, but wrestling with a difficult set of choices which required considered political and technical decisions. On more than one occasion, Philippe Maystadt, the Belgian Finance Minister, proposed elegant solutions to what seemed to be impossible dilemmas. By late afternoon, we had concluded our business. In St Patrick's Hall, I informed the international and European press that we had made great progress and were on course to complete the design of the Stability Pact in time for the Irish summit in December.

There had been a lot of speculation about whether or not Ireland would meet the criteria and be able to join the single currency on day one. If we were going to be in that league, then interest rates on Irish bonds and loan notes issued by the NTMA would fall as Ireland converged towards the Deutschmark and the single currency. The potential savings were enormous, given the size of our national debt, which reached its height of 128 per cent of gross national product in 1987 and was at 88 per cent and falling by 1994. Paddy Mullarkey was particularly anxious about the perception of Ireland, not necessarily by domestic commentators, but more critically by London and Frankfurt-based financial journalists. Diligently, he ensured that the Irish embassy staff in Bonn followed up unfavourable mentions or exclusions of Ireland in news stories about the currency project. The erring journalists were fully briefed by an Irish diplomat about the country's rapidly improving economic performance.

During the Saturday lunch for ministers, Jean Arthuis, the French Finance Minister, raised for the first time the issue of an inner council of euro currency ministers. His idea was that the economic governance of the new eurozone was equally as important as the successful introduction of the single currency. After all, the project was named 'economic and monetary union'. He wanted these ministers to meet before the ECOFIN proper and agree their approach on a number of relevant issues. There was quick support from Germany and the Netherlands, but Ken Clarke and Yiannos Papantoniou were less happy. It smacked to them of a club within a club, from which they would be excluded. I raised some doubts myself about this two-tiered concept. In response, Theo Waigel, who was sitting beside me, asked, sotto voce, what was I worried about. Ireland after all, was going to be in the founding group of countries.

Later in Dublin Castle I reported to Paddy Mullarkey and other senior civil servants about what had happened during the ministerial luncheon. After I described the French proposal, Noel O'Gorman, second secretary at the Department of Finance, confirmed that a similar idea had been tentatively raised at Sir Nigel's Monetary Committee, of which he was a member. But Mullarkey really got excited when I described the German Finance Minister's comments. In fact, he asked me to repeat what Waigel had said. For the secretary general of the Department of Finance, this was great news and proof positive of the growing credibility of the Irish position.

I have always been curious about the workplaces of other colleagues and took a particular delight, when I had the opportunity, of visiting the Capitol Building in Washington, the Westminster House of Commons and the spectacular Hungarian parliament in Budapest. When it came to selecting a venue in Dublin for the large dinner on the Saturday, the newly refurbished dining room in Leinster House was the obvious choice. Once some minor irritating difficulties were got out of the way, I ensured that for the first time the elegant Palladian building, formerly the palace of the Duke of Leinster, was open on Saturday evening to the guests and to the many Irish civil servants who had helped to make the presidency successful. A string quartet greeted people as they came into the impressive two-storey high entrance hall. If they wished, they could explore the building and visit the Seanad and the Dáil chambers. When finally seated in the dining room, they received three differently prepared sides of Irish salmon, a main course of traditional corned beef with vegetables, followed by a selection of fine Irish cheeses. The dessert was a compote of autumn berries. Making people comfortable, at ease with themselves, while proudly presenting the best in things Irish was an important part of what I wanted to do.

As we approached Christmas, it became evident that the political decisions taken in September had cleared the way. There were three formal ECOFIN meetings before the European Council meeting was held in Dublin Castle on 13 and 14 December. Looking back through the official conclusions of those meetings, it is clear that the Monetary Committee made rapid progress in preparing the detailed documents for ECOFIN on the third and final stage of EMU.

The European Council in Madrid, the year before, had formally recognised that Stage III could not be achieved by 1997, the original target. It did confirm, however, that it most definitely would happen on 1 January 1999. By this time, based on the reports from the European Monetary Institute, the decision on what countries met the criteria would be taken early in 1998.

On 2 December, in Brussels, we failed to get political agreement on matters outstanding on the Stability Pact. Waigel had been delayed because he was attending the funeral of a close friend and colleague in Bavaria. Readily I agreed to defer the item, saying that we understood, in Ireland, the political culture of funerals. In his place at the time was Jürgen Stark, the State Secretary for Finance, who had attended most of the ECOFIN meetings. His position was unusual in that it was half political and half senior civil service. Nevertheless, he was a clear authority on these issues and had the ear of the German Bundesbank.

When Waigel arrived, I adjourned the meeting so that Stark could brief him on what had happened and to prepare him for the work on the final details of Stage III. But when the meeting resumed, it was early evening and the mood was wrong. Waigel simply was not in a position to do business. The fact that he felt he was being hurried on the outstanding issues meant that I could not get German agreement. I had hoped for substantial progress, but I was not surprised by Waigel's response. The European Council meeting was now less than two weeks away. So, realising that no further progress could be made, I closed the meeting; but, in doing so, I announced that we would have a resumed attempt at finding agreement at a special ECOFIN meeting, which I now convened for 12 December in Dublin Castle.

The following morning I flew to Madrid. Richard Ryan, Ireland's energetic ambassador, had established a Spain–Ireland Business Club to promote commercial relations between the two countries. At his invitation, I had agreed to speak on the single currency and the topicality of the issue ensured a large attendance, including the media. Fresh from Brussels the day before, I gave an up-to-date account of how things stood. By now, Spain had a new centre-right government, led by José María Aznar with his Minister for Finance, Rodrigo Rato. All the economic indicators suggested that both Spain and Portugal would now qualify to join the single currency, but everyone in Madrid knew that the political will to proceed was critically dependent on Germany getting a Stability Pact with sufficient safeguards that would enable Kohl and Waigel to sell it.

When we met in Dublin on 12 December the momentum for progress had grown. Soon into the meeting we were down to three remaining issues, with the French and Germans failing to agree. I had made arrangements for food to be provided and so we adjourned at 7.30 p.m. At that stage, I went round the council room and approached Waigel and Stark. Quietly but firmly, I asked them if they were prepared to do business and if so would they please do it tonight. They indicated that they would. Paddy Mullarkey had been particularly helpful in drafting a presidency compromise, but the Germans had also just proposed an alternative compromise to me which they wanted to put to the meeting. At Paddy's suggestion, I ran the German proposal first to let them know that, while we were trying to accommodate them, they could see for themselves the extent of opposition to their position. The way was then clear to run the Irish presidency proposal, which was accepted.

Despite the progress we were making, I had been utterly distracted by something that occurred during that night of our meeting. For some time, going back to before the Irish presidency, there had been tension between the Tánaiste's advisers and mine. I was not directly aware of this but Ciarán O'Mara kept me regularly informed, particularly after the Labour programme managers' and advisers' pre-cabinet meeting on Monday evenings. Some of the advisers felt that their Labour Finance Minister was too strict in controlling expenditure. But both Ciarán and I knew that we had to ensure that Ireland's budget figures enabled the country to qualify for the euro. The big prize down the line would be currency stability and historically low interest rates. In addition, our successful running of the economy was envied by others. It had never grown so fast – 8.3 per cent in 1995 – and unemployment was falling rapidly, as was inflation. Perhaps this high-profile success, which attracted a lot of positive media comment, was resented by the people around Dick on his behalf. As Minister for Foreign Affairs, he was extremely busy, particularly during the presidency, but he also had to contend with the Northern Ireland peace talks, his responsibilities as party leader, and mind his demanding and distant Kerry North constituency. The memory of the four-vote survival in 1987 was still very prominent. To keep all these different activities going was incredibly time-consuming and exhausting. As a result, Dick was a terse and tight time manager. There was little room for informal space and chats or reflection, which would have helped us to understand what we were all doing.

At 11.30 p.m. that evening, Ciarán O'Mara told me to take a call from Dick Spring. I moved from the presidency chair to the side wall of the conference room in Dublin Castle and took the mobile. Dick informed me that the talks on the national pay deal with the social partners, which had been going on for some months, had reached a critical point. This was news to me. We had been resisting, in Finance, the scale of the pay demands coming from the unions. I was looking for public sector productivity improvements and other economies to ensure that we would continue to meet the criteria for membership of the single currency and to maintain budgetary discipline, especially with regard to public service pay. John Hurley, the secretary with responsibility for the pay talks, and I intended to stretch the negotiations over the New Year, making it appear as difficult as possible before we would agree to the inevitable compromise.

But now Dick was saying that Bill Attley, general secretary of SIPTU, was telling him and Taoiseach John Bruton that the higher figure on the table simply had to be accepted. Even more difficult than that: it had to be accepted that very night. The one remaining working week before Christmas would be used to sell the deal to the relevant trade-union officials and make the necessary preparations for the balloting of all members early in the new year.

I was being gazumped and bushwhacked right at the time of the critical discussions which were going on at ECOFIN. Despite being furious with Dick, I also knew that I was powerless. The Taoiseach and Tánaiste had agreed to the pay deal.

It was a very angry president who resumed the chair of the ECOFIN meeting and, with my breath spitting fire, I told Paddy Mullarkey what had happened. Turning my attention to the meeting again, it was now clear that, even though the French and Germans had made substantial progress, both finance ministers felt that the residual burden of this political task was too heavy for them. So at my recommendation, we decided to refer the outstanding matter to the heads of government, who would commence the European Council meeting the following morning. The ECOFIN meeting finally finished at 3.00 a.m.

At 8.30 a.m., back in my office after a few hours' sleep, I took a call from Dick. Before he could begin to speak, I let out a roar at him and proceeded to have the one and only intense, awful row we ever had. I told him he could do the bloody job himself, if he wanted, because I was on the point of resigning. I must have been at some pitch because Hannah O'Riordan not only closed the door into the office, but ushered the civil servants working around her out of their room and up to the cafeteria for a sudden coffee break.

I got into the car with a quiet Ciarán O'Mara, Denise Rogers and

Joe Lennon at 9.15 a.m. I was seething with anger and didn't speak. Nashie didn't open his mouth either. As the car travelled in angry silence through the city, I reflected on the growing tensions between the Tánaiste's office and my own. Was it rivalry between our advisers or did Dick resent my increased power as Finance Minister? Was he envious of my growing economic reputation and command of my department? I could not see why he should be, because I felt that he was doing such a terrific job in Foreign Affairs, particularly on Northern Ireland. We arrived in Dublin Castle close to 10.00 a.m.

To signal my annoyance with Dick and John Bruton, I did not enter the council room until exactly 10.30 a.m. I had stood in a meeting complex of Dublin Castle having a cup of coffee with Denise. The place was packed with prime ministers, heads of government, foreign and finance ministers, civil servants and EU officials. The stairway down to the large ante-room, adjacent to the main meeting room on the basement level, was crowded. When the television camera crews were finally ushered out by the government press secretary, John Bruton as President of the European Council opened the meeting, with Dick on one side and myself on the other. Dick and I did not exchange a single word.

When the report of the previous night's ECOFIN meeting was heard, with the suggested referral back to the heads of government that they should make the final compromise, there was some dismay. Prime ministers started to consult with each other. In effect, there was a de facto adjournment. At once ministers began discussing with officials. John Bruton turned to me to know if it was possible to have one last go at finding a solution. By this stage Kohl was talking to his close friend and neighbour Jean-Claude Juncker, asking him to go off with the presidency and the disputing ministers to see if a compromise could be reached. In turn, I went over to Gerrit Zalm, who was sitting beside Dutch prime minister, Wim Kok, and asked him, as the incoming ECOFIN president, to leave the room with me.

A small group of finance ministers, led by me, left the council meeting room looking for a place to resume our negotiations. Fortunately David Byers, manager of the Dublin Castle complex, came to our help. Realising we needed a quiet and secure room, he led us down a series of corridors and into a meeting room.

As we were beginning our meeting, Ken Clarke's head came peering around the door. Instinctively, I called on him to come in and join us, his comments from an earlier time still in my head. Beyond doubt he was respected and admired by us all. His good humour often lightened a tense moment and he handled, with style, the contradictions of his pro-European views and the formal position of his government – but at no stage ever letting down the official British position. Soon we were into the detail, arguing very familiar points and clarifying issues. Jean-Claude was immensely helpful, switching effortlessly from German to French and back to English. We were making slow but steady progress. Then Gerrit intervened vigorously.

'Look,' he began, 'we are at the edge of success. This position now is really the only one that can be achieved. I can tell you for sure that the Dutch presidency will not be able to improve on it. There is a mood to do the business now, just before Christmas. I can't guarantee you that we'll be able to recreate that mood again.'

The French and German ministers looked at each other, anxious to agree but nervous to accept. I again pressed them to reach out and, with the urgings of Jean-Claude and the very solid encouragement of Ken Clarke, they did.

I now had an agreement. But first Theo Waigel and Jürgen Stark wanted to inform Kohl. Likewise, Jean Arthuis wanted to run his compromise past Jacques Chirac. We went back to the main complex to find that the council was now in recess. Close to the large staircase a group soon gathered around Kohl and Chirac with all their advisers. There was tension and excitement as hurried conversations took place. Would the two heads of government agree? There, with the bulk of the compromise incorporating the German numbers and figures, Chirac asked for one addition. He wanted the word 'growth' somewhere so as to emphasise employment. At last it was agreed that the new entity would be called the Stability and Growth Pact.

Now back in formal council session, the deal, happily announced by the Irish presidency, was formally accepted and agreed. It was all over. The Dutch presidency would complete the legal technicalities and the European Council would sign off the project in Amsterdam in 1997. Early in 1998 the qualifying member states would be known. Ireland had once again run a very successful presidency, and my contribution had been central. The political success of negotiating the Stability and Growth Pact was a major part of it.

In Ireland, we were facing an election year and campaign plans were being devised, though I was not involved in the detailed planning. One question that was discussed informally among ministers was the preferred date of the election. Should it be in June or in the autumn? Economically, things were continuing to improve. Brendan Lynch kept telling me that the department's internal economic projections and forecasts were excessively cautious. At the same time, the public knew that the mandate of the government ran out in November 1997. Demands for increased expenditure on a whole range of matters were now being articulated by vested interests and lobby groups. They knew well how to pressurise government backbench TDs, let alone government ministers. Having seen the way I had been treated in relation to the social partnership talks, I feared that we might have been put under extraordinary pressure during the summer and early September. This led me to support the earlier time of June.

In the end, it was a June election, and the Rainbow Coalition was defeated. Bertie Ahern and Mary Harney were able, with the help of four friendly ex-Fianna Fáil Independent deputies, to form a government with a working majority. The election result also meant that Labour had lost most of the gains of 1992.

The new government would not be formed until 28 June, after the European Council had completed its work. This had been informally agreed between the party leaders so as to facilitate a satisfactory participation by Ireland in the European Council, which was completing its work under the Dutch presidency. The inter-governmental conference was to conclude with the Amsterdam Treaty, and the final technical decisions on the single currency still had to be decided. Irish continuity was considered important by all concerned.

Given the extraordinary performance of the Irish economy since 1995 and the success of the Irish presidency the following year, my European colleagues could not understand why we had not won the general election. I tried to explain to them the complexities of Irish politics but their blank faces indicated that I was not making sense, at least to them.

Why did we lose? I wrote soon afterwards that we had failed to convey a clear and concise message on the issue of income tax in our manifesto. In an unprecedented front-page editorial towards the end of the campaign, the *Irish Independent* declared in its headline that 'It's Payback Time'. The simplicity of Fianna Fáil's income tax options to a 20 per cent standard rate and a 42 per cent higher rate had a clarity that everyone could readily understand. By contrast, our joint programme, between the three outgoing political parties, of broadening tax bands and reducing rates, while socially more progressive, was just not as easily understood by the electorate.

However, I think there was a deeper reason which was felt but not readily expressed by large sections of the electorate who rejected us in 1997. By going into government with Fianna Fáil back in 1993, we were perceived by a large anti-Fianna Fáil vote of having betrayed their trust and also the resounding mandate which they had given to us – thirty-three seats! Notwithstanding what we had actually said in our manifesto of 1992, combined with Fine Gael's post-election attitude to Democratic Left in the coalition talks, that section of the electorate felt, I believe, very angry with Labour and were simply waiting to punish us. When we then broke with Fianna Fáil in 1994 and formed the Rainbow Coalition without the mandate of a general election, I believe we proceeded to alienate a section of the electorate, including large sections of Fianna Fáil supporters and members of the trade-union movement, who had been happy with the left-of-centre Fianna Fáil/Labour coalition. Whatever about the manifestos and the difference in taxation policy, perhaps it was the perceived shifts in Labour's political alliances that were the principle cause of our defeat.

Chapter 19

Leader of the Labour Party
1997–2002

It was overcast and rain threatened, or at least a soft drizzle seemed to be certain. In the distance the deer of Dublin's Phoenix Park could be seen through the trees. Close by, Conan was running from tree to tree, searching for squirrels and calling on Liz and myself to help him. But that Sunday, we were discussing a search of a different kind – the leadership of the Labour Party.

The previous Wednesday, 5 November 1997, Dick Spring had announced his intention to retire from the leadership after fifteen years. He had held a conference the following Friday, in which he bade farewell to the large assembled group of parliamentary colleagues, friends and supporters. There was a vast media turnout and much sympathetic coverage over the weekend.

The question now was who would succeed him. I had been deputy leader for eight years. I did not expect, when Dick had been elected leader back in 1982, to ever become leader because he was four years younger than me. But now I had to make a decision. Did I want to be leader? Was I prepared to campaign hard to win the votes of the parliamentary party and the general council – a total of sixty-four votes – who would make the choice? It was not a decision that I could make on my own. A number of things had recently happened and I was not sure if I could be the type of leader which the party needed. From the evening of the announcement, Liz and myself considered the situation. Many people close to me, particularly Denise, Ciarán and others, were very anxious for me to go for the job.

The June 1997 general election saw Labour lose seventeen of the thirty-three seats we had won in 1992. While I was not too surprised that we had lost the election, I was horrified at the defeats suffered by some prominent members. Niamh Bhreathnach, one of the best ministers for Education the country had ever had; Eithne Fitzgerald, who had pioneered the radical Freedom of Information Act; and Joan Burton, who had highlighted development co-operation work in the Third World, all lost their seats. Other hard-working deputies, like Joe Costello, Brian Fitzgerald, Seán Ryan and John Mulvihill, were not returned. In Cork South-Central, Toddy O'Sullivan, a Minister of State and former Lord Mayor of that wonderful city, was defeated for the fifth and last seat. There was no doubt that Labour had delivered substantially on the issues on which we had campaigned. We had clearly demonstrated our ability to manage the economy and create the resources necessary to implement our promises, but it simply had not worked.

In Bloomfield House, just outside Mullingar, over two days in early September 1997, the parliamentary party met to review what had happened but, more importantly, to look towards the future. Mary Robinson's mould-breaking and innovative seven-year presidential term was up that autumn. She had succeeded in redefining the role of president and, consequently, the potential of an office which had previously been restricted and which had made little impact on the Irish people. Before her term was completed she had resigned and gone to Geneva to be the United Nations High Commissioner for Human Rights. The mood at our meeting was mixed and the discussion about a possible Labour candidate for the Áras was stilted. Many people present were aware of Michael D. Higgins' interest, or at least his eagerness to be asked. But that did not happen. Others, many of whom were critical of Dick Spring on a regular basis and repeated their criticism in our post-mortem on the election, wanted him to repeat the magic of the 1990 presidential campaign. The meeting ended inconclusively.

The political stability of the new minority Fianna Fáil/Progressive Democrat coalition government was unclear. There was a lot of speculation about corruption allegations, which questioned the duration of the government. Pressure began to build in the early autumn and ultimately led to the resignation of the Minister for

Foreign Affairs, Ray Burke, on 7 October, in response to his own government's decision to establish a tribunal of inquiry into the substantial allegations of planning corruption in the Dublin county area. As we left the shores of Lough Ennell and Bloomfield House, Dick had a mandate from the parliamentarians present to come up with an acceptable candidate for the presidential election, because nobody present was prepared to put forward a name.

When, some days later, Adi Roche, the charismatic Chernobyl victims' campaigner, was announced as Labour's prospective candidate, there was both surprise and delight. The first opinion poll placed her very well against the probable Fianna Fáil candidate, Albert Reynolds, and Fine Gael's candidate, Mary Banotti. She looked credible and strong. It seemed that Dick Spring had done it again. Or had he? The tight three-candidate race was challenged by Dana – aka Rosemary Scallon – the legendary Eurovision Song Contest winner of 1970. She had succeeded in persuading four local authorities to nominate her, a significant political achievement in itself.

As the race unfolded, Fianna Fáil's former Taoiseach Albert Reynolds was shafted by its new Taoiseach when the party realised that he could be beaten. More to the point, Bertie Ahern feared that, if Albert won, he might prove to be a dangerous meddler in the delicately balanced peace process, which Albert Reynolds had done so much to drive. The return of Fianna Fáil to government in June had very conveniently been followed, a few weeks later, with the announcement by Sinn Féin/IRA of a new ceasefire. The original ceasefire of 1994 had been shattered with the destruction and loss of life in Canary Wharf on 9 February 1996, allegedly because the British government was dragging its feet in advancing the talks.

Fianna Fáil discarded their former Taoiseach and supported their own Mary Robinson lookalike: Mary McAleese. She was a well-known academic lawyer and a former current-affairs reporter with RTÉ. Originally from Belfast, McAleese was now teaching in Queen's University. She had been added to the Fianna Fáil Dublin South-East ticket in the 1987 general election, where she had polled poorly. In the summer of 1997, she launched a persuasive campaign to win the Fianna Fáil nomination. At the beginning, few people thought that she had a chance, but still she swept to victory. With the Fianna Fáil presidential candidate declared, the contest was now dramatically changed. The nation was presented with four women and one man – Derek Nally, a retired garda, who strongly identified with Victim Support, a group dedicated to obtaining justice for the victims of crime, had successfully followed Dana's local authority route for a nomination.

Adi Roche quickly emerged to be very good at what she did, but sadly she was not equipped for the job on offer. When the votes were counted on 31 October, her humiliating fourth place behind Dana was very hard on her. But the damage, politically, was greater elsewhere. Whether he had already decided that he would go the following year, when his second six-year term as leader was up, or was prompted to earlier action by the disastrous presidential election results, only Dick can say. But go he did, and his successor was to be chosen the following Thursday afternoon.

After announcing his resignation, Dick called Brendan Howlin and myself, the two likely leadership candidates, into his office. Whatever happened, we agreed that we would provide no entertainment for the media by campaigning against each other on the airwaves. Instead, we would confine our energies to the sixty-four electors, comprising members of the parliamentary party and the national council, in the knowledge that whatever the outcome, we would afterwards have to work together.

As Conan continued his search for squirrels in the Phoenix Park, Liz and I discussed the implications of my standing. As deputy leader, I did not have that much extra to do and, besides, from the beginning Dick had run a tight ship, even after I was elected deputy leader in 1989. Could I stay on in that post? I wondered aloud, but dismissed it as I heard myself say it. If I did not want to run for the top job, then maybe I had been too long in the number two slot. The implications for us were real. Ministerial office was very hard on family life. Looking back now at a crowded diary, I remember just how intense that time had actually been. Conan was three and entering a new phase and Liz, understandably, was torn between the family's needs and the future possibilities. However, she knew the leadership was something that I had always wanted and that I would not be happy with myself and with my family if I did not at least try for it.

Walking purposefully towards the car with Conan perched on my shoulders, we had reached a decision. Over a very welcome cup of coffee in the café of the newly opened National Museum in Collins Barracks, our minds were decided and we started to formulate our plans. I would campaign hard for the leadership, which I thought I could win. We agreed that we would give it our best. If it worked out, fine; if not, we would, as a family, move on to other things. An IMS opinion poll published some days later, but before the Thursday election, showed that I was clearly the public's preferred candidate. Some months later, this was a matter of some controversy, but happily it did not cause any damage to the close working relationship between Brendan and myself.

When the votes were counted on 13 November, I had won comfortably: thirty-seven to twenty-seven. Immediately I proposed that Brendan Howlin be elected deputy leader. This was accepted by all present. The meeting was then concluded and we went across, through Leinster House, to the National Gallery for a press conference. In the days before the leadership vote, and reasonably confident of the outcome, I had asked Ronan O'Brien, the parliamentary party research officer, to prepare a draft speech for the press conference to which we were now heading. On the way to the press conference, I asked him if he would take on the role of chef de cabinet to the new leader of the Labour Party. His answer was yes, and he did an excellent job. At home the night before, as we discussed the prospect ahead of us, Liz urged me to make sure that there was a reference to Frank Cluskey in my remarks. In agreeing with her, I said that Corish could not be excluded either for all sorts of reasons, not least for the very presence of Brendan Howlin. She then came up with the reference to the two of them somewhere up in the socialist sky, looking down favourably on the outcome of this electoral contest. It was a line that was picked up by many of the media.

Brendan Howlin was magnanimous in defeat. The speech he had prepared, he told the gathering in the National Gallery, was now in the shredder. He won great admiration for his positive, sincere and unscripted congratulations. When we had concluded the press conference, the initial response of the media to the leadership result was warm. The following day, by pure coincidence, Brendan and I met in the corridors of Leinster House and had an unplanned lunch together. There, in the privacy of the small dining room, we agreed our approach on a number of issues. I was happy to reassure him about his own role for the future, and indeed that of others who were close to him. As we discussed the issues which confronted us, we discovered, not really to our mutual surprise, that we had similar views on what way to proceed.

To begin with, we were now facing two by-elections which would be held in the new year. Jim Kemmy, the Labour deputy for Limerick East, the larger-than-life socialist, had died suddenly in September and, when the Labour Party decided to call the by-election, it was decided that the consequential North Dublin by-election, caused by Ray Burke's resignation, would be held on the same day.

At Brendan's suggestion, I agreed to the idea that a special conference to signal the new direction of the party should take place after the by-elections. It would be a one-day event, a showcase within which we could present, both to ourselves and to the wider public, the post-Dick Spring Labour Party.

In the meantime, before Christmas, a good deal of immediate work had to be done. Ronan O'Brien proved to be a very good choice as chef de cabinet. The same age as my son Malachi, he had come straight into Leinster House from UCD in 1992 to work with Derek McDowell, the new Labour deputy for Dublin North-Central. In fact, he was part of a most impressive group of Labour Youth activists, including Michael McLoughlin, David Leach, Conal McDevitt, Fearghal O'Boyle, Amie Tallon, Aidan Culhane and Des Cullen. They reminded me in so many ways of myself years before. Because I was going to have someone working close to me on a daily basis, I made the deliberate choice to jump a generation. I also wanted to send a clear signal to the parliamentary party that mine would be a very different kind of leadership. Ronan knew them all. He also had special qualities. Immensely mature for his age, he could see around complex political corners. I do not recall ever meeting anyone with his experience who possessed the same level of political wisdom. In time, I came to admire and respect his judgement and was frequently guided by him. The perception, in latter years, that Dick had been run by an impenetrable group of non-elected personalities grated with some members of the parliamentary party. Within the tight constraints of resources that existed at that time, I was able to promote Ronan, Tom Butler and Denise to new positions.

Both Ray Kavanagh, general secretary, and Marion Boushell, deputy general secretary, of the Labour Party were supportive. A member of Dublin South-East for many years, Ray was enthusiastic about my victory. He wanted the best for the party and for me. I looked at the resources being used in 17 Ely Place, Labour's head-quarters, to see how it could be better connected to the parliamentary party on the one hand and the party on the other. The disconnected head office was always a complaint, real or imagined, from members around the country. Indeed, when canvassing in the course of pursuing the leadership, I met time and again with the same point and I was determined to do something about it. Right from the start I had many plans, including the renovation of the headquarters building. Despite the inevitable resistance to change, especially when it can be inconvenient, the work was done. Because of the small nature of the building, in retrospect I think I expected too much from the project. But we did make it more effective.

Back in Leinster House, I also made a number of physical changes to the layout and furniture. These were done not only to improve working conditions, but also to send a signal that things were changing demonstrably. The open door to my office on the top corridor of the 1932 extension was a message to all who passed by. There would no longer be a sentinel at the gate! We did however implement a new, more modified version of management control when we moved to the new Leinster House offices in 2000. Nevertheless, the underlying message remained.

Tom Butler, a Labour Party activist, had joined the press office in 1993 when he left Trinity College. With the change of government, he was the parliamentary press officer, working closely with Ronan O'Brien. Clearly, Tom had an ability for appreciating presentation and the visual aspects of the job. With tact and professionalism he persuaded me to change the frames of my glasses. The existing ones, he allowed me to conclude, made my face appear to be more plump and fat than was desirable. The sheer demands on a public figure to avoid adverse media comment, in the non-political sections of an increasingly indifferent printed media, were a revelation to me. How you were seen to be seen, let alone perceived, can and does influence the casual throwaway comments by a journalist! When polled, by chance, the following day, a voting citizen may offer an authoritative assessment based on nothing you have either said or done, but merely on how you look, through the eyes of some journalist.

By the end of November, the new team had settled in. The main focus was on the immediate by-election contests, in addition to the day job of parliamentary opposition. The new Taoiseach, Bertie Ahern, was very nervous in the chamber at the start of the new Dáil session. In addition, the Tánaiste, Mary Harney, was highly defensive. She had run a populist campaign, as party leader, and made a number of gaffes. As a result, her party lost seats, including that of Michael McDowell in Dublin South-East. He bitterly criticised her leadership and subsequently let his membership lapse, effectively leaving the party he helped found.

The obvious candidate for Dublin North was Seán Ryan, who had lost his seat the previous June. In Limerick East, former Senator Jan O'Sullivan was the candidate. She had originally been known as one of Kemmy's Femmies, a reference to the radical, progressive and courageous stands on women's rights that Jim Kemmy had taken over the years, much to the discomfort of the conservative class in that city. Now, with some time on our hands, and in control of the date, we did our research.

Jack Jones, an ex-army officer from Tipperary, had been to the forefront of market research in Ireland. He had set up the Market Research Bureau of Ireland (MRBI) many years previously, principally to service the growing commercial demand for detailed and scientific market research. In the past he had done work for the Labour Party and we turned to him again for information and to help us run the campaign. We wanted to know what the level of support was in the two constituencies. When the fieldwork and research were completed, Ronan O'Brien, Ray Kavanagh, Pat Magner, Tom Butler and myself met with the team from MRBI.

The news they presented was good. Seán Ryan was so far ahead in the polls that he could not lose, unless he publicly blew it away. Henry Haughton, as the director of elections for Seán Ryan, knew precisely what was needed and did a superb job. Jan, on the other hand, had a struggle in front of her. The combined Labour vote in Limerick East the previous June had been 4,568; John Ryan of Democratic Left had 3,403 and former Senator Mary Jackman of Fine Gael had 3,084. The Fianna Fáil vote was distorted by Willie O'Dea's huge personal following, and the likelihood that he would field a weak candidate – to avoid serious competition for himself within Fianna Fáil at subsequent elections – meant that there would not be a serious Fianna Fáil contender. The message was that with a good methodical campaign, Labour could win Limerick East as well. Joe Kemmy, Jim's brother and director of elections, had come separately to a similar conclusion.

The party in Limerick did a slow reflective canvass before Christmas, calling on every door, spending time to explain the importance for the city and their families of holding on to the Labour seat. When the campaign officially started in the new year, the harvest of that pre-Christmas canvass in Limerick East was waiting to be collected. I worked intensively in both campaigns. On polling day, 12 March 1998, I was in London at a PES leaders meeting and, in anticipation of the good news, arranged to fly first to Shannon and then on to Dublin to be at both counts and celebrate a stirring double victory. In the end the win in Limerick East was as comfortable as that in Dublin North. When pressed to comment on this success, less than six months after becoming leader, I responded by saying that I felt like Napoleon, who was fortunate to have lucky generals.

At the same time, we had been doing some preparatory work in advance of the special conference held in Jurys Hotel in Ballsbridge, on Saturday, 28 March, where we celebrated our by-election successes and paid tribute to the late Jim Kemmy. In my speech, I wanted to focus on the future and to eschew the politics of personality or the most recent political scandals. With the help of a number of people, I amassed an array of data illustrating the near future that was facing us as a nation and as a people. My theme for the leader's speech was similar to what I had been saying in 'Ireland 2010' and indeed a comment that I had made in an interview immediately after the leadership contest.

> *In ten years' time, this country is going to be as rich as Finland or Denmark is now. The question is what kind of society are we going to have? Do we want to become like California, where 80 per cent of people are well off and all pay low taxes, while 20 per cent of the population are excluded and antagonistic towards the better off? It is a rich society but not a secure one. Or, do we want to be a secure society where there is proper public provision for all, with everybody sharing the fruits of economic growth?*

Looking back on that observation eight years later, I was fundamentally wrong about only one thing – the timing. Within six or seven years we had reached the Scandinavian levels to which I referred. But Mary Harney's infamous assertion that Ireland was closer to Boston than Berlin had been confirmed by the policies of the Fianna Fáil/ Progressive Democrat coalition government. My message was right but my delivery at that conference was poor. In front of a warm and willing audience, a good speech was badly communicated.

In his last speech as leader, Dick said that the left in Ireland was too weak to be divided by two competing left parties. His call for the eventual unity of the left, which was clearly desirable, was perhaps now possible with his departure. In the days after my election as leader, there was much focus on what he had said. I received a warm message of congratulation from Proinsias De Rossa, who asked me to meet him. When we did, it was a formal private encounter. Close co-operation was considered by both of us as highly desirable. We agreed that, if possible, a policy foundation should be established, shared by our two parties, dedicated to developing a clearly left critique of Irish society. This would generate radical policy options that could be promoted independently of our parties so as to generate a vigorous debate, free of narrow partisan electoral constraints. This was an idea warm to my heart, and we readily agreed to pursue the matter further.

A carefully drafted press release from both Labour and Democratic Left was released and attracted considerable attention. A working group, chaired by Robin Wilson of Democratic Dialogue in Belfast, was brought together to explore and report on the foundation proposal. They did a good job and we got their report in the new year. Sadly, however, its scale was way beyond our resources and our political priorities.

Some days after I had met Proinsias De Rossa, I received a phone call from Pat Rabbitte, who was in his office in Kildare House across the street from Leinster House. It was a quiet Friday before Christmas and he asked if we could meet; he wanted to talk to me confidentially and not in the gaze of other people, even in the privacy of the members' bar. The Labour parliamentary meeting room was down the corridor from his office and I suggested that we met there in fifteen minutes.

The door opened and a slightly furtive Rabbitte entered. After the usual greetings he pledged me to confidentiality and said, a few times, that he was there entirely in his own personal capacity. He just wanted me to hear something that I might not have heard. Welcoming the meeting between De Rossa and myself, he then went on to say that something much more fundamental than a declaration of closer co-operation might be available between the two parties. I listened attentively.

A lot of things had happened in recent years. The landscape of left politics had changed. Pat Rabbitte had recently attended the funeral of Michael Enright, an old friend and political contemporary who had died tragically in a car accident. Michael had devoted his adult political life to trying to carve out a Dáil seat in Wexford but never came near it. At the social gathering of his political friends after the funeral, the talk turned from Michael's life to the future of many of those present. As I continued to listen, Pat looked at me straight, 'If you were open to it,' he said directly, 'we could be talking about a merger of our two parties and not just co-operation. The Labour name, the Labour brand,' he went on, 'has a historical validity and tradition which could never be replaced. We tried it in Democratic Left and it did not work. A merger is now possible with you as leader. While Spring was there, it simply was inconceivable.'

I did not demur from his analysis, but neither did I show the excitement that had started to rise within me. In the past, I had been involved in discussions with Jim Kemmy's Democratic Socialist Party when it merged with Labour, and even more so with Declan Bree and his Independent Sligo–Leitrim organisation when it finally joined in time for Declan to win a Labour seat in 1992. Now something on a far bigger scale was being intimated to me as being possible, however remotely. The four Democratic Left deputies were excellent parliamentarians, senior politicians who were supported by very able and highly committed members.

'There is a minor problem on the horizon,' I said in reply; 'the two by-elections. Democratic Left's John Ryan strong presence in Limerick will be tested. Any suggestions of our conversation becoming public before that's concluded would be disastrous.' Pat agreed and as he left the room I was absorbing the implications of what had been communicated.

On 20 March 1998, eight days after Jan O'Sullivan's and Seán Ryan's overwhelming victories, I got another call from Pat Rabbitte. I was at home that afternoon, catching up on some domestic work, including planting potatoes. He was in Leinster House, but was anxious to meet me.

'Are you going for a pint?' he asked.

'I could be,' I replied, 'but in O'Reilly's in Sandymount, not in town.'

We agreed to meet there at 5.30 p.m. Liz was preparing dinner and Conan was playing with his Lego at the kitchen table. 'I'm going into O'Reilly's to have a pint with Pat Rabbitte. I expect it's about the other thing. I'll be home no later than seven.'

'Good luck,' she responded.

I arrived first in O'Reilly's and went into the back, near the door to the garden, ordering a pint as I passed the bar. Paul, the proprietor, brought it down to me and was chatting when Pat arrived. Another pint was soon produced and Paul wished us well, saying that the drinks were on the house. Pat soon got to the point. 'This thing that I spoke to you about has moved much more quickly than I thought. Limerick simply confirmed it for us. If a strong, dedicated hard-working guy like John Ryan cannot do it, then where are we going?'

He asked me if I was open to moving forward. He produced a document prepared, I later learned, by Philip O'Connor, a senior Democratic Left member and a specialist in international and European affairs. 'Read that section there,' he indicated.

The piece was a commentary on the evolution of the European Project and the positive future of the Party of European Socialists, with, in passing, some kind references to me. 'What's this?' I said half jokingly. 'Flattery?'

'No, no, but an indication of the way thoughtful people in our party are reacting.'

Having got my assurance again that this was a confidential conversation, we were interrupted before I could resume. A man, whom I recognised but whose name I could not remember, greeted the two of us warmly. He turned to me and said he wanted to thank me for doing the 'other thing' and placed two pints in front of us. When he had gone, I asked Pat to continue. He looked at me intensely as he laid his cards on the table. There were many people on his side who wanted to do business but they needed reassurance. If the project advanced, would I be generous? Would they have a role? Would we respond openly? I had no difficulty in immediately replying, 'For my part, most certainly yes.'

Then as we continued to talk another man came over. 'I hope that you two guys are talking about what you should be talking about,' he said. 'The Rainbow was a great government and the sooner you get back in there, the better.'

Then as we moved to discuss tactics and logistics, Paul O'Reilly arrived with two more pints. 'From one of your admirers,' he said.

'Jaysus, Ruairi, I'll have to come here more often,' Pat said.

'I wish you would,' I responded; 'it's not usually like this.'

Back home, Liz was laughing when I finally came through the hall and down the stairs.

'Where's Conan?' I asked.

'Next door with his Nanno, but wait till you hear what he has said to her.'

She then related how his grandmother had told her that when Conan was sitting on the couch beside her, he turned and said, 'You know, Nanno, my Dad has very strange friends.'

'Why?' she asked. 'What do you mean?'

'Well,' he replied, 'last week he was in London having lunch with Tony The Bear and now he has just told Mamma that he was going into Sandymount to have a pint with Pat The Rabbit!'

This decisive, but informal, contact with Pat was soon followed by a formal exchange between Proinsias De Rossa and myself after the special Labour Party conference had taken place in Jurys. It seemed to me that, initially, Proinsias was quite reluctant and distant about the whole idea. Because of promptings from within his own party, I believe that he finally agreed to set up a group comprising representatives from Democratic Left and the Labour Party to explore the question of closer unity, if not an actual merger.

I asked Brendan Howlin to lead our team and work began before the summer recess. But the real hard work took off in the autumn and Brendan kept me fully informed. To my surprise, De Rossa had nominated Eamon Gilmore to head up the Democratic Left team to negotiate on their behalf, even though Pat Rabbitte had been the number two minister in the Rainbow Coalition. As it turned out, Brendan and Eamon got on well and real progress was made in time for a comprehensive report to be given to the executive and general council of the Labour Party which met in Buswell's Hotel on 24 September.

Travelling back from Cork, where Brendan and myself were

working in the by-election campaign caused by Hugh Coveney's unfortunate death the previous March, I took the opportunity of the lift with Brendan to review matters. We discussed the issues of the merger and the resistance of some of our members. Pat Upton in particular was utterly opposed to the merger, but, when pressed, could give little constructive argument why. He just didn't like the people and didn't like the idea. It was not unlike his position, back in 1992, when we had to decide whether to go into government or not. At that time, he was against all the options, putting forward strongly held views, but offering no constructive alternative.

In contrast, Róisín Shortall's opposition was at least understandable. From where she was, there was simply no room for two left seats in the now three-seat Dublin North-West constituency. De Rossa's intentions, with regard to the next general election in this constituency, were not clear, but we expected him to contest the European Parliament election in June 1999. It was suggested at one stage that he might consider moving to the new Dublin Mid-West constituency, a three-seater which had emerged from the recommendations of the Electoral Boundary Commission. Labour had no incumbent there, yet there was a large working-class and left vote between Lucan and Clondalkin, the two main population centres of this big constituency. However, when pressed on this, Proinsias rejected it, on the basis that, having examined it in some detail, all he could see was a lot of sheep! This was not a reference to the constituents, but to the substantial hinterland that stretched far south up into the Dublin Mountains around Saggart and Newcastle.

Understandably as it turned out, Bernie Malone was completely opposed to the merger because she saw that, in all probability, De Rossa would want to run for the European Parliament and win the seat she now held. She came to see me on 29 October, by appointment, to discuss her concerns. By this stage considerable progress was being made and I was anxious for the project to succeed. She used all the usual ploys, but I told her firmly that as far as I was concerned the party was bigger than any one individual, myself included. This was a unique opportunity and any attempts by her to actively oppose the measure would be vigorously countered by me. While I had some sympathy for Róisín Shortall, I had very little for our MEP. In my opinion, Bernie had already done very well by being co-opted, in the first instance, to the vacancy caused by Barry Desmond's promotion to the Court of Auditors in Luxembourg. In truth, she got the co-option only because at the time the two people ahead of her, Joan Burton and Paul Mulhern, were already committed when we were in government after 1992. Indeed Bernie had been very unco-operative with head office. In addition, I also had the memory of her behaviour during the course of the European Parliament elections of 1994 and her outrageous attitude towards Dick Spring, when he promoted Orla Guerin as a candidate. As far as I was concerned, I was not going to lose any sleep over Bernie Malone.

The Cork South-Central by-election intervened in the progress of our talks. Democratic Left had, however, given a very positive signal by not putting forward a candidate, unlike earlier in the year in Limerick East. Our candidate, Toddy O'Sullivan, did well but, when the votes were counted on 24 October 1998, he had not done well enough. Young Simon Coveney won the seat, combining his youth with a huge sympathy vote related to the death of his father.

Meanwhile, Brendan Howlin and Eamon Gilmore proceeded to make progress, narrowing the issues to what level of posts the Democratic Left deputies would get as part of an enlarged parliamentary party. That prospect would require me to make a front-bench reshuffle and, consequently, reallocation of responsibilities. It soon became apparent that Pat Rabbitte was very keen to be the new Finance spokesperson, but, as far as I was concerned, Derek McDowell was doing a good job. Besides, I had worked hard when I was the Finance spokesperson in the early 1990s to ensure credibility regarding Labour's economic and financial abilities. To assign an ex-Democratic Left deputy that responsibility would send out the wrong signals. In any case, Derek was a close ally and adamant about staying on as Finance spokesperson. When we held the line in the negotiations, Democratic Left accepted it as a fait accompli.

There were two outstanding issues which remained to be resolved and little progress was being made, since both concerned Proinsias

De Rossa. Was he going to run for the European Parliament and so forgo standing for the Dáil in the next election? That in a sense was the easier of the two issues. We anticipated correctly that he did want to go to the European Parliament and envisaged that both he and Bernie Malone would be on the ticket together.

But what does an ex-party leader do in a new party having allowed his party to merge with a larger one? There was strong loyalty to and support for De Rossa within the parliamentary group, particularly from people like Liz McManus and senior figures outside it, such as Des Geraghty and Rosheen Callender. It was about status and perception. At this point, Brendan Howlin proposed to me that we should create a new position of President of the Labour Party within the merged party. It would be filled at our national conference by direct vote of the delegates and it would obviously convey status and recognition for De Rossa. I liked the idea and agreed to it in principle, as indeed did the rest of the group of advisers around me.

Still, in relation to both these issues there was no movement from Proinsias. Eamon Gilmore, and to a lesser extent Brendan Howlin, got quite nervous. Finally, I received a hand-delivered letter from De Rossa rejecting our offer of the presidency of the party. Meanwhile, Brendan Howlin and Pat Magner were on their way to continue negotiations with Eamon Gilmore and Pat Rabbitte. Wasting no time, I phoned Brendan, who was now on the plinth in front of Leinster House and called Brendan and Pat back to discuss De Rossa's letter. After intense discussion, I decided that we would ignore the letter and see what happened. The two Labour negotiators continued with the negotiations. No reference to the letter was made by either side. A collapse at this stage was simply inconceivable. In some ways, Eamon Gilmore and Pat Rabbitte had already, psychologically, joined the Labour Party.

But I resisted the suggestion from some in my own quarter to encourage a collapse in the negotiations and to accept individual applications for membership. I wanted the generous spirit, which I had promised some months back, to inform the whole project. The opposition within the party continued. They argued that it would not necessarily bring about real net gains. But for me, the merger was about openness and growth. In effect, Democratic Left wanted to merge, to join with dignity. How could we keep the door closed? How could we assert that the party was full and that there was no room for them? Both inside and outside Dáil Éireann, they had talented and committed members. The existing Parliamentary Labour Party was not exactly bursting with a hungry and talented team. In the end, Proinsias arrived at an agreement in a manner similar to the way we had negotiated the Department of Social Welfare Estimates in previous years.

The merger negotiations ended on 20 November 1998, exactly one week after I had been a year as leader of the party. Days later, the Labour Party general council voted fifty votes in favour, with two abstentions, to the terms of the merger. The week previously, at the Democratic Left executive, there were thirty votes in favour, four abstentions and one vote of opposition. The special conferences for the Labour Party and for Democratic Left to enable individual delegates to ratify or reject the proposed merger took place on the same day, 12 December. Labour's delegates met in the National Concert Hall and there was an overwhelming vote in favour, with 90 per cent of the delegates giving their endorsement to the project; over in the Shelbourne Hotel, Democratic Left obtained an endorsement of 89 per cent.

In the National Concert Hall, Michael Moynihan, a former minister of state showed no signs of his age with the passionate speech of approval which he gave to the merger. It was a rousing endorsement of what was proposed and one from which I drew great personal strength. Michael's daughter, Breeda, had succeeded him in Kerry South, but the continued commitment of his political and trade-union values was manifest with every word he uttered.

One sad contribution, as far as I was concerned, came from Brian Fitzgerald from Meath. In articulating his opposition to the merger, he made reference to his concerns about the way in which the SIPTU merger had unfolded. He was from the old FWUI wing of the trade-union movement and still carried some of the angst of those animosities. Even so, Jimmy Somers, the first directly elected president of SIPTU, made a constructive and strong speech in favour of the merger and, in the process, gently but firmly rejected the suggestions that Brian Fitzgerald had made.

With her usual skill, Anne Byrne, the events organiser for the Labour Party, had organised an entertaining and positive social event in the Riverside Centre on Sir John Rogerson's Quay, where both parties came and celebrated the collective decisions that had been made so overwhelmingly to bring Labour and Democratic Left together. Listening to Jimmy Somers and looking at the obvious pleasure amongst prominent trade unionists, I realised that the Labour/Democratic Left merger had also put an end to the political divisions that had haunted the trade-union movement.

We had identified a number of constituencies where there was both a strong Labour and Democratic Left presence. The candidate strategy for the locals, but even more importantly for the general election, was agreed in an implementation document, which in turn was an integral part of the merged party. In many cases, local election candidates had already been selected by both parties, before the conclusions of the merger talks. We now had the difficult task of trying to rationalise this, so as to get the optimum number of candidates, relative to our electoral strength.

Our national organiser for a number of years, Pat Magner, was given the task of making this happen. I had known Pat for a long time, but only really got close to him after Toddy O'Sullivan's November 1979 by-election campaign. Pat was the dynamic director of elections who effectively oversaw the return of the Labour Party in Cork city. By now, just over a year in the leader's job, it was with Pat that I travelled the country to every constituency, not once or twice but at least three or four times between November 1997 and the May 2002 general election. Looking at the intensity of the diary now, I realise just how many miles we covered, local visits we made, media interviews we gave and deputations we received. Where possible, I would use the train, especially to Cork and Limerick, but after those two locations, we travelled in Pat's Volvo.

In the course of those long visits across the country, Pat and I had many conversations, frequently about the intricacies of how to manage candidates and the outstanding difficulties that existed in the core constituencies where we had agreed to field two candidates, one from each side of the merged party.

The merged party had a special one-day meeting in the Round Room of the Rotunda Hospital on 24 January 1999, to launch the new logo and offer a new vision of what Ireland could be, and how the left had a unique contribution to make as well as the ability to deliver it. Even allowing for the optimism of that coming together, there was a real sense that Labour – an invigorated Labour – could play a key role in the Ireland of the future. After all, it was Labour's agenda that had dominated the political landscape for the best part of that decade.

While the politics of opposition and holding the government to account in the Dáil was our weekly task, we were also looking at the local and European elections in June, less than six months away. A national conference was to be held over the May Day weekend in Tralee. As ever, I was surrounded by supportive and talented people. Ronan O'Brien continued to play a central role as my main adviser. The merged party inherited the skills and dedication of Tony Heffernan, who had worked in Leinster House since 1982. He was now the parliamentary director of the Parliamentary Labour Party, having previously been press officer with Democratic Left. In reality, he did nearly everything from drafting press releases, preparing parliamentary questions and dealing with media enquiries. His passionate commitment to radical politics was masked by his quiet personality, methodical work practices and an incredible knowledge of political history and well-filled files. He was and remains an important addition to Labour's team.

Tom Butler got me to do preparatory work for the leader's speech at the Tralee conference. The issue of immigration was one of the themes beginning to surface across the country. In order to dramatise and make it relevant, we decided that a refugee should speak in the middle of my televised speech. Fardus Sultan-Prnjavorac, a Croatian refugee from Bosnia and Herzegovina, who had been granted asylum in Ireland, electrified the conference with her contribution. The mood, at that my first national conference, was good. From there until polling day on 11 June, it was simply full steam ahead. Proinsias De Rossa was comfortably elected on 11 June 1999 as the Dublin MEP, polling twice the number of votes of his running mate, Bernie Malone, but our other Euro candidates did poorly. The result at local level was uneven, but generally, disappointing.

Other changes were occurring too. Ray Kavanagh resigned as general secretary of the Labour Party in July 1999 after thirteen years in the job. Following a process of public advertisement, Mike Allen, the general secretary of the Irish National Organisation of the Unemployed (INOU), applied for and got the job of general secretary. Effectively, he had created the INOU, and I was delighted that he had joined us. It meant that we now had a good administrator as well as an authoritative line into the community and voluntary sector. This was an increasingly important part of the social partnership structure, and Mike had played a large role in developing it.

On 22 February 1999, I was in my office in Leinster House, reviewing some documentation and looking forward to having lunch with Jim Downey, a senior political journalist and an old friend. Tom Butler had set up the lunch, one of a regular series I was having with political correspondents, and when he came into my office, I thought he was going to review the likely conversation topics with me. Instead, ashen-faced, he told me that he had heard that Pat Upton, a member of the parliamentary party, had had a heart attack in UCD's Veterinary College where he was a lecturer. Our worst fears were confirmed. Pat did not regain consciousness and was later pronounced dead in nearby St Vincent's Hospital. We were stunned. These are the worst of times, when all normalities are savagely cast aside. But Pat's death was news and I reluctantly agreed to do an RTÉ television interview for the *6.01 News*. Politicians have a reputation for ruthlessness and for being without feeling. But when I was asked to respond to the news of Pat's sudden death, I could only express sadness and shock, combined with a concern for his wife and four children. When the female interviewer then asked who would run for Labour in the by-election, I think I was more annoyed than surprised, and my angry sentiments, clearly expressed, were shared by many who saw the broadcast.

Six months later, the question could properly be addressed. In August when staying in Roundstone, I rang Caroline Hussey. She was a friend and professional colleague in UCD of Dr Mary Upton, a science lecturer and the sister of our deceased deputy for Dublin South-Central. In response to my questions, Caroline thought that, yes, Mary might run, and that she would make enquiries on my behalf. Some weeks later I met with Mary in Leinster House. After some days of reflection, she agreed to be the candidate for the Dublin South-Central by-election. We already knew from polls that she had an excellent chance of victory. But I had to convince party member Eric Byrne first. Eric was the former Democratic Left TD who had lost his seat in the previous general election in the same constituency. It took me a considerable time to persuade Eric and his supporters to stand aside and let Mary run. My strategy was that we could in fact win the two seats at the next general election. Constructively, Eric with his very reluctant supporters agreed to this. On 27 October, we won the by-election comfortably with 28 per cent of the vote. The strategy appeared to have been vindicated because two seats in a five-seater, where the quota was 17 per cent, now looked really possible.

There were two more by-elections, both, unusually, in the same constituency – Tipperary South – and exactly twelve months apart. Labour's Michael Ferris died in 2000 and Fine Gael's Theresa Ahern in 2001. I was at home in my study on 20 March when the phone rang and I was surprised to hear the familiar voice of Dick Roche, a Fianna Fáil TD for Wicklow, on the other end. He was ringing from Portugal, where he was attending a parliamentary conference, with the shocking news that Michael Ferris, a member of the parliamentary party, had died suddenly. Fortunately, Michael's wife Ellen was there with him at the time but his death was a very hard blow for her and their daughter.

Labour did not win either contest: Ellen Ferris put up a good fight in 2000 and Cllr Denis Landy bravely carried the flag in 2001. But, for a variety of complex reasons, the party had been defeated in Clonmel, its birthplace, by an Independent ex-Labour man, Séamus Healy, and his Workers and Unemployed Action Group. He holds the seat to this day. By-elections can be difficult for parties but they do offer a chance to promote a new candidate and, whatever about the internecine rivalries among incumbents and challengers, the party leader has a dominant role to play.

I wanted to give a lot of attention to the policy platform of the party. We knew that there would be no snap general election, as in 1992. In all likelihood, it would be in June 2001. Frequently over lunch in the Leinster House cafeteria, Independent deputy Tony Gregory asserted to me that it would be the following year. A constituency colleague of the Taoiseach, he held the view that Bertie would go to the very end – and he was right.

This gave the party considerable time to develop our ideas and to bring forward a range of radical and well-thought-out policies on health, immigration and policing, as well as a detailed spatial strategy to co-ordinate the major infrastructural challenges facing the country. Given my planning background, I knew how important it was to have our transport and other major services properly planned and well co-ordinated. The modern application of socialist values involved enshrining concepts like equality into practical law. For example, we developed detailed policies on education and childcare. Likewise, people with disabilities would have the legal right to support and assistance contained in legislation. Public opinion research and the representations which we were receiving from colleagues in the parliamentary party, and from my constituency visits across the country, confirmed the correctness our own value-based analysis.

Underpinning this interventionist and redistributive set of policy measures was a core economic document entitled *New Direction, New Priorities 2001–2004*. In unambiguous terms, it set out the macro-economic framework within which we proposed to progressively increase public spending in a coherent and non-inflationary manner, thus providing us with the resources to implement our policies. Some of these we had already published, others were still in preparation, but all would be contained in our manifesto. Admittedly, we had the best professional and political help with this seminal work. Never before had the Labour Party produced something as comprehensive and as well costed as the manifesto on which we were now engaged. Richard Humphreys, working closely with Ronan O'Brien, prepared the initial draft.

But we were not in favour of lavish spending proposals in the run-up to an election. My experience of Enterprise and Employment and latterly of Finance had demonstrated the need for a rigorous system of ensuring value for taxpayers' money. We proposed in line with the increase in expenditure, the establishment of an Evaluation Unit, styled like of the EU Structural Funds Evaluation Unit, which had been such an innovation in the Irish public service. One dramatic background statistic to our manifesto was the increase in Ireland's per capita income against the EU average income. In 1990, as our economy struggled, we had 73.3 per cent of the average; by 2000, we were 15 per cent above that average, and rising. The money was there, provided it was well harnessed and properly spent.

This was an awesome threshold on which to stand. For most of my political life, the Labour Party simply could not do the things that really needed to be done in coalition, because we did not have the resources. The nation was comparatively poor and Labour lacked the political strength to challenge or change the situation. In the 1980s, we had fought a successful rearguard action in slowly turning around the economy but only with a lot of political pain. Having largely done the job in government with Fine Gael between 1982 and 1987, it was Haughey and MacSharry who claimed the credit.

In the 1990s, the strategic imperative was to get within the solidarity and strength of the single currency with its promised low inflation and low interest rates. But we were now in the eurozone and all our enthusiastic, if not optimistic, expectations for Ireland were coming to pass. One hundred and fifty years after the Famine, we were now a rich country. Imagine trying to tell the Sudanese today that in less than five generations they would be as rich as the Swiss! There were no longer economic barriers to the social programmes and policies which we were proposing and for which there was an overwhelming need and public demand. We just had to present our policies honestly, clearly and enthusiastically, or so we thought.

Good policy content needs clear design and effective promotion. We were strong on the first, but we needed a good deal of help with the rest. I met Gary Brown of Target Marketing in the late 1980s when he was one of the founders of the Irish Direct Marketing Association. At that time, I was working to get Barry Desmond elected to the European Parliament, and Gary Brown was at the start of a very successful marketing career. When I became leader, our friendship strengthened and I gladly accepted his offer to help. Over time Gary Brown, Ronan O'Brien, Pat Magner and Mike Allen deepened and reinforced the party's corporate image.

When the tide for a June 2001 election had passed, it was obvious that the following year would see a late spring/early summer contest. The lines had now clearly been drawn. We had a buoyant economy and a government immersed in sleazy allegations from different tribunals, including the dubious practices of substantial corporate donations, of which Fianna Fáil were the main beneficiaries. Many unsavoury revelations emerged from the various tribunals, but particularly from the Flood Tribunal. It found that Ray Burke, among others, had received corrupt payments. Labour moved a Private Member's Bill in May 2000 to have corporate donations to political parties terminated and a system of public financing for political parties put in place to sever, once and for all, the financial links between business and politics. But Fianna Fáil, immune to any shame that might emerge from the flow of revelations and assertions, simply refused to ban corporate donations to political parties. Combined with our comprehensive policy programme, we included clear commitments on finance, business donations and the need to clean up politics as we approached the last autumn before the general election.

The dominant strategic issue which concerned us, right from my becoming leader, was that of coalition. Which party would Labour go into government with, in order to implement some, if not all, its policies? From my first press conference as leader, in the National Gallery in 1997, I kept that option open. We had come out badly from the previous general election, which we had contested as part of a three-party pre-election coalition pact. We lost nearly all the gains which we had made in 1992, when we had stood as an independent party.

By the autumn of 1998, with my integrated team of advisers, we were ready to consider our strategy and worked on it over the ensuing months. On 12 July 2000, we took the day off, away from Leinster House, so that we could have a think-in on electoral options in the spacious Nerney's Court offices of IMPACT, the public services union in Dublin. We concentrated on the import-ance of what the next government would do, and how it now had the wealth and resources to implement the detailed policies we were continuing to develop. Slowly, but clearly, we converged on an elec-toral strategy.

Our opposition partner, Fine Gael, was floundering in the polls. John Bruton, their leader, was going nowhere. Despite his repeated private requests for a pre-election pact, I held to our independent and separate policy position. There were clear policy divisions between Labour and Fine Gael, and more were to emerge. If I agreed to a pre-election pact, then every subsequent Labour Party policy initiative would be challenged at the press conference with one question: Had Fine Gael agreed to this? If not, the implication was that it would not be part of a programme for government.

The real question was not who would be in the next government, but what that government would do. We wanted to dominate the 'what' of that new government and so we decided to fight the election on our distinctive radical policies. The more support we got for them from the public, in Dáil seats, the more our issues would dominate the 'what' agenda of the next government. This was now clear in our minds, but what about our own party and the public?

Even though we ourselves were focused on the programme of the next government, we knew that many of our members had strong views about our possible partners. So too had the public. Since some motions for our national conference in September 2001 had already been submitted on this issue, we decided to take it head on.

A leadership motion, outlining the open strategy decided at Nerney's Court, was tabled and accepted by the party's executive. If passed, all other motions referring to other options would fall. We all recognised that this was the key theme of our conference and so we decided to give it centre stage. The 11.00 a.m. to 1.00 p.m. slot on the morning was to be televised live and it was there that we agreed to place the debate, and so communicate not just to delegates but also to the wider public. It was high risk, but so too was our electoral strategy.

The conference was held in City Hall, Cork, on the last weekend in September 2001. A compromise motion from the party's executive on the issue of abortion was narrowly rejected on the Friday night. My wife Liz had voted, in accordance with her own long-held views, in support of the position of the Labour Women's National Council, which the compromise motion proposed to dilute. The narrow defeat for the leadership had been assisted by the leader's wife! Some angry advisers close to me demanded to know what was going on. Did this mean that we might be in trouble on the big issue the following morning?

'No it did not,' was my reply and I was right.

Saturday morning's debate was intense, intelligent and extensive in its range of arguments and the passion that conveyed them. It was about strategy, not principle. It was about power, not position. It was about what we would do in government, and not about who would be with us in government. The leadership had an overwhelming majority and the minority opposed, with a few exceptions, accepted the outcome. What was left now was the long march to the election campaign proper, which started the following week. Once more, a series of constituency visits were lined up to consolidate candidates and reinforce morale. Meanwhile, Pat Magner and Ita McAuliffe began the preliminary planning of the leader's election campaign tour for when the Dáil was dissolved. Posters, campaign slogans, literature and promotional material had been prepared in the meantime, under the supervision of Ronan O'Brien and Mike Allen.

Back in February 2001, after a long and bitter campaign within Fine Gael, John Bruton had lost a hotly contested vote of confidence and was forced out of the leadership of the party he loved. It was savage to watch, even from the safety of the sidelines. For weeks, if not months, before there had been snipings and rumblings in the party about the former Taoiseach's lack of electoral appeal. The polls were not good for Fine Gael and Jim Mitchell had once again started to publicly voice doubts about Bruton. He had done this before in the mid-1990s, only to fail in his coup attempt then. As a consequence, he was excluded from the Rainbow Coalition cabinet in 1994.

Now, equipped with an anonymously funded poll, the findings of which undermined Bruton, Mitchell was at it again. Since the late 1990s, Jim courageously overcame a life-threatening illness and had been the star of the Public Accounts Committee's DIRT Inquiry. As chairman of that constitutionally important committee, he drove it with a manic energy and, in record time, produced a report which revealed the shocking extent of bogus non-resident, tax-evasion accounts held by thousands of Irish citizens. Worse still was the complicit involvement of our banks, including the state-owned ACC Bank. The amount of monies recouped and the speed of the committee's work had made Jim Mitchell a public hero.

I admired his courage but not his politics. He was a populist anti-socialist who, on occasion, possessed an erratic and contradictory mind. Michael Noonan, Mitchell's soon-to-be ally, was quite different. Calm and committed, a firm Minister for Justice in the 1980s, he had had the misfortune to be appointed Minister for Health in 1994. This was when the hepatitis C blood transfusion scandal was beginning to break. Against, I believe, his better instincts, Michael Noonan had taken the conservative adversarial legal advice proffered to his department. Under no circumstances could the minister say that he was sorry or the department apologise for mistakes that had happened, even though they knew nothing about them. That would be the same as admitting full liability with the consequent horrendous financial costs of an unquantifiable kind. But I think, in retrospect, even Michael Noonan would agree that his handling of the issue was far from his finest hour.

Now in the heave against Bruton, a dream ticket to replace the former Taoiseach and return Fine Gael to government glory was unveiled. Noonan and Mitchell offered to lead a revitalised party – if elected. Following a long and emotional meeting of the Fine Gael Parliamentary Party, Michael Noonan was elected as the new leader and immediately announced that Fine Gael would no longer accept corporate donations. Only then did he talk to his party officers and discover the true state of the party finances, which were dismal.

Worse still, leaked documents revealed that Fine Gael had apparently received a major donation of $50,000 from Telenor, a Scandanavian company in business with Denis O'Brien's Esat Digifone, which became the surprise winner of the second mobile phone licence competition, and which was awarded the contract when the Fine Gael TD Michael Lowry was the Minister for Transport, Energy and Communications in 1995. However, soon after that government decision, Lowry was forced to resign when it emerged that he had conspired with one of his major clients, Ben Dunne of Dunne Stores, not to pay tax. It became clear that, following his resignation from the cabinet, Lowry had lied to the Dáil when he denied having an offshore account. One of Fine Gael's great advantages, that of ethical superiority to Fianna Fáil, was being eroded rapidly.

Worse was to come. The Fine Gael party proposed that the small shareholders, who had lost out badly on the Fianna Fáil/ Progressive Democrat overenthusiastic privatisation of the state telecom company, Eircom, should be compensated for their losses. In addition, the aggressive and heavily protectionist taxi-plate owners in Dublin, who had stubbornly resisted numerous attempts to liberalise the system and increase the number of taxis, had a major setback. The court had found that there was no legal restriction to local authorities issuing new plates. Overnight the resale value of their plates, which had been as high as £80,000, was wiped out. Soon anyone with £5,000 could acquire a taxi plate. Naturally, the taxi federations were in uproar and populist Jim Mitchell announced a compensation package for these heavy-handed monopolists.

If I was amazed at this nonsense, Fine Gael supporters were horrified. When I was on a constituency visit in Carrick-on-Shannon with Declan Bree, some days after the Mitchell announcement, an ex-Fine Gael supporter declared unreservedly for Labour. I asked her why and she replied that her former party might as well set up a stall outside Leopardstown Racecourse to reimburse disappointed punters! Right through the summer and into autumn, support for Fine Gael did not improve. Some, who had doubts about our electoral strategy, now breathed sighs of relief that we were not attached to what appeared to be a sinking ship.

We decided early in the new year that we would have a one-day conference in March in Dún Laoghaire to utilise the party's entitlement to live television coverage on RTÉ 1. The theme of the conference would be the launch of our six-pledge card, a Blairite device which we openly copied from New Labour in Britain. The six pledges, based on our manifesto, had been carefully researched using our own members as well as professional focus groups. The issues were central to our values, and how they were to be presented and characterised was important to us.

Our first pledge was about health. 'Free GP health care for all. As Labour delivers a high quality health system based on need, not continued health apartheid.' During the course of my many visits and interviews around the country, it was clear that health, in all its manifestations, was the public's major concern, displacing employment and crime. The cost of a visit to a GP, for which two-thirds of the citizens had to pay, was often a deterrent to attending the doctor. This resulted in sick children and their parents clogging up the outpatients and Accident and Emergency sections of our hospitals. Primary health care, properly resourced, together with a comprehensive information system linking patients to hospital records and health support systems nationally, could transform our people's health profile. The killer punch for me was the revelation that the state held a better record on the health status of the national herd of cattle than it did of its own citizens! Every time I used that line, the effect was electric, or so I thought. Schools, childcare, carers, poverty and housing were the themes of the other pledges. For all, we had detailed and workable policies to implement the pledges. All were costed and all were eminently affordable.

The Dún Laoghaire conference was a great success. I felt it was the best leader's speech I had delivered. We choose to have it broadcast an hour before the *6.01 News* and so got the *Nine O'Clock News* as well. Ronan O'Brien's speechwriting skills had developed, and he had found the rhythm of my delivery. That evening we were all in good mood and felt that we could not have been better prepared.

On 10 April, Michael Noonan asked to see me. Not surprisingly, he was very anxious to do a pre-election deal. I subsequently wrote that I thought he was desperate for something from us. At our meeting, he began with a review of his party's prospects across all the constituencies, but I knew that he was being overly optimistic. He then made a suggestion: in addition to a pre-election pact between our parties, there would be a joint ten-point policy statement. I listened to him for a while, and then declined his offer, repeating the party's well-known position. My preference was for a government with the Greens and Fine Gael, and told him so. Privately, I had been increasingly put off by the behaviour of the Fianna Fáil ministers and I personally could not see myself working comfortably with some of them, even if Labour secured a good programme for government. I told Michael that a Labour/Fine Gael/Green coalition would be my publicly stated preference, both before and during the course of the election campaign.

Given the opportunity, I then raised with Michael my serious policy concerns about the statements coming from Jim Mitchell in relation to Eircom and the taxi-plate owners. He told me, in confidence, that Jim was seriously ill. This explained, in part, some of Jim's exuberant utterances, and the Fine Gael leader went on to make it very clear that, as and from then, whatever about the dream ticket, he was in full control of the leadership. As he was leaving my office, Michael turned and said, more in sadness than in anger, that if we two did not get into government together after the next election, then neither of us would be leaders of our parties the following Christmas.

At last, in a slithery way that did Bertie Ahern no credit, the Taoiseach shuffled into a virtually empty Dáil chamber as a Wednesday adjournment debate was ending, and announced the dissolution of the Twenty-Eighth Dáil on 24 April 2002 at about 9.00 p.m. There were no courtesy calls, as would be normal, from the Taoiseach's office to inform opposition leaders of the intended announcement. It was a studied form of non-communication, and though I did not realise it at the time, was an indication of how the entire election campaign would be run.

We had had our first pre-election launch that same afternoon. A special Labour election press conference centre was established in the Royal Hibernian Academy in Ely Place, right beside our party headquarters. We intended to have a daily press conference and policy launches throughout the entire campaign. At last we were up and running. Now, with the announcement of polling day for 17 May 2002, Pat Magner's detailed choreographed national tour, complete with helicopters, cars and battle bus was started. Like a middle-distance runner in training for a championship race, I was a mixture of nerves and pre-contest tiredness. This, as Tony Farrell used to tell me, was the body conserving energy for the real contest. It was a good sign of mental and physical fitness, he would say. And politically speaking, I felt that I had both.

From the beginning, the long-awaited election campaign had an air of unreality about it. P.J. Mara, Haughey's former press officer, was the Fianna Fáil director of elections, and his opening remarks at his party's campaign launch perfectly combined both the cynicism and professionalism of Fianna Fáil. To a glitzy soundtrack, on a screen behind a panel of government ministers, as the press launch started, he was heard to say, 'It's showtime', and so it was. There was practically no political interaction between Labour or Fine Gael and the government parties during the campaign. The leaders' debate on RTÉ had, at Fianna Fáil's insistence, been held off until nearly the end of the minimum three-week campaign. Disputes about the accuracy of figures and budgetary projections and the viability of spending programmes, which dominated the first week of the campaign, became the property of economic commentators because the political corres- pondents were bored and non-engaged. Despite our best efforts, the campaign into which we had put so much energy did not catch the imagination of the public. While Labour had an excellent start, as the campaign progressed it became obvious we were not mobilising public support. Then a published opinion poll changed everything. Fianna Fáil were at 45 per cent and would lead the next government no matter what else happened, and perhaps, they might even form a one-party government. Labour at 12 per cent and Fine Gael at 23 per cent were not at the races. The issue now, so famously and brilliantly put by Michael McDowell, now back in the Progressive Democrats, was 'One-party government – no thanks.' His climb up the lamp posts of Ranelagh, with that iconic poster, was the turning point, although at the time it was hard for me to see it.

We continued energetically to hold well-thought-out press con- ferences detailing what the next government could and should do. The public, through the media, appeared more concerned with who the next government would be. Once that opinion poll was published, they certainly did not want Fianna Fáil on its own, and swung to the Progressive Democrats. Besides which, hadn't they been assured by the Taoiseach, the Minister for Finance and the Minister for Health that hospital waiting lists would be eliminated within two years and that an extra 2,000 gardaí would be recruited to combat crime, with no tax increases? There was therefore no need to redirect funds from the recently established National Pension Fund scheme in order to overcome our social problems. When the debate between Ahern and Noonan finally took place, it was too late. The election campaign had been running for two weeks. The opinion polls had been published and most people had probably made up their minds. In my opinion, Michael won the debate, but Bertie won the prize.

Fine Gael's collapse from fifty-four to thirty-one seats over-shadowed Labour's poor performance. Despite the merger, we did not increase our seats. In the process, we lost Dick Spring and Michael Bell when Sinn Féin took their seats. Derek McDowell was defeated by a populist Independent, Finian McGrath. The day of the election count was a nightmare. The early indications were that I might lose my seat. I thought of June 1981 and Frank Cluskey's double defeat from both the Dáil and the leadership. With my family around me, we waited together over lunch for the phone calls from Dermot Lacey and Ciarán O'Mara, who confirmed that I would be elected. However, my vote in Dublin South-East had been greatly reduced. I was lucky to survive in a constituency which for the first time in the history of the state did not return a Fine Gael deputy. Despite Dermot Lacey's exception-ally hard work as my director of elections and the enthusiasm of my election team, the perception that I was safe, combined with my absence from the constituency for sixteen out of twenty days, was a major handicap.

The real winners were the Independents, the candidates around the country who promised to save this hospital or that factory. Faced with the choice of giving the extra seats to Labour to implement the policies which it appeared to want, the public chose Independents, or the Greens, Sinn Féin or ultimately the PDs. In effect, anyone but us. I simply could not understand it. I could not connect what I had heard repeatedly over the previous three years, from a wide variety of people across the country, with the way the people had actually voted. As leader, I had taken the Labour Party into the general election with twenty-one seats and we had emerged with the same number – it was just not good enough.

I was exhausted and very disappointed. We had pressurised

Dick Spring to stand one more time. Now, the best deputy the Kingdom ever had had been rejected by the electors of Kerry North in favour of a convicted gun runner and a member of the Army Council of the Provisional IRA. I was heartbroken for people like Kathleen O'Meara, Eithne Fitzgerald and Joanna Tuffy, who had worked so hard over the previous four years. Likewise, in Carlow– Kilkenny, Jim Townsend and Labour were effectively denied a seat because of inaccurate coverage by the *Carlow Nationalist* newspaper, which said that their poll showed that no Carlow candidate could win a seat. The poll did not convey that exact message; it did show that the Carlow seat would go to Jim Townsend.

However, as the dust settled, and my emotional wounds began to heal, I reflected on the mood of the country and the decision of the voters. Why would they change, after five years of unprecedented growth and a huge increase in incomes for nearly everyone? An opinion poll taken just before the election recorded a level of 61 per cent satisfaction with the performance of the government. After all, housing affects only those without a home, and not everyone is a carer. The disabled in Irish society are for most people already in a world of their own, and anyway childcare is really the direct concern of the parents and grandparents.

The majority of the people who exercised their sovereign right to vote on 17 May 2002, may have, over the previous years, expressed multiple concerns to me and others, but in the absence of any clear alternative government, they seemed to want to remain with the one they knew.

My term of office as party leader was due to expire in November. After the election my immediate reaction was to resign after the new government was formed, but I was persuaded not to. In retrospect, I am glad that I did not.

On 27 August 2002, I made my formal announcement to a different audience and in a different climate. The lies and deceptions of Fianna Fáil's campaign promises had already become apparent. My decision was tinged with a sense of disappointment and regret, for the lost opportunities which could have been provided by our success. I was also acutely aware of the consequences of my decision for some of the people immediately around me, and that did cause me quite a lot of concern. Nevertheless, it was more than compensated for by a sense of relief that the huge burden of responsibility as leader, combined with the relentless schedule, would no longer be mine.

Chapter 20

Looking Forward

'There you are Ruairi,' said an old friend and constituent as I was going through the supermarket in Sandymount, with my list in one hand and the trolley in front of me. 'What are your doing now? Are you retired or what?'

'No, Frances, I am not,' I replied. 'I'm still on the team but I'm no longer captain.'

'And how do you feel?' she asked.

'Well, to be honest, I'm delighted, because now I can read and do the things that I want to do, which I couldn't when I was leader.'

When Pat Rabbitte was elected leader, after my term ended in October 2002, I became the Labour Party spokesperson for European Affairs, a logical step as I was vice-president and treasurer of the Party of European Socialists. My interest in the future evolution of Europe and Ireland's role within it has deepened since my first involvement. I became chairperson of European Movement Ireland and an executive member of the Institute of European Affairs.

I am still very active in politics and I intend to remain so. Freed of the direct and demanding responsibilities of leadership, I find that I can now play a wider and more reflective role. There is a continuing need, in my view, to re-engage people about the relevance of politics and democracy to their everyday concerns. I find myself availing of my chance to talk, particularly to young people, about the importance of democracy and public life.

I still retain the same sense of excitement as I first experienced forty years ago in Michael O'Leary's election campaign. But time moves on and, with it, the issues of the day. I look now at what concerns people, in contrast to the past. But some things do not fundamentally change: society will only improve and develop if people remain connected and committed. That is the real task of politicians, in or out of office, and political parties, in or out of power. Sometimes I become depressed by the low standing of politics and politicians in the eyes of the public, but I realise that the relationship of its very nature with a democracy cannot be static.

The original arrival of democracy in Europe was hesitant and, in many cases, very unstable in its initial outcomes. We should remember that Hitler's Nazi party received a substantial democratic mandate, which enabled him to become chancellor, before he abolished democracy in Germany. Likewise, communist parties in Czechoslovakia and Hungary won a significant level of electoral support after the end of the Second World War. The extremes of fascism and communism were, in some respects, the result of the citizens' distrust of democracy, particularly when it failed to solve social problems, such as high unemployment or fear of foreigners. That distrust is the dominant characteristic that, to this day, is shared by the far right and the hard-left in Europe.

But do the terms right and left mean anything now in our modern globalised world? Many commentators would like us to think not. Socialism is now clearly dead, they argue. Yet the Party of European Socialists is the largest political party on the continent. The collapse of the Soviet empire was the end of history, as far as Francis Fukuyama was concerned – meaning that liberal democracy was now the only way now to run a modern successful economy.

The neo-conservatives, the new right, would like us to believe that the end of history has arrived and that the market has triumphed. Whether it is the Progressive Democrats in Ireland or the Republican Party in the United States, they and their conservative allies around the world hold a view that people should have as little government interference in their lives or economy as is possible. This is the familiar cry heard in conservatively owned media for 'less government' and even 'less Europe'.

The right know what they are doing and they have mobilised a new vocabulary to advocate it. This is because the strong and the dominant thrive in a disorganised world and an open-market economy. They do not want the state to regulate the economy, beyond maintaining a minimum framework of rules to sustain civic order. The efficiency of market forces and the wisdom of the so-called 'the invisible hand' will in time, it is asserted, solve all problems. Anything else, right-wing pundits proclaim, is a return to the past with its legacy of clumsy government intervention and failed state companies. There is, they would have us conclude, no alternative.

I profoundly disagree. I refuse to surrender to the belief in the mysterious workings of the market or accept that humanity cannot politically organise or manage its society and economy to achieve desirable outcomes. I reject the view that governments should not interfere and that the state should not intervene. The entire legacy of the left, before the achievement of democracy, was about winning state power so that it could do precisely that. The values of socialism – democracy, equality and social solidarity – could not in the past and cannot now be achieved without state intervention and government action deliberately constructed to correct or reverse the momentum of some market forces. Of course, there are many areas for which the markets are the most effective and efficient methods of operation but they are not for everything. In my opinion, the state should remain as a player in the market economy through the ownership or control of some key companies. That role must be clearly separate from the independent task of market regulation for which the state has ultimate responsibility. There is a big difference in setting out what needs to be done and how exactly it is achieved. This is where the intelligence and the sophistication of the political process interconnects with the skills and professional abilities of the public service.

For example, Irish people should compare the availability of electricity in the past and access to broadband across our country today. The Irish state used the ownership of the ESB, a state monopoly company, to achieve a socially desirable objective – rural electrification – which was the product of a political decision. This electrification was a deliberate act which ignored market demand

and distorted prices by cross subsidisation between urban and rural customers. As a result, everyone has access to electricity, an essential prerequisite of modern society.

By contrast, broadband will only be made available by private companies obeying market rules not political direction. This important modern communication infrastructure is not accessible in many parts of the country because, we are told, of a lack of demand. This euphemism means that there are not enough people in an area willing to pay a profitable price that will justify the investment by private companies. After all, they remind us, they have a duty to their shareholders and to their banks. As a consequence, large towns, particularly in the west of Ireland, have little prospect of attracting inward investment because they do not have access to broadband.

I can think of many other economic areas where a small island nation like Ireland must ensure that the state is capable of acting commercially so as to secure the future of the country. As an island, off an island, off the continent of Europe, we have natural barriers and natural protections.

Our island location enables us to proclaim our military neutrality, secure in the knowledge that we don't have to finance our army to ensure it. But that same location also means that we must maximise direct access to the island. For example, the ownership of Aer Lingus enables the state, if necessary, to maintain that access. The proposed sale of Aer Lingus means the loss of control and, with it, the ability to intervene in the market. To retain control, we need a profitable airline that answers to the real needs of all of its stakeholders, the Irish citizens.

Since 1997, when the Rainbow Coalition, in which I was Minister for Finance, was defeated, Ireland has had a contradictory political experience. From 1994 we had substantial economic growth averaging at 8.5 per cent. No other OECD or EU country has had such good fortune. In my opinion, we have failed to transpose that private wealth into the necessary public infrastructure and services upon which we, as a society, depend. Returning to J.K. Galbraith's famous phrase, the past eight years of our centre-right Fianna Fáil/

Progressive Democrat coalition government have ensured the emergence of 'a society of private affluence and public squalor'.

Our public infrastructure through a combination of bad planning, inept management, political interference and ideological conflict lags seriously behind our economic achievements. I frequently get angry at the boasts of government ministers when they defend the failure of the Irish health or education services with the plaintiff plea that they are spending more money now than ever before. The concept of value for money has disappeared. The money is not wisely spent, it is wasted on unnecessary projects. Whether is it health care, housing, environmental protection or the provision of childcare, we have failed to utilise our new-found wealth to resolve these issues. Some sectors are not easy to deal with and others will take time to reform, but what angers me is the lack of political will and ministerial competence. Today, amongst the world's developed countries, Ireland has the second highest per-capita income and, paradoxically, is now the second most unequal society. Pride of place for the most unequal society goes to the United States of America. Clearly, we have travelled a long way in our migration from Berlin to Boston.

Ireland's internal social, environmental and infrastructural needs cannot be met in isolation from the other states in the European Union. The phenomenon that we face is completely new. The level and range of market and economic activity has moved beyond the frontiers of the nation states within Europe and the rest of the world.

As the impact of globalisation continues to affect people's lives in the developed world, there is a growing demand to have the state or the European Union do something about it. The transfer of well-paid jobs in France to cheaper labour markets, known as the process of 'delocalisation', was cited by French commentators as a part explanation of the victorious no vote in their recent referendum on the European constitutional treaty.

To minimise the stresses of adjustment to the new world economic order we, as a human community, will have to do much more than simply liberate markets. In my opinion, we need to find a way to civilise global capitalism in the twenty-first century, in the same way that social democracy civilised European capitalism in the last century. Failure to do so will create many social victims and economic losers, and has the potential to undermine in the future the very stability of the countries concerned.

The world in which I grew up has happily disappeared. I have no nostalgia for the recent Irish Celtic past, which, in my opinion, imprisoned the country in a fog of impoverishment and intolerance. I remember meeting Irish emigrants at an IDA-organised lunch in Chicago where a person of my generation who had left Ireland in the late 1950s asked if our native land still controlled by a conservative cluster of families and dominated by the Catholic Church. My response, as Minister for Finance at the time, was clear: Ireland was now a progressive, prosperous, post-Catholic society. When challenged, I cited the new wealth and opportunities we had created. The government no longer felt obliged to consult the Catholic hierarchy in matters of social legislation. Ministers no longer feared the belt of a crozier when developing policy.

I have, so far, being very fortunate in my political life. I have been a minister in a range of departments and a number of governments. But holding office is not the only pinnacle of political life. The interaction between the public and the state is the centrepoint where the citizen and the politician frequently meet. The role of the public representative in listening to the concerns of a person and negotiating with the public service is a very big part of my work. Many commentators, who can well look after themselves, deride the amount of time and energy that Irish politicians give to advocacy on behalf of their constituents. They claim that this is time spent at the expense of our duties as legislators. I disagree. For many people unfamiliar with the intricacies of a state bureaucracy, their deputy is their only accessible and sympathetic intermediary. I have always enjoyed that aspect of my work and regard it as the other side of the coin to grand policy initiatives when in opposition or complex programme implementation when in government. The sense of achievement, of being relevant and effective, is manifest when the problem of an individual is solved as a result of work I did on their behalf.

It is not, as some cynical commentators would assert, getting something delivered to which the citizen was entitled to in the first instance. On the contrary, it is using my political powers of advocacy and knowledge of the public service to ensure that a citizen's case is properly heard and justly dealt with. When the outcome to a constituent's problem is positive, I have a sense of achievement because the rights of the citizen have been vindicated. 'Whatever can we do to thank you?' they frequently ask. 'Just keep voting for me' is my response, knowing that they may not have done so in the past while hoping they will do so in the future.

Being a politician confers the right to enter people's lives or have the public enter yours. My face is familiar to a total stranger who knows that they can approach me. In the supermarket or on the street, I am greeted and frequently told by people what they think of the state of the world or what action I should now take to correct it. They feel they know me as they recognise me from the television and feel I have been a frequent visitor to their home.

One benefit of being a politician, which I did not foresee at the beginning, was the access that foreign travel gives to a public representative in another land. There is an enormous difference to being a tourist to a foreign country and being a member of an official delegation. I have had the opportunity to be an official observer at elections in Zimbabwe and Pakistan, to participate in democracy workshops in Namibia and Niger in Africa, as well as official visits to a number of other continents. These occasions give access to decision-makers in the country, to hear of the problems they face and by observation to compare how better they organise their societies than we do. By contrast, and more frequently now, I am reminded when I visit other countries of just how fortunate we are at home and often reflect to myself on the homeward journey how lucky I am to be alive at this time.

There are many dimensions to a political life; it has its full share of frustrations and challenges, opportunities and great personal setbacks. But taken together, the balance of the outcome is immensely positive as far as I am concerned.

I reaffirm my belief in politics and the necessity of citizens to engage and to intervene.

One of the big problems social democratic parties have witnessed, across Europe and possibly beyond, is the distrust by the people in political action and intervention. Low voter turnout, poor political behaviour by a minority of politicians, mostly Fianna Fáil in Ireland's case, and a destructively critical press with few exceptions, have eroded the broad public trust in democratic politics. But I say to the many people who have stopped voting: do you believe that market forces will deliver equal pay for women, build infrastructures for the whole community, respect the environment and deal effectively with global warming?

Will the appeals from global pop stars to 'Make Poverty History' mobilise a new generation of political activists and bring about the changes which we want? Will the same young people who attend such mass gatherings and concerts mobilise their votes in subsequent elections to transform their expectations into political directions? We have to hope so.

I am optimistic for the future and humanity's ability to make fundamental social changes. The engine of change is clear. It is democratic politics. The advocacy of ideas, the mobilisation of support, the pursuit of democratic power and the implementation of change is the path that we must follow. It is a continuation of a journey in politics.

Bibliography

Allan, Mike, *The Bitter Word Ireland's Job Famine and Its Aftermath* (Dublin, Poolbeg) 1998.

Arnold, Bruce, *What Kind of Country Modern Irish Politics 1968–1983* (London, Jonathan Cape) 1984.

Bainbridge, Timothy, *The Penguin Companion to European Union, 3rd edition* (London, Penguin Group) 2002.

Bell, Gwen, (ed.) & Jacqueline Tyrwhitt, *Human Identity in the Urban Environment* (Pelican Books, London) 1972.

Blake, Peter, *Le Corbusier Architecture and Form* (Pelican Books, London) 1963.

Boland, Kevin, *Up Dev!* (Dublin, Kevin Boland) no date.

Brittan, Samuel, *Capitalism with a Human Face* (London, Fontana Press) 1996.

Camus, Albert, *The Rebel* (London, Hamish Hamilton) 1953.

Connolly, James, *Labour in Ireland: 1. Labour in Irish History 1910, 2. The Real Conquest of Ireland 1915* (Dublin, Sign of the Three Candles) 1966.
    — *Socialism and Nationalism* (Dublin, Sign of the Three Candles) 1966.

Crosland, C.A.R., *The Future of Socialism* (London, Jonathan Cape) 1964.

Davies, Norman, *Europe: A History* (Oxford, Oxford University Press) 1996.

Desmond, Barry, *Finally and In Conclusion, A Political Memoir* (Dublin, New Island) 2000.

Doxiadis, C.A. & J.A. Papaioannou, *Ecumenopolis the Inevitable City of the Future* (Athens, Athens Center of Ekistics) 1974.

Dudley Edwards, Ruth, *The Pursuit of Reason – The Economist 1843–1993* (London, Hamish Hamilton) 1993.

Fanning, Ronan, *The Irish Department of Finance 1922–58* (Dublin, Institute of Public Administration) 1978.

Fanon, Frantz, *The Wretched of the Earth* (London, Penguin Books) 1967.

Finlay, Fergus, *Mary Robinson A President with a Purpose* (Dublin, The O'Brien Press) 1990.

Fischer, Ernst, *The Necessity of Art A Marxist Approach* (London, Pelican Books) 1963.

Galbraith, John Kenneth, *The Affluent Society* (London, Hamish Hamilton) 1958.

— *The Culture of Contentment* (London, Penguin Books) 1992.

Garaudy, Roger, *The Turning-Point of Socialism* (London, Fontana) 1970.

Garton Ash, Timothy, *The Polish Revolution Solidarity* (London, Alan Lane) 2004.

Garvin, Tom, *1922 The Birth of Irish Democracy* (Dublin, Gill & MacMillan) 1996.

Gaughan, Anthony J., *Thomas Johnson* (Dublin, Kingdom Books) 1980.

Glenny, Misha, *The Balkans 1804–1999* (London, Granta Books) 1999.

Goodman, Robert, *After the Planners* (London, Pelican Books) 1972.

Hobsbawn, Eric, *Age of Extremes The Short 20th Century 1914–1991* (London, Michael Joseph Ltd) 1994.

Horgan, John, *Labour The Price of Power* (Dublin, Gill & MacMillan) 1986.

— *Sean Lemass* (Dublin, Gill & MacMillan) 1997.

Hussey, Gemma, *At the Cutting Edge; Cabinet Diaries 1982–1987* (Dublin, Gill & Macmillan) 1990.

Hutton, Will, *The World We're In* (London, Little, Brown) 2002.

Jenkins, Roy, *Churchill* (London, MacMillan) 2001.

Kennedy, Geraldine (ed.), *The Irish Times Nealon's Guide to the 29th Dáil & Seanad* (Dublin, Gill & Macmillan) 2002.

Kennedy, Paul, *The Rise and Fall of the Great Powers* (London, Unwin Hyman Ltd) 1988.

Keogh, Dermot, *Twentieth-Century Ireland Nation and State* (Dublin, Gill & MacMillan) 1994.

Kiberd, Declan, *Inventing Ireland* (London, Jonathan Cape) 1995.

— *Irish Classics* (London, Granta Books) 2000.

Larkin, Emmet, *James Larkin Irish Labour Leader 1876–1947* (London, Rutledge & Kegan Paul) 1965.

MacEntee, Sean, *Episode at Easter* (Dublin, Gill & Son) 1966.

MacGréil, Mícheál, *Prejudice and Tolerance in Ireland* (Dublin, College of Industrial Relations) 1977.

MacMillan, Margaret, *Paris: Six Months that Changed the World 1919* (New York, Random House) 2003.

Manning, Maurice, *James Dillon* (Dublin, Wolfhound Press) 1999.

Nealon, Ted, *Ireland: A Parliamentary Directory 1973–74* (Dublin, Institute of Public Administration) 1974.

Nealon, Ted, in association with Frank Dunlop, *Ted Nealon's Guide to the 21st Dail and Seanad* (Dublin, Platform Press) 1977.

Nealon, Ted . Séamus Brennan, *Nealon's Guide 22nd Dáil & Seanad Election '81* (Dublin, Platform Press) 1981.

— *Nealon's Guide 24th Dáil & Seanad 2nd Election '82* (Dublin, Platform Press) 1983.

Nealon, Ted, *Nealon's Guide 25th Dáil & Seanad Election '87* (Dublin, Platform Press) 1987.

— *Nealon's Guide 26th Dáil & Seanad Election '89* (Dublin, Platform Press) 1989.

— *Nealon's Guide 27th Dáil & Seanad Election '92* (Dublin, Gill & Macmillan) 1989.

— *Nealon's Guide 28th Dáil & Seanad Election '97* (Dublin, Gill & Macmillan) 1997.

Pettit, Philip (ed.) *The Gentle Revolution: Crisis in the Universities* (Dublin, Sceptre Books) 1969.

O'Toole, Fintan, *After the Ball* (Dublin, New Island) 2003.

Porter, Michael E., *The Competitive Advantage of Nations* (London, The MacMillan Press) 1990.

Revel, Jean-François, *Without Marx or Jesus* (London, Paladin) 1972.

Rudofsky, Bernard, *Architecture Without Architecture* (London, Academy Edition) 1964.

Sassoon, Donald, *One Hundred Years of Socialism, The West European Left in the Twentieth Century* (London, Fontana Press) 1997.

Stephens, Philip, *Politics and the Pound* (London, Papermack) 1997.

Sweeney, Paul, *The Celtic Tiger* (Dublin, Oak Tree Press) 1999.

— *Selling Out? Privatisation in Ireland* (Dublin, New Island) 2004.

Tawney, R.H., *Religion & the Rise of Capitalism* (London, Pelican Books) first published 1926.

Thody, Philip, *Alber Camus', 1913–60* (London, Hamish Hamilton) 1961.

Tressel, Robert, *The Ragged Trousered Philanthropists* (London, Penguin Classics) 2004, first published 1914.

Wilson, Edmond, *To the Finland Station* (London, Fontana) 1972.

Yeates, Pádraig, *Lockout Dublin 1913* (Dublin, Gill & Macmillan) 2000.

Index